SO-ASP-988

52

Waterwalks in Israel:

40 new one-day walks and hikes

Joel Roskin

The Jerusalem Post

IMPORTANT NOTICE and DISCLAIMER: Safety precautions are a necessary concern regarding all outdoor activities. No guidebook can alert you to every possible danger. Nor can a guidebook aim to adapt itself to the individual limitations of the reader. The routes described in this book are not guarantees that any particular hike is safe for your party. When you engage in an outdoor activity, you assume responsibility for your own safety. All of the outings in this book require the appropriate supply of water. You must leave the details of your route with at least two people, either a friend or an official. Awareness of particular hazards will be required due to changing topographical, political and seasonal factors. Keeping informed on current conditions and exercising common sense are the keys to a safe, enjoyable trip.

The writer and publishers of *Waterwalks in Israel: 40 new one-day walks and hikes* disclaim any responsibility for the conditions of the trails, roads and places described in this book, or for the safety or security conditions in the area. Visitors touring the area or following the hikes described in this guide do so at their own risk. The map and hike descriptions in this book must be supplemented by a topographic map of the region and proper hiking equipment as described.

ISBN:

© Copyright 1996

Maps: Gil Paran
Editing: Jeff Seinfeld
Design & Layout: Judith Fattal
Photographs: Joel and Nitza Roskin

ISBN   965-356-033-6   מסת"ב

This book is in your hands thanks to my wife Nitza who constantly supported and assisted the long process from before its beginning until publication. She sacrificed normal daily routines, never complaining about my odd working hours or my lack of steady income. Aviya, born during the writing and hiking, has also contributed to the effort by being so calm and inspiring.

The guidance and support of my parents, Dr. Michael and Lessa, so essential to my first two books, continued with this one. My sister Aviva joined me through the most rainiest hike of them all and also helped proof-read. Jeff Seinfeld not only hiked but also edited the book and offered many constructive comments. Special thanks go to Gil Paran, who combined patience and expertise putting together the maps. I also cannot forget the Earth Sciences librarians of the Hebrew University who assisted me, even though I was no longer a student. Last, but not least, this book could not have taken shape without the companionship of my friends who patiently but not effortlessly shared my pace on the trails.

Joel Roskin

Beersheba, 1996

Table of Contents

Kinnarot Valley and the Bet She'an Valley

Jerusalem Hills

Judean Desert

Negev

Introduction

About the Book

The aim of *Waterwalks in Israel: 40 new one-day walks and hikes* is to make Israel's trails along various forms of water accessible to the English-reading hiker. Beyond getting you onto the trail, I hope that the subjects discussed on each hike related to the specific landscape will add color to the route.

Israeli water hikes superficially resemble comparable hikes in other countries, but here they have a lot more meaning attached to the scenic beauty. While some hikes follow rushing streams and lagoons in the North, others run between small layer springs in the Jerusalem Hills which have for centuries sustained small farms. Hiking along the Dead Sea is totally unique and desert oases exemplify the impact of natural water on the desert.

Being a small country lacking true wilderness, every part of Israel is accessible in a one-day hike (except in the Negev). Water routes are usually no longer than a few kilometers long. Thus, the book offers concise routes to the most beautiful places. This makes many routes suitable for families, while some are only for experienced hikers.

A number of things make this book different from other guidebooks to Israel (including those in Hebrew):

1. *Waterwalks in Israel: 40 new one-day walks and hikes* (along with its prequel, *A Guide to Hiking in Israel*) is the only walking and hiking guidebook in English that offers routes from North to South.

2. Its routes can usually be reached by public transportation and those who take private transportation are usually not required to walk a back-and-forth route.

3. Beyond the technicalities (which can be complicated), the book tries to broaden the hiker's appreciation for each locale's aspects: geology and geography, history and archaeological finds, and outstanding or common plants and animals.

Each hike begins with a general outline to help you choose your route and make preparations. While you prepare, spend time reading the discussion of the geography. The history, which has left some of its tracks along every hike, is intertwined with the geography.

The life forms which are described in detail are usually seen along the route. Try to find them along the way! Since many common plants and animals are found along more than one hike, the plant and animal index in the back of the book can help find the page where a detailed description appears.

Information on interesting sites along the way is also included.

The regional introduction adds additional insight helpful for each hike, emergency telephone numbers, suggested overnight solutions, and sites worth visiting.

1

The hikes in this essay do not encompass all of the popular water hikes of Israel. The Central Golan streams; Nahal Gilabon, Nahal Zavitan, Nahal Yehudiya, Nahal Daliyot (Gamla) and Nahal El Al were described in my previous book, *A Guide to Hiking in Israel.*

A number of wide, slow-moving rivers and streams drain through the Coastal Plain into the Mediterranean Sea. The Coastal Plain also marks the centralization of the Jewish population of Israel. The human presence has not helped nature. A majority of the land is built or farmed by man. Leftover land and water have become disposal sites with water being severely damaged. Pollution and sewage have practically killed the natural biota of these environments.

These streams and rivers have recently entered the national forum and it seems that a slow comeback is imminent. Still, water routes are limited to short walks along small enclaves of undisturbed landscape. The proximity of the coastal streams to the urban center of Israel, the highly unstable environment and the strong affiliation of these regions with everyday life have compelled me to abstain from describing these routes.

I have also avoided the waterscapes of the Hebron and Bet El Hills of Judea, Samaria and the Central Jordan Valley, due to the uncertain politics and security in their populated regions.

Geography

The State of Israel covers only 21,000 sq. km. Its maximum length is about 480 km. between the far North, the Hermon, and the southern tip, Taba (south of Eilat alongside the Gulf of Akaba). Its width averages around 80 km., an hour's drive. Being so narrow it is remarkable that the State has a national watershed; to the west the streams drain into the Mediterranean Sea and to the east into the Syrian-African Rift. The national watershed runs in a fairly straight north-south line along the "backbone" of the country. The backbone is composed of the mountainous sections: Negev, Judea, Samaria, Galilee and the valleys between these regions. The only Israeli regions east of the Syrian-African Rift are the Golan Heights and the southern parts of the Hermon Mountains.

The Syrian-African Rift is a valley cut deep into the earth's crust. It is certainly the country's most outstanding large-scale geological-geographical feature. It has many outstanding water environments. The intense starkness and salinity of the world's lowest spot, the Dead Sea, and the beauty of the Sea of Galilee (Lake Kinneret) are the most well-known.

The sharp elevation changes down to the Rift, along with its vast drainage system, has created many profound waterscapes on its sidelines. A majority of this book's routes are along the streams and sites associated with the Rift.

The Rift's low elevation hosts high temperatures and relatively low amounts of precipitation. The eastern slopes of the backbone of the country, facing the Rift, are characterized by an increase in temperature and decrease in precipitation which intensifies closer to the Rift.

Although the streams which run westward of the national watershed toward the Mediterranean are usually less spectacular and more polluted, a number of them are also described.

Outside of the deserts, Israel's climate is Mediterranean, with 500-1000 mm. of precipitation in winter with occasional snowfall above 750 m. Israeli summers are rainless. The Negev, compromising half of the country, is part of the global desert belt. Being a narrow country running north-south, climatic changes are quite apparent as one travels south: it gets hotter and dryer. This usually can be seen (ignoring human impact) by the density of vegetation cover.

Nature Preservation

Every square meter of Israel is precious. The country is both small and densely populated. The increasing population and modern development have accelerated the turnover of open fields and forests to construction sites. For example, in 1994, 100,000 dunams of agricultural land were allocated to construction. At this rate, in the next decades most of central Israel's open expanses and forests will probably disappear. These trends accentuate the importance of keeping what remains in its natural state.

Fortunately, Israel has many (but very small) nature reserves and many of the hikes in this book are in them. Due to their popularity and minute size, the Nature Reserves Authority has strict regulations such as entrance fees, limited hours, the prohibition of fires and food, and walking limited to the trails only. Some reserves are closed to the public. Instructions are posted on signs. Please follow them.

Here are several guidelines regarding all of the hikes:

1. Refrain from littering and burying litter. Buried litter is later dug up, eaten and strewn about by animals. Bring plastic bags to carry out everything brought in.
2. Bury human waste with dirt (not stones). Burn (bring matches) and bury soiled toilet paper.
3. Campers should bring a supply of firewood from home. Extinguish fires thoroughly, bury the ashes and smoldered rocks. Fires are prohibited in reserves.
4. Please leave archaeological and geological artifacts where they are found.
5. Neither disturb nor feed wild animals. Keep a distance from nesting birds. Intimacy can be harmful for both.
6. Leave pets and loud instruments at home.
7. Take care not to contaminate any water, anywhere.
8. Report environmental crimes to the Nature Reserves Authority or to the Society for the Protection of Nature in Israel.

A number of the hikes pass through private property. Do not forget to close gates. Please refrain from crossing agricultural fields and picking orchard fruit. Bedouins store their belongings in a casual manner throughout the countryside. Items which may seem neglected to you may be useful for others. At sites holy for any religion, please behave accordingly and wear modest clothes.

Israel's Main Nature Preservation Groups

Society for the Protection of Nature in Israel (S.P.N.I.), head office address: 4 Hashefela Street, Tel Aviv, 66183.

Nature Reserves Authority (N.R.A.), head office address: 78 Yermiyahu Street, Jerusalem, 94467.

Using This Book

The goal of this guide is to get you onto the trails and to make the hiking experience meaningful. Hiking with this book is simple but demands a basic understanding of how to use it.

Before choosing a hike, read all of that hike's information, including the route description in order to make sure you know what is waiting ahead.

The length of a hike does not always correlate with its difficulty. As you plan, take note of the "Hiking time," which is an estimate for a group of five (large groups substantially slow the pace). The hike length is only an estimate: a kilometer in a maintained nature reserve does not demand the same effort as a kilometer in the desert.

One-way hikes are problematic for one-car parties. A volunteer of the whole group has to rewalk the hike. The few one-way trips therefore are also back-and-forth routes (don't forget to double the length of hike). In any case, one-way hikes are usually short trips. On longer one-way routes there is usually public transportation back to the starting point.

The hot Israeli summers make hiking always better in spring and fall in the Mediterranean regions and in winter in the desert. For some hikes, waiting for the "Preferred season" can really make a big difference. Hikes which are good for "All year" usually offer shaded sections along the way.

Hikes suitable for "All" mean that the route poses no difficulties such as climbing ladders, falls and ropes, or crossing boulders and streams. Thus, families with children can estimate the hike's suitability based on its length and time. Hikes suitable for "Experienced hikers" include minor obstacles as mentioned above, difficult terrain and/or serious elevation gains or losses.

Before you go, make sure you understand the route. The listed hiking and touring map is obligatory. Being prepared with the "Special preparation" makes the hike more comfortable.

The regional introductions are important for every hike and can be read at home. Besides geographic, biological and historical information, they include emergency telephone numbers. These numbers are liable to change! I have mentioned some of the nearby interesting places which do not require hiking and have included a partial list of reasonable overnight options. It is not meant to be an endorsement.

Transportation

Accessibility was one of the criterion I used to select the hikes. "Public transportation" generally refers to buses which serve almost every settlement. It also refers to the sherut cab service which usually follows main routes. Private transportation refers to any vehicle without four-wheel drive.

On one-way routes a single car allows easy access to the starting point but poses a problem for the way back. So I have described many interesting loop trips, but this is not always possible. Thus, a one-car party needs to return the same way or sometimes follow a shorter but less attractive way back.

Buses can be boarded at the main town or city of the region. Usually, a bus running to the local countryside stops throughout the town and at junctions and villages along its route. Bus fares, numbers, and departure and travel times vary. You must seek this information prior to the hike. Often a single bus line includes several hikes in a region.

Adapting the described hikes to the present bus routes sometimes involves additional walking to-and-from the starting and ending point, usually not more than an hour.

Trails and Maps

The described hikes run along marked and unmarked trails, dirt roads, gravel roads and paved roads. Occasionally, you may walk short distances cross-country.

The marked trail is most common; gravel roads, dirt roads and recently-paved roads are also marked. The marker is known as a "sandwich": two painted white lines about 20 cm. long with a colored line—red, blue, black or green—sandwiched between them. Each color signifies a different trail. There is no correlation between mark color and trail difficulty. These trail marks are painted on signs, rocks, barrels, trees, paved roads and other structures. Trail heads sometimes have specific signs.

The marked trail is not always easily recognizable. Sometimes, the markers are spaced so that from one marker you can see the next while no clear trail connects them. Sometimes the route is so clear that markers are spaced (especially on dirt roads). Unfortunately, sometimes the trail and markers are both unclear.

Since the beginning of the decade, the Israel National Trail project has been working on a single trail across Israel, north to south. Some of the I.N.T. is along pre-existing trails while other parts are new paths. The I.N.T. mark is a distinct orange and blue intertwined triangular-like mark. Some of the hikes in the book head along part of the I.N.T.

Hiking and touring maps are topographical maps with a 1:50,000 scale. At the time of writing this book, the first English edition was being produced. Hiking and touring maps are essential assets for all hikes in this book.

The specific hike maps in the book do not include the quantity of information found in a topographical or hiking and touring map. Landmarks are denoted by numbers within the text, in coordination with the specific hike map. Exact route details cannot appear on the maps. If you feel you have departed from the prescribed route, calmly retrace your steps until you recognize your previous surroundings.

Clothing and Equipment

Israel's rocky terrain is known to be rough. Good footwear is extremely important. Gym shoes are fine. Sandals should not be worn. Adventure sandals are good for walking in water, but on rocky trails hazards such as thorns and sharp stones tend to find themselves between the foot palm and sandal. A simple pair of rubber and cloth boot known as Paladium is the cheapest shoe available in Israel. It is good for hiking and water walking but the cloth tends to tear. This boot used to be Israel's national hiking shoe. Never go hiking with a new pair of hiking boots. Always break them in before hitting the trail.

The sun in Israel can burn your skin quickly. Over-exposure (a relative issue) to the sun is not healthy and no one is immune. A light-weight hat with a brim is a must for all seasons. Light-weight slacks and long-sleeved shirts are good to have on days of long exposure, although shorts and short-sleeved shirts are more comfortable.

Most of the hikes are along water, and waterscapes tend to be affiliated with vegetation. Always equip yourselves with long attire, especially in the hilly regions, where the summer evenings are usually cool. A number of routes offer swimming. In water it is recommended to wear shoes or sandals, in order to guard your feet from sharp objects.

In the winter bring a change of clothes, specially a change of shoes and socks. It is best to dress in warm, light layers which can be peeled off as the sun climbs and then rewrapped as the day grows cool.

To be adequately prepared, the following should be included in your backpack on every hike: water, food which does not easily spoil, sun cream, toilet paper and matches in a waterproof container, compass, map, flashlight, pocket knife, first aid, phone tokens and telecard, plastic garbage bags and this book. Do not forget the "Special preparation" noted in each hike outline.

Suggested items are: binoculars, camera, thermos or gas stove with hot drink packets, additional guidebooks, Bible, mosquito repellent and sunglasses.

Water

The importance of this vital issue cannot be over-exaggerated. Dehydration and heatstroke are the primary hiking hazards in Israel. Dehydration is caused by a loss of body liquids. Lengthy exposure combined with physical activity, without enough water, can easily bring on dehydration which can lead to death. Heatstroke can even occur if you are drinking an adequate amount of water. Dehydration can come along suddenly with little warning. If a slight headache develops, or if urine is bright yellow or orange, it is time for a rest and at least a one-liter water supplement.

Rest in the shade and drink constantly, even when not feeling thirsty. Make sure that the rest of your party is doing the same.

Water is always the best liquid to drink. It is sometimes needed for other purposes like cleansing wounds. Juices which induce thirst are also good as they keep you drinking. Carbonated drinks are not recommended; the gas fills you up, cutting down your liquid input.

Prepare your water on the eve of departure. Storing your water in the freezer can keep the water cool throughout the hike. Before hitting the trail, drink a substantial amount of liquids (also after the hike). Though most water sources are not defined as polluted, they are not recommended for consumption. Water purification tablets can solve the problem, but purified water is like drinking swimming pool water.

A hike should always end with spare water. A hike that is concluded with no water left is a warning sign that you did not drink nor carry enough. Next time, add an additional liter (at least!) to your calculation.

In the summer don't hike in the desert. In the winter, 4 liters of water will do for a day hike in the desert. In fall and spring, 6 liters are sufficient. In the Mediterranean regions, 4-5 liters of water are needed during the summer, while in the winter, 2-3 liters are enough.

Safety

Though hiking exposes people to many different circumstances, an accident at home is more likely than something happening on the trail. Before going on any hike, check into the nearby field study center to learn up-to-date news about the area. Leave your names, number of party members, particular medical instructions for individuals of your party, if any, and your chosen route.

Here are important guidelines for hiking in Israel:

1. Hike in groups of at least five members. In case something happens, more than one person can treat the problem while two more can run for help.

2. Leave your route written out, including expected arrival time with at least two people you can trust, and on your cars windshield. Lock your car. Try not to leave valuables inside, and if so, in the trunk.

3. Wear a hat, use sun cream, and rest in the shade.

4. Supply yourselves with plenty of water. Drink natural sources at your own risk.

5. Before sitting down, climbing a wall, shoving your hand into dark places, and donning shoes, look out for scorpions and snakes.

6. Do not befriend wild animals as you may misunderstand each other. Upon meeting a leopard (currently, only in the Judean Desert and Negev) retreat posthaste (they have never attacked people, but who knows?).

7. Finish the hike before sunset. Sunset times are listed in the daily newspaper. If lost at night, stay put, light a fire, and wait until morning. In day, retrace your steps to the last point recognized on the trail, re-orient yourselves and continue on. If you cannot make out the continuation, return to the starting point.

8. A few hiking routes pass close to minefields. Minefields are fenced in, usually with barbed wire. Along it at undefined intervals are 2 types of signs: small red triangles or yellow and black signs with a written warning.

9. Remnants of the country's intense military activity are common in many places. Do not touch any unfamiliar item. Don't forget to instruct the rest of your group, especially children.

10. Do not enter firing zones without an official permit (obtainable at S.P.N.I. offices).

11. When walking along a paved road, stay outside its shoulders, heading against the direction of traffic.

12. Please come prepared and drive carefully.

In the winter

13. Do not hike in foggy conditions.

14. On damp days try to stay dry and watch your step—the trail can be very slippery.

15. Beware of flash floods. On rainy days, do not walk in narrow canyons. Clear skies in the Judean Desert do not mean clear skies in the Judean Hills. When rain is expected in the Judean Hills, do not under any circumstances enter the Judean Desert wadi beds.

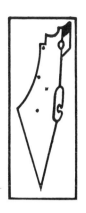

Northern Golan and the Hermon Mountain Range

Geography — Northern Golan

The Golan Heights is really the western part of a region known from biblical times as the Bashan, which is tenfold the Golan's size (today the Bashan is under Syrian control). The Golan is only 1,200 sq. km. Two thousand years ago the Jewish residents used the terms "Upper Golan" and "Lower Golan," but modern convention counts three subregions: northern, southern and central. The latter two form the ancient area of Lower Golan.

Northern Golan is therefore the equivalent of Upper Golan and covers about 250 sq. km. Its natural boundaries are between Nahal Gilabon or the contour (elevation line) of 700 meters in the south, northbound to Nahar Sa'ar. Its western border is the Hula Valley, like the rest of the Golan. Its eastern border is upper Wadi Rukad, a bit east of the Israel-Syria border.

Northern Golan differs from the rest of the region in its pronounced relief and numerous volcanic cones forming the most prominent features. Har Varda at 1226 m. above sea level is its highest spot, higher than any point in western Israel (west of the Syrian-African Rift).

The subregion is built of Eocenian sedimentary rock covered by numerous layers of basalt. Unlike elsewhere in the Golan, here there are no "windows." Windows expose sedimentary rock where the surface basalt has either not covered the earlier strata or that the basalt has eroded away. Volcanism in the Pleistocene created mountains and cones, releasing flows of lava. There is evidence that volcanic activity took place not far east of the Golan only 4000 years ago. Between eruptions, thousands of years passed and soil developed on the basaltic surface. In the Northern Golan there was tectonic stability; only minor faulting has taken place on the plateau during, between and after the volcanic episodes. Hiking down some of the canyons, one sees the different lava flows with dark red soil between them. Some of these ancient soils, known as paleosols, are aquicludes, a source of springs.

The eruptions made their mark. A series of lava flows has covered Northern Golan with basalt. Volcanic mountains protrude 50-200 m. above their surroundings in recognizable lines from north-northeast to south-southwest. Small craters, known as jubas, are evident in the northern parts of the region. Other types of volcanic rock, tuff and scoriae, also appear at certain places. The most recent lava flows have helped to flatten the topography.

The soil is mainly of coarse grains. Carbonate is absent, an uncommon phenomena in Israel. Ordinarily, volcanic soil is very rich and good for agriculture. But the ample rainfall has eroded much of it, exposing the bedrock. Furthermore, the absorbant soil becomes very muddy in the winter and cracks in summer. The contraction of the soil uplifts bedrock fragments. These two factors impede plowing. The land is thus better suited for grazing. Nonetheless, the western slopes hold small valleys that have collected topsoil ample for agriculture. The loose volcanic soils on the mountain slopes are also suitable for growing crops.

Hermon Mountain Range

The Hermon Mountains form Israel's highest region surpassing 2,000 m. In fact, other than the peak of the Lebanon Mountains (surpassing 3,000 m.), the Hermons are the highest mountains from Turkey to Yemen. Since only 7% of the range is in Israel, it is mistakenly perceived as one mountain, not a region or mountain range. It actually stretches 50 km. north of the Golan and its average width is 20 km. Like the Golan, it covers over 1,000 sq. km. Its borders are the Syrian-African Rift to the west, Nahar Sa'ar and the basaltic Golan to the south. To the southeast it drops to the Damascus Basin. Beyond the Zebdani Valley stretches the Anti-Lebanon Range to the northeast.

The Lebanon-Syria border runs along the Hermon watershed, dividing the area equally between the two. A quarter of the range, including its 2,807-meter peak, is a demilitarized zone where United Nations troops are stationed.

The Israeli Hermon is a nature reserve of 70,000 dunams, composed of three ridges running southwest-northeast: Si'on, Siryon and Hermon (also known as the Hermon Shoulder). The latter two run down from Mitzpe Shelagim at 2,224 m., Israel's highest point. Between the three ridges run deep gorges: Nahals Si'on and Guvta. Both drain into Nahar Hermon just below its source, Banias Spring.

The Hermon is a huge anticline. Its formation is connected to the northward movement of Transjordan in relation to Cisjordan and the fact that west of the Hermon, the Syrian-African Rift bends east. The Hermon section of Transjordan eventually hit the Rift, and consequently buckled and rose, elevating ancient strata from the depths of earths crust.

The original uplift was 4,000 m. Today, over 1,000 m. of rock have eroded, exposing ancient strata. The main component of the range is Jurassic sedimentary rock. Rock of this age is rarely exposed in Israel.

The prevailing Hermon soil is yellow terra rossa. Along the lower slopes are colorful sandstones and clays from the Cretaceous. Here and there rocks revealing volcanic activity appear.

The combination of limestone and large quantities of precipitation (mainly snow) has produced heavy karst activity. This has caused the slowly melting snow water to seep into the underground caverns and emerge at the base of the range. This explains the lack of springs and perennial streams in the upper parts of the range. Karst weathering also creates the subtle landscape of the Hermon. Only during peak snow melt season does the excess water trickle down the steep deep wadis, creating a unique waterscape of streams.

Climate

The Hermon's climate is quite similar to the Northern Golan's at equivalent elevations (up to 1,200 m.). Besides elevation, the climate here is determined by the regions slope to the west, toward the Mediterranean Sea, and the distance from it.

The climate at elevations exceeding 1,000-1,400 m. differs from anywhere else in Israel, as a large proportion of the precipitation is snow. At 2,200 m., the mountains receive 1,600 mm. of precipitation, a majority of it being snow. At higher elevations there is an increase in precipitation and wind speed and a decrease in temperatures (0.5-0.6° centigrade, every 100 m.). The Hermon summer is dry and hot during the day.

Northern Golan is known for its notorious winter weather and comfortable summers. It is closer to the Mediterranean than most people think, only 50 km. Since it slopes to the west and southwest, it faces the sea and the air coming from it. This single factor gives the region a Mediterranean climate with dry summers, rainy winters and moderate temperature spans.

In Northern Golan the average temperature ranges from 2°C in January to 15° in July—a 13° span. In Safed, which is closer to the Mediterranean but not facing it, there is a 16° temperature span. In Acre, on the coast, there is a 12° span.

Since Upper Golan is closer to the Mediterranean than the Lower Golan, it is more humid. The daily Mediterranean breeze climbs the Upper Galilee during late morning. It descends into the Hula Valley, heats up, and expands as its humidity decreases. Upon rising to the Upper Golan towards sunset, the air cools and becomes more saturated. Clouds are therefore common, even in the summer.

The summer nights are dew-laden, for the dark basalt cools more rapidly than light-colored sedimentary rock, causing condensation of the rising humid air. Soon after sunset, very mysteriously, fog covers the crests of the volcanic peaks. There are 170 dew nights per year. In the early morning, the Bashan plains to the east quickly heat up and suck in air from the cooler Golan, causing strong easterly winds.

Upper Golan receives up to 1,200 mm. of precipitation annually due, in part, to the proximity of the Hermon. Snow is common in the winter.

Vegetation

Climate is the biggest factor influencing plant life. In a defined geographical location, climate is mainly a product of the elevation. From the Hermon's base to 1,200 m. the vegetation resembles that of western Israel. An important difference is that since the Jurassic sedimentary rock is uniform and has few layers of marl, the vegetation in the lower Hermon is less variated than at similar elevations in Israel.

At higher elevations the plant life is unique. However, these elevations are beyond the scope of the present book.

Northern Golan's vegetation is Mediterranean. The moist weather made this region one of the richest regions mentioned in the Bible along with the Carmel, Hermon and Lebanon. Then it was covered by a thick green forest. Today, most of the Golan is open fields, but the Northern Golan is partially covered with trees. This is due to the poor soil, not being high priority for human use.

The Phoenicians are the first known loggers in the region: "Of the oaks of Bashan have they made thy oars," (Ezekiel 27:5-6). During the rich Roman-Byzantine Jewish settlement 2,000 years ago in Central Golan, the forests were severely cleared for land and wood. Throughout the years, local residents kept using the natural old-growth wood. The deforestation accelerated when the Ottoman Empire brought new peoples to the wild region. They cut trees for the wood, fuel and charcoal industries. The Circassians led the effort, cutting down the remaining forests for homes and field expansion. When the Syrians turned the Golan into a military zone fifty years ago, they banned logging and put the forests on a comeback. Still, only 3% of the Golan is covered by forest, compared to 18% just one hundred years ago.

The Northern Golan forest is primarily of the common oak and Boissieri oak association. Odem Forest, west of Mas'adeh and Buk'ata, is still one of the only forests in Israel. A hundred years ago it covered the whole Northern Golan. The Odem is not a dense forest and many species accompany the common-Boissieri oak association. Most of the trees are deciduous. The Syrian Pear and wild plum inhabit moist parts. The Atlantic terebinth can be seen here and there and the spiny hawthorn is common in sunny areas. Since the soil has neither marl nor carbonate, some members of the Mediterranean forest are absent like the strawberry tree, mastic terebinth, laurel and buckthorn. The terebinth is also rare, appearing only in Nahar Sa'ar. The snowbell is very common, especially along the slopes.

The shady forest is rich in all types of vegetation. It hosts many creepers, such as the wild asparagus, green brier, raspberry, honeysuckle, madder and birthwort. The yellow blooming Spanish broom bush, often seen in Jerusalem, is native to the region. Many annuals and geophytes also inhabit the forests. A number of rare orchids can be seen, like the helleborine.The openings between trees are full of different grasses. Mushrooms are also common. Two rare protected species of wild flowers are the Greek cyclamen that blooms in winter and the Lebanon iris that blooms in spring.

In some deforested areas, other plants have taken over. Along the lower western slopes for example, the Christ thorn jujube and lotus jujube association appears at Banias (350 m. above sea level) and runs down to the shores of Lake Kinneret (200 m. below sea level). It seems that this association has replaced the Tabor oak and Atlantic terebinth tree association that has been logged. The jujubes are sturdy trees, withstanding fire and logging.

Knotweed and rest harrow are common plants in deserted agricultural fields and terraces.

Wildlife

When Israel gained control of the Golan and southern Hermon in 1967, large mammal life was practically absent. Heavy hunting had taken its toll. The last sighting of a Syrian bear was in 1917. Only wild boar, prohibited by Moslem dietary law, remained along with some vultures.

Today, mammal life has made a strong comeback, enduring the development of new roads, infrastructure and heavy military activity. For some animals, the firing zones are actually comfortable places as they are rarely visited by people. There are both Mediterranean and Iro-Siberian species. Generally speaking, the mammal life today differs only slightly from the Galilee's (see regional introduction there).

Salamanders live in springs and other bodies of water. A number of reptiles like the tortoise and gecko are colored in darker shades in the Golan than elsewhere, an adaptation to the dark soil and rock. The rare green lizard, a dweller of cool forests, is found in Odem Forest. The Palestine viper is found in Northern Golan. There is an opinion that the Asian viper, confirmed in Turkey, also resides here.

There are no endemic birds in the Northern Golan nor unique aviary species. The birds are mainly common forest songbirds. In the open fields, common raptors include three species of kestrels (falcons) and the Egyptian vulture, Griffon vulture and long-legged buzzard. Since cliffs are not common features, large birds of prey prefer to live elsewhere, although they have been seen in Northern Golan and Hermon. The small pools and Berekhat Ram hold wintering duck flocks which remain until late spring. Wigeon, tufted duck and pochard ducks are all present in good numbers. Common, too, are wintering finches and chukars in open fields. A rare wintering bird is the Radde's accentor.

The white-throated robin is rarely seen anywhere in Israel, including Northern Golan and lower Hermon. In the Hermon they nest at altitudes of 1,400-1,900 m. The robin's relative, the black redstart, also nests in the Hermon above 1,400 m. In the Hermon, the woodlark and blue rock thrush commonly nest up to 1,500 m. The sombre tit, found in maquis, has a large habitat span of 800-1,700 m. The rock nuthatch is extremely ubiquitous in Nahal Si'on and Nahal Guvta. The rock sparrow is also common.

Human Involvement

Golan in Bashan was a city of refuge (Deuteronomy 4:43). The region acquired the city's name during the Second Temple period. It is not known where the city of Golan stood. Golan may be connected to the word *golah*, "exile," or to the Arabic *julan*, which means a region of nomadism.

Throughout history, Golani settlement has been intermittent. Yet the region has always been a link between east and west with a number of ancient routes crossing it. Northern Golan's ancient route is today Road 99, which rises from the Hula Valley at Banias and runs eastward towards Damascus, just south of the protruding Hermons.

During the Paleolithic times, before many of the volcanic eruptions, humans roamed Northern Golan. Sites have been found in exposed windows of Eocenian rock. During the Neolithic period it seems that people were less common. It is possible that volcanic instability kept them away.

During Chalcolithic times, the Golan was intensely developed. Many small villages remain, most of them by sources of water in Lower Golan. Following the end of the third millennium, the region remained uninhabited for nearly two thousand years. It was resettled only during the Hellinistic period. In the meantime, the Northern Golan was roamed by nomads.

During the First Temple period, the Golan was a buffer zone between Israel and Aram. The nations of Geshur and Ma'akha, established in the 11th century, are mentioned in Joshua (13:11) as being between Hermon and Gilead. Their exact location is unclear, possibly east of the Golan with Ma'akha in the north. King David captured Aram, Geshur became an ally and Ma'akha was subordinate to Israel.

When rich Jewish settlements appeared in the Golan during Hellinistic times they avoided Northern Golan, maybe due to its thick forest.

Following the Moslem conquest in 636, the Golan community dwindled and nomadic tribes invaded, mainly from the Syrian Desert. The few settlements which remained were not in Northern Golan. During Crusader times the Golan was a buffer zone between the Crusaders and the Moslems. During the short Mameluke period the region belonged to the Damascus province and Kurds and Turkomans arrived. Northern Golan was fiercely ruled by a Bedouin tribe for a few hundred years.

In the 15th century, the demographic vacuum began to suck in minorities. Druze, coming from the north, settled at a number of spots and founded Ein Kuniyeh. In the 17th century, Alaouites founded two villages, Ein Fit and Za'urah, on the slopes near the Banias-Damascus road.

In the 1830s things picked up. Egyptian rule began to curb the Bedouins and create new settlements of Egyptians, Sudanese and Samarian refugees. Egyptian rule ended in 1841 and the Bedouins regained control, harassing new settlers and halting development. The Kurds took advantage of Ottoman land registration rules and gained official ownership of a majority of the Golan.

In 1871-1878 Turkey tried to stabilize the region by transferring Circassians from Bulgaria. The new settlers received land and financial assistance. They first settled in a khan in the town of Kunaitira and soon afterwards established 12 large villages in Upper Golan along with smaller estates. Each family received 70-130 dunams of land, a pair of oxen and seeds. The hard-working Circassians planted vineyards and orchards on the mountain slopes and cleaned basalt boulders from the fields. They built large homes with slanted red-tile roofs. Their fierce courage thwarted Bedouin attacks and after 7 years the two groups held a *sulha*—an appeasement feast. In 1879 the Circassians expanded into Lower Golan.

The Hermon also has a long history of settlement. The name, possibly derived from the Arabic *haram* (holy), is mentioned 13 times in the Bible. The term Ba'al-Hermon refers to pagan worship in connection with the region. Other names in Jewish literature include Hermonim, Siryon, Si'on, Mount Snow. Today the Arabs call it Jabl Sheikh—since the snow-capped mountain is similar to the white hair of an old man.

Although traditional crops kept settlements below 1,500 m., the higher elevations were grazed in the summer. The region also offered rich forests, harnessed for fire wood and charcoal. The summer ice trade between Cairo and Beirut was also a local occupation from ancient times until the introduction of electricity under the

British Mandate in 1920. Har Kahal, above Neve Ativ, has lead sulfide mines, used for makeup and ceramics coloring. Nineteenth-century travellers through Majdal Shams described the local women as "painted women" due to their blue makeup. The rough conditions never gave way to the development of large towns. Majdal Shams, at 1,200 m., is the largest settlement today after Hatzbaya, Lebanon.

Survey archaeology has revealed over 40 settlements on the Israeli Hermon. Coins have been found dating to the Roman-Byzantine period, when economic growth characterized the region.

The Jeturite nomads mentioned in I Chronicles 5:19 are the first people known to live here. I Chronicles 5:23 adds:

> And the children of the half tribe of Menasheh dwelt in the land; they increased from Bashan unto Ba'al-Hermon and Senir, and unto Mount Hermon.

The Jeturites are described in the book of Maccabees as being pursued by Jonathan the Hasmonean. The Hasmoneans captured part of their region and imposed conversion. Later, Jews married into Jeturite families.

The Jeturites maintained their independence for over 1,000 years, until 20-30 B.C.E. when the Romans subdued them, slowly taking control of the rugged region. The Jeturites joined Roman forces as hired soldiers. After the Moslem conquest and the subsequent Bedouin invasion, the Jeturite culture disappeared.

Archaeologists have also found remnants of synagogues at a number of places on the Hermon. The mosaic at the Rehov synagogue by Bet She'an mentions a number of sites in the Hermon area, defining the northern border of Israel in regard to the sabbatical year. One site is mentioned as "Tarnegola above the Caesarea." Caesarea is Banias, so it must relate to some place in the nearby Hermon.

Since the 11th century the Hermon has been the home for Druze, seeking refuge from violent Moslems. Christians have also settled the region, mainly Greek-Orthodox and Greek Catholics. Most of the Christians dwelt in Druze villages like Ein Kuniyeh. Both minorities mainly settled on the western slopes while Moslems, fewer in number, lived on its eastern slopes, facing Damascus.

Until the late 19th century Jews lived in the Hermon, mainly around the Lebanese town of Hatzbaya. They traced their ancestors back to the Roman-Byzantine period! The community has been documented throughout the centuries by travellers diaries. The Cairo Genizah (cache) also talks about Jews of the Hermon. The community broke up due to religious tensions between Jews, Moslems, Christians and Druze. Most of the Jews joined the settlements sponsored by Baron Edmond de Rothschild in the Upper Galilee. Today many of their offspring can be identified by name—Hatzbani.

In 1948 the Golan became a military area and many of the residents were hired by the Syrian army, building military infrastructure. In 1961, 111,340 people were listed in the Golan, 78,281 in the Kunaitira district. The people resided in 272 villages, 115 of them holding less than 50 people.

In the mid 1960s the Syrians tried to divert Nahar Hermon to a canal running along the slopes of the Golan. Their goal was to dry up the Jordan River. Their plan would have seriously cut the water supply for the N.W.C. that was facing completion. Israel responded militarily and halted the project. Not much later, in 1967 and 1973, many of Israel's most bloodiest battles took place in this region.

During the first four days of the Six Day War, Israel fought Egypt and Jordan, while the Syrians steadily shelled the villages of northern Israel. A committee of the villages and kibbutzim met with members of the government requesting a military move in order to put a stop to 19 years of Syrian shelling. On the fifth day of war, June 9th, after the battles ceased on the Egyptian front, Israeli troops began to take the Golan. The main impetus took place in the Northern Golan as forces began to ascend the plateau from Kefar Szold.

On June 10th, Golani Brigade forces took Banias and continued up to Mas'adeh and Kunaitira. Part of the force landed by helicopter on the Hermon, taking it without a battle. Moshe Bril's tank brigade headed north from Banias and captured the low plateau, north of Tel Dan. By 10:00 the Syrian resistance collapsed and, at 14:00, Kunaitira was taken without a fight. The war ended at 18:00. Of 40,000 people residing in the Golan before the war, 34,000 fled to Syria.

The Yom Kippur War in 1973 was a different story. The Israeli Hermon fell to the Syrians. They landed with helicopters, surprising the Israeli troops and killing many. Only 15 days later, after a previous failing attempt, was the Hermon reconquered by Golani and paratroopers suffering heavy casualties.

While the Lower Golan fell to Syria, fierce tank battles led by regiment commander Avigdor Kahalani in the southern parts of Upper Golan maintained Israeli positions. Not far from Buk'ata, a company of half-tracks ran into an ambush and was mutilated by Syrian commandos. Due to the proximity of Upper Golan to Syria's capital Damascus and the success in blocking the Syrian attack, Israel's counter attack sprang from there. During October 13-22, the I.D.F. broke into Syria from Northern Golan and took control of the Hermon and the region south of it, reaching 40 km. from Damascus.

The new position of the I.D.F. pushed the Syrians towards a cease-fire, which was only officially reached six months later. During the winter of 1973-1974 the I.D.F. was constantly under artillery attacks and smallscale ambushes.

Jewish settlement began in the Golan in the 19th century, but collapsed after WWI. Immediately after the Six Day War, kibbutz members ascended to the Golan and began to herd cattle. At first they resided in deserted Syrian army camps. Less than a year later, the Labor government approved settlement. Kunaitira was settled first as it was known that settlements would eventually mark the border. The first settlers suffered from security problems; Syrian shelling and terrorist infiltration. Ten years later there were 25 settlements with 3,500 people. Today there are 33 and over 13,000 Jewish residents.

Two Druze villages in the Hermon slopes and two more in Northern Golan are the only communities who which not flee during the Six Day War. Following the war the villages held 6,400 people, today there are 17,000. Agriculture does not provide enough jobs and many seek work in northern Israel, though there are many periodically unemployed. When the Golan was annexed to the State of Israel in 1981, the Druze resisted, fearing that, were the Golan to fall again to Syria they would be branded "traitors."

Water

Berekhat Ram (see Hike 2) is the outstanding hydrological feature of Northern Golan. Otherwise, the waterscape is concentrated along small canyons which drop to the Hula Valley.

The regional springs emerge off seasonal aquicludes that develop on layers of clayish earth between basalt flows. This earth is actually weathered basalt that developed into soil before it was covered with another lava flow.

Karst features of the Hermon allows water to percolate underground, thus limiting sources of water. A number of small springs do emerge around Ein Kuniyeh, off Jurassic clay, sandstone and volcanic rock.

In spite of the altitude, it seems that there were never glaciers on the Hermon, as there are no typical features of mountain glaciation. This is interesting because Pleistocenian glaciation features have been found on the mountain tops of southern Sinai at lower elevations. It is possible that the strong karst weathering has erased evidence on the Hermon.

Depending on the seasonal rainfall, but usually in April and May, Nahal Sa'ar, Nahal Si'on and parts of Nahal Guvta fill with cascading snow water. The water seeps through the karst terrain and at certain spots bursts forth. The waters of Nahal Sa'ar tend to be chocolate color due to the loose earth of agricultural fields that it drains. The quality, temperature and rush of these waters, makes it a unique phenomena for Israel.

Hiking in the Northern Golan
and the Hermon Mountain Range

It is about a four-hour drive to the region from the center of the country. Access from the west is on Road 99 from Kiryat Shemona and Road 977 from Goma Junction, leaving Road 90 just south of Kiryat Shemona. Coming from Central Golan, Road 978 runs north from Nafah and Road 86 runs along eastern Golan.

The upper parts of the Hermon is a closed military area and entrance requires written permission from the I.D.F. That is why the hikes in this book miss some of the region's coolest spots.

Infrequent public transportation is centralized at the Kiryat Shemona central bus station.

The slopes of the region have a typical Mediterranean climate: hot, dry summers and cool, rainy winters. The plateau of Northern Golan, where Berekhat Ram lies, suffers harsh winter weather but enjoys a mild summer. In the spring, water is abundant and the hills are green. Like everywhere in Israel, spring is the most beautiful hiking time. In summer and fall, the region is dry and hikers must carry all of their water needs. Along the canyons it is especially important to follow the marked trails, for free descent along Golan canyons has caused many fatalities. The strong currents of some of the freshwater streams may look inviting but can be treacherous.

The hikes run along private property belonging to the Druze. The Golan Druze, known to be pro-Syrian, are usually friendly. By Berekhat Ram you may notice cherry groves. Due to their high value, the Druze keep an eye on the orchards.

Important Phone Numbers (area code 06)

<u>S.P.N.I. Field Study Centers and Information</u>

Hermon F.S.C., by Kibbutz Senir:	06-941091, 951523
Golan F.S.C., Katzrin:	961233/4
Keshet, Moshav Keshet:	960560/505
Information Center and Tourism Reservations—Golan:	177-022-7595
Bet Ussishkin Regional Museum:	941704
Regional Nature Reserves Authority:	971918

Safety Assistance

<u>Police</u>: 100   <u>Ambulance</u>: 101
Kiryat Shemona: 943444   Kiryat Shemona: 944334
Mas'adeh: 981888
<u>Army</u>
Gibor: 941055   Northern Command: 979370, 979253, 512356

Sites worth Visiting

Mount Hermon Ski Site.
Northern Golan Dairy, Ortal.
Druze-Style Hospitality, Ein Kuniyeh 982386. It is worthwhile strolling around the
       village, it has a unique atmosphere.
Nimrod Fortress National Park on Road 989.
There are many tourist sites around Katzrin in Central Golan.

Overnight Options

<u>Indoors</u>
Nearly all of the Golan settlements have bed & breakfast or other types of
       overnight accommodations.
S.P.N.I. Field Study Centers, see above.
Neve Ativ Holiday Village—a number of hotels.
<u>Outdoors</u> (with water)
Nebi Hazuri Picnic Site, see Hike 4.   Katzrin Camping (Central Golan).

Gas Stations

In the towns of: Mas'adeh, Buk'ata, Majdal Shams and Katzrin (in Central Golan).

Nahal Hemdal and Ein Gonen

See map on page 22

Points of interest: *A hike along Northern Golan's western slopes, offering fabulous views of the Hula Valley and the Upper Galilee. In the spring, the colorful wildflowers, bubbling springs and basaltic canyon with three waterfalls are most spectacular.*

Length and nature of hike: Option 1: Ein Gonen: 4 or 5 kilometers, loop trip. Option 2: Nahal Hemdal: 4 kilometers, loop trip. The two options can be combined for either a 8- or a 9-kilometer hike.

Hiking time: Option 1: 3 hours. Option 2: 3 hours.

Preferred season: Winter and spring.

Suitable for: All. Crossing Nahal Hemdal when flowing is for experienced hikers only.

Maps: Golan and Hermon hiking and touring map.

Special preparation: Shoes for wading in water and swimsuit on warm days.

Starting point: For hikers arriving by public transportation, Kibbutz Gonen.

Starting & ending point: Turnoff to gravel road off (Ma'atz) Road 918, between kilometer posts 25 and 26.

To reach starting point:

Arrival by private transportation: Road 918 runs along the contact of the eastern Hula Valley with the western slopes of the Golan. Access to this road coming from the north is from Gonen, or in the south from Kibbutz Gadot. Park the vehicle by a gravel road that veers to the west, toward a grove of trees and where a dirt road heads up to the east (1).

Arrival by public transportation: Buses do not make it to the starting point. They reach Gonen from Kiryat Shemona. From there to the route it is a kilometer. At the end of the hike, it is another 2.5 km. back to Gonen.

From Gonen, head up Road 959 towards the Golan Heights. At the first sharp curve to the left, a blue-marked dirt road leaves south. Take the dirt road, and after 1 km., cross Nahal Gonen. Fifty meters beyond, reach an intersection (4), continue straight (south) on the dirt road. Continue as described in "To begin hike": at "This road gently ascending . . ."

Geography

This hike traverses the western slopes of Northern Golan. The slopes are actually fault escarpments, part of the series of parallel faults belonging to the Syrian-African Rift. Along some of the faults springs have emerged. These faults have occured between episodes of lava flow; some of the older faults are only recognizable by landscape features (a sharp slope flattening out) since later flows (today basalt) have covered the fault.

Parallel faults, all in a north-south direction, have profound influence on today's landscape. Tel Urfiyeh, for example, is a block that has been thrust upwards with faults on both of its sides, east and west. This phenomena is known as a horst. A number of these horst-hills appear along the western slopes. Small valleys have appeared between the horst and the descending slope to its east. These valleys have accumulated with soil and people have used them for farming, cattle pens, roads etc. Since the formation of the Rift (and due to it), a sharp altitude change has developed between the Hula Valley and the Golan plateau. This differential has given the descending streams more energy, causing them to cut into the rock, creating canyons. The ancient canyon of Nahal Hemdal cut a wide valley into one of the first basalt layers of the Golan, set down over a million years ago (Golan Formation). Between thirty and sixty thousand years later, a lava flow (Muweisse Basalt), originating in the eastern part of the Golan, reached Nahal Hemdal and filled in part of the valley. This can be seen from the trail, by the descent to Nahal Hemdal, looking upstream. Since then, the stream bed has cut into the recent flow, creating today's narrow canyon.

Plants and animals

Lupine (*Lupinus*): One of the most outstanding wildflowers in Israel. The mountain lupine blooms in early spring. Its dark blue flowers create a strong contrast with the green landscape.

The lupine (*turmoose* in Arabic and Hebrew) is well-known worldwide. In Israel there are four main species, two of them growing in the Nahal Hemdal vicinity: the mountain lupine (*Lupinus pilosus*) and the thinner-leaved, lighter-colored *Lupinus angustifolius*. The mountain lupine officially grows throughout the Mediterranean regions of Israel. It is common along the slopes of the Golan and the Lower Galilee, especially by ancient tels and abandoned settlements.

The flowers grow in an arranged cluster at the top of the stem. The distinctive finger-like leaves are coated with hairs. The 1 cm. seeds come in a 5-8 cm. long pod, quite similar to a pea pod. The lupine flower has an interesting device to attract insects. The petals form a shape of a "boat" with two "oars" and a "sail." The boat encloses the anthers, hidden by the oars. The sail stands upright and sports a white patch in the middle. Dark streaks lead from its periphery to the center of the flower, where the petals form a short nectar tube.

The oars offer a landing platform for an insect. The small dark streaks and white spot of the sail lead the insect to the nectar. The white patch becomes purple after pollination, like a traffic light turning red. It seems that blue and white attract insects more than blue and purple.

The entire plant contains a poisonous substance called lupinin. The seeds of all species are edible after being boiled in water a number of times. They are best served salted or soured. They are eaten as snack food, once a favorite in the Middle Eastern market. Even today they are sold in the open market of Jerusalem. Traditional medicine uses the seeds for opening the intestines and worm treatment. Seed ash is used to expel lice.

The lupine is mentioned in the Mishna: (Shabbat 18:1) regarding its *halakhic* status in context to its removal during the Sabbath "...and the dry lupine, because its a poor-mans food."

Egyptian vulture (*Neophron percnopterus*): This common bird of prey is easily distinguishable by its black and dirty-white colors. Its wings are 0.5 m. long and wingspan three times that. The bird's bill is yellow and legs are long and pink.

Its range includes all the warm regions of the main continents. In Israel it is a common migrant and summer resident throughout the country. It occasionally winters in the Negev.

This bird eats carrion and refuse, but sometimes may vary its diet with slow-moving creatures, such as tortoises. It breaks eggs by dropping them.

These raptors arrive in the Golan only at the end of March. They usually build their nests in crevices, out of coarse branches and line them with scraps of refuse or food. Two eggs are laid in early spring. Incubation, by both parents, lasts about 40 days. At 75 days, the chick flies for the first time. Usually only one chick reaches maturity. In early autumn, the birds migrate to Africa.

Waterfalls in Nahal Hemdal

History

The canyon of Nahal Hemdal was never suitable for agriculture. Thus, no remarkable materialistic evidence has been found. Sporadic, smallscale settlement has taken place along the Golan slopes, such as by Ein Gonen.

On June 9th, 1967, the fifth day of the Six Day War, the assault on Syrian-held Golan began. The main pressure was applied in the north where the first Israeli forces reached the sloping plateau. In the Nahal Hemdal area, Golani and NAHAL infantry forces captured the Urfiyeh fort, opening access to the Golan Heights and ending the threat that the fort had made on Israeli farmers in the Hula Valley.

Two brigades ascended Road 959, north of Nahal Gonen. The steep paved road at the top intersects with the T.A.P. Line Road which was quickly taken to the south by the Har'el Brigade. This movement captured the Central Golan.

During the Yom Kippur War the Nahal Hemdal area was one of the few spots in the Golan spared from battle.

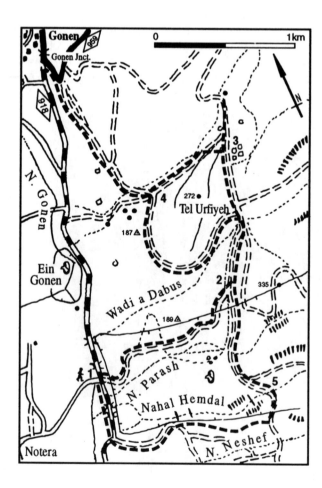

Hike 1, Nahal Hemdal
and Ein Gonen

Site description

Ein Gonen: A miniature paradise offering two streams of water fed from many springs. The springs emerge from a layer of ancient soil. The soil was quickly covered by a flow of lava and today is exposed along the slope. Total annual discharge reaches 5 million cubic meters. The springs fluctuate between 100-200 liters per hour, depending on the season.

The water is excellent for drinking, but due to the cattle, is not worth a try. On site are ruined water channels, ruins of a flour mill, fruit trees and shade. The tall thin trees, leafless in winter, are called ulmus, a rare specimen in Israel. Tall ulmus trees grow by the Dan springs. The larger and taller trees are eucalyptus. The site is known as Ein Mamoon in Arabic, after a village of the same name. Explore, wade in the water and enjoy this little-known site.

Nahal Hemdal: A nature reserve of 1,143 dunams. The stream, in Arabic known as *Wadi Hanzal*, descends 800 m. over ten kilometers, and drains into the Hula Valley. The wadi carries water only during the winter and spring, leaving the stream bed poor in vegetation. In early winter, the snow to pink colored blossoms of the almond tree initiate the blooming season.

The cliffs of lower Nahal Hemdal home different birds of prey such as the Egyptian vulture. Some of the cliffs reveal hexagonal basalt columns (*meshushim*).

To begin hike:

The gravel road leads to a cluster of eucalyptus trees where the settlement of Notera was established and abandoned. Across Road 918, head up the wide dirt road onto the slopes of the Golan. The steep road passes jujube trees. Looking up to the east, note a change in the steepness of the slope. The change is due to a north-south fault. Parallel to the fault runs a dirt road, toward which you are heading. In the spring, lupines color the green fields with hues of blue. After 1 km., and 200 m. of ascent, reach a T-intersection (2). To the north, large spurge bushes bloom in late winter through spring in unique, bright yellow colors.

Both options begin here. Option 1 leads to Ein Gonen and returns to this intersection. Option 2 heads south to Nahal Hemdal and ends at the starting point.

Option 1: Take a left on the blue-marked dirt road heading along the contour. The small hill across the wadi ahead and a bit to your left is Tel Urfiyeh. This modest hill was a Syrian fort until 1967.

After 500 m., cross a wadi and go through a gate. Continue on the dirt road by a cattle pen. Exit the pen arena via another gate (do not forget to close them), pass sabra cacti and continue on the dirt road which begins to descend to Wadi el-Katzeb (Nahal Gonen). At a sharp curve to the left, leave the road, heading straight on the wide trail into the grove of Ein Gonen (3).

After maximizing the time at Ein Gonen you can return to the T-intersection (2) the same way you came. If time is not a factor, add an hour to the hike: descend along Nahal Gonen for a kilometer. This can be done along the stream or in the stream (for the adventurous). Otherwise, from the intersection, descend the blue-marked dirt road on the southern slope. Along the way, enjoy views of the Hula Valley and eastern Upper Galilee. The pointed hill straight across Hula Valley is Keren Naftali, 510 m., where a Greek temple once stood.

Where the dirt road crosses Nahal Gonen (4), go left on the dirt road. This road, gently ascending, eventually curves around Tel Urfiyeh. The plant with dissected wide leaves at its base and a 1-2 meter shear stalk is the giant fennel, untouched by cattle and man. Its dry stalk burns slowly.

Return to the blue-marked dirt road by the cattle pen. Go right, back to the T-intersection (2). It is possible to return to the starting point the way you came or continue as described below—option 2.

Option 2: Head south on the blue-marked dirt road. This was the Syrian patrol road until 1967. The road crosses Nahal Parash after 350 m. and begins to ascend to the crest of Nahal Hemdal. Where the road sharply curves left (east), follow the blue mark onto a wide path that drops to Nahal Hemdal. Head off to the right and catch an unsatisfying vista of the impressive canyon. Note the cave at the top of the southern bank, a rare phenomena in basalt. Here the viper's bugloss blooms boasting violet-red one-inch flowers.

Descend to the crossing. Above this small canyon ran a bridge, part of the Syrian patrol road. A flood destroyed the bridge in 1968. During periods of strong flow and on wet days when the going is slippery, it is dangerous to cross the stream. If so, there are other options:

1) The least exciting option: to return to the starting point, head back the way you came.

2) The easy option: descend along the slope above the northern cliffs of the stream. This way is interesting and offers good views of two of the three waterfalls. The comfortable descent is at your own risk! Along this route there is a vista of the southern cliff of the lower canyon, where raptors nest.

3) The long and tiring, but most interesting, option: head up the northern bank of the stream along its upper canyon (or along the dirt road) for 500 m. and then cross the stream. Head south along the southern bank until rejoining the blue mark at the top of the short steep ascent from the stream bed. Continue as described below:

If the crossing is manageable, cross the stream and ascend the southern bank. Above, reach the continuation of the Syrian patrol road. The blue mark descends to the right (west) along the top of the canyon's cliffs, offering a few glimpses of the canyon's secrets. Take it. The trail does not enter the canyon.

After descending a steep slope, the main trail runs by a dirt road which you can also follow down to Road 918. Take a right on Road 918, and after about 500 m., return to the starting point (1).

Berekhat Ram

Points of interest: *A round blue lake beneath the slopes of the Hermon Mountain Range, encircled by the peaks of the Golan Heights, surrounded by cherry and apple orchards.*

Length and nature of hike: 4 kilometers, loop trip, encompassing the lake. Berekhat Ram is surrounded by private property. Thus the hike sticks to roads most of the time. The speciality of the hike is the landscape, unique in Israel.

Hiking time: 2 hours.

Preferred season: All year. In the winter, temperatures are often close to freezing.

Suitable for: All.

Maps: Golan and Hermon hiking and touring map.

Special preparation: Swimsuit and fishing pole.

Starting & ending point: Druze town of Mas'adeh.

To reach starting point:

Arrival by private transportation: Drive to Mas'adeh. Road 99 leads there from Kiryat Shemona. Road 98 leads there from the Central Golan. At the junction of these two roads in Mas'adeh, head northeast on the continuation of Road 98 for 1 km. to the restaurant (3). Park there and begin the hike as described in the second paragraph of 'To begin hike.'

Arrival by public transportation: Take the (infrequent) bus from Kiryat Shemona central bus station to Mas'adeh. Descend on Road 98, before the police station (1) (there is no bus stop). Take a left through the narrow street heading east past a few homes. After 150 m., the paved road exits the village and descends to a small wadi. Continue down and up the other side to a junction with a dirt road arriving from the right (2). Here follow 'To begin hike.'

Geography

Berekhat Ram, 940 m. above sea level, is an elliptical lake, 850 m. at its longest and 600 m. at its widest. It is surrounded by basalt and layers of volcanic ash (tuff and scoriae). The water is 6-10 m. deep. Because it has no drainage system and no outlet, the waters must have an underground source. In other words, the pool is a window into the underground water system.

The origins of this crater-like depression has been postulated by many. According to one explanation, it came from the karstic dissolution of a nearby limestone stratum. But this would make the lake a doline, which is not the case. Today, the prevalent theory is that the lake sits in a caldera, or collapsed volcano, similar to many smaller ones in the area known by locals as juba. The source of the basalt flow lining the northern rim of the lake is from a nearby volcano. The tuff and scoriae are most likely from the volcano of Berekhat Ram. The tuff reaches a thickness of 38 m.

Following the Six Day War, the lake was declared a nature reserve of 1,100 dunams. The entire surrounding area is private property, making nature conservation around the lake problematic. The lake is used as a reservoir: stream flow of upper Nahar Sa'ar is dammed and pumped in. From here, water is transferred to reservoirs in the Northern Golan and to nearby fields. About 500,000 cubic meters are pumped annually.

Several rare water plants grow along the shores. Carp were introduced in 1958.

Plants and animals

Apple (Malus Sylvestris): The Hebrew name, *tapuah*, occurs five times in the Bible as a tree or fruit and six times as a place. Here is one well-known example (Song of Songs 2:5):

Sustain me with raisins, refresh me with apples; for I am sick with love.

Biblical botanists have debated the identification of the *tapuah*. In II Chronicles 2:43, Tapuah is used as a personal name. Some have applied the name to be an apricot or bitter orange. Tracing back the origin of apples in the Middle East, no prehistoric traces have been found. Arabic identification of the *tuffah* as the apple strengthens the assumption that everybody is talking about the same thing. Pliny's *Historia Naturae* mentions red and white apples from Syria. Wild apples have been found in Turkey. Thus, apples may have been wild plants in neighboring Lebanon. It seems that apples reached Israel 4,000 years ago.

The apple tree is stately, reaching a height of 8-12 m. It has elliptical or roundish leaves. The white flowers, 3-4 cm. in diameter, grow in clusters of four to six. This species seems to have widely bred and domesticated so that hundreds of strains were developed and are grown throughout the temperate regions of the world.

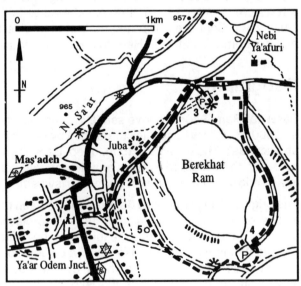

Hike 2,
Berekhat Ram

26

History

Berekhat Ram, one of the few lakes in the Middle East, has been heavily documented throughout history. During Hellinistic times, the pool was known as Phiala, meaning bowl. It belonged to the county of Panias.

Josephus Flavius writes that it is the source of the Panias (Banias). Actually, the waters feed only the small springs around Ein Kuniyeh. Talmudic sages called it the Sea of Panias.

An Arab folk tale tells about a prospering village of wicked people where Berekhat Ram is today. One day a holy man passed by and was refused a place to rest and food. The following day on his way out, he left a curse: "May the village sink into the ground with all its inhabitants." Sure enough, the earth sank and the hollow that was formed filled in with water—what we know as Berekhat Ram.

Berekhat Ram and the
Hermon Mountain Range

H.B. Tristram, who ascended to Berekhat Ram via Nahar Sa'ar, explicitly describes Berekhat Ram of the 1860s:

> In about three hours we came upon a bare but well-watered plateau, all basalt. We here crossed the stream, up the gorge of which has crept, and passed a wretched Bedouin village—Mezra'ha. From this we immediately descended into a wide shallow basin, in the center of which was a deep oval lake—Phiala.

> We walked round it in twenty minutes. The enclosing hills were bare, except on the south, which was clad with large flowering shrubs and small trees. There was no marsh, but rich verdure, with many lumps of black scoria on it, fringed it to the water's edge. We were in the center of an enormous extinct volcano ...

> To the east side of this basin the limestone hills rose bold and lofty, but on the other three sides a mass of scoria, lava, and basaltic blocks had partially decomposed into a rich black earth.

> Frogs (*Rana esculenta, L.*) by thousands upon thousands swarmed in and round the lake, and their croak was deafening. On every stone and along the edge they sat in serried ranks, bolting into the water before us as we stepped, while hundreds of water snakes (*Tropidonotus hydrus, Pall.*) wriggled from under them, but not a stork or heron to rule them.

A fringe of rushes and water-weeds lined the slimy pool, which was shallow for a few feet, and then became suddenly deep. The water was icy cold, and swarmed with leeches, which were adhering in numbers to every stone. Immense numbers of warblers and red-backed shrikes were breeding on the southern slopes, and in three or four hours we obtained about twenty nests, chiefly the Orphean warbler and lesser whitethroat.

To begin hike:

Enjoy your first view of Berekhat Ram. One hundred meters above the junction, to the north, is a small juba. (Berekhat Ram, recall, is possibly just a larger version). Take a left along the newly-paved road, running for 600 m. above the lake to a junction.

Take a right along the road (that leads to the Israel-Syria border). Immediately to the right (south), a paved road leads to a restaurant, gift shop and boat rental (3) overlooking the lake. To the north lies Ya'afuri Valley, named after the tomb of Ya'afuri (a Druze saint), 250 m. to your north. The valley is the border between the Golan Heights and the Hermon Mountains. Upper Nahal Sa'ar runs among the apple orchards of Majdal Shams in the valley.

After 200 m., take the first dirt road to the right. Ascend the basalt ridge from behind the restaurant. Go left at the intersection for 100 m. and join a partially paved road. Take it to the right, descending along private orchards to the rocky shores of the lake.

Along this part of the lake it is possible to swim and fish.

The eastern slopes (left) are of colorful volcanic tuff. Head along the road to the pumping station (4). Beyond the station the lower scoriae cliffs are visible, dropping to the water.

At the gate, begin to follow a green-marked trail to the left. The rock here is sedimentary, a rarity in Northern Golan. Above the station, reach a dirt road intersection. Go right (leaving the green mark), parallel to the ridge crest. The ridge is of tuff.

Along the way, step off to the right and feast your eyes on the best views of Berekhat Ram: to the north, the southern shoulder of the Hermon holding the Druze town of Majdal Shams. To the northeast note Har Ram (1,182 m.) and to the south, Har Keramim (1,190 m.). Both mountains are of scoriae. Behind Mas'adeh lies the Odem Forest, one of the few true forests of Israel.

After 250 m., the road splits. Take the right option, towards the white water tank on the 1,000-meter ridge (5). From the water tank, the road descends along cherry trees to the road from Mas'adeh (2), passing remnants of a Syrian army camp. En route, note the layers of soft, light-colored tuff rock, ideal for water collection.

Nahar Sa'ar

See map on
page 31

Points of interest: *A seasonal river of melted snow, cutting a gorge along the contact of Hermon and Golan.*

Length and nature of hike: 4 kilometers, loop trip or back-and-forth. For hikers coming with public transportation add a kilometer to and from the starting point. A one-way route is also feasible.

Hiking time: 2-3 hours.

Preferred season: Winter and spring, when the river is rushing.

Suitable for: All.

Maps: Golan and Hermon hiking and touring map.

Special preparation: Swimsuit.

Starting & ending point: Parking lot before Gesher Hayedidoot on the road leading to the Druze village Ein Kuniyeh.

Ending point for hikers going one-way: Sa'ar Falls by the junction of Roads 989 and 99.

To reach starting point:

Arrival by private transportation: Between Banias Spring Nature Reserve and Mas'adeh on Road 99, turn off towards Ein Kuniyeh. The turnoff is by kilometer post 19, at a sharp curve in the road. After the sharp turn to the right, it is worthwhile parking the car and enjoying a grand view of Nahar Sa'ar below, Ein Kuniyeh, and the Hermon Range in the north and east. Due north, and a bit higher than where you are, stands the impressive Nimrod Fortress.

Arrival by public transportation: At the time of writing, no public bus reaches the starting point (Ein Kuniyeh). Take the (infrequent) bus from Kiryat Shemona central bus station to Mas'adeh. Get off at the turnoff to Ein Kuniyeh and descend the paved road for 1 km. to Gesher Hayedidoot (1).

Geography

Nahar Sa'ar clearly marks the border between the Golan Heights and the Hermon Mountain Range. The river bed runs northwest and includes a number of water-falls.

The water cuts between the basalt of the Golan Heights and the Jurassic and Cretaceous sedimentary rock of the Hermons. Along this line stands a frozen relic of a lava flow from only 14,000 years ago. The basalt emerged from Berekhat Ram and surged down the ancient Nahar Sa'ar all the way to Nahar Hermon. Nahar Sa'ar since then has cut into the basalt, creating a canyon, 10-30 m. deep, along most of its course.

The river begins at Ein Sa'ar, 1,035 m. above sea-level on the Israel-Syria border. In the summer, 140 cubits of water emerge every hour, and are fully used for agriculture. Then the barren stream bed reveals dark boulders, coated with white calcium carbonate that comes from the river's waters that have seeped through carbonate rocks of the Hermon. In winter, discharge increases seven fold and Nahar Sa'ar becomes a raging torrent.

An 11,000 dunam nature reserve includes Nahar Sa'ar and some of its slopes.

Plants and animals

Snowbell (*Styrax officinalis L.*): This common tree has many names: snowbell, styrax or storax. It is mentioned in Genesis 30:37 and Hosea 4:13:

> They sacrifice on the tops of the mountains, and make offerings upon the hills, under oak, styrax and terebinth, because their shade is good.

It is a deciduous tree, 3-6 m. tall. The oval leaves are about 5 cm. long, green on the upper face and white-hairy beneath. The whitish color of the leaves, visible from a distance, is the source of the Hebrew name, *livneh*—white.

The tree has its leaf-break in March and begins to bloom in April. Its droopy, bell-like white flowers resemble those of the orange tree. The fruit is a one-seeded, hard, wooly green drupe in a nut shape which turns yellow when ripe. The fruit holds fort in the fall with the shedding of the leaves. The large poisonous seeds are used by fishermen to stun fish.

The snowbell is often found with the oak and terebinth plant association through-out the Mediterranean parts of Israel, especially at low elevations.

History

An ancient route runs along Nahar Sa'ar from Damascus to Banias. Although the French Mandate paved today's road upon the ancient one, ancient milestones were found by Tel Dan.

Tristram ascended to Berekhat Ram via Nahar Sa'ar in the 1860s:

> May 16th was devoted to a most interesting excursion to Birket et Ram, the Lake Phiala of Josephus, east of Banias. Our track lay up the north side of a deep glen. The hills on the left were lofty, but, excepting the massive ruin of the castle, not picturesque; and we had occasional glimpses of Hermon, ribbed down all the ravines with snow, while the higher and exposed portions were already bare.

> The nearer view in its present transition state was by no means striking or grand, like its distant majesty in winter. The absence of all bold peaks or granite points, as well as of timber (except of the smallest size low down), renders Hermon far inferior in grandeur to mountains of equal height in the Alps or Pyrenees. And yet it rises from its base nearly 10,000 feet.

We passed the flourishing village of Ain Kunyeh. Our course was on limestone rocks, comparatively bare, though relieved by many patches of mulberry and olive groves. Close to us, on our right, a mountain torrent tore down on a rugged bed, while the opposite side of the ravine was a mighty lava current, black and rugged, but with soil of great fertility, clad with a mass of trees and brushwood.

Site description:

<u>Ein Kuniyeh</u>: The smallest, oldest and most picturesque of the four Druze villages in the Northern Golan and Israeli Hermon, with 1,500 residents. Kuniyeh means cypress, once a common tree in the region.

Remnants of an Early Bronze village have been found and ruins of a couple of churches are also evident in the village. A sacred tomb of Jethro's sister Sit, one

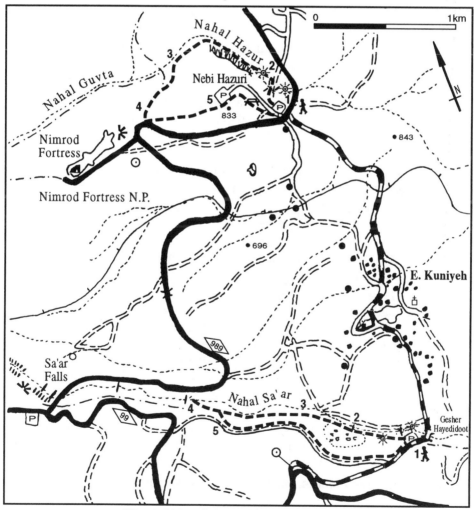

Hike 3, Nahar Sa'ar and Hike 4, Nahal Hazur

of the most revered places for Druze, stands at the western side of town. A number of springs emerge off the unique strata in and around the friendly village.

Gesher Hayedidoot (The Friendship Bridge): Also called Gesher Hashalom (The Bridge of Peace). Syria dynamited the bridge in 1967, cutting off Ein Kuniyeh. The Israeli administration quickly rebuilt it, hence its name.

To begin hike:

From the parking lot (1), descend west towards remains of a flour mill above Nahar Sa'ar. On your left grow snowbell trees. By the mill, note the wide water channel. At the arched opening you can see where the water dropped from the chimney. Note another mill across the way.

Continue on the green-marked trail which hugs the edge of the gorge. Along the trail round thorny burnet and calycotome bushes grow, blooming in yellow during the season when the river runs. Behind the rock wall lay remnants of a village (2). Today edible Mediterranean fruits remain, such as sabra, olive and grape.

Alot of terebinth and snowbell trees grow along the cliffs down to the river. This is the only place in Israel where snowbell trees dominate a forest. Arabs believe that ghosts dwell beneath the trees and they leave them untouched.

Two hundred meters from the mill, the Sa'ar drops a waterfall. A hundred meters farther down trail, the ruined village ends and you enter an expanse of viper's bugloss. In early summer it blooms in whitish-pink colors along its stalks that can reach 2 m. in height.

Closer to the stream sprout fig trees which ripen in late summer. The stalks of hollyhock blooming in shades of purple in May usually signify the end of spring.

One kilometer from the starting point, the marked trail curves left, jutting above the shallow canyon. Here the vast field ends as the ridge to the south descends toward the river. The trail curves back right. Look at the basalt cliff dropping to the Sa'ar and note hexagonal columns, called *meshushim* (3).

About 150 m. from the *meshushim*, look for Road 99 across the river. When you see the paved road it is a sign that you have reached the area where you head up to the dirt road which runs parallel to the marked trail and a bit above it. Where a number of animal trails sharply veer left and a rock wall stands 30 m. above, head south (left) along the animal paths to the rock wall above, holding the dirt road (5). But before heading back, it is worthwhile continuing on the marked trail which descends 200 m. to the river bed by a waterfall (4) (there is another one 100 m. upstream). The pool beneath the waterfall is perennial and swimming is feasible.

For hikers arriving by public transportation it is possible to continue on the marked trail that follows the southern bank, for 1.5 km ending at Sa'ar Falls at the junction of Road 989 and Road 99 (there is a bus stop), making the hike one-way.

To return to the parked vehicle, head to the dirt road and go left. The road gradually ascends along the base of the steep southern slope.

There is a nice view of the Hermon: Ein Kuniyeh; Nebi Hazuri, the tree capped hill, to its left; and, further left, Nimrod Fortress. If you look between Nebi Hazuri and Ein Kuniyeh you can see the upper parts of the Israeli Hermon (treeless slopes over 2,000 m. above sea level) between Hermon Shoulder to the right and Siryon Ridge to the left. To the north stands the protruding peak of Mitzpe Haramata at 1,200 m. and, east of it (right), other peaks of Si'on Ridge. Ahead to the southeast, look for the fringe of Odem Forest at the edge of the sheer drop to Nahal Sa'ar.

After 800 m. a dirt road veers to the left. Continue on the main dirt road to the paved road, past oak forest with calycotome and wild asparagus. Go left on the paved road to the starting point (1) and right, back to the junction if you came by public transportation.

Oak trees of Nebi Hazuri (Hike 4)

33

Nahal Hazur

4

See map on page 31

Points of interest: *A narrow gorge of trickling water beginning at two ruined flour mills, a deep ravine shaded by boulders and thick vegetation. Views, a memorial and an ancient oak grove around a tomb.*

Length and nature of hike: 3 kilometers, loop trip.

Hiking time: 3-4 hours.

Preferred season: All year.

Suitable for: Experienced hikers.

Maps: Golan and Hermon hiking and touring map.

Special preparation: Swimsuit in the spring, binoculars.

Starting & ending point: Nebi Hazuri Picnic Site, right off Road 989, past kilometer post 5. Water is available.

To reach starting point:

Arrival by private transportation: From Road 99 by kilometerpost 15 at Sa'ar Falls, turn off to Road 989 immediately crossing Nahal Sa'ar. After 5 km., turn left to the parking lot of Nebi Hazuri, by a clump of impressive trees (1).

Arrival by public transportation: Take the infrequent bus from Kiryat Shemona towards Neve Ativ. Ask to get off at Nebi Hazuri (1).

Geography

Upper Nahal Hazur runs by a unique geological unit known as the Guvta Eruptive. The unit is mainly volcanic breccia from the Lower Cretaceous. Between the Roman bridge and the main road, the river runs through shales and marls from the late Jura and Lower Cretaceous. These impermeable rocks expose underground water. Beyond the Roman bridge, a fault runs in a northeast direction initiating the canyon which is out of hard Jurrasic sedimentary rock.

The unique geology make this the only perennial stream in the Israeli Hermon. During the month and a half following the rainy season, the stream has a considerable amount of water. Most of the hiking route is along cracked Jurassic limestone which induces infiltration. The disappearing waters most likely reappear at the Banias Spring. The uniformity of the hard Jurassic rock is the reason that no real waterfalls are present along its course; waterfalls often occur along faults or where a hard layer of rock overlays a softer layer.

Along its one-kilometer canyon ending at the merge with Nahal Guvta, the stream drops about 100 m., a steep incline. The stream's Arabic name is "Oleander Wadi." The presence of oleanders and the remnants of flour mills prove that the stream has been running for years.

Plants and animals

Spanish broom (*Spartium junceum*): The bush, of the pea family, reaches 3 m. It has leaves only in the winter, so that its common appearance is of ropy green branches—similar to the desert broom bush, the *rotem*. Thus its Hebrew name, *ahirotem* meaning the brother of the *rotem*.

Its bright yellow flowers, 2 cm. large, bloom in late spring. Although lacking nectar, the flowers are nonetheless pollinated by insects. When the insect lands on the "oars" of the flower the pollen is released, covering the whole insect.

Spanish broom is native to northern Israel but can also be found in the country's center. It grows at high elevations, mainly on chalk soils (rendzina).

Humans use its flowers for aromatic oil and yellow dye, its branches for weaving baskets, and various parts of the plant for herbal medicine.

History

Nebi Hazuri lies on an ancient road that ascended from Banias towards the Hermon. Crusaders built Nimrod Fortress, overlooking the road, to control the whole region. Between 1129 and 1164, the fortress exchanged hands several times between the Moslems and Crusaders, finally falling to the Moslems. In 1219, the ruler of Damascus destroyed the fort in fear of it being recaptured by the Crusaders (the same thing was done to the walls of Jerusalem). The site seems to have prospered during Mameluke times.

H.B. Tristram describes the site

> More than once we visited Kulat es Subeibeh, the noble castle of Banias. We were at once struck by its strong resemblance, both in situation, in plan, and in actual style, to the castles of Kurn [i.e., the Monfort in Nahal Keziv] and Shukif [the Beaufort in Lebanon]. The latter can be distinctly seen from it… The castle is difficult of access, and is in many parts in admirable preservation.

Site description

Nebi Hazuri: Sheikh Uttaman el Hazuri is commonly known as Nebi (prophet) Hazuri. The site contains the tomb of Hazuri and of a few other Druze holy men, plus 73 developed oak trees up to 300 years old. The trees average 100 years.

According to the Bible, pagan worship was common beneath such trees. The trees are *haram*, and it is strictly forbidden by Arabs to harm the trees or the fallen branches. There are a number of stories about people trying to collect wood at Nebi Hazuri only to find their hand withering.

The site is holy to the Druze, a *Makam*. Druze continue to come on pilgrimage, with the belief that Hazuri will help fulfill their personal prayers.

Hazuri, according to Druze tradition, was a peace-loving man. Hazuri would give salt to people passing by. The salt would cause evil people to lose their way while peace lovers enjoyed the salt.

In 1974 the Jewish National Fund established a picnic site to accompany the new road from Banias.

To begin hike:

The wooden sign at the edge of the parking lot (1), describes the memorial for fallen soldiers of the Egoz Elite Unit and lists the sponsors. Look across Road 989 and note the colorful strata. That type of rock is partially responsible for the appearance of running water in Nahal Hazur. From the sign, a dirt road heads up and along the ridge to the memorial.

A wide blue-marked trail also begins here. Take it and descend to Nahal Hazur. Cross the stream on a bridge, assumed to be Roman and follow the marked trail on the eastern bank. The trail passes two ruined flour mills (2). It then descends into thick Mediterranean forest, criss-crossing the steep shady ravine. Half a kilometer from the mill, as the wadi curves west, notice that the running water has percolated into the gravel. Oleander bushes appear along the way, hinting that underground water is close to the surface.

Occasionally through the thicket you might glimpse Nimrod Fortress, hovering above the deepening cleft—an impressive sight. Around this point look for the trail to the southern slope (to the left) (3). It is not a good idea to miss this turnoff. There are two landmarks: a Syrian acer tree stands just prior to the turnoff and the trail is marked by two white lines (an empty sandwich).

Follow the new trail on level elevation through a patch of Spanish broom. It joins a marked trail ascending from the wadi, a bit farther down from where you left it. The trail, marked in blue and sometimes black, steeply climbs southwest, passing through a deserted olive grove with wild asparagus. Reach the fence of the Nimrod Fortress National Park and go left to a curve on Road 989 by the park entrance (4).

Topographically the spot is a saddle between Nimrod Fortress at 786 m. above sea level and Egoz Elite Unit Memorial hill at 833 m., the next stop.

Head 50 m. up Road 989. By post 989, veer to the left; 20 m. below the road runs a clear trail. Take it to the right and ascend the moderate slope through Mediterranean forest. Farther up, the vegetation dwindles and the trail is poorly marked between two scraggly lines of stones.

At the top (5) enjoy the encompassing view. The memorial extends toward Nebi Hazuri, along a gravel trail adorned with plaques describing each fallen soldier. Take it to Nebi Hazuri (1).

Back at Nebi Hazuri it is interesting to peek into the room holding the tomb of Hazuri.

Upper
Jordan Valley

Geography

The Upper Jordan Valley has two main subregions: the Hula Valley and the Rosh Pina Sill. (Some call the narrow Jordan River Canyon east of the Rosh Pina Sill a third subregion, but I connect it to Kinnarot Valley.)

The Hula Valley is the best-known part of the region. It is almost completely encompassed by hills. The steep ridge towering 800 m. above the Hula is the Naftali Chain, part of the Upper Galilee. This is the largest elevation drop in western Israel. To the east rise the slopes of the Hermon Range and the Northern Golan Heights. To the north between Hermon and Galilee lay the Metulla Hills (500 m. high), creating the valley's northern border. The Rosh Pina Sill, rising a meager 100-200 m. above the valley floor, blocks the valley from the south. The valley measures only 25 x 8 km., but drains 1,470 sq. km., 675 of them from the Hermon. The Hula is 71 m. above sea level.

Lake Hula appeared thanks to the Rosh Pina Sill, a natural dam in the south that blocked the upper Jordan River. The sill was formed hundreds of thousands of years ago when lava flows descended into the Rift valley.

The lake has become swampy due to two main reasons: 1) The inflow of water has deposited tremendous quantities of sediment. 2) The Jordan River, which drains the Hula Valley, cuts into the Rosh Pina Sill, steeply dropping to the Kinnarot Valley. The Jordan drains the water but not the sediments which create the swamps.

The lake-shrinking process is quick in geological terms—two meters a year. If Lake Hula had not been artificially drained, it would naturally clog up in 5,000 years.

The extermination of the lake in the 1950s brought on profound changes to the region and to Lake Kinneret. The soils that consequently appeared are unique for Israel. They are black alluvial swamp soils rich in organic material and peat. In recent years, due to the draining of Lake Hula, the peat has undergone subsurface combustion, severely hurting the valley's agricultural potential. Lake Hula had an important effect on the quality of Lake Kinneret's waters. A majority of the waters draining into the Kinneret originated from Lake Hula. The sediment settling process which occured in Lake Hula released sediment-free water to Lake Kinneret. Today, the absence of this natural filter is causing the Kinneret to fill up with sediment. At the present rate, the Kinneret will turn into a swamp in a few thousand years.

The hikes in this section take place along the northern part of the Hula Valley. The area is composed of three levels of basalt and travertine, descending from north to south. These sediments were deposited in the Pleistocene. The basalt drained into the region from the nearby mountains. The travertine is evidence of large bodies of water with vegetation that covered the valley. Tel Hai and Moshav Yuval are situated on the upper level. On the middle step lies Tel Dan and Kibbutz Ma'ayan Barukh. The third step is the location of Kibbutzim Dan, Dafna and Hagoshrim. Along this step runs the ancient road to Banias and today's Road 99.

Climate

The basin-shaped valley is in the rain shadow of the Upper Galilee and is protected from winds. Though relatively close to the Mediterranean, the Hula Valley climate is a continental one, with heavy heat hovering over the ground in summer when maximum temperatures exceed those along the coast (maximum is 35 degrees). Summer nights are comfortable.

The Hermon Mountain Range, when covered with snow, creates cold waves in the valley. Cold air settles in the valley. Winter nights yield frost, thus limiting the variety of plant species in the valley. In January the mean temperature is 11°C.

The average annual temperature at Dan is 20.2°, similar to Beersheba! Annual precipitation drops toward the center of the valley, from 750 mm. at Dan, at the northern rim, to 450 mm. at the center.

Vegetation

The plant life reflects a combination of two climatic factors. One is the north-south gradient—it is hotter in the south. The second factor is the west-east gradient—the descent from the mountains of western Israel corresponds to a temperature increase.

The Upper Jordan Valley is the only part of the Syrian-African Rift in Israel with Mediterranean vegetation. This can be divided into three groups:

1. Relicts of natural vegetation. Huge Tabor oaks and Atlantic terebinths grow along the valley sides and slopes. These trees are remnants of a plant association which covered the slopes of the Golan and Gilead hundreds of years ago before being logged. The jujube association along with a few other thorns such as the Syrian notobasis, the rolling gundelia and golden thistle are consequences of long-term human involvement.

2. Agricultural vegetation and disturbed fields. These include apples and irrigated and fodder crops. The frost that collects during a few winter nights eliminates the ability of sub-tropical species to develop. That explains the absence of bananas and citrus fruits. Tropical annuals, such as sugar cane, rice and cotton, do grow well through the hot summer (though sugar is not a profitable business in Israel).

3. Water vegetation. Before its drainage, Lake Hula offered the most variated water vegetation in Israel.

The most striking feature of plant life throughout the Upper Jordan Valley are belts of plant associations. Each association differs in composition according to its distance from the water. Upon the stream boulders maidenhair ferns grow. Stream bank vegetation includes willow, common reed and Persian reed. Holy bramble survive a few meters from the banks. Farther from the water are a number of summer-bloomers such as the yellow lesser elecampane (inula) and pitch trefoil, which has pale mauve blossoms.

Along Lake Hula in water less than 2 m. deep, the famous papyrus reed reigns supreme. It is accompanied by the knotweed. On the lake's outskirts one finds the purple loosestrife and oleander.

The Hula Valley has some of Israel's rare plants: the papyrus reed, the yellow nenuphar (whose floating leaves cover quiet water), and the rare white water lily.

Wildlife

The Upper Jordan Valley is rich in water-related species, especially waterbirds, migrating birds, mammals, amphibians and fish. Hundreds of thousands of birds fly through the valley twice a year. The Hula Nature Reserve is one of Israel's best wildlife watching sites.

The migrant white pelican is one of the most famous fowls. Other birds of special interest include spotted eagles, hen harriers, and merlins; breeding marbled teals and mustached and clamorous reed warblers. There are often large numbers of waders, cranes, storks, gulls, ducks, herons and egrets as well.

The European otter, extinct from the coastal streams, still lives in the Hula Valley and its drainage area. The coypu is a large rodent indigenous to South America that looks like a huge rat. It was brought to Israel in 1951 from South America for its fur. The hot climate here was found to harm fur quality. However, the coypu found no obstacles on its way to a majority of Israel's waterscapes.

Egyptian mongeese can deal with snakes, but prefer to find their lunch in the water. They can be seen on the ramps of fish ponds in early morning and late afternoon. The wild boar, Israel's largest mammal, takes advantage of the rich waterscape roaming the thick swamp vegetation and often resting in shallow water.

A few mammals spend most of their time on dry land, such as the Indian crested porcupine, the marbled polecat and the quick bushy-tailed beech marten. The wildcat and jungle cat are common nocturnal mammals.

Israel's largest fire salamander population is at the source of the Dan. A species of frog was defined in the eastern part of the valley in 1941. Since then, the frog has never been found. The rest of Israel's amphibians are also found here.

The sources of the Jordan today contain rainbow trout that were brought to Kibbutz Dan fishponds from the U.S.A. Escaping trout have successfully found a home in the cool rivers. A few specimens have even made it to Lake Kinneret.

Hula Valley used to be infested with a number of types of mosquitoes. The malaria-spreading anopheles was eliminated well before the draining of Lake Hula. The tufted mosquito (after the males tufted antennae) does not sting humans. Its reddish larvae is a dietary staple for fish.

Human Involvement

Heavy human involvement has marked the Upper Jordan Valley for over 5,000 years. Even before then, people enjoyed the lush valley; a Stone Age grave of a man and dog buried together was revealed at Einot Einan, a main Hula water source.

International trade routes have passed through the valley since the fourth millennium. Along the western fringe ran a section of the famous Via Maris. Via Maris was the most important trade route of the old world. It connected Egypt with Mesopotamia, and contributed to the prosperity of the cities of Dan and Hatzor during the second millennium B.C.E.

Two other ancient roads crossed right through the valley: south of Lake Hula crossing the Jordan River at Gesher Benot Ya'akov, and north of the lake ran the Tzidon-Damascus Road via Banias. Both of these roads continued towards Damascus. Today they are paved, although only United Nations officials can continue to Damascus.

The region is mentioned many times in the Bible. The tribe of Dan captured Tel Dan, known as La'ish, around 1,100 B.C.E. (Judges 18:7-30). Since then, Dan has represented Israel's northern border. King Solomon included the valley in his eighth district—"the land of Naftali." In 733 Naftali fell captive to Tiglath-Pileser III, king of Assyria (II Kings 15:29).

The Assyrians used the Upper Jordan Valley as a marker between two districts. When the Hellenists arrived, they drew the line between the Ptolemaic and the Seleucid dynasties. The Greeks named the valley *Oulatha*. (The name carried into the Talmud, where the region is called "Hulata of Antiochia"). In 198, the Seleucids declared victory in a battle with Egypt and annexed the sources of the Jordan. The victors renamed Dan as Antioch (after the Seleucid king), established a pagan temple at what was then Panias and founded the town Dafna nearby.

With the Hasmonean Revolt in 165 the Seleucids lost control of the region. In 104 it was captured by Alexander Janneus, who destroyed Antioch. With the Roman conquest in 63 B.C.E., Pompeius returned the Upper Jordan Valley to the Jeturites along with Panias. Around 20 B.C.E., Augustus presented Herod with the city of Panias, who built a temple there and developed the surrounding region. Philip, Herod's son, inherited the Golan and Upper Jordan Valley. He built his capital at Panias, causing the famous city of Dan to wilt. Roman roads and bridges were constructed in the region. Today, a Roman bridge still stands on Nahar Senir, on the Lebanese border. Following the death of King Agrippa II in 93 C.E., the region left the hands of the Herodian dynasty and became part of Roman Syria. (In Jewish law, Dan is part of Israel but Panias is not.)

The Talmud mentions red rice as a local crop, ca. 135 C.E. Cotton achieved rice's popularity in the Early Arab period. Jews and Arabs also cultivated papyrus for paper, ropes and mats. Panias was called Banias by the Moslems.

Jewish communities in Banias were documented in papers found in the Cairo Genizah (cache) of 1044-1055. They were annihilated by the Crusaders, who reduced the region to a frontier land between themselves and the Moslems. The Crusaders tried to control the region, for they saw the Banias as a base for attack on Damascus. They built a number of forts in the encompassing mountains. They may have also been motivated by a mistake: they identified the region as the biblical Waters of Marom which is actually in the Upper Galilee.

At the end of the 12th century, the region again fell to Moslems, who did not develop it much. So, like most unsettled regions in the Middle East, the Upper Jordan Valley fell into Bedouin hands. The Ghawarineh tribe settled along Lake Hula, living off fish, water buffalo and mat weaving.

Due to the lack of Arab villages, late-19th century Zionists purchased land more easily here than in other regions. In 1883, Yesod Hama'alah was the first Jewish settlement, established south of Lake Hula. Although malaria and Bedouin attacks made life extremely difficult, the settlement thrived with the help of Baron Rothschild and even developed friendly relations with some of the Bedouins.

By WWI, the region again came under dispute. In 1916, the secret Sykes-Picot agreement, dividing the Ottoman Empire among the Russians, French and British, allocated the sources of the Jordan to the French and the rest of Palestine to the British. During WWI, the British took control of the entire region, but withdrew to Rosh Pina in accordance to Sykes-Picot.

The British brought Faisal Ibn Hussein into the war by promising him the kingship of a united Syria, including Palestine (of then) and Lebanon. However, the French took over Damascus and expelled him. Many Syrians still see themselves as rightful rulers of Lebanon and Israel. In 1920, heated talks between the British and French resolved the border in the Upper Jordan Valley which became the Israeli border in 1949.

Even after the establishment of the State of Israel and the cease fire agreements of the Independence War, Syria continued to invest energy in taking control of the Jordan River water supply. Their efforts (dams and diversions) caused military retaliation by Israel. The Six Day War's capture of the Golan solved many of Israel's water problems with Syria.

In 1951-1957 Lake Hula was drained, giving Israel many new acres of agricultural lands, initially the most fertile in the country. Since then, underground combustion of the peat has damaged the lands. A quarter of Israel's fish ponds are in the Upper Jordan Valley.

The drainage and imminent death of Lake Hula motivated nature lovers to organize and create the Society for the Protection of Nature in Israel. The S.P.N.I.'s first project was to save part of the lake as a nature reserve. In the 1960s the tributaries of the Jordan were declared nature reserves, just in time to save the streams from being pumped and annihilated. Today the efficiency of the drainage of Lake Hula is not apparent and part of the valley is being flooded with water in order to create a new Lake Hula which will be utilized for recreation.

Water

Israel's richest water environments are in the environs of the Upper Jordan Valley. About 1,500 million cubic meters of water drain into the valley annually. This equals Israel's annual consumption. Here are the only real cold-water streams in

Israel, originating from the snow of the Hermon. Lake Hula is one of only three natural freshwater lakes (the other two are Lake Kinneret and Berekhat Ram).

While the valley drains large amounts of water by Middle Eastern standards, it also has a number of its own water sources. Recall that it lies on the Syrian-African Rift and is lined with faults. These faults release spring water at many locations. Altogether there are over seventy springs with an average annual output of over 100 million cubits. The waters are utilized today for irrigation.

Today, the Jordan River does not run a natural course through Hula Valley. It is diverted for fishponds to two side channels. After the channels converge, the water continues in an artificial conduit. The river resumes its natural course only by Gesher Benot Ya'akov, and even there, it runs in a canal.

Hiking in the Upper Jordan Valley

The Valley is about a 4 four hour drive from the center of the country. The main access road is Road 90, leading north to the town of Kiryat Shemona. Coming from the Upper Galilee it is possible to descend to Road 90 on scenic Road 86 or 899. Three decent roads cross the valley from west to east: Road 99 towards the Hermon and Northern Golan, Road 977 to the Northern Golan and Road 91 to the Central Golan. All of these roads pass by small settlements. A number of smaller roads dissect the region.

The region is quite accessible. The central bus station of Kiryat Shemona central-izes public transportation to the region.

The many settlements dispersed in the valley are situated by the many water-scapes. It makes for many refreshing sites, but not necessarily hike routes. Rather, the best hikes run along the main streams. Please note: Nahar Hermon and Nahar Senir in the winter are powerful streams making swimming dangerous. Due to the proximity to civilization, it is not advisable to drink from the waters.

Today, there are many innertube floating and boating enterprises in the region. Floating down the streams on an innertube can be highly enjoyable though often it involves crashing into thorny bramble bushes, constantly getting one's behind jolted in shallow water and occasionally getting entwined in submerged vegeta-tion. At the time of this writing, some of these recreational companies did not always maintain strict safety standards.

The hot valley temperatures demand large quantities of liquid consumption during hikes, even when the rush of cold water accompanies the route.

Important Phone Numbers (area code 06)

S.P.N.I. Field Study Centers and Information

Hermon F.S.C., by Kibbutz Senir:	941091, 951523
Bet Ussishkin:	941704
Regional Information, Paz Gas Station at Mahanayim Junction:	935016
Upper Galilee Tourist Information:	945633
Regional N.R.A.:	971918

Safety Assistance

Police: 100   First Aid: 101
Kiryat Shemona: 943444   Kiryat Shemona Ambulance: 944334
Army:
Gibor: 06-941055   Northern Command: 979370, 979253, 512356

Sites Worth Seeing

Museums:

Bet Ussishkin Regional Museum in Kibbutz Dan on Road 99.
Prehistory at Ma'ayan Barukh on Road 99.
Farmers House, Metulla, at end of Road 90.
Tel Hai, on Road 9977 just off Road 90 by kilometer post 472-473
Hashomer House, Kefar Gil'adi, on Road 9977 1 km. off of Road 90.
Wildlife at Kefar Blum, 4 km. off Road 90 at Goma Junction.
Prehistory, Shamir 3 km. north of Road 977.
Hatzor Museum, Ayelet Hashahar on Road 90.

Nature Reserves and National Parks:

Hula Nature Reserve, off Road 90 by kilometer post 453-454.
Ein Ta'oh pool Nature Reserve (Jahula spring) on east side of Road 90, 800 m.
north of Koah Junction.
Tel Hatzor National Park, on Road 90 by kilometer post 447-448.
Hurshat Tal National Park, on Road 99 by kilometer post 5-6.

Others:

Derovrovin Farm, Yesod Hama'alah, off Road 90 by kilometer post 476-477.
Dag al Hadan restaurant, north of Road 99 by Kibbutz Hagoshrim.

Overnight Options
Indoors

(Many settlements offer private rooms with kitchen facilities.)
Youth Hostels: Rosh Pina, Tel Hai, Safed
Other Hostels: Hermon F.S.C., by Kibbutz Senir
Kibbutz Ayelet Hashahar, Kibbutz
Ma'ayan Barukh
Guest houses: Kibbutz Hagoshrim,
    Kibbutz Ayelet Hashahar, Kibbutz
    Kefar Blum
Outdoors
Hurshat Tal National Park
Metulla Picnic Site, by the starting point
    of Hike 9, 'Nahal Iyon'

*Officers Pool
(Hike 5)*

Gas Stations

Kiryat Shemona; Gesher Senir, on Road
99 (Hike 8); Mahanayim Junction on
Road 90

5 Banias Spring and Upper Nahar Hermon

See map on page 48

Points of interest: *A large spring which emerges from beneath ruins of a pagan temple into pools along a picnic site and becomes a rushing torrent beneath tall trees. The river passes many archaeological and historical remnants.*

Length and nature of hike: 3 kilometers, loop trip.

Hiking time: 1-3 hours.

Preferred season: All year.

Suitable for: All

Maps: Golan and Hermon hiking and touring map.

Special preparation: The hike is in a nature reserve. Please follow the signs. Swimming is prohibited in Nahar Hermon.

Starting & ending point: Entrance to Nahar Hermon (Banias Spring) Nature Reserve. Entrance fee.

To reach starting point:

Arrival by private transportation: Drive to the Nahar Hermon Nature Reserve, 13 km. east of Kiryat Shemona on Road 99. Enter the reserve and park in the parking lot to the right (1).

Arrival by public transportation: Take bus towards Neve Ativ from the Kiryat Shemona central bus station. Get off at the Nahar Hermon (Banias Spring) Nature Reserve. Enter and cross the parking lot (1).

Geography

Nahar Hermon, also known as Nahar Banias, is the eastern tributary of the Jordan River. It drains 190 sq. km., mostly the Israeli section of the Hermon Mountains. Its tributaries are the three large wadis draining the Israeli Hermon: Nahal Si'on, Nahal Guvta and Nahal Sa'ar.

The waters of Banias Spring originate deep beneath the Hermon. They run underground through karstic systems and emerge at Banias Cave (400 m. above sea level) at the base of the Hermon. Although the spring subsides in fall and winter, the river's annual discharge averages 120 million cubits (half that of Nahar Dan). Almost half of this volume comes from the tributaries. Banias Spring itself yields 75 million annual cubits. Water temperature does not exceed 16° and salinity is only 12 mg. chlorine per liter.

Nahal Hermon is 8 km. long. It descends over 300 m. along a 4 km. basalt canyon beginning not far from its source. Its lower parts, in the Hula Valley cut into layers of travertine, deposited by an earlier, wider stream.

Plants and animals

Nahar Hermon is lined with impressive plane trees and many rare plant species. Many types of fish are found in the river. Rainbow trout, carp and tilapia, common in the lower parts of the river are refugees of fishponds.

Capoeta damascina: This fish is common throughout the Jordan River system and in the unpolluted streams of the Coastal Plain. Known as _hafaf_ in Hebrew, it prefers rapid water and can jump waterfalls up to 1.5 m. _Capoeta_ has small scales, a low mouth and a pair of barbels on the side of the mouth. It reaches up to 30 cm.

It feeds mainly on algae that it scrapes off rocks. It tends to mate in ephemeral streams that only flow in the spring. The female digs a small hole and lays eggs there.

Oriental Plane (_Platanus orientalis_): This tree is the most impressive of all water plants in Israel. Today, the plane is found only in northern Israel, where it is fairly common. It is especially conspicuous in the riverine forest. Aged specimens, 20 m. tall and 1 m. or so in diameter, are found by permanent streams such as Nahar Hermon, Nahar Senir and Nahal Ammud.

The plane's Hebrew name, _dolev_, is based on the Aramaic _dilba_, a name preserved in Arabic. In the Bible, the tree is mentioned as the _armon_, most likely from the word _aroom_, meaning naked, reflecting the fact that the tree's bark peels off easily.

Generally deciduous, the hand-shaped leaves are covered with sharp and readily-removable hairs which are poisonous to the skin and eyes.

History

During biblical times Banias was uninhabited.

The town is first mentioned as Panias by Polivius, a Roman historian (198-177 B.C.E.). He describes a battle in 200 between Egyptian (Ptolemid) and Syrian (Seleucid) Greeks.

The Greeks brought Pan, god of music and goat herds, to the town and built a pagan temple by the river's source. The town was named Panias and flourished. Josephus Flavius mentions that Augustus gave Panias to King Herod. Herod's son Philip, who ruled the area, expanded the city and called it Ceasarea Philippi, mentioned in the New Testament.

When Agrippa I ruled all of Israel, Ceasarea Philippi lost some of its grandeur. Agrippa II made the city capital again and changed its name. In 181 the city was renamed Panias. The Talmudic rabbis knew the city as Aspamia, Apamia, Apamias and Kaysaryon.

During the Great Revolt (66-70 C.E.), the Romans imprisoned the Jews of Panias. Nevertheless, the Jewish community survived, according to the Talmud (Sukka 1:9), Rabbi El'azar ben Horkanus visited the city and found learned Jews such as Rabbi Yohanan ben Elai.

By the end of the 2nd century of the Common Era a majority of the city's inhabitants were pagan worshipers, a minority Christians and Jews. Judaism saw Panias as the boundary of the land of Israel.

Byzantine tradition lends Christian importance to Panias, based on Matthew 16:13-20 and Mark 8:27-30, where the people of Caesarea Philippi recognized Jesus. Jesus and his disciples arrive, fleeing from Herod Antipas, king of Galilee. In the 4th century, Christians were still a persecuted minority and their churches were vandalized. In the 4th and 5th century, however, Panias had an important episcopacy that participated in church councils and the city became an important focus of Christian pilgrimage.

Panias became "Banias" upon Moslem conquest in the 7th century, for there is no "p" in Arabic. The Moslem geographer el Ya'akubi writes that Banias was the capital of the Golan, competing with Damascus in its wealth and quality of life.

The Cairo Genizah (cache) of 1055 describes Jewish life, including a Jewish court (*bet din*) in Banias that it calls the "state or fort of Dan." Other documents mention two communities, a Kara'ite and a Babylonian. They all left the city before the Crusader invasion, most likely to Egypt.

In 1920, Banias Spring created the main conflict for the committee that decided the border between the British Mandate and the French Mandate. The French prevailed. In 1941, Australian forces won Banias from Vichy-controlled Syria. In the 1960s the Syrians planned to divert the waters of Banias along the slopes of the Golan to the Yarmuk River in order to deprive Israel of one of its essential water sources. Israel successfully retaliated in what is known here as "The War Over The Water."

On June 10th, 1967, the last day of the Six Day War, Golani Brigade forces quickly conquered the small village of Banias where a Syrian fort stood.

For all of its physical beauty, Banias may be of greatest interest to readers of the New Testament. H.B. Tristram expressed this point-of-view in the late 19th century:

> But there is one thing that impresses Banias more deeply on the heart than its beauty, its ruins, or its natural history. Into the coasts of Caesarea Philippi our Redeemer came. Among these rocks St. Peter confessed His divinity—that confession which was the "Rock of the Church..." The situation is indeed magnificent, with tall limestone cliffs to the north and east, a rugged torrent of basalt to the south and a gentle wooded slope for its western front. Banias is almost hidden till the traveler is among the ruins. These are not remarkable, the best preserved being the old Roman bridge over the impetuous stream which has hewn out its channel, the black basalt to the south.

During the last few years the site has been extensively excavated. The main finds are the pagan temple by Banias Spring, a water aqueduct above the spring and many urban structures to the south. The finds are planned to be renovated.

Site description

Banias Spring and Cave: The spring usually emerges outside of the cave but during rainy years the cave fills with water. Earthquakes have damaged part of the outer rim, creating a pile of rubble at the cave's entrance.

Above the cave, not far from the observation point, ran a water aqueduct to the northwestern villa suburb of Banias. The aqueduct was built in the first century and repaired a number of times. Here, in springtime, blooms the blue hyacinth squill.

Pan's Temple: Located by Banias Cave along the cliff. Eleven layers have been uncovered, from early Hellenistic times until the 19th century. Notice the five statue niches carved into the cliff. Three of these include Greek inscriptions. The niche on the right refers to Galerius, a priest of Pan. Above it is a large inscription from the third century stating, "the city council and the household of Agrippa the son of Mark the magistrate."

A four-line inscription in the base of the niche by the cave relates to Pan and Echo, the mountain nymph. This inscription is dated 87 C.E.

Nebi Khadr: The white tomb has an ideal vista of the reserve. *Khadr* is Arabic for green, vividly describing the surroundings. It also means Elijah. Near the tomb are remnants of 20th century structures and various fruit trees.

Officers Pool: This swimming pool, one of five such pools built along the slopes of the Golan, was used by Syrian officers during 1948-1967. It is possible that the modern pool is based on an ancient one, for an affluent Panias neighborhood stood along the nearby stream in the fourth century B.C.E. (based on archaeological finds of private homes with mosaic floors nearby.) In Arabic, the pool is known as the "Pool of the Sweet Spring," for its spring-fed waters are warmer than Nahar Hermon.

Sheikh Sidi Ibrahim: The domed tomb is built around the trunk of a Tabor oak. The large tree has been untouched due to its presence at a holy site. Sheikh Sidi Ibrahim was believed to be responsible for weights and measurements in the Banias *shuk* (market), sometime during the Ottoman period.

Today, Druze and Arabs make pilgrimages to the tomb, holding festive banquets. Access is from Road 99. During the writing of this book, entrance from the Road was forbidden due to nearby archaeological excavations.

To begin hike:

From the far end of the parking lot (1) there are a number of trails. To the right, a steep trail leads up to the rim of the cliff to a new observation point (2). If it is not too hot, the view is worth the effort — a nice view of the reserve, along with a broad vista of the northern Upper Jordan Valley, the Naftali Chain to the west, and the slopes of the Hermon to the north and east. From the observation point, return to the parking lot (1).

Follow the trail towards Banias Cave and Pan's Temple (3). The area may be closed due to renovations. Cross the headwaters and head up stairs beneath terebinth trees to Nebi Khadr (4). The site is sometimes locked as it offers a back entrance to the reserve.

Return to the kiosk by the parking lot and head along the pools for 100 m. Schools of *capoeta* are visible. Black snails are also abundant, a sure sign of the water's purity. The bur reed that grows here is not a common denizen in Israel. The tall trees are (planted) silver poplars.

Cross the river on a bridge. Looking downstream, note how a channel leads some of the waters along the restaurant. The channel leads to Matruf Mill. Follow the wide trail between thickets of bramble and caper to the merger of Nahal Guvta and Nahar Banias. Here, walk beneath two bridges—a modern one holding Road

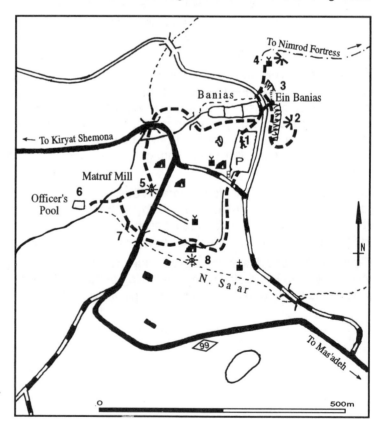

Hike 5, Banias
Spring and Upper
Nahar Hermon

99 and a Roman one coated with travertine. Overlooking these bridges, across the river, is a tall Crusader fortress hidden by greenery. Look for it. Its location controlled the ancient bridge.

Continue on the riverside trail. Pass a hydroelectric power station that supplied the Syrian town of Banias with electricity (there is a huge willow here) and soon reach Matruf Mill (5). This flour mill is the only water-powered mill active in Israel. The mill is maintained only for tourism, but residents of Mas'adeh and Ein Kuniyeh used it until recently.

Continue the trip by taking a right on a stepped path leading back to the river. To your left is the Crusader wall of Banias. Other remnants, such as aqueducts, terraces and columns are probably originally Roman. After about 200 m. hit a trail junction full of signs. The left turn is the return path for the loop trip. The right option continues 1 km. downstream to Banias Falls (see Hike 6, Banias Falls and Central Nahar Hermon) along aqueducts, deserted flour mills and luxuriant vegetation. The trail to Banias Falls is clear and if you have time (45 minutes at least) it is worth the walk. In any case, take a right, cross the stream and head left on a wide trail to Officers Pool (6).

Return to the trail junction and head right toward Nahar Sa'ar. Where old pavement leads left from the path, go right onto a small path and descend to the Sa'ar. Melted snow feeds the stream in springtime, but in summer it is barren. At this spot (7) there is a small gorge holding a shady, serene pool year-round. The pool holds rich water life; watersnakes, frogs and fish.

Return up to the trail and take a right. Along the way note the fruit trees: lemon, fig, grape and more. Reach the bridge over Nahar Sa'ar. The bridge connects the southwestern Crusader tower of the wall of Banias to the northern bank of the Sa'ar. The masonry can easily be recognized as Crusader. Below the bridge are remains of the concrete bridge, blown up by the Syrians during their hasty retreat in 1967.

The trail heads along Nahar Sa'ar, ascending wooden stairs. Pass over an aqueduct and reach a large structure to your right, an impressive Crusader gatehouse, still intact (8). This was the entrance to the Crusader town of Banias. Imagine a bridge over Nahar Sa'ar leading right into the gatehouse. It was intact a hundred years ago. To your left is Sheikh Sidi Ibrahim. Explore!

Continue on wide trail to the southeastern corner of Crusader Banias, marked by a tower. Above you is a Maronite church. Take a left in a Crusader moat. Pass another tower. Another interesting structure is right across from the reserve entrance. It represents at least seven different periods of construction, from Roman (probably) to Syrian.

From here it is worthwhile visiting the archaeological dig if allowed. A commercial center with arched roofed stores has been revealed. It was built by Herod Philip and later used by the Crusaders. Carefully cross the main road back to the reserve entrance (1). On the left of the booth are remains of a Byzantine church.

6 Banias Falls and Central Nahar Hermon

*See map on
page 52*

Points of interest: *A rushing waterfall, and a series of shady
river gorges.*

Length and nature of hike: 2 kilometers, loop trip.

Hiking time: 2-4 hours.

Preferred season: All year. In winter the going is very muddy.

Suitable for: All.

Maps: Golan and Hermon hiking and touring map.

Special preparation: A change of socks and shoes in the
winter. Swimming is prohibited in the reserve.

Starting & ending point: Nahar Hermon (Banias Falls) Nature
Reserve. Entrance fee.

To reach starting point:

Arrival by private transportation: Drive to the Nahar Hermon (Banias Falls)
Nature Reserve, on Road 99 by kilometer post 12. Take a right (there is a sign)
and follow the road for 1 km. to the reserve. Park in the parking lot (1).

Arrival by public transportation: Take bus towards Neve Ativ from the Kiryat
Shemona central bus station. There is no bus stop at the Nahar Hermon (Banias
Falls) Nature Reserve so ask the driver kindly to stop by the turnoff. Walk the
entrance road 1 km. to the parking lot (1).

Geography

Nahar Hermon along this route descends a canyon, whose slopes are of basalt
and travertine. The lower part of the canyon is of basalt belonging to the upper
parts of the Golan Formation. Basalt of this formation covers large sections of the
Golan Heights. This basalt came from the Golan Heights at least 75,000 years
ago. The lava forming the basalt originated from one of the volcanic mountains
that dot the Golan. Through this hard rock the river creates a narrow canyon.

Above the Golan basalt is the Kefar Yuval Travertine. The erodible rock has been
dated by its organic remnants to 72,000 years ago. It is most likely a remnant of

a large and deep Lake Hula which covered the whole valley. It usually appears as a 30-meter slope.

Along the top of the canyon's northern slope appears the tip of Sa'ar Basalt, which originated from Berekhat Ram, rolled down Nahal Sa'ar into and down Nahar Hermon. This occurred 15-30,000 years ago. The hard basalt creates a ledge of about 10 m. Above Sa'ar Basalt is a thin layer of travertine known as Senir Travertine. Here stands Kibbutz Senir.

For more information see Hike 5, 'Banias Spring and Upper Nahar Hermon.'

Plants and animals

Willow (*Salix alba*): The willow is rather common along the banks of perennial streams and by springs in central and northern Israel. In the northern parts of the Jordan River, willows dominate the stream bank vegetation and towards the south give way to the Euphrates poplar, which is tolerant of saltier water.

The willow is a deciduous tree that sheds its oblong leaves at the end of the summer. The flowers are arranged in a spike, males and females on different trees. The minute greenish flowers appear in early winter, when the landscape is devoid of flowering plants, while the many seeded fruits mature in early summer.

There are two main species in Israel, even though the differences between them are sometimes blurred due to hybridization. *S. alba* is a more northern species, demanding a more temperate climate. *S. acmophyla* is more heat tolerant.

The identification of the biblical *arava* with the willow is unquestionable. Willow boughs are one of the four species of the festival of Sukkot—the Feast of Tabernacles: "And you shall take on the first day, the fruit of goodly trees, branches of palm trees, and boughs of leafy trees, and willows of the brook; and you shall rejoice before the Lord your God seven days." (Leviticus 23:40)

The willow has been mistaken for the Euphrates poplar (*tzaftzefah*) for centuries. In Psalms 137:2, "On the willows where we hung up our lyres," the scripture is most likely talking about the poplar. The Talmud says that after the destruction of the Second Temple, the *arava* became *tzaftzefah* and vice versa.

History

Upstream of Banias Falls are a couple of ruined flour mills. Beyond the falls, the river runs in a canyon (with a short spurt in a narrow gorge). This has made the waters of the river difficult to utilize. Strong flash floods have wiped out any human relics. Thus, we know of little human activity along this part of Nahar Hermon. For more information see Hike 5, 'Banias Spring and Upper Nahar Hermon.'

To begin hike:

From the entrance booth, proceed to the lookout point. Enjoy the view of Nahar Hermon and all three ridges of the Israeli Hermon. To the south are the slopes of the Golan where fierce battles took place in 1967. The two eucalyptus-topped hills were Syrian forts, taken by tanks and the Golani Brigade. There is a tale regarding Eli Cohen, Israel's most famous spy who was hung in downtown Damascus before the Six Day War. Working at a high position in Syria's defence department, he advised the army to plant eucalyptus trees to "camouflage" their bases. Israel owes much of the success of the Six Day War to his work.

Descend to the left, to the Banias Falls (2). Then take the trail by the riverside. After 150 m., reach a junction by a bridge. The trail crossing the bridge (3), runs 1 km. upstream on the southern bank to the Banias Spring. Continue west along Nahar Hermon on the black-marked trail. After passing through a cattle gate find yourself high above the river which winds through a shady gorge. Look across and note a small, densely green wadi feeding the river with a trickling waterfall. As the trail curves right, reach a sign where a stepped trail descends to the river (4).

The short, steep descent is slippery when wet. At the bottom lies a Syrian (Russian-built) tank that fell into the canyon in 1967. On a hot day the spot is ideal for refreshment. Return up to the marked trail and go left. The curve ahead is a good spot to review the different geological layers of the canyon. By the tank, the river has cut into Golan Basalt. The main part of the slope is out of crumbly Kefar Yuval Travertine. At the top of the slope above the curve, a small ledge of basalt can be made out—Sa'ar Basalt. Above it, covering the plateau, is Senir Travertine.

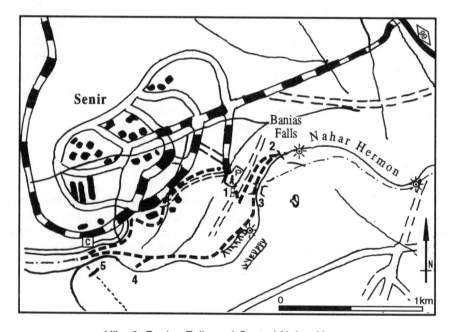

Hike 6, Banias Falls and Central Nahar Hermon

Nahar Hermon

The trail curves a bit and by a green N.R.A. sign a trail heads up to the right (5). Take it and soon pass through a few Tabor oak trees. Upon reaching the plateau go right on the gravel road. (Taking a left on the gravel road leads you to the Senir F.S.C.). Pass the Senir cemetery. The orange balloons on the electricity wires are markers for helicopters.

Reach the access road to Senir. Take a right to the entrance gate. The kibbutzniks feel that they have become part of the nature reserve. They therefore request hikers not to enter. Go right, around and alongside the cattle pen. On the other side of the pen, go left at a T-junction. By the kibbutz fence is a clear dirt road heading northeast. Take it to the right and, after 250 m., reach the parking lot (1), ending the hike.

7

Nahar Dan

See map on
page 59

Points of interest: *A rushing stream which emerges from an ancient city surrounded by a tall forest of many tree species. The forest is blanketed with cool pools and rivulets.*

Length and nature of hike: 1 kilometer, loop trip. Arrival by public transportation demands an extra kilometer of walking to and from the reserve.

Hiking time: 1-2 hours.

Preferred season: All year.

Suitable for: All.

Maps: Golan and Hermon hiking and touring map.

Special preparation: Swimsuit. Swimming is allowed only in the 'wading pool.'

Starting & ending point: Entrance to the Tel Dan Nature Reserve, located 1.5 km. north of Road 99. Entrance fee.

To reach starting point:

Arrival by private transportation: Turnoff to the Tel Dan Nature Reserve, from Road 99 by kilometer post 9. Pay, enter and park.

Arrival by public transportation: Take bus from the Kiryat Shemona central bus station to Kibbutz Dan. Get off, walk into Dan via the main gate. Take a left onto the external road, walk 250 m. and exit the back gate. This paved road runs through avocado plantations. After 300 m., reach the trout and salmon farm. Go right through an open gate into the parking lot of the Dan Nature Reserve. Before beginning the walk please pay the entrance fee.

Geography

The most plentiful spring of the three sources of the Jordan, Nahar Dan yields 240,000 million cubits of water annually. Unlike Nahars Senir and Hermon, Dan has no drainage basin and thus no floods. The water's temperature is 14.5-16°C. The waters originate in the Hermon Mountains.

Nahar Dan's headwaters are a nature reserve of 391 dunams, including Tel Dan. At Tel Dan's western slopes, five small springs emerge into small rivulets. These springs emerging above valley level are not yet understood. It seems that they have been shaped by humans. The river's main spring emerges northwest of Tel Dan.

The river, lined with basalt boulders and cobbles, heads southwest averaging ten meters in width and only 0.5 m. in depth. Eventually, the river flows into a channel, three meters deep.

Plants and animals

European Otter (*Lutra lutra*): The European otter is the only type of otter in Israel. It is Israel's largest freshwater mammal and is mainly found in perennial streams of the Syrian-African Rift. There are occasionally reports of otters in the coastal streams. They are also seen near trout ponds of the Dan, evidently looking for an extra helping of fish. Israel's population is currently around 100. The European otter is a protected animal.

The European otter belongs to the family that includes polecats, badgers, honey badgers and martens. All are predators with cylindrical bodies, short legs and tiny ears.

The adult otter weighs 9 kg. and is 70 cm. long. Its long tail adds another 45 cm. (the male is longer than the female). Otters are fitted for their aquatic environment. The fur is fine-haired and very dense, capable of trapping air bubbles, and thus staying dry underwater. The flat head, lithe body and small ears give it good hydrodynamic qualities. Its webbed feet ensure rapid movement in the water.

The otter is totally dependant on steadily flowing streams, where it is a master. Its eyes, nostrils and ears are positioned above water when swimming. At the base of its whiskers are sensors which warn it of currents and obstacles ahead. Thus the otter can move at night, when it is mainly active.

The otter live in a den dug into the stream bank with an opening above ground at one end and under water at the other. Thus, they can slip straight into the underwater world where they can stay for eight minutes. During the day, the otter passes time hunting, sunbathing and giving acrobatic performances.

Otters are territorial animals. They mark their territory on hard objects with secretions from its anal glands. Sexual maturity is reached at age one. The otter has no breeding time, though only one litter is produced annually. Life expectancy is 12-15 years.

Otters are sometimes vegetarian but usually prefer fish, small birds, mammals and even insects.

Holy Bramble (*Rubus sanguineus*): Commonly known as raspberry or blackberry. It is a common species in the central and northern parts of Israel, growing along streams, swamps, springs and by spots with high underground water. The Hebrew name is *petel*. The plant is not mentioned in the Bible, but the Bible does refer to thorns as *tzinim*, which most likely refers to bramble. The book of Luke mentions the bramble explicitly.

It is an evergreen, erect or twining, and very intricately branching prickly bush. It has hooked prickles all over the stem and the branches. The leaves have three-to-five leaflets, and the flowers, grouped at the branch tips, have five pink-to-white, 6-9 mm. petals each. The edible fruit is a a small reddish-black berry of many one-seeded fleshy drupelets that ripen at the end of the summer through the fall.

History

H.B. Tristram described the region in 1863-1864:

> A ride of three miles from the bridge brought us to Tell Kady ("the mound of the judge"), which thus in the significance of its name, still preserves the ancient Dan ("judge"). On the higher part of the mound to the south, tradition places the temple of the golden calf, and ruined foundations can still be traced. Nature's gifts are here poured forth in lavish profusion, but man has deserted it, Yet it would be difficult to find a more lovely situation than this, where "the men of Laish dwelt quiet and secure." "We have seen the land, and behold it is very good...A place where there is no want of anything that is in the earth" (Judg. 18; 9,10).

> Its western side is covered with an almost impenetrable thicket of reeds, oaks, and oleanders, which entirely conceal the shapeless ruins, and are nurtured by "the lower springs" of Jordan; a wonderful fountain like a large bubbling basin, the largest spring in Syria, and said to be the largest single fountain in the world, where the drainage of the southern side of Hermon, pent up between a soft and a hard stratum, seems to have found a collective exit. Full-grown at birth, at once larger than the Hasbany which it joins, the river dashes through an oleander thicket.

Site description

Garden of Eden: Natural pools up to 1 m. in depth which contain a lot of sediment from the slow current. The garden ends where the water noisily seeps underground in a doline-like hole, possibly connected to an ancient drainage system. A forest of laurel grows here. Usually the laurel does not exceed four meters in height, but here it can be found up to 15 m. Black and yellow fire salamanders populate the quiet pools.

Lower Thicket: The waters come from the main stream along an ancient canal. Here grow Syrian ash trees up to 15 m. along with laurel. Buckthorns, usually only two meters high, grow ten meters here. Many other trees and creepers of the moist Mediterranean forest and some rare plants grow here.

Tel Dan: A large tel of 200 dunams, 204 m. above sea level. The name, in both Hebrew and Arabic (*Tel el Ka'azti* or *Kady*) means judge. Identification of the tel was found during the digs of 1967-1977—an inscription dedicated to "El that is at Dan."

The dig exposed remains from the Early Bronze up to the Roman period. Its southern slope has a wide, ten-meter-tall wall and gate from the Israelite period.

During biblical times, the city's gate was probably the center of things. All of the city's guests and merchants passed through it. People leaving for and returning from voyages passed through it. It was the place to pick up the recent news from the outside wall. Many biblical phrases relate to the gate "Then went Boaz up to

Nahar Dan

the gate..." (Ruth 4:1), In those days while Mordecai sat in the king's gate..." (Esther 2:21).

One entered the city from the east, via a gate into a square and along a cobble road up to the top of the tel where another gate was found. The lower gate was found to have four cells, most likely for the guards, and a stone bench nearby, possibly for the city's elders. Some think that it was an enclosure for the king or a place of worship. A unique structure with decorated bases in its corners stood next to the bench. It apparently held poles for a canopy.

Archaeologists found 13th and 14th century walls, floors and rock graves containing fifty skeletons of men, women and children. Fragments of a Mycenean chariot jug is one of the most unique finds from this period. The reconstructed jug and many other artifacts are on display at the Israel Museum in Jerusalem.

Israelite settlement left remains of pots, jugs and walls. The Israelite town was burnt in the mid-11th century. The rebuilt town included bronze melting furnaces.

By the springs in the north, archaeologists have exposed the remnants of a Roman dam. The dam elevated the water level and directed it through clay pipes to a springhouse (exposed to the right of the spring thicket by the large terebinth tree). Nearby stands a walled, 18-square-meter Israelite "four-horned altar," possibly the work of King Jeroboam, son of Nevat. The platform was used through Hellinistic times.

With the development of Panias in the Roman period, Dan declined and was eventually abandoned. The site is currently being excavated and renovated.

To begin hike:

There are clear hiking trails through this shady gem of a reserve and a route description is not essential. A detailed brochure received upon entering gives a good general introduction to the reserve. The above explanations should complement the brochure. It is interesting that the mound of Tel Dan is the same size as the whole walked route in this reserve.

Begin at the kiosk (1). The eucalyptus trees were planted by members of Kibbutz Dan in 1939. Follow the trail along the river to the end of the picnic site. Veer right to the ruined water channel which runs parallel to the entrance road. Take a left to the trailhead (2). Go left and return to the riverside beneath a Syrian ash tree. Here begins the section known as the Lower Thicket.

Follow the trail to the right. Note the overgrown artificial terraces. The pipe by the Byzantine channel leads water to Moshav She'ar Yeshuv. The turnoff here can shorten the hike, but the short-cut includes only the renovated Arab flour mill and the wading pool. It is worthwhile only for those who are pressured for time.

Here are the best views of the torrential river (3). It may be possible to see ferns, a rare sight in Israel, growing on boulders between the rapids. The *Thelypteris palustris*, known in Hebrew as "marsh fern," is found here and in the Hula Nature Reserve. It reaches 1 m. in height. The family of this fern includes 500 species throughout the world. Further along the trail a rivulet comes in from the hill on the right. It drains the sinkhole. Tall, white-barked silver poplars shade the environs.

Head up to the west and on the left is an artificial sinkhole (4) which swallows a large proportion of the upper rivulets. The function is unclear. The trail continues over a stream to the Garden of Eden and veers to the right. Many springs emerge between the trail and the slopes of Tel Dan. The springs, called El Ka'atzi after the tel, collect into the stream that runs south parallel to the trail. The slope is appropriately known as the Moist Slope. These springs coming from the man-made hill are not understood.

A trail veers off the main route to the left. Ascend into the open, to a lookout point on Tal Dan (4). Notice the burnt terebinth tree to the left of the ascent. During the 1940s, Jews from Syria, Lebanon and Iraq secretly entered Israel from here, led by the Palmach. The large tree served as a landmark. The view from above encompasses the southwestern slopes of the Hermon Range, the Golan Heights, northern Hula Valley and the Naftali Chain of Upper Galilee to the west.

Return to the trail and continue. The El Ka'atzi springs are now led into a channel which reaches the flour mill. and continues towards Kibbutz Dan. The trail crosses the channel and reaches the mill from below. Along the way, the short-cut trail rejoins us. Continue past the mill and note the grind stones used as pavement. Reach the wading pool (5) and enjoy a refreshing dip. From the pool, it is easy to head back out (1). This is also the departure point to see the excavations of Tel Dan, but make sure you have coordinated the visit with the ranger and, if there is a current dig, with the archaeologist.

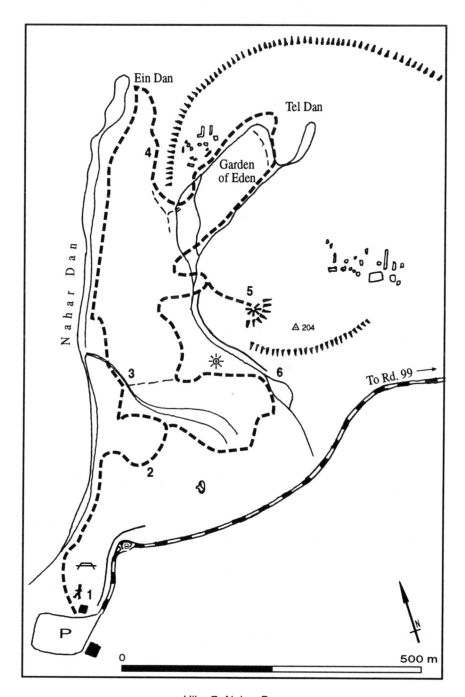

Hike 7, Nahar Dan

Nahar Senir

See map on
page 64

Points of interest: *A cool and clear gently cascading stream between developed river vegetation.*
Length and nature of hike: 3 kilometers, loop trip.
Hiking time: 2-4 hours.
Preferred season: All year.
Suitable for: All.
Maps: Golan and Hermon hiking and touring maps.
Special preparation: Swimsuit, clothes for walking in water (optional).
Starting & ending point: Henyon Ha'abuvim (Ma'ayan) picnic site.

To reach starting point:

Arrival by private transportation: Take Road 99 to the bridge over Nahar Senir (Gesher Senir or Gesher Hadolev), between kilometer post 5 and 6. Just before the bridge, turn north toward Ma'ayan Barukh (there are orange signs). Immediately park at the Henyon Ha'abuvim parking lot (1).

Arrival by public transportation: Take bus from Kiryat Shemona central bus station to the settlements off of Road 99. Get off at the turnoff to Ma'ayan Barukh and proceed to the Henyon Ha'abuvim parking lot (1).

Geography

Nahar Senir drains 630 sq. km. It is the largest of the three tributaries of the Jordan River. Its own tributaries begin as far as 50 km. into Lebanon, on the western flanks of the Lebanese Hermon Range. The river is called *Hatzbani* in Arabic, after its source in the Hatzbaya Valley, the cradle of the Druze religion, by the town of Hatzbaya. In the summer, the waters are utilized for irrigation by Lebanese farmers. Then, the Israeli Nahar Senir is fed only by the Vazani Springs, which burst forth at 280 m. above sea level, beneath the Israeli Alaouite village of Ghajar.

Discharge wise, Nahal Senir is the most fluctuating stream of the three Jordan sources. A rainy winter can release over 300 million annual cubits of water while following a drought, less than 50 million cubits will run downstream. Average annual discharge is 135 million cubits. Following floods, discharge is 250 cubits-per-second and only 0.6 cubits-per-second at the end of the summer when water temperature rises. Discharge from the Vazani Springs is 45 million cubits per year.

The Israeli portion of Nahar Senir from the border to Gesher Senir on Road 99 is a nature reserve of 1,335 dunams. It can be divided into two sections: along the northern section, the river cuts a deep ravine (though not a canyon), into a "young" basalt flow which originated in Lebanon. Two kilometers north of Gesher Senir, Nahar Senir runs beneath the ancient Jisr el-Ghajar (*Jisr* is Arabic for bridge). Half a kilometer south of Jisr el-Ghajar, the basalt section ends and the stream enters the Hula Valley, where it cuts into travertine lined with basalt boulders, deposited by an ancient stream. This is where part of Nahar Dan merges.

Nahar Senir winds its way for 5 km. south of Gesher Senir, where it merges with the Dan-Hermon River by Kibbutz Sdeh Nehemiah and becomes the Jordan River.

Plants and animals

Many rare plants are found along Nahar Senir. Two common Mediterranean water plants that resemble one another are the willow herb and the purple loosestrife.

Purple loosestrife (*Lythrum salicaria.*): The Latin name and the Hebrew, *shanit*, refer to the flower's color, similar to blood but usually lighter. Loosestrife has a worldwide distribution. It is a dominant streamside plant in the U.S., even though it originates in Europe. The bush reaches 3 m., sprouting quickly in the spring, usually in open wet areas such as marshes.

The flowers grow throughout the summer in a cluster along the ends of the standing stems.

The young branches and their leaves are edible. The flowers are used in folk medicine. Loosestrife is therefore commonly grown in gardens.

Willow herb (*Epilobium hirsutum*): The name *aravrava* (in Hebrew) is derived from its similarity in leaf-shape (up to 9 cm. long) and environment to the willow. It can be found along waterways throughout Israel north of Beersheba.

The grasslike plant sprouts each spring to 2 m. In the winter, the plant wilts down to the root. Its 5-petal pink-red flowers bloom at the end of the stems as single flowers between May and December.

Long-Headed Barbel (*Barbus longiceps*): Named after two pairs of barbels, one above its upper lip and the other by the sides of its mouth. The long and narrow fish is covered with small scales and reaches 50 cm., occasionally 70 cm. It is found in large pools and lakes along the Syrian-African Rift and in Syria. It lives near the bottom and feeds on invertebrates and small fish. It uses its barbels to detect food.

During the mating season the fish run up small tributaries, even ephemeral ones. The long-headed barbel can be seen in groups of males surrounding and rubbing against one female. The female digs with her tail a small hole and deposits the eggs, fertilized by the nearby males. She then digs another hole a bit upstream and the loose debris covers the fertilized eggs. About 60 tons of long-headed barbels are fished commercially every year in Lake Kinneret. Its relative, the large-scale barbel, is found only in deep, slow-moving water and commercially yields 50 tons annually.

History

The name Senir is the Amorite name of the Hermon:

> Which Hermon the Sidonians call Siryon and the Amorites call it Senir (Deuteronomy 3:9).

It also may refer to the Lebanon Mountains and also the Hermon:

> Come with me from Lebanon, my spouse with me from Lebanon: look from the top of Amana, from the top of Senir and Hermon from the lion's den from the mountains of the leopards" (Song of Songs 4:8).

I Chronicles 5:23 confirms this geography:

> ...and the children of the half tribe of Menasheh dwelt in the land; they increased from Bashan unto Ba'al-Hermon and Senir, and unto Mount Hermon.

The verse relates to Senir as being in the proximity of Hermon.

The short section of Nahar Senir (of the hike) does not yield many historical stories. Tel Mamzi is the only sharp evidence of nearby settlement. Less than a kilometer north of Gesher Hatzinorot is Jisr el-Ghajar, today reinforced with concrete since it is part of the Israel Defense Force's patrol road.

A basalt boundary rock was found by the bridge with a Greek inscription:

> Diocletian and Maximian Augustus and Maximium, emperors, commanded that this rock, which borders on this fields of the Hersimian farms, be laid with the supervision of Elias Statutus, who is in charge of the places mentioned.

Elias was governor of the province of Phoenicia between 293 and 305. There may be a connection between the farm field and the settlement of Tel Mamzi.

In the 1960s, Syria tried to divert the waters of the Senir along with the other sources of the Jordan. Israeli tanks retaliated. The Six Day War relieved Israel from the fear of losing its most valuable water sources.

H.B. Tristram, the English clergyman-naturalist who ranks among the most important of the 19th century Holy Land explorers, writes:

> Jisr el Ghajar on the Hasbany, here a turbulent mountain torrent of the brightest blues as it dashes among great volcanic boulders, hemmed in by walls of basalt, very different from the brown steady volume that rolls between mud banks below. It is a lovely spot, the banks overhang with oleanders, honey suckle, clematis, wild rose and Oriental plane. Their perfume charged the atmosphere, and the bulbul and nightingale vivid in rival song in the branches above, audible over the noise of the torrent.

Site description

Tel Mamzi: The reed-covered mound represents a settlement established in the Roman period. Even though it has not been excavated, based on clay sherds it seems that the village was abandoned in the Late Arab period.

Gesher Hatzinorot: "Pipes Bridge." This bridge is supported by two pipes that lead water from Nahar Dan to the nearby settlements.

Nahar Senir

To begin hike:

Cross the lawn and head north onto a wide trail. Pass a lone eucalyptus. The trail is marked with a local trail mark. After 100 m. a marked trail leads right to a pool in Nahar Senir (2), your first view of the river.

Return to the main trail heading north. The trail continues along the edge of an open field. Here is a nice view of the surrounding mountains: the Hermon to the east and the Ramim Cliffs to the west. Hollyhocks bloom in late spring-early summer along with tall purple clovers.

In the middle of the field, the trail veers right (there is a sign and arrow) into the thicket and splits. Take the left option, soon running along the base of the reed-covered Tel Mamzi. Here is a good place to catch sight of a kingfisher. If you have time, it is worthwhile to explore the dead-end trails that descend to the right to Nahar Senir. Pass a pumping station and reach an open area with a N.R.A. sign and trash can, shaded by tall trees. Here Gesher Hatzinorot crosses Nahar Senir (3).

Cross the river and begin to head downstream along the eastern bank. There is no marked trail but it is hiked every year by thousands.

The trail immediately crosses a small rivulet. It comes from Nahar Dan and is known as the northern Senir ditch. Before reaching the rivulet's mouth into Nahar Senir, note a large slab of cement, torn from one of the upstream bridges.

The trail runs along a cliff of travertine and basalt boulders. Two of the creepers hanging from the tall plane trees is the Grecian silkvine and grape vine. In Israel, the silkvine is found only here and along Nahar Hermon. Its 2 cm. flowers are violet outside and green inside.

The trail climbs up to the plateau on the left and returns to the riverside by the southern Senir ditch (4) which feeds the Si'on Farm. The trout farm offers a wedding garden and a fish restaurant, Dag al Hadan, that you will pass. The passage over the second ditch demands acrobatics to keep your shoes dry.

One-hundred-and-fifty meters downstream, reach the Eshed (5). Here is the most popular rest stop of the route. The water is deep, ideal for swimming, and the large rocks are adorned with maidenhair fern, ideal for sunbathing. In the water it is easy to see *capoeta* fish and possibly barbels.

The trail continues downstream, not always loyal to its immediate bank. Close to the river, on a small beach, stands a lone purple loosestrife bush, blooming all summer long. Three hundred meters from the "Eshed" brings you to a valley. Here, by some eucalyptus trees, the stream widens in the winter and spring. A nice pool (known as the "first pools") ends the riverside trail section (2). Continue south on a dirt road between the river vegetation and the eggplant (formerly cotton) fields to your left. Reach Road 99, carefully cross Nahal Senir on the bridge and return to the starting point (1).

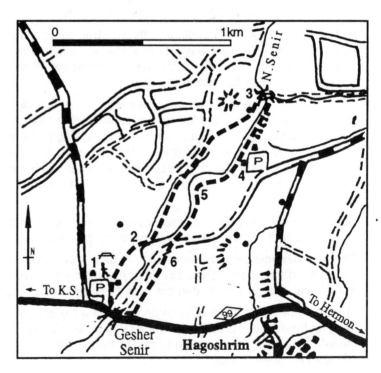

Hike 8, Nahar Senir

9

See map on
page 70

Nahal Iyon

Points of interest: *A stream containing a series of canyons initiated by waterfalls with rare wildflowers and bird life, right between the pastoral village of Metulla and the border with Lebanon.*

Length and nature of hike: 2.5 kilometers, one-way; 5 kilometers, back-and-forth).

Hiking time: 2 hours each way.

Preferred season: All year. In the summer the stream is dry but it is still a beautiful hike.

Suitable for: All.

Maps: Golan and Hermon hiking and touring map.

Special preparation: The hike is in a nature reserve. Please do not stray from the designated trails. Two vehicles will make the trip comfortable, as one can be parked at the ending point.

Starting point: The hike can be done in either direction. The one-way trip described here is downhill. The trail head is at a N.R.A. entrance booth by a gate through the eastern fence of Metulla. Entrance fee.

Ending point: N.R.A. entrance booth and parking lot off Road 90 by kilometer post 476-477.

To reach starting point:

Arrival by private transportation: Drive into Metulla via Road 90. Pass the entrance gate. If you want to drive the scenic road along the village's fence that runs parallel to Nahal Iyon, take the first right and again take a right turn. Follow the winding road for 2.5 km. to the starting point (1).

To reach the starting point quickly, take the second right, cross Metulla, pass the police station and (to the right) reach a fence by a grove of eucalyptus trees with picnic tables. The starting point is a bit to the right.

Arrival by public transportation: Take bus from Kiryat Shemona to Metulla. Ask to get off by the police station. From there, follow the road to the fence. By the eucalyptus grove find the starting point along the fence (1).

Geography

Nahal Iyon runs through the western section of the Syrian-African Rift along one of its north-south faults. Three geological units are exposed along the route. Eocenian chalky limestone creates the canyon of Iyon Falls. The canyon opens up to soft Senonian marly chalk. The lower part of the last canyon section, ending at Mapal Hatanur, is of hard conglomerate.

Faults dividing the hard and soft strata have created falls along the stream bed, such as Mill Falls, where hard conglomerate is confronted with soft marl.

Plants and animals

Fragrant mint (*Mentha longifolia*): Grows in Israel along ditches and water courses, and in swamps. Like most water plants, it blooms in the summer. The perennial herb is mentioned in the New Testament twice, in Matthew 23:23 and in Luke 11:42.

The mint is a perennial herb, 40-100 cm. tall, covered with tiny hairs. Its main stem branches in its upper section, each branch terminating in a spike of minute purplish-pink flowers. The leaves are grayish-green and toothed along the margin.

Commonly used as a condiment and as seasoning for meat, mint was probably far more popular in the past when people tried to flavor their tasteless food. *M. Longifolia* is the most common of the three mint species in Israel. It is also used for medicinal purposes, such as infusions and for pain relief.

Rock Dove (*Columba livia*): The ancestor of the domestic pigeon. It resembles the pigeon in shape and size, but its pattern of colors is less varied. Its overall color is bluish-grey with a tendency toward green on the head. The tip of the tail is black and on the wings are two black bars. On the neck of a mature dove there are glossy shades of green and metallic grey.

The dove is mentioned 32 times in the Bible as a symbol of beauty and innocence of a loved one. The Song of Songs includes the dove a number of times, for example: "Thou hast doves eyes" (1:15). A pair of doves was also a modest sacrifice in the Temple. A woman was obligated to bring a pair in thanksgiving for childbirth.

This creature is common in most parts of the world. Due to domestication of the species it is hard to distinguish between natural and human-helped distribution.

In Israel the rock dove is more common east of the watershed, from Metulla to Eilat. A hundred years ago they were very common in the Nahal Arbel and Lower Nahal Ammud area by Lake Kinneret (based on H.B. Tristram). The population has since dwindled.

The birds sometimes fly 20 km. from their nests in search of food. Though they reside in cliffs, they seek food and water in fields and open areas. They are vegetarians.

Nesting season runs from March until August, usually in ravines of rocks but also in wells and caves. During that time, two to three broods are hatched. Only 2 eggs are laid at a time, hatching after 12-18 days. The male incubates during the day, the female at night. For 5-6 days following hatching, the chicks drink pigeon milk and softened seeds.

History

One kilometer south of the route stands Tel Avel Bet Hama'akha, 414 m. above sea level. The tel was a Canaanite town, later taken by the Israelites and settled through Hellenistic times. It is mentioned numerously in the Bible. The site has not been excavated.

The village of Metulla is named after the Druze village of *Um-Taila*—"mother of the tel." *Taila* might also come from "to look" in Arabic describing the scenic location. The town was settled in 1896 on lands bought by representatives of Baron Edmond de Rothschild. At first the settlers suffered Druze raids. During WWI the Turks attacked them and, in the 1920s, Arab rioters assaulted the village, bringing on evacuation.

During WWII the British prepared their anti-tank line along the canyon of Nahal Iyon. Even today, anti-tank obstacles remain in the region.

The region is recognized as the "Pass of Iyon" mentioned in the Jerusalem Talmud, an important identification as it marks a boundary of the Promised Land. Two thousand years later, Jews from Syria and Lebanon were smuggled into Israel in the 1940s via Metulla, right by the starting point.

Metulla is currently a village of 100 families. Though lying on the Lebanese border, Metulla is a resort town, offering motels and hotels, a sport center, ice skating rink and other facilities.

Site description

Nahal Iyon Nature Reserve: The reserve begins at the fringe of Bik'at Iyon at a bridge blown up by a Palmach unit in 1946 on the "Night of the Bridges." It hugs the stream and is 400 dunams and 2.5 km. long. Nahal Iyon drops 125 m. in elevation along the reserve.

Nahal Iyon's Arabic name, *Dardara*, relates to its torrential nature as it means surging or drumming. It also is known as "Wadi of the Fleas," possibly describing the leaping water and waterfall spray. The latter name may also relate to the bugs which develop in the pools during the summer. Nahal Iyon originates at the Lebanese town of Marjiyon, 7 km. north of Metulla. It drains 30 sq. km., some of which receive large quantities of precipitation. The stream runs into the western part of Hula Valley. Today it is drained to the western drainage channel of Hula Valley, west of Moshav Bet Hillel. In the winter the stream yields 0.3-1.5 cubic meters-per-second, while following storms it can reach 26 cubic meters-per-second.

Mill Falls: Waterfalls with significant elevation differences like Mill Falls are usually in a canyon rather than out in the open. The open vista of the falls is due to the exposure of erodible marl beyond (the path descending to the fall runs on it). People took advantage of the fact in creating a mill without needing to lay a long water channel system to gain relative elevation. The water was diverted right before the fall and the utilized water fell along the same cliff face.

The Tanur Waterfall, Nahal Iyon

Baron Edmond de Rothschild purchased the mill along with other real estate in the area at the end of the 19th century. He renovated it turning it into the only Jewish-owned water mill in Israel. Usage stopped during WWI. Following the war its wooden wheels were replaced with iron ones but it did not last long: in 1920 Metulla was attacked so frequently by Arab neighbors that the settlers eventually left. After their return, they did not restart the mill.

The pool at the base of the falls is perennial, for a small spring, Ein Sukra, emerges here. Until 1957, the water quenched the thirst of Mettulaites during the summer.

Mapal Hatanur: The 30-meter fall is the largest in the Upper Galilee. The short narrow gorge following the falls represents the distance that they have retreated from the clear fault line between the hard rock of the canyon and the soft Senonian marl downstream.

The Hebrew tanur is a mistaken translation of the Arabic name of the wadi, *Wadi Hammam*. *Ham* is hot in Hebrew so the large waterfall was thought to be the source of the wadi's name as it resembles an Arab pita oven, a *tabun*. Thus, the falls were named Ha-tanur—the oven. *Hammam* in Arabic does mean a hot place or hot baths but it also means doves. The wadi is most likely named after the rock doves which were a very common sight in Israel before fire weapons were introduced. The cliffs of Nahal Arbel (that runs into Lake Kinneret north of Tiberias) is also called Wadi *Hammam*, after the doves.

To begin hike:

Being a popular stream, the route is extremely clear and does not require step-by-step description. Do not let children run ahead! There are many cliffs and falls! The route is one-way so it is possible to head opposite as described here. The description is the downhill version.

Descend on the trail to the stream bed. At the bottom, go left 50 m. to the base of nine-meter Iyon Fall (2). A concrete wall was built above the falls by the British in order to dam the stream and supply their forces with water. Continue downstream on the path. The stream bed widens after 200 m. because the prevailing strata is soft marl. To the left, beyond the orchard, is the Lebanese border. Cross the stream and pass through a clump of eucalyptus trees, planted by the settlers of Metulla. Three hundred and fifty meters from Iyon Falls the trail leaves the stream bed, which deepens a bit before dropping 20 m. at Mill Falls (3).

Before the descent to Mill Falls, note the trail leading from Metulla to your present position. Today, the entrance to Metulla is blocked by a security fence. Enjoy the view of Mill Falls and its namesake flour mill to the left. Follow the trail to the pool below. Just past the pool are remains of a dam and pumphouse used to collect the waters to Metulla until 1957.

Continue downstream. Again, do not let children run ahead! The path runs snugly between the small canyon cliff and rich water vegetation. Mint is found here. The stream runs between walls of conglomerate, cemented residue of the ancient Nahal Iyon.

Four hundred meters from Mill Falls carefully cross the next canyon on a bridge. Across Nahal Iyon is a mediocre viewpoint of the next waterfall, Cascade Falls (4). Cascade Falls are a pair of falls, 9.5 and 5 meters high respectively. The slope above the trail at Cascade Falls is known as Squill Hill. In the autumn, it is adorned by hundreds of squills. In the spring, bellflowers and snapdragons, both protected wildflowers, bloom nearby.

From Cascade Falls the stream runs in a deep gorge. Follow the trail above it (do not attempt to approach the gorge rim!). Before steeply descending, pass along the cemetery of Metulla, an interesting place to visit (the entrance is from inside the village). Descend to the stream by a trail intersection. Go left and dead-end at the pool of Mapal Hatanur (5). Here, a small trickle of water runs down the stream bed year-round, offering habitat for fish, amphibians and other aquatic life. Just before the dead-end, a trail leads up to an observation point. If you decide to follow the short ascent, it loops back to the trail farther downstream.

If you have to return back to your vehicle at the starting point, return the same way you came. To finish the route, a wide trail leads from Mapal Hatanur to the parking lot (6) which is 400 m. from Road 90, and less than 1 km. south of the entrance to Metulla where you can catch a bus back to Kiryat Shemona.

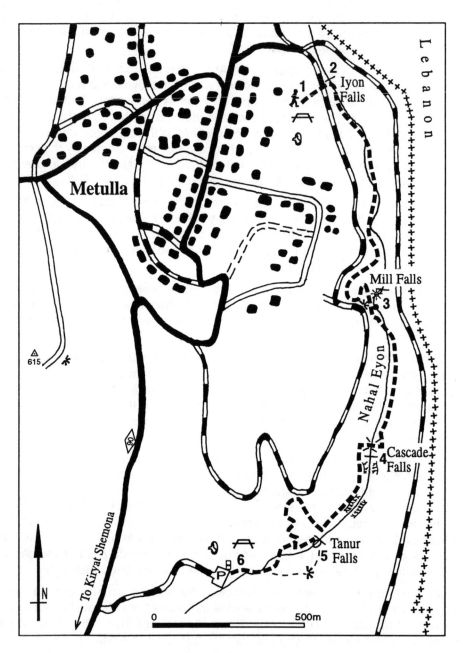

Hike 9, Nahal Iyon

Upper Galilee

Geography

The Upper Galilee is the most mountainous part of western Israel (west of the Jordan Valley). Its geographical boundaries are quite clear. Its northern geographical border is the Litani River in Lebanon, known as the *Kasamiya*—the divider. From the Litani, the region stretches to the Bet Hakerem Valley in the south, the Upper Jordan Valley of the Syrian-African Rift in the east and the Coastal Plain in the west.

It is a small region, only 690 sq. km., and can be divided into three subregions: central, western and eastern. The central subregion mainly consists of the Meron Mountain Range, where over half a dozen peaks surpass 1,000 m. in elevation. The Merons have steep eastern and southern slopes rising 700 m. above their surroundings.

The elevation of the Meron Range induces harsh winters which affect the landscape and hydrology of the entire Upper Galilee. The mountain rocks are Cenomanian and Turonian limestones and dolomites. These hard carbonate rocks create here karst phenomena, such as sinkholes as deep as 100 m. Due to the cracked appearance of these rocks, water infiltrates and emerges outside and below the region in the form of streams such as in Nahal Keziv and Nahal Ammud. In the mountains themselves, only small springs emerge.

Central and western Upper Galilee are distinguished by the Peki'in Valley. In the west, the lithology is also of Cenomanian and Turonian rock. The landscape is of parallel ridges in an east-west direction dissected by V-shaped canyons, 100-200 m. deep. The ridges gradually slope to the west, usually less than 5 degrees. Thus, there is a a great view from every ridge to the west and usually to the north and south.

A few of the stream beds between the ridges originate along east-west faults; the crack of the fault widened into a stream throughout time. Among some of the streams springs emerge. Nahal Keziv, which drains large portions of the Meron Range, is the only stream originating from outside the subregion.

The eastern Upper Galilee is also mountainous, 700 m. or more above sea level. The region is the southern continuation of a syncline which runs north into Lebanon. The large streams of Nahal Ammud and Wadi Duba in Lebanon take advantage of the synclinal axis. Between the two, Nahal Dishon drains the northeastern corner of the Meron Range to the east. Naturally, the syncline is covered with strata, younger than the structures of the other sections of the Upper Galilee. Softer lithologies; Eocenian chalk and limestone and Senonian chalk, prevail. Some of the areas are covered with Neogenian basalt flows.

The most prominent structure in the eastern subregion is the Canaan Mountain Range reaching 955 m. at Har Biriya. The town of Safed covers its southwestern slopes. The soft lithologies of the mountains are covered with planted pine trees.

Climate

Being the northernmost part of western Israel, and one of its most elevated regions, the Upper Galilee is known for winters with violent storms and moderate, sunny summers. Due to the large amounts of rainfall, the region is usually affected less than the rest of the country by drought.

Wind velocities of 120 km. per hour have been measured at the peaks of the Canaan Range. Snowfall occurs approximately five times per winter at elevations above 700 m. There are 70-80 rainy days. Annual precipitation reaches 1,000 mm. at the high peaks of the Meron Range. Lower elevations pick up 600-800 mm. of rainfall. Humidity in the winter is similar to the Coastal Plain, about 60%.

In May, *sharav*s depress humidity by 30-40% causing strong evaporation, and the surface of the soil dries rapidly at the beginning of summer. Dewfall is bountiful in the western Galilee (200-250 nights per year) due to its proximity to the Mediterranean Sea. Eastern Galilee has only sparse dewfall.

Annual temperature averages 15° at the peaks of the Meron Range and 16.1° in Safed in the Canaan Range.

Vegetation

Due to moderate human involvement throughout history, central and western Upper Galilee are thickly covered with Mediterranean maquis, more than any-where else in Israel. The rainy winters have also played a part, assisting damaged vegetation to recover quickly. The climate creates an environment yielding a large variety of species in comparison with other Mediterranean parts of Israel. The thick vegetation seems to be everywhere, not offering many open spots for blooming wildflowers to survive. There is a common Israeli phrase: "I love the green Galilee blooming with colorful flowers in the spring." It applies to the Lower Galilee whose blooming open fields abound with a rainbow of colors in the late winter and spring. The Upper Galilee is covered with evergreen maquis.

Vegetation distribution in the western and central subregion mainly depends on slope and soil. As throughout Israel, the shaded slopes facing north hold dense vegetation, while the south facing slope is more barren. The soil is a reflection of the prevailing lithology. In the eastern subregion, plant variety is mainly influenced by the microclimate, such that the same plants grow on different slopes and soils within a given climate.

There are two main types of soils common throughout the greater region: rendzina and terra rossa. Rendzina are yellow-grey soils which form on marl and chalk. Their water economy is inferior to the terra rossa. Yellow rendzina soils originating from marl hold strawberry trees and Boissier oak, where there are also layers of dolomite. Rendzina soils originating from chalk are the natural domain of the shallow-rooted Aleppo (Jerusalem) pines. Natural Aleppo pine can still be found in a few spots in the western and central Upper Galilee.

Open fields of rendzina soil hold plants of the *Labiatae* and *Cistaceae* families. The *Labiatae* family includes aromatic spices such as sage, thyme and savory.

The rockrose and smaller sunrose bush are common members of the *Cistaceae* family. Many rare orchids also prefer rendzina.

Terra rossa soil is more abundant than rendzina. The brown-red soil forms upon a limestone-dolomite substrate. Generally, one finds the oak and terebinth association on terra rossa soils. In the Upper Galilee, many other trees enrich these thick maquis. Many of them belong to the *Rosaceae* family, such as the Syrian pear, wild plum and mountain ash. Laurel and Syrian ash also are common.

Open fields hold thorny burnet bushes, thorny calycotome, sage and short buckthorn tree. Many geophytes are common, such as the squill and cyclamen. Marjoram is also abundant and aromatic.

In the eastern Galilee, large sections are covered with planted forests of pine, usually on rendzina soils. The natural oak-terebinth association on rendzina is supplemented with snowbell trees and on terra rossa soil with the Atlantic terebinth.

Wildlife

The Upper Galilee's wildlife is of a northern Mediterranean and Iro-Siberian origin. There are, however, a few representatives of other climates. The Syrian rock hyrax, honey badger, bulbul, laughing dove and small dark blue Palestinian sunbird, all originate in Ethiopia. The Indian crested porcupine is from Asia. The light-green tree frog comes from an Irano-Turanian background.

Bats and rodents are the most common mammals in the region. Of these, two common types represent northern regions: the dormouse and the vole. Dormice live amid the maquis while voles thrive in open fields (and agricultural fields, which they damage). The vole shares the open field with the Palestine mole rat, whose small mounds you may notice.

At the turn of the century, a number of mammals were extinct from the region: the Syrian bear, the roe (Carmel) deer, the Persian squirrel and the small-spotted genet. Since 1948, leopards and striped hyenas have also disappeared from the Galilean landscape. A few wolves are the only large predators left. Middle-sized predators include the jungle cat and wild cat, badger, beech (stone) marten, marbled polecat and Egyptian mongoose. The European otter seems to have recently become extinct from the waterscapes.

The wild boar, Israel's largest mammal, is still a common sight. Although hunted, it manages to survive well. Due to the dense vegetation of the western and central Upper Galilee, mountain gazelles are only seen in the eastern subregion.

Amphibians have fared much better than large mammals. In the Upper Galilee, all six of Israel's species are found: the fire salamander, newt, stream frog, tree frog, green toad and Syrian toad.

Reptiles are also abundant. The only poisonous snake is the impressive and deadly triangular-headed Palestine viper which lives in rocky walls, often near settlements and chicken coops. Other common snakes are the black snake and coin-marked snake which looks similar to the Palestine viper. The spotted green lizard is a rare lizard in Israel, but quite common in the shady maquis of the Upper Galilee. The quick lizard, agama, gecko land tortoise and chameleon are as common here as in the Lower Galilee and Jerusalem Hills.

As for fowl, the Upper Galilee has a majority of Israel's species. Nonetheless, little has been written about them because the nearby Hula Valley is the regional birdwatching magnet. A large number of maquis-loving birds are common, such as the jay, blackbird and woodpecker, whose different melodies ring out among the thickets. Due to the extensive maquis cover, raptors are relatively limited. They seem to be more abundant in the eastern sections where there is a less thick vegetational cover.

Human Involvement

Little is known of the prehistoric periods in the Upper Galilee. While hundreds of artifacts have been discovered, sites are rare. One site in Nahal Keziv has yielded significant Neolithic remains (5500 B.C.E.).

The most interesting Canaanite site is a large stone mound, traditionally called "Jethro's Cairn," northwest of Kibbutz Parod. This cairn was part of a large stone wall on a ridge overlooking a spring. Since no buildings were found, archaeologists concluded that this was a shelter for goats and sheep, similar to finds in the Lower Galilee and Golan. Dolmens, usually dated to the Mid-Canaanite period, were discovered in the eastern part of the Meron Range. It thus seems that settlement in those days was primarily nomadic, with highly developed burial practices.

The Phoenicians built towns alcng the coast and also penetrated inland. Kabri, for instance, was a town on the Coastal Plain destroyed around the 8th century B.C.E., possibly by the tribe of Naftali.

A thousand years of only modest construction in the mountains preceded the settlement of Naftali in the 12th century B.C.E.: "Neither did Naftali drive out the inhabitants ... but he dwelt among the Canaanites, the inhabitants of the land" (Judges 1:33). While the Canaanites and Phoenicians held towns in the fertile valleys and plains, Naftali settled the forested mountains. Fifteen sites have been found hinting toward small family farm settlements upon strategic locations, such as ridges. As years went by, the Israelites gained more control over the land, abandoned the small farms and founded Israelite cities.

In 634 B.C.E., the settlement was destroyed and exiled by the Assyrian King Tiglath-Pileser III. For hundreds of years the central Upper Galilee remained sparsely populated. People congregated by the main tels. In the eastern region, Jewish settlement began again during Hasmonean times.

The Meron Range became re-inhabited only in the Roman-Byzantine period when the western subregion became a populous Christian enclave, and the east had a renewed Jewish settlement. It seems that Jews were forced out of the western Galilee by government supported Christians. Nevertheless, both populations prospered with olive oil being the main source of revenue. The Rama-Peki'in-Sasa-Baram line represents the border between Jews and Christians. The Meron Range clearly distinguishes between the two regions. Nine settlements in the

Meron Range were constructed, still being smaller than the ones at lower elevations. Hurbat Hotam, in Har Peki'in above Nahal Keziv was the large settlement of the time in the Meron Range.

With the Moslem conquest in the 7th century, both Christian and Jewish populations declined. The Moslems brought in newcomers to populate abandoned towns. Since there are few finds from the two centuries following the conquest, it seems clear that development did not take place. Resettlement came again with the Crusaders, who constructed estates, especially in the west. The Mamelukes continued the process in the 13th and 14th century. Three of their agricultural settlements in the Meron Mountains persevered until the 19th century.

The Druze who are today closely associated with the region first settled the Galilee in the 13th or 14th century. They chose remote sections, as far away as they could get from their Moslem persecutors. Today, 16 out of 18 Israeli Druze villages are in the Galilee.

In the 16th century, Safed, in the eastern Upper Galilee, became the pulsating heart of the Jews of Israel. Many famous rabbis, some of whom were forced to leave Spain at the time of the Inquisition, wrote great kabbalistic and *halakhic* tomes here, investing the very cobblestones, some say, with an aura of mysticism The saintly Rabbi Isaac ben Solomon Luria, resided in Safed and revealed the graves of many Jewish sages throughout the Galilee.

Safed prospered at the expense of smaller villages, as the weakening of the central Ottoman government, plagues and Bedouin attacks took their toll. Rabbi Israel Bek and his son, of Safed, attempted to settle the ruins of the Druze village Jermak by Har Meron in the early 19th century. The attempt, the first Jewish one in the Galilee for hundreds of years did not last long. Real development did not happen until after WWI. First, a Franco-British resolution fixed the Lebanese border. Then, in the 1930s and 1940s, Jewish settlements sprouted in the region. The best-known are Hanita and Yehiam in the west and Biriya, by Safed, in the east. These settlements were the impetus for the region's inclusion in the state of Israel by the United Nations Partition Resolution of 1947.

During the War of Independence, 60% of the Galilean Arabs fled. A few villages were also evacuated. The Druze stayed, for during the war they had changed sides and joined Israel.

In the 1950s the Negev topped the settlement agenda, due to David Ben Gurion's southern push. Nevertheless, 20 settlements were founded in the Upper Galilee, mainly due to its proximity to the border.

Between 1957-1965, the north came to the top of the national agenda. The Syrians began to build a water diversion canal in the Golan. The Arabs of the Galilee, recovering from the blow in 1948, began to form extremist political movements and engage in violent demonstrations. Israel began urban settlement in the Lower Galilee but only smallscale settlement in the Upper Galilee.

During the Six Day War, Israel increased its size by 400% and soon the Galilee was forgotten. Following the Yom Kippur War in 1973-1974, the Upper Galilee began to return to the headlines, as the Palestinian Liberation Organization implemented numerous assassinations in northern towns and settlements.

In the late 1970s and 1980s, without active government encouragement, the Jewish Agency, launched a settlement campaign, creating some 30 small communities (*mitzpim*). Each mitzpe has a distinctive atmosphere, providing a high quality of life away from the urban intensity. A mitzpe usually houses 5-50 families. This costly project spawned the construction of hundreds of kilometers of roads, many of them private access routes to the tiny villages. The goal was to change the Arab-Jewish population ratio, but the effort brought only 10,000 new people into the region, far from a significant demographic change. It became clear that construction of settlements will not demographically change the Galilee.

Today, the Jewish Agency is again planning another 30 or so settlements there. Their goal is not clear. If the plan is executed, the Galilee will be packed with dozens of tiny settlements and its few wild areas will be totally decimated. The Galilee's fragile ecological balance will be shattered.

Water

The Upper Galilee is a region of many naturally flowing streams. Since 1948, the large springs have been pumped. Agreements between the N.R.A. and the Israel Water Planning Authority (Tahal) saved the waterscapes from total demolition; a trickle of water is released in the pumped streams enabling a short lane of natural waterscape to survive. In any case, many water-loving plants and animals have disappeared from the region.

Among the streams, many springs emerge. Due to their low topographic position, the waters were never intensively exploited for agriculture, but for flour grinding mill operation. Thus, ancient settlements usually depended on water cisterns.

A few meager springs also emerge in the Meron and Canaan Ranges. Rainwater percolates through the cracked mountain rock, emerging upon marl layers. These springs are often marked by fig or poplar trees.

Hiking in the Upper Galilee

The Upper Galilee is one of the few regions in Israel where hiking is relatively comfortable in the summer. This is due to the elevation, and quantity of shade. The streams also create a cool atmosphere. In the winter, the weather is often balmy and the trails muddy and slippery. After a heavy snowfall, a snow-hike in the Meron Range is unique for Israel (see hikes in, *A Guide to Hiking in Israel with 40 selected one day Hikes*).

Upper Galilee is about 4 hours by vehicle from the center of Israel. Three roads run east-west in the Upper Galilee:

1) Road 85 runs along its southern fringe. Along it break off a number of roads which climb into the Upper Galilee to meet Road 89: (Tefen) Road (854) connecting Karmiel with Ma'alot, the scenic, Road 864 through the village of Peki'in and Road 885 towards Safed.

2) Highway (and Road) 89 cross the region from Nahariya to Safed. Road 899 winds its way through northern Upper Galilee.

3) Road 886 runs through the eastern Upper Galilee towards the Upper Jordan Valley and the Ramim Ridge.

Public transportation is from Safed to the eastern Upper Galilee and from Nahariya (also *sherut* cabs) to the western Upper Galilee. An infrequent bus line runs between Safed and Nahariya on Road 89 through the Meron Range. Buses from Haifa to Kiryat Shemona run through the Bet Hakerem Valley and Safed.

Until now, the region was in many ways the fringe of Israel. The narrow, winding roads are an example. Currently, they are under improvement. Be careful, especially in the winter when snow, sleet, rain and fog (also in summer) obstruct vision and stability on the roads and trails.

There are many marked routes. Since you can not wander farther than six kilometers from a settlement, water sources are always closely available. In any case, a day's hike demands 5 liters in summer and 2 liters in winter. Although most of the spring water is clean, it is best to stick to canteens.

Important Phone Numbers

S.P.N.I. Field Study Centers and Information

Har Meron F.S.C.:	06-980023, 06-989072; fax: 06-987723
Western Galilee (Akhziv) F.S.C.:	04-823762; fax: 04-823015
N.R.A.:	04-978825

Safety Assistance

I.D.F Northern Command, Safed:	06-979253, 06-979370
Nahariya Police:	100, 04-920344
Nahariya Ambulance (Magen David Adom):	101, 04-823333
Safed Police:	100, 06-978444
Safed Ambulance:	101, 06-930333

Sites Worth Visiting

Museums:

Safed Old City and Museums.
Biriya Fort at Har No'azim, 2 km. north of Safed on paved road to Amuka.
Tefen Industrial Zone, (and museums) on Tefen Road 854, south of Ma'alot.
Hanita Museum, Kibbutz Hanita.

Nature Reserves and National Parks:

Bar'am National Park, 2 km. north of Bar'am Junction off Road 89.
Rosh Hanikra, National Park, end of Road 4 at border with Lebanon.
Har Meron Summit Path, 5 km. off Road 9.
Hurbat Mahoz and Hurbat Heshek: above kilometer post 12 on (Tefen) Road 854.
Keshet (Arch) Cave: trailhead is 2.5 km. along Idmit Road from junction on Road 893.

Others:

Rashbi (Rabbi Shimon Bar Yohai) Tomb: behind Moshav Meron, 1 km. south of
    Meron Junction.
Peki'in Druze Village and Ancient Synagogue, along Road 854.
Mitzpe Harashim, 2 km. west of Road 864.

Overnight Options

Indoors

Many settlements offer private rooms with kitchen facilities.
S.P.N.I. Field Study Centers, see above.
Youth Hostels: Akhziv, by the Mediterranean Sea, 5 km. north of Nahariya; Safed.
Hotels: In Safed and Nahariya.

Outdoors

Parod Recreation Grounds, at sharp curve on Road 865, by kilometer post 34-
    35 (see Hike 14).
Nahal Meron Picnic Grounds, at sharp curve on Road 865, by kilometer post 42.
Meron Picnic Grounds, 800 m. east of Meron Junction on Road 89.
Upper Nahal Ammud Picnic Grounds, 1 km. north of Road 89 between kilometer
    post 47-48.
Dalton (Ein Zetim) Recreation Grounds, 2-3 km. north of Road 89 on Road 886.
Hammama Picnic Grounds, across from Har Meron F.S.C.
Har Meron Picnic Grounds, by summit on Har Meron 4 km. past Hammama Picnic
    Grounds.
Recreation Ground, off Road 89 by kilometer post 12.
Nahal Sarakh Picnic Grounds, off Road 899 across from Geranot Hagalil turnoff
    (see Hike 10).
Har No'azim Picnic Grounds, by Biriya Fort, north of Safed.

Gas Stations

In the towns of: Safed, Karmiel, Ma'alot, Nahariya. By Rama on Road 85, and at
    Meron Junction (Road 89 and 886).

Nahal Sarakh and Nahal Betzet

*See map on
page 84*

Points of interest: *Fascinating archaeological finds, a stalactite and stalagmite cave, and a rich waterscape of pools beneath a canopy of vegetation, between thick forests and towering cliffs.*
Length and nature of hike: 5 kilometers. one-way.
Hiking time: 5 hours.
Preferred season: All year.
Suitable for: All.
Maps: Upper Galilee hiking and touring map.
Special preparation: Flashlight, swimsuit.
Starting point: Nahal Sarakh Picnic Grounds, off Road 899.
Ending point: Kibbutz Eilon, off Road 899.

To reach starting point:

Arrival by private transportation: Take Road 899 (known as the Northern Road since it runs south of the Israel-Lebanon border) to the village of Geranot Hagalil. Just east of the turnoff to Geranot, between kilometer post 13 and 14, turn north (left if you are coming from Nahariya) onto a gravel road (1). The gravel road eventually veers west as it partially encompasses a pine-forested hill. The road dead-ends at the Nahal Sarakh Picnic Grounds (2).

To return to your car at the end of the hike: either retrace your steps from (6) (heading back on the same trail offers a slightly different perspective of the area), or catch a bus to Geranot Hagalil and follow the instructions in 'Arrival by public transportation.'

Arrival by public transportation: From the Nahariya central bus station a bus line runs along Road 899 to the region's settlements. Get off at the entrance to Geranot Hagalil (1) and follow by foot as mentioned above in 'Arrival by private transportation.'

It is also possible to ask the bus driver to stop where the road straightens out after a curve to the right, some 400 m. before the entrance to Geranot Hagalil. Across the road to the North begins a blue-marked trail (there is a small sign) which leads to the Nahal Sarakh Picnic Grounds (2).

Geography

Nahal Betzet is the northern-most stream of Israel, west of the national watershed. It holds a nature reserve of 7,650 dunams. Part of its northern watershed coincides

79

with the Israel-Lebanon border. Its southern watershed is Nahal Keziv's northern one. The lush watercourse has a drainage area of 123 sq. km., from northwest of the Meron Range to the Mediterranean Sea.

Nahal Namer and Nahal Sarakh are ephemeral tributaries of Nahal Betzet. Nahal Namer, originating in Lebanon, merges into lower Nahal Betzet. Nahal Betzet is a dry stream east of the Nahal Sarakh-Nahal Betzet joint. Half a kilometer west of this joint, the stream yields perennial flow emerging at Einot Karkara. The springs yield between 20 to 70 cubits per hour (about 1 million cubits annually). Today the watercourse stretches for 1.5 km. It ends where the water is pumped up to Kibbutz Eilon.

Nahal Galil and Nahal Sarakh cut into the Sakhnin Formation of dolomite, well-known for its karstic phenomena. Similar to Nahal Keziv, the watercourse section of Nahal Betzet is in the relatively-impermeable chalk of the Dir Hanna Formation, (Rosh Hanikra Member). Upon hill tops and ridge crests in the area, such as at Har Okhman and Hurbat Din'ila lies exposed massive limestone of the Bina Formation which is the same formation upon which the Old City of Jerusalem stands. This formation, found throughout Israel, is one of the main sources of building stone.

Plants and animals

Fern: *Sarakh* means fern, and you will find rare ferns along the shaded slopes of Nahal Sarakh. Today the stream bed is heavily hiked; to find these plants it is best to head up the moist north-faced slopes or tributaries.

Dryopteris villarii is an impressive fern, boasting stiff leaves, 20-60 cm. long. The sporangiums are found in two rows on side arteries on the underside of the leaf. This is the only fern in Israel that grows on slopes rather then alongside water or in rock cracks. Found also in the Golan, this fern gives a European atmosphere to the few Israeli forests where it is found.

The *Asplenium adiantum-niggrum* fern has triangular leaves up to 50 cm. long. It sprouts from cracks in rocks in the thick forests of the Golan, Galilee and Carmel. One specimen has even been found growing out of cracked granite rock by the Santa Catherina monastery in the arid Sinai mountains. *Asplenium adiantum-niggrum* is one of 700 sub-species of Asplenium. In Europe the Asplenium was used against black death. The black stalk of the fern gives its scientific and Hebrew name: *Asplenium Shahor*. The evergreen, dark dissected leaves are shiny while their undersides have spores along the main arteries. The sporangium open between March and July.

Leopard: *Namer* in Hebrew is leopard. Years ago, in Nahal Namer leopards often preyed on sheep. The last leopard reported was in 1963, when a Bedouin shepherd from the nearby tribe of Arb El-Armasha, knifed one.

Jay (*Garrulus glandarius*): The distribution of the jay in Israel is constantly widening. Once found only in the open forested or tall-tree areas of Judea, Samaria and the mountainous Galilee, today they nest throughout the non-desert regions, including cities.

Olive presses at Hurbat Din'ila

The jay belongs to the crow family, which is the most developed of the songbirds. It has a unique combination of colors which vary throughout the different biotopes. In Israel the main colors are an active black tail, white posterior and blue and white wings. The bird is over a foot long and sounds a recognizable "skaak skaak" and a ringing "kyuu." It also imitates other bird and animals noises. Officially, the jay chatters rather than sings, hence the Latin name.

During the nesting season the jay tends to be quiet when it lays 2-6 9-gram speckled green eggs. The birds usually live alone or in small groups but in the spring are seen in flocks. This bird is a true omnivore but prefers acorns.

History

Betzet is one of the towns in the county of Tyre mentioned in the Mishna (tractate Shevi'it). The town is identified as the ruined village of El-Batza where today stands the development town of Shlomi. During the Byzantine period, the western Galilee supported affluent Christian communities. Two ruins along the hike, Hurbat Karkara and Hurbat Din'ila testify to the fact. Nahal Betzet is known in Arabic as Wadi Karkara. The people of these villages supported themselves from olive oil. Based on the quantity of oil presses found in these ruins, it seems that large portions of the region which are today forest were then olive orchards. Single olive trees appearing among the wild trees may be ancestors of Byzantine trees.

Upper Nahal Sarakh hosted the army of Fauzi el-Kaukg'i retreat northward during the 1948 Independence War. In October of that year, the Israeli Defense Forces conducted the successful Hiram Operation, capturing in 60 hours the whole Upper Galilee.

I.D.F. forces headed out of Nahariya and Safed surrounding the enemy in a pincers fashion. Kaukg'i's famous "Rescue Army" lost the battle at the Arab village of Tarshiha and began retreating northward via an ancient Crusader route, squeezing out just before the two I.D.F. forces closed in on them. The route heads from the ruins of the King's Fort in todays village of Mi'ilia via the village of Elkosh (then Dir el-Kassi) and upper Nahal Sarakh, to the Turon Fort by the town of Tivnin in Lebanon.

Site description

Hurbat Din'ila: At 393 m. above sea level, very impressive remains of an olive oil industry and other facilities have been exposed. The site was first settled in early Roman times as a square 1 dunam compound. It flourished during the Byzantine period when the complex expanded to 4.5 dunams (90 m. diameter). During the Crusader-Mameluke period, Hurbat Din'ila was reoccupied and the buildings and olive presses were repaired. The large number of olive presses clearly explains the villages income.

Sarakh Cave: Also known as the Ookam or Xylophone Cave. Near the upper exit of the cave was once a row of red (from iron precipitation) stalactites hanging down from the ceiling. It was possible to 'play' music on them by hitting them lightly giving out a glassy ring. Visitors stole these unique wonders years ago. This cave is in hard dolomite of the Sakhnin Formation. Cracks in the hard rock allowed seepage of water and carbonic acid that slowly weathered away the soluble rock. With the incision of Nahal Sarakh in the strata, the cave was exposed.

To begin hike:

From the picnic grounds (2), it is worthwhile heading up to the top of the pine forested hill (that the gravel road encompasses) to Hurbat Din'ila. Return to the parking lot and follow the blue-marked trail which begins by a sign. The trail heads north along the watershed of Nahal Sarakh, and Nahal Hagalil. As you pass beneath a clump of pine trees, look for a subterranean cave. It was possibly used for burial.

Half a kilometer from the picnic grounds you reach Nahal Sarakh. Follow the blue trail along and in the wadi. Here the jay can be heard and seen in the dark forest. Reach the Sarakh Cave (3) after 1 km. along the stream bed, easily deduced from the many colorful 'trail markings' of garbage. Nahal Sarakh is one of the more popular hiking routes in the North. The cave is on the right, behind a big boulder. The opening is clear and can be comfortably entered. The cave can be explored along two main routes:

The short option: follow the main hall and take the second right which leads back out.

The long option: gives access to explore most of the caves treasures (what remains of them). With the aid of a flashlight, follow the main hall up the ladder (note stub of stalagmite at bottom of ladder) and then take a right climbing up a bit more. Here you can feel a draft from the exit. At next intersection take a right and crawl out of the cave. Looking back in, note the crack in the rock from the ceiling upwards. This crack allowed water to seep down and create this part of the cave. Descend carefully to the cave entrance.

Continue down Nahal Sarakh 400 m. to Nahal Betzet (4). At the Nahal Betzet-Nahal Sarakh joint, a black-marked trail heads up Nahal Betzet and then climbs its steep northern slope to Hurbat Eirav where there is a grand green view of Nahal

Betzet and of the western Upper Galilee. The trail is for experienced hikers only and should take 1.5 hours, round-trip.

Take a left westward along the blue trail, down Nahal Betzet. Oleander bushes appear in the stream bed marking the existence of water. The trail crosses upon a large rock which is interestingly coated with a layer of flint. Here on your left is a mass of rock fragments, most likely consolidated by carbonate solution.

The large fragments hint that their source was most likely not the stream bed, rather slope debris. The source of the carbonate solution was probably running water. Today the southern slope (the north face) of Nahal Betzet is densely forested, meaning that mechanical erosion of rock debris is scarce, due to the vegetational canopy and the soil cover. The formation of the rock seen here most likely took place when (or after) the landscape was an open, non-forested one. For example, after a fire, or during an agricultural/pastoral period such as the Roman-Byzantine.

Before Einot Karkara, a cliff of soft gray marl and white chalk is on your left (Dir Hanna Formation, Rosh Hanikra Member). These marl layers are similar to the layers on which Einot Karkara emerges. Einot Karkara, the source of perennial Nahal Betzet, emerge in the stream bed amidst tall oleanders, 900 m. west of Nahal Sarakh. The trail soon brings you to the active stream shaded by large plane trees (5). About three 'rest and refresh' stops line the next 500 m. of the trail. To add excitement, it is possible to walk in the stream itself. Either way, the running water ends by a rectangular cement pool.

The trail hugs the southern bank until reaching the eastern side of a eucalyptus forest. Amongst the forest stands the pumping station which pumps the water to Kibbutz Eilon. Here begins a trail to Hurbat Karkara: a short red-marked trail leaves the western side of the eucalyptus forest, encompasses the pumping station and ascends amidst the pine forest on the southern bank of Nahal Betzet to the ruins of the Byzantine settlement. Recently, many remnants of oil presses have been revealed. Return back to main trail.

Follow the white-marked trail beneath pipe on the left as you enter Nahal Hagalil (6). Immediately take right, along fence, leaving Nahal Hagalil and reach parking lot. Take the paved road which ascends to Eilon. Along the way, by the curve to the right you can view eastward the pine-forested hill by the starting point, and below it Nahal Hagalil. Further up there is a memorial section for Maya, a teenage girl from Eilon who was kidnapped hitchhiking in Jerusalem and was found dying, burnt in the forest below the Ein Kerem Hadassah Hospital.

After passing through the gate into the kibbutz you can stop at the 'Bedouin' tent. If you are a small party, continue straight through the kibbutz until reaching the entrance along Road 899 (7). Otherwise, take a left along the circumference road to the entrance of Eilon (7).

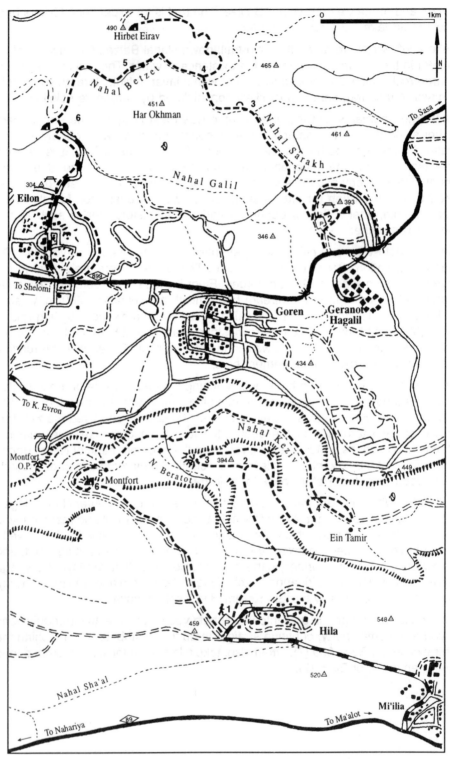

Hike 10, Nahal Sarakh and Nahal Betzet, and Hike 11, Nahal Keziv

Nahal Keziv

See map on page 84

Points of interest: *A bubbling stream shaded by tall trees and thick Mediterranean forest dotted with flour mills and a 13th century Crusader fortress. Madonna lilies bloom in late spring.*

Length and nature of hike: 9 or 10 kilometers, loop trip.

Hiking time: 6-8 hours.

Preferred season: All year.

Suitable for: All.

Maps: Upper Galilee hiking and touring map.

Special preparation: Swimsuit and flashlight.

Starting & ending point: Parking lot before the entrance to Mitzpe Hila.

To reach starting point:

Arrival by private transportation: From (Nahariya-Safed) Road 89, 16 km. east of Nahariya, turn into the village of Mi'ilia, and follow the main road as it curves left, passes a school on the left, narrows and exits the village. The road, 1 km. from the curve in the village crosses the dry Nahal Sha'al on a small bridge. A half kilometer from the bridge the paved road turns sharply to the right. After 200 m., park on your left at the trailhead, a loop gravel road parking lot lined with large stones, one of them marked with a black trail mark (1).

Arrival by public transportation: The Nahariya central bus station has many bus lines passing Mi'ilia. It also may be possible to take a bus from Haifa or Safed. *Sherut* cabs at bus prices are also available from Nahariya. The *sherut* cabs can be picked up also along the main roads. Get off at the main entrance to the village of Mi'ilia. From here, follow the instructions above in 'Arrival by private transportation.'

Geography

Nahal Keziv is the largest and longest stream in the Upper Galilee, west of the national watershed. Nahal Keziv heads west, draining into the Mediterranean Sea. The stream bed, most of which flows only after rainstorms, is 20 km. long and drains 140 sq. km., 120 of them being in the central Upper Galilee where annual rainfall reaches 1000 mm. This is where Nahal Keziv's tributaries drain the majority of the Meron Range and the Peki'in Valley. The western half of Nahal Keziv forms a narrow channel with no large tributaries. Here the three main springs of Nahal Keziv emerge: Ein Ziv, Ein Tamir, and Ein Hardalit where Nahal Keziv opens into the Coastal Plain.

The stream's natural discharge is 600 cubits per hour in the winter and 100 cubits per hour in the summer. This fed 12 km. of stream bed graced by rich water vegetation, kinged by tall plane trees. The waters of Ein Ziv have been trapped since 1952. In 1959, a water pumping project in Nahal Keziv was completed: including a dirt road running along the bottom of the canyon, connecting Ein Ziv to Ein Hardalit with a 24" pipe. Ein Tamir though, was not touched. The piped water is led to the Kefar Barukh Reservoir in the Jezre'el Valley. Today, barely 3.5 km. of flowing water remain—where the hike takes place, (west of Ein Tamir), averaging 100 cubits per hour. This is just enough to maintain the speciality of the place.

The relatively flat ridge above Nahal Keziv is out of dolomite of the Sakhnin Formation. The lapies formations in this dolomite accompany you at the beginning of the route. The canyon of Nahal Keziv cuts into chalk of the Rosh Hanikra Member of the Dir Hanna Formation. From the starting point of the hike you can make out the white chalk ridge of Rosh Hanikra to your northwest (the source of the name for the Rosh Hanikra Member).

Plants and animals

Madonna lily (*Lilium candidum*): The Madonna lily, also known as the white lily is the most glorious wild flower in Israel, due to its unique size, height, color and aroma. The plant is a geophyte, reaching 1.5 m! The stalk holds 5-20 white flowers, over 10 cm. long which release a strong aroma, mainly nocturnally. Thus pollination is done by moths. The Hebrew name, *Shoshan Tzahor*, is derived from *shesh* (six)-the number of petals. It blooms in May-June.

The natural region of the lily is in the Eastern Mediterranean Basin. In Israel it is rare, found only at 6 patches in the Carmel, in two patches in the Upper Galilee (Nahal Keziv and Har Peki'in) and along the slopes of the Hermon Range. The species has 80 wild genera and 50 garden genera. In Israel only one genus is found.

> I am the rose of Sharon and the lily of the valleys. As the lily among thorns, so is my love among the daughters (girls)." (Song of Songs 2:1, 2) "Thy two breasts are like two young roes who feed among the lilies."(ibid. 4:5)

The lily is mentioned many times in the Bible and represents beauty and aroma. For centuries, the biblical lily was understood as being a rose. Today it is clear that the biblical lily does not refer to a rose, yet there are still doubts, if the biblical lily is the flower found above Nahal Keziv. Solving this problem involves adapting the descriptive biblical text to botanical finds: today we find the lily blooming in late spring amongst thorns, after the spring flower carpets have already wilted. On the other hand, the lily has been found only in densely forested areas, not in the valleys. It is possible though, that the flower's distribution was once a lot more encompassing.

During the Middle Ages, Christians saw the flower as a symbol of purity and dedicated it to Mary. Crusaders collected lily bulbs, thus bringing the plant close to extinction. Only the most hidden members survived. Only in the second quarter of the 20th century the lily was found in the Holy Land by the northern village of Metulla, after years of searching.

Its shape inspired architectural shaping of columns for the temple. In the Mishna and other books from the Roman period the lily also was a symbol of beauty.

Forest dormouse (*Dryomys nitedula phrygius*): This cute looking rodent has characteristics running between those of mice and squirrels. In Hebrew the small rodent is known as *Namnaman haetzim*-the tree dozer. The scientific name is the "beautiful-shiny mouse of the forest god."

The nests resemble bird nests. Look for them in the trees of a typical oak and terebinth forest. The nest is made out of leaves and is coated with tree bark, built 1.5-3 m. above ground. Sometimes the dormouse simply moves to a bird nest. Nests come in groups of 2-6. Distance between sets of nests is hundreds of meters.

The dormouse reaches a length of 9.5 cm. with its tail length a bit shorter. Typically it weighs only 25 grams! It has a light brown coat and white undersides. The eyes are surrounded by a dark brown or black stripe. Its diet includes acorns and other fruits, seeds, invertebrates and bird eggs. During cold weather, hibernation takes place as body temperature drops to a stable 13°. In Europe, hibernation takes place through the whole winter while in Israel only on exceptionally cold days will the rodent take a few days off. When in danger, the small creature will utter a dull hoarse gargle.

History

Keziv is a modern name given to the stream by the government name committee. South of the stream's mouth into the Mediterranean Sea, lies Tel Akhziv which in the Mishna is known as the city of Keziv. It is said of Keziv that it has never disappointed its waters—as the root of the Hebrew *kazav* is disappoint. The site of Keziv is first mentioned in the book of Genesis 38:5—a birthplace for one of Judah's sons, "And she again conceived and bare a son and called his name Shelah, and he was at Keziv when she bare him."

Upper Nahal Keziv is known in Arabic as Wadi Hoobeiz which means one who secludes himself from society, like a monk or ascetic. The name is after Sabalan, a Druze prophet who lived by himself atop the hill known today as Nebi Sabalan. The part of Nahal Keziv followed in the hike is known as Wadi Kurn, meaning small horn, most likely named after the horn shaped ridge of the Montfort. Due to the rough terrain of Nahal Keziv, there are no important ancient routes along the stream, thus no battles have taken place by its waters. Until 1948, 12 flour mills were active along the stream, used by residents of the nearby Arab villages. The decrease in the Arab population, the modernization taking place in Israel, and the utilization of Nahal Keziv's waters, quickly made the flour mill business a non-profitable one. After 1948 only one mill remained in use for a few years.

H.B. Tristram describes Nahal Keziv and Montfort on an early December day in the late 19th century:

We turned to the left up the Wady Kurn, through which a bright mountain stream rushes to the sea, which it enters near the town of Zib. At the entrance to the valley we saw two fine tawny eagles. By and by we came to an ancient water mill nestled in a luxuriant but wild and unfenced orange grove.... we found the river which was swarming with fish.

It is very difficult to give a written description of this almost unknown ruin— a sort of miniature Gibraltar of the olden time, isolated as the rock of Calpe yet it still more strongly reminds one of the situation of Constantine in Algeria but on a much smaller scale. Imagine a tongue of rock standing out between two ravines, upwards at 600 feet high, its sides almost perpendicular and scarped to the waters edge. Its platform, almost 200 yards long and not more than from twelve to twenty yards wide... Time however has had little to do with the ruins of Kulat-el Kurn for the chiseling of the stone work is fresh and sharp as when the walls were first undermined and thrown down...

Most beautiful of all the way was the delicate cyclamen, nestling itself under every stone, and lavish of its lovelyness with its graceful tufts of blossoms varying in hue from purest white to deepest purple pink.

Site description

<u>Ein Tamir</u>: *Tamir* (Aramaic and Hebrew) means hidden, accurately describing the source. Today, from Ein Tamir the perennial flow of Nahal Keziv begins. Discharge averages 45 cubits per hour. The spring emerges by the contact of two geological formations, Sakhnin and Dir Hanna. Nahal Keziv cuts deep into the formations, exposing this contact upon which underground water flows, and at Ein Tamir emerges. The tunnel of Ein Tamir seems to be natural though there are similar

The popular pool of Nahal Keziv

man-made tunnels like these at numerous springs throughout Israel. It is possible that the tunnel is man made and that all the signs of construction have been dissolved throughout the years. It is an exciting experience to wade up the tunnel to the source. During high flow there is a section where one has to dive beneath the low ceiling!

Montfort: The Crusader fortress, 120-180 m. above Nahal Keziv, first served as an agricultural farm mansion and only later as a fortress as no Crusader border or main road ran near Nahal Keziv. The farm was founded in the mid-12th century and belonged to the Feudal estate whose headquarters (Kings Castle) were in Mi'ilia. As the farm prospered, its importance increased and was named 'New Kings Castle.' After Saladin's victory over the Crusaders at Karnei Hittin in the Lower Galilee, the fort also succumbed to him. Five years later 'New Kings Castle' was recaptured and restored.

Montfort was sold nine years later, in 1228 to the German-Tevtonian Order. During this period the name Montfort came to be, meaning the fort of the mountain. In German the Tevtonians called it *Shtarkenburg* "strong mountain." In the 13th century the Crusader headquarters in the Holy Land was in Acre. Since the Tevtonian Order was disliked by the other two orders, they were exiled to the Montfort taking all their treasures and archives. In 1266 the fort withstood a Mameluke siege. With the help of Popal donations, Montfort was enlargened and fortified. In 1271, five years after the Mameluke Sultan Bibers sieged the Montfort for the first time, Montfort fell. The Bibers engineering force, collapsed the fortress' southern wall bringing the knights to surrender in a week. The Montfort archives were transferred via Acre to Tirol in Austria where they still are today.

Montfort was dug in 1926 by the New York Metropolitan Museum. Most of the finds were taken there. A few artifacts are at the Rockfeller Museum in Jerusalem. Roman pottery shards and coins were found along with some of the forts stones. The hewn stones, having masonry typical of the Herodian period, led researchers to believe that the fort was first built during the Roman period. The archaeological dig exposed rich Crusader artifacts: weapons, armour, colored glass, coins and shards. Currently, Montfort is being renovated.

To begin hike:

The trailhead (1) offers a moderate vista of the upper western parts of the Israeli Upper Galilee: Israel's border with Lebanon, 6 km. to the north, the Mediterranean Sea 14 km. to the west, with the city of Nahariya laying on the coast. Where the (Soolam) ridge drops to the sea, to your northwest, you can make out Rosh Hanikra with its exposed white chalk lithology.

Follow the easily distinguishable black-marked trail through low kermes oak maquis as you begin the descent toward Nahal Keziv. Note two stages of growth on the oaks. There is the basic tree shape, and along the trunk there is new growth. The trees have been shaped by goats who feed on oak. Oak trees trimmed by goats and sheep will never achieve a tree shape; instead they spread and form a bush shape. The trees seen here have 'made it' but their bottoms are constantly harassed. The trail here is wide and well trodden by hikers and also by flocks of

The entrance to Ein Tamir

sheep and goats from the nearby Mi'ilia. In the fall, dark purple crocuses appear.

After a bit more than 1 km. reach a trail intersection (2). Here you have 2 options:

1) The black trail continues straight down to Nahal Keziv. This option saves you 20 minutes of walking, but offers nothing new.

2) The blue option lengthens the route by 1 km., but is worth the extra steps. It presents beautiful views of Nahal Keziv in all directions, including the impressive Montfort fortress. During the late spring, Madonna lilies bloom along the blue trail which encompasses a ridge (3) surrounded in three directions by wadis. At one time the trails environs were cultivated, olive trees as evidence still remain. This trail reconnects to the black trail, 300 m. further along the black trail from the first intersection.

From the reconnection note how the forest thickens as the tree height rises. Here is a good place to notice nests of the forest dormouse. Soon you will be able to hear the rustle of Nahal Keziv. Upon reaching the bottom follow the trail to the right and find the most popular pool of Nahal Keziv, shaded by plane and Syrian acer (maple) trees (4). Enjoy! Today the source of the stream is only Ein Tamir. To reach Ein Tamir, either follow the stream bed or take a right on the green trail on the northern bank for 300 m. It is an exciting experience to follow the tunnel (with flashlights of course) to its end.

Return to the popular pool (4) and continue westward along the stream. Note the remnants of a structure on the northern bank, most likely of a mill. The trail reaches an open rock stage decorated with a couple of boulders. Here the stream is at its deepest, about 2.5 m. as it cuts a small narrow gorge through the hard chalk (Rosh Hanikra Member). Here is an ideal spot for a dip and tan. Be careful, do not attempt to jump into the water!

Willows grow along the stream. Where plane trees are not present in Nahal Keziv, willows replace them. In my opinion around here the stream flow was reduced for some time killing the plane trees. Note how younger plane trees appear in this area. Today the N.R.A. makes sure that a sufficient amount of water flows annually along this section.

The path soon recrosses to the southern bank and follows the contact of Mediterranean flora with Mediterranean water-loving flora. The wide trail is actually upon a stream terrace! At one time, most likely during the Pleistocene, the stream bed was at the elevation of the trail. Note on your left another step of about 1 m., another terrace. Also note rocks on your left whose shape resemble water currents. The carbonate rock is called travertine. The travertine contains plant stem imprints, and sometimes prehistoric flint artifacts and mammal remains. Cross the stream where a trail departs up to Kibbutz Goren to the north. You continue along the black trail which widens into a dirt road. After crossing the gravel stream bed (around here the water has percolated into the gravel), you will come across the ruins of a water-powered flour mill on your left. The building was later used for other purposes. Note travertine in a dripping shape on the western side of the water channel (by the trail). When the dirt road hits the reactivated stream bed (5), you have reached Ein Matzor. Ein Matzor is not actually a fresh spring; the water that infiltrated into the gravel stream bed upstream reemerges here. The water is potable.

From here a red-marked trail ascends up the northern bank to the Montfort lookout point, its continuation heads up the southern bank to the Montfort. Those who suffer from hyper-activity can hike up to the Montfort lookout point for a postcard view and then hike back down.

Here, less than 1,000 years ago, stood an impressive dam. Note sturdy remnants of it on both sides of the stream bed. Imagine a lake east of it which filled up the whole valley. A water channel ran on top of the dam. Along the western side of the southern mass of built rock lays a huge piece of travertine separated by a few inches from the hewed stone, but lying exactly parallel to it. Just behind stands a huge building with Gothic styled arches which was most likely a flour mill, storage building and sleeping quarters for farm workers during the inhabitancy of Montfort.

There are two options to get to the Montfort (6): explorers can head straight up from the dam through the oak forest (you may come upon a trail connecting the dam and the Montfort). The simpler option is to follow the red dirt road up to the Montfort. Note how the dirt road was constructed: hewed out of the mountainous side and terraced on the open side. Enjoy the seaward view. Note how lower Nahal Keziv is more desolate than the area just hiked. This is due to a number of factors: lower elevation (thus a higher annual temperature), less deep and steep slopes as the wider stream valley becomes more exposed to sunlight, and lack of stream water.

At dirt road intersection take left as you walk beneath the Montfort (6). Note sewage disposal chute at the bottom of the fort. Explore the Montfort from bottom to top and note the inaccessibility of the structure. Starting at the bottom, pass by openings to the cellars. Continue up to the main floor of the structure. On the western side stood the church and miscellaneous rooms, living quarters and a weapon factory. At the top of the fort stood the main tower, overlooking the Montfort's weak spot—the ridge to the southeast. Here, below the Montfort, you can discern the outline of a moat, now full of debris from the tower.

From here follow the red trail along the northeastern bank of the green wadi. Fifty meters after the fort there is a flat wide shady spot, ideal for a rest (even though you just made a stop above). Note the interesting crevasse in the rock. Here begins a hidden trail that descends down to the structures by Ein Matzor. Continue along the red trail (note, it is an ancient hewed path) and connect to the modern gravel road. The gravel road has been recently built for the purpose of reconstructing the Montfort. Continue up and out of the forest through young olive plantations to the sharp curve of the Hila road, and back to the starting point (1).

See map on page 97

Points of interest: *The hike boasting views of the eastern Upper Galilee all the way to Lebanon, numerous springs emerging along a steep wadi, a pond, remnants of a magnificent ancient synagogue and other relics, begins at a modern Arab village built upon an ancient Jewish settlement.*

Length and nature of hike: 7 kilometers, loop trip.

Hiking time: 6 hours.

Preferred season: All year.

Suitable for: All.

Maps: Upper Galilee hiking and touring map.

Special preparation: Swimsuit.

Starting & ending point: Entrance to the village of Jish (Gush Halav).

To reach starting point:

Arrival by private transportation: The village of Jish is located right off (Safed-Nahariya) Road 89, 4 km. north of Meron Junction. Drive into the village via the main entrance. The route begins at the second street to the right (1). Park nearby. On your left, 50 m. ahead on the main street, there is a minimarket with a small parking lot.

Arrival by public transportation: Take the Safed-Nahariya bus. Get off at the entrance to the village of Jish. Head up the main street. The route begins at the second street to the right (1). If you pass a minimarket on your left that has a small parking lot in front, you have gone too far.

Geography

Nahal Gush Halav runs north, into Nahal Dishon, which is the second largest wadi in the Israeli eastern Upper Galilee (Nahal Ammud is number one). Nahal Gush Halav is a short, steep stream; it drops 300 m. along 4 km. The stream's upper parts run along the contact between the edge of the Dalton Plateau and rolling chalk hills (which the Dalton Plateau covers).

The Dalton Plateau, 9 sq. km., is a layer of basalt originating from a volcanic eruption which formed Har Yohanan. The eruption occured after the Neogene, most likely near in time to other magmatic events like the formation of the basalt cover of the Golan Heights.

The lithology of Gush Halav's slopes and of the village of Gush Halav is Upper Senonian chalk and clay. The wadi of Ein Alva runs along the contact of this strata with Eocenian chalk and limestone, that composes the wadi's northern slope. Along this contact, Ein Alva emerges. The clayish Senonian strata is the aquiclude. The spring which forms a pond in Nahal Halav also emerges upon the same contact.

Plants and animals

Fig (*Ficus carica*): The fig is one of the two Israeli members of the *Moraceae* family. Although it originates in southeast Asia, it has been well-known in the Middle East for a long time. The Egyptians began to cultivate the fruit 4,700 years ago. Fig remnants in Israel date back to the Neolithic period. In contrast to most other fruits, the fig has been used as a basic food, due to its high calorie content. Dried figs have 255 calories per 100 grams.

The fig is mentioned numerously in the Bible, from the Garden of Eden, where Adam and Eve clothe themselves with the large hand-shaped leaves through the books of the prophets, who portray each man sitting under his fig tree and vine. This image has been used to symbolize ideal prosperity and peace. In the five books of Moses, the fig is defined as one of the seven species with which the land of Israel is blessed. Fig cultivation is also mentioned in Greek and Roman texts.

The best growth conditions are in a typical Mediterranean climate—hot summers and cool rainy winters. Israel has very few natural figs, known here as the field fig, which usually grow in cool, moist and shady spots. Field figs grow individually, never forming a grove or forest.

The fig is not a true fruit, rather a meaty, pear-shaped skin that holds a cluster of flowers. They ripen during summer, usually in dark purple shades.

Rabbi Dr. Moses son of Maimon (Maimonides) mentions figs a number of times as good for constipation. The fig is known to cure many ailments and weaknesses.

Two-thirds of the fig market is invested in dried figs. Israel imports dried figs from Turkey. Before 1948 there were 100,000 dunams of fig plantations, but today the branch is neglected. In Judea and Samaria a few people still grow figs, as in Nahal Gush Halav.

History

Gush Halav, first inhabited in Canaanite times, is not mentioned in the Bible, although the Mishna does refer to it a number of times. In tractate Arakhin 9:5, Gush Halav is said to be a wall-surrounded village since the times of Joshua. After the destruction of the First Temple, it was inhabited either by remnants of the exile or a bit later by Jews returning from Babylonia.

The village was much more important during Second Temple times. Yohanan ben Levi, known as "Yohanan from Gush Halav," helped lead the Great Revolt against

Rome (66-70 C.E.). Josephus Flavius writes that he went to Gush Halav to assist in preparations but Yohanan turned him down.

Gush Halav was then the last village in northern Israel to fall into Roman hands. Josephus tells that the Roman commander Titus, along with a thousand horse-ridden soldiers, arrived there on the Sabbath. Titus offered the residents a peace treaty. Yohanan ben Levi accepted but asked Titus to wait until the end of the Sabbath. Titus, accepting Yohanan's word, returned to camp at Kedesh and Yohanan lead the town's inhabitants south toward Jerusalem. Only some of them arrived there safely.

After the revolt, Gush Halav was resettled and prospered, mainly in the silk, olive and olive oil industries. In the Jerusalem Talmud (tractate Shevi'it), it is said that one eats olives on the Sabbatical year (when land must lie fallow) until the olive crops of Meron and Gush Halav end.

Tradition holds that the rabbinic pair, Shemaiah and Avtalion, who were heads of the Sanhedrin court in Jerusalem during the second half of the 1st century B.C.E., are buried west of the village entrance.

During the 10th and 11th centuries, Gush Halav was a large village inhabited by Jews. In 1170 the famous traveller, Benjamin of Tudela mentions a presence of some 20 Jews in the village. In the 13th century the village had acquired an Arabic name, El Jish. In 1672 the village is described by a Turkish traveller as a Druze village of one hundred houses. Later, as a result of a war, the settlement was abandoned and Maronite Christians from Lebanon settled in. In the mid-19th century there were Jewish land ownerships in Gush Halav. In 1837 a strong earthquake shaked the Upper Galilee killing 235 people in the village.

By the British Mandate, Moslems had reached a slight majority in the village. During the Independence War in 1948, Jish became one of the most fortified bases for Kaukg'i's "Rescue Army." The Israel Defense Forces captured the town in the fall, during the Hiram Operation, following a bloody battle in which Kaukg'i received assistance from the Syrian Army. Some of the villagers, mainly Moslems, left to Lebanon, while Maronite Christians of nearby Biram and Ikrit found refuge in Jish. By 1978 there were 2,200 people in Jish, 87% of them Christian (mainly Maronites, with some Greek Catholics), 13% Moslems, and no Jews.

There are a number of explanations for Gush Halav. Today, a cheese has the name. Literally, it means a block of milk. *Halav* or *helev* can also refer to tallow. The name may refer to the bright white milky chalk upon which the village is built, a sharp contrast to the adjacent black basalt of the Dalton Plateau. The word *halav* may also describe the local richness in olive oil.

Site description

The ancient synagogue above Nahal Gush Halav remains as a 19x18 meter square. The building faces south, toward Jerusalem. The main entrance is also in the southern wall, which is an unusual placement for a synagogue. The western wall most likely had an opening also.

Upper Galilee oak forest

The building has only a few significant remains. A lower piece of a framehead lies by the entrance; the inside is decorated with a bird of prey whose spread wings are draped with a chain of flowers. Three rows of columns stood in the main hall. The column on the right when entering has the Aramaic dedication, "Joseph Bar Nahum made this (the column) he shall have a blessing."

European travellers first described column heads in 1861 and the first archaeologists arrived in 1905. In 1977, Prof. Eric Meyers dug the site again and concluded that the synagogue had two stages of construction, hundreds of years apart. He also found remnants from a number of historical periods beginning from the Bronze. The original synagogue was constructed on the base of a building from the 2nd century B.C.E. and had two floors. A grand synagogue was built in the 3rd or 4th century and it is the source of what is now seen. On the western side is an uplifted area, most likely from where prayers were conducted. A sherd with the Greek name Aristus was found, possibly the builder's signature. The large hewn stones are from then. Meyers also found two thousand bronze coins from the 4th or 5th century. The building was later reduced in size and most likely in use until the 8th century when an earthquake destroyed it.

Due to land ownership reasons, the archaeological excavations have not yet revealed the hidden relics of the nearby fig groves, most likely where the synagogue users lived.

To begin hike:

Take the second right turn from the main street, heading northeast (1). The street soon becomes a dirt road which exits the village and gradually descends along the western slope of Nahal Gush Halav. Look for the green trail mark. On your left you pass a cave full of debris. It was most likely used for burial.

Looking east across the valley, view the western fringe of the Dalton Plateau, made out of dark basalt. The dark stones lying around the dirt road are basalt rocks from the Dalton. These stones were used for terraces as they are more weather resistant than the local chalk and clay. Slightly above the plateau and in the distance, it is possible to make out the peak of Har Yohanan, 885 m. above sea level, topped with water reservoirs.

After the dirt road cuts into the slope, a very unclear path veers to the right along a shallow gully. Here used to be a service road for access to Ein Gush Halav. If you are the explorer type, follow the path(s) to the spring, which emerges in a small cave, built up during different periods. The structure next to the source is a pumping facility.

Return to the dirt road and continue on it as fig groves appear to your right. Note that the stone walls are made mainly out of basalt and that some of the (ancient) stones are nicely cut. After about 200 m. from the descent to Ein Gush Halav you will see an opening in the stone wall on your right and a trail leading through it toward the ancient synagogue, some 75 m. east of the dirt road (2). It is possible to glimpse the column heads of the synagogue from the road. Follow the short trail through the fig grove to the impressive ruins.

Past the synagogue there is a nice view of hard chalk cliffs on the other side of the stream. The layer of softer clay beneath the cliffs is most likely the water-impermeable layer (aquiclude), which holds the underground waters of the Nahal Gush Halav springs and seepages. In the cliff there are two faults, one of which continues west through Gush Halav.

Return to the green-marked dirt road, take a right and descend along it. At a sharp turn to the right, just above and to the left, lie two small pools, the source for the spring water running onto the road. This layer spring is known as Ein Bardi. *Bard* means cold in Arabic.

As the dirt road hugs the active stream you will soon come across a gate in a fence. Go through it and cross the stream. Here you can see typical stream vegetation, such as the common reed with its hollow segmented stalk and the narrow reedmace that also has round stalks but also long, narrow, pointed leaves. Head up across the open field until you hit a wide trail. Go left and gradually ascend, heading along the southern bank of Gush Halav's main tributary.

Three hundred meters after leaving the stream, you should arrive at Ein Alva, which emerges from a closed cement structure (3). If you are lucky, the lid will be open and you can enjoy a refreshing swim inside. Hikers are usually limited to a primitive shower. Notice remnants of an ancient pool and stairs on both sides of the closed pool. The tall trees below the spring are cottonwoods (poplars). To add to the refreshment, a few fruitful walnut trees grow a bit up the wadi.

From Ein Alva, follow the path on the wadi's northern bank, back to Nahal Gush Halav. It is possible to recross Nahal Gush Halav on a washed-out pipe bridge and continue down the green route, or follow the stream on its eastern bank and merge with the green dirt road about 300 m. further downstream.

Follow the marked trail along the northeastern bank to the ruins of a water-powered flour mill. The slope across the way has a number of small landslides; during periods of rainfall, the clay, dissected into thin horizons, becomes saturated with water and literally slides and gives way.

Before reaching a third mill, make out a prominent line in the landscape which runs above the trail along the slope. This is all that remains of the water channel, high

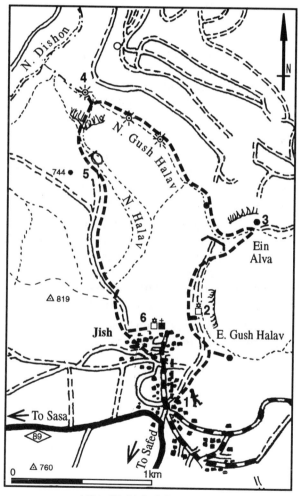

Hike 12, Nahal Gush Halav

enough to reach the mill at its top. It seems that these ruins are not so antique, no more than 200 years old.

After the third mill, the trail crosses the stream through bramble patches and reaches Nahal Halav, a steep gully arriving from the left (south). Just beyond, across Nahal Gush Halav, there is another mill (4).

Leave the green trail and head up the gully. At the elevation where the gully is lined with trees you should find yourself on the western (right) side where there is a clearer, zig-zagging trail. Reach a fenced-in vegetable patch and head around its left side. The cliffs above offer a nice rest spot and view of Nahal Gush Halav and Nahal Dishon (to the north).

At the cliff base the trail is clearer as it veers away from the gully and briefly negotiates the chalk cliffs. Continue along the now shallow Halav wadi, past a few almond trees, and ascend the artificial embankment damming the wadi (5). Here emerges a spring, forming a pond. Swimming is at your own risk! From here there is a nice view of the Lebanese border.

From the pond, an unclear dirt road heads gradually up the western bank, towards Jish in the south. Head that way. The road is full of fossils. Farther up, the vista changes and includes Lebanon in the north, the Hermon and the Golan Heights in the northeast and east, and Mounts Adir and Hiram in the west. After crossing a watershed, the outskirts of Jish appear ahead and the Meron Mountains loom further to the southwest.

Just before the village entrance a road veers left, to the Catholic Mar Butrus Church (6). You can head up for a nice view. Outside the courtyard you can see neglected remnants of the synagogue that stood here during the Roman-Byzantine period in the exact site of the present church.

Return to the road that enters Jish, or head straight down and explore the village. Notice the use of ancient bricks and other interesting masonry in some of the buildings. From the road that enters town, descend on the newly-paved street until an intersection, where you go right onto the main street back to the starting point (1). Just off the main street on your right is a monument to Rabbi Meir Katzon, traditionally known as Rabbi Meir Ba'al Haness, whose tomb is south of Tiberias.

An impressive tomb, traditionally believed to be of Shemaiah and Avtalion is found north of Road 89, west of the main entrance to the village.

13

Nahal Ammud

See map on page 104

Points of interest: *This pearl of the Upper Galilee offers a tremendously rich waterscape of pools and small waterfalls accompanied by variated botany, restored water channels and farms, visited by a great variety of humans and animals.*

Length and nature of hike: Option 1: 9 kilometers, (semi) loop trip.

Option 2: 11 kilometers, loop trip.

Hiking time: Option 1: 6-8 hours. Option 2: 7-10 hours.

Preferred season: All year.

Suitable for: Option 1: All. Option 2: Experienced hikers.

Maps: Upper Galilee hiking and touring map.

Special preparation: Clothes for walking in water, swimsuit.

Starting & ending point: Main entrance to the Safed cemetery.

To reach starting point:

Safed's cemetery lies below the Old City. Its main entrance is at the bottom.

Arrival by private transportation: Drive through Safed toward the new industrial zone and before reaching it, turn right onto a street (no name). (From the street there is a nice view of the Meron Mountains.) After some 750 m. you will reach the gates of the cemetery (1).

Arrival by public transportation: It is possible to walk from the Safed central bus station to the Old City and from there descend along or through the famous cemetery to its gate at the bottom. Another option is to take a city bus that reaches the new industrial zone. Before the industrial zone, get off on Lehi Street where a (no name) street turns off to the right. Follow it for 750 m. to the gates of the cemetery (1).

Geography

Nahal Ammud's drainage basin is only 125 sq. km. but its initial elevation is higher than any other wadi west of the Jordan. Its tributaries wind from the steep eastern slopes of the Meron Mountain peaks (over 1,000 m.) and the western slopes of the Canaan Mountains (close to 1,000 m.) to Nahal Ammud at 600 m. Nahal Ammud itself winds 22 km. down to Lake Kinneret at 210 m. below sea level. The descent makes Nahal Ammud a steep stream by Israeli standards.

En route, the stream creates a number of striking canyons. At the end of its last canyon appears the Ammud, the pillar, giving the stream its name (see Hike 17, 'Lower Nahal Ammud'). During the rainy season over 2 million cubits of water flow down the stream. Its watercourse also includes over 10 springs of different types and sizes.

Nahal Ammud is geographically unique, as its north-south direction has no competition in the Israeli Galilee. The upper parts run between the uplifted block of the Meron Range, composed of Cenomanian hard dolomite and limestone, and the Canaan Mountains (of Safed), made of soft Eocenian chalk and limestone. The canyon sections of upper Nahal Ammud cut into hard Cenomanian dolomite of the well-known, quarried Sakhnin Formation and, farther down, into Turonian limestone of the Bina Formation. The less glorious section of central Nahal Ammud is a wide valley through soft Senonian chalk and marl.

Lower Nahal Ammud defines the border between the Upper and Lower (eastern) Galilee. In this area the stream creates a canyon in hard Eocenian limestone. Until recently, Ammud carried water year-round. Today all three of its main springs are harnessed to supply water to the Safed region which in "exchange," supplies the stream with sewage.

Plants and animals

Pink (*Dianthus pendulus*): The pink is a well-known garden flower. Some know it as a carnation. The pink is found in Europe and Asia in Mediterranean and Irano-Turanian phytogeographic zones. There are 300 different species, eight of which are found in Israel, in rocky mountainous areas. In late summer the pink flower stands out sharply in the dry brown landscape. The flower has five petals, 10 pollens and two pistils.

Dianthus pendulus is a dwarf shrub lacking a tree-like trunk. It is found in very moist cliffs in the Carmel and Galilee. The purple-dotted pink flowers are easily noticeable. The flower has a distinct aroma and the fruit is used as a spice.

Syrian rock hyrax (*Procavia capensis*): The small mammal is a descendant of the elephant family and originates in Africa. The species most likely reached Israel via the Syrian-African Rift. It has proliferated throughout the Galilee.

The hyrax is usually found in vegetated areas adjacent to boulder piles or cliffs. Sometimes one hears groups of these cute creatures on a tree, munching leaves. In 3-4 hours of intensive eating a hyrax can supply himself with its daily needs. The rest of the day is usually spent resting. Sunbathing members watch for predators. Sunbathing also helps regulate the highly fluctuating heat of these mammals.

A dominant male member rules a herd of females and cubs. Subordinate males keep a distance. The dominant male controls a fixed territory and has first pick in mating.

The hyrax, *shafan in Hebrew*, also known as a rock-rabbit, is mentioned a number of times in the Bible and has been variously mistranslated as hare, coney and rabbit. Psalms 105:18, describing the creations of the Lord, says, "The high hills are a refuge for wild goats (ibexes), and the rocks for the hyrax." The animal is also mentioned in Proverbs 30:24-28 and in a number of Rabbinical texts (midrashim).

These middle sized mammals are quite unusual. While their social life resembles herds of large mammals, their size and homes in tunnels place them with smaller rodents. Hyrax body metabolism is similar to reptiles and desert mammals, which makes life easier in warm conditions. In Nahal Kedesh, north of Nahal Ammud, the hyrax population jumped from 80 to 450 after a series of mild winters. Two successive harsh winters decreased the population to only 40 members! They can eat plants avoided by most other creatures, an adaptability asset.

Lately, hyrax distribution has expanded in Israel. This is due to two reasons. First, intense development (even in towns and villages) has created many artificial rocky slopes, ideal for hyrax. Second, the reduction of raptors and carnivores has also limited some dangerous enemies.

The hyrax, like nearly all the wild mammals of Israel, is a protected species.

History

Nahal Ammud has been consistently inhabited, from prehistoric times when people camped in caves and hunted in their front yards, through later periods when the stream became a source for garden irrigation and water-powered mills, until today when the lone occupant is the N.R.A. ranger and his family.

Along the lower stream there are many caves with ancient human remains. The first, a collection of skulls and bones, were found in 1925 by a British archaeologist. He classified this type of *homo sapiens* as *Galilean*. Since then, numerous prehistoric human finds have been found, especially in the Carmel Mountains.

In the 16th century, the ancient town of Safed, 300 m. above and 1 km. to the east of Nahal Ammud, became the cradle of the Kabbalah and the home of the Zohar. Jews who fled the Spanish Inquisition established the town's flourishing spiritual and economic status. Safed was one of the largest centers in the Ottoman Empire for the production of quality woolen cloth. Over 7,000 of the 25,000 inhabitants worked at about 500 looms, six dyeing plants and at least three water-powered fulling mills.

The fulling mills processed the main stage in finishing the wool cloth. Only one remains, at Tahunet el-Batan (see "Site description" below), the only remnant of this flourishing textile industry. The cloth was transported to and from Safed by donkey via Nahal Sekhvee. By the mid-17th century the French and English weavers had captured the market and Safed's industry and population declined.

Nahal Ammud has a number of names. The Jews of Safed knew the stream as Nahar Dilbai, the "river of plane trees." South of the trail to Sheikh Koves it is known as Wadi Leimon, named after the lemon trees. Even today you will find many fruit trees by the stream. Wadi el-Tawahin in Arabic means "stream of the mills" after the twelve mills along its upper portions (and three more mills along a short reach of Nahal Meron before its merge with Nahal Ammud). Some of these mills were active until 1948. They were mainly used in the winter and spring when discharge was at its maximum. At such times, a mill could grind 25-100 kg. of produce in an hour. A peasant woman can grind by hand 1 kg. in about an hour.

Tristram passed by Nahal Ammud a number of times during his tour of the Holy Land in the late 19th century. He observed:

> Wadi Leimon, a narrow gorge which the sun never penetrates, walls the rapid brook on each side so closely that we often had to ride in the bed of the stream. The cliffs are perforated with caves at all heights, the secure resting places of hundreds of noble griffons, some lammergeyers, lanner falcons and several species of eagles. But no description can give an adequate idea of the myriads of rock pigeons. In absolute clouds they dashed to and fro in the ravine, wheeling round with a rush and a whirr that could be felt like a gust of wind.

> One tall isolated pillar stood out, an island in the ravine, tenanted by griffons on all sides.

Today Safed uses the Ammud waters. When water was first pumped it supplied half of the town's needs. Today with the growth of Safed, it supplies less than a third. Safed sewage flows into Nahal Ammud at two locations. The first is by Ein Seter, where sewage purification pool overflow (sludge) runs into the stream. The second is in Nahal Akhbara which drains into central Nahal Ammud, a stream of sewage coming from Safed is discharged in the fall and spring.

Site description

Ein Po'em: The "pulsating spring" in Hebrew. In Arabic it is known as the spring of the Genie. Ein Po'em is a karstic spring which works according to the physics law of connecting vessels: water from various underground tunnels and streams collects into an underground pool. The pool is connected to the outside by an upside-down V-shaped tunnel. The water level in the pool has to reach the level of the bend in the V in order to be released. Water discharge lasts until the underground pool's level drops below the V-shaped tunnel.

The Arab tradition says that the spring is inhabited by a genie, who drinks the water when thirsty. When the genie is finished drinking, the water overflows. In all of Israel only two other perennial springs of this type are known, Ein Gihon, the spring of ancient Jerusalem in the City of David, and Ein Fawar in central Wadi Kelt, east of Jerusalem.

In winter the spring's output can occasionally reach 1000 cubits per hour. In summer output averages 100-200 cubits per hour. Drought can dry the spring. Today, half of its waters are released into the Ammud.

Ein Yakim: Named after an order of priests who served in the Second Temple and who, after the destruction, settled in the vicinity. In Arabic the spring is known as Ein Tina, the "spring of the fig."

Ein Yakim flows year-round. Average discharge is 800 cubits per hour. As with most springs, discharge decreases in the summer. Excess water, after pumping, is released into Nahal Meron and the water channel. In the 1930s the British built a large pumping station at the spring to supply Safed. When the Arab riots resumed in 1936-1939, the British added a police station atop the ridge to the south to guard the important site from sabotage. Today Ein Yakim includes picnic grounds, an information center and a kiosk for the 100,000 annual visitors.

Tahunet el-Batan: Known in Hebrew as *Mavtesha* (place of beating clothes). The Arabic name, *el-Batan,* incorporates the memory and purpose of one of the two types of machines used by the Safed textile industry in the 16th century. The word *batan* comes from the Spanish, for "fulling mill"—a place where woven (usually woolen) cloth is beaten, pressed and trampled in order to tighten and thicken the weave. Once woven, woolen cloth comes off the loom with small gaps between the warp and woof and must be made uniformly compact. In ancient times this was done by beating the wet cloth with staves, a task often performed by women near streams and springs.

In the stream bed, 50 m. upstream of the building, there are remnants of a dam. From the dam, a stone channel directed the water to the mill. The channel broadened before the opening of the mill funnel. The water dropped down the 7.4-meter funnel and turned a vertical water wheel which rotated a beam. Along the beam were clusters of two or three wooden cams or paddles. Rotation of the cams lifted wooden mallets that were suspended from above. The descending mallets pounded the woven cloth which was placed in a tub. The wool cloth was thus cleaned of foreign matter (and tightened). The cloth (probably) was brought and returned to Safed via Nahal Sekhvee.

Before being converted for fulling, the mill was used to produce flour. After the textile industry declined, it again served as a flour mill. Throughout history the mill has belonged to the government or religious establishment.

To begin hike:

From the cemetery gate (1), head north on the road (right, upon exiting the cemetery). Soon the road becomes a dirt one and begins descending towards Nahal Sekhvee. The gentle slopes at this part are due to the soft lithology—chalk and marl of the Har Tzefat and Ein Zetim Formations. When the road splits by a grove of olive trees, take the left option, passing a cattle pen. One kilometer from the starting point you arrive at Nahal Sekhvee (2).

Take a left onto the green-marked trail along the wadi which cuts into the hard sedimentary rock of the Bina Formation. As you descend, you may notice vegetation that represents moister conditions at certain spots in the stream bed.

The trail tends to prefer Sekhvee's southern bank. Two-hundred-fifty meters down the wadi, another wadi arrives from the north. Note the piles of limestone rock beneath the small cliffs. This accumulation is known as talus or scree and each pile represents periods of erosion. Here also is the contact between the Turonian (Bina Fm.) and the older, Cenomanian sedimentary strata. The wadi deepens here. It is one of the few beautiful Galilean wadis that remain relatively untouched.

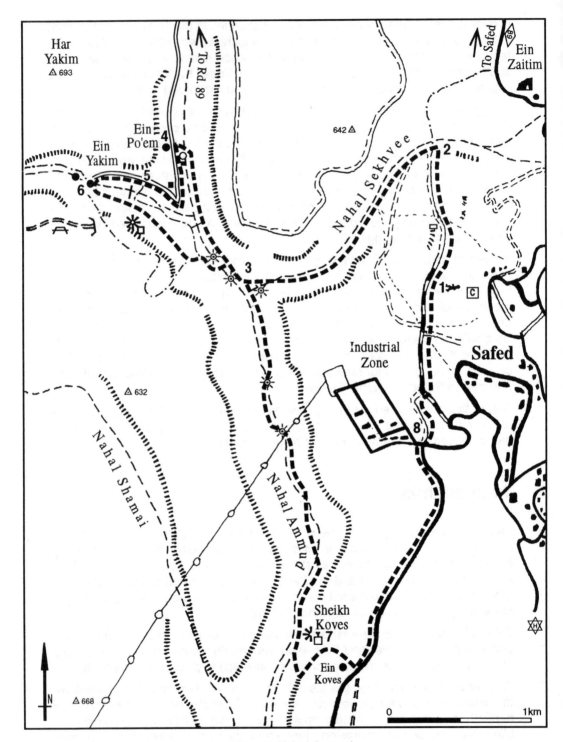

Hike 13, Nahal Ammud

Along this part of the Sekhvee, the trail is actually an ancient one. Note the cobbles, the width of the stone steps and the slickness of the stones on the path, evidence of many feet and possibly carts. During the 16th century and most likely during other periods the wadi seems to have been the major route from Safed to Nahal Ammud.

In the fall, hundreds of the two types of pinks bloom along lower Nahal Sekhvee. Before the merger with the Ammud, the Sekhvee widens a bit into a "Garden of Eden" displaying nearly every wild fruit tree in Israel, including lemon, date, olive, almond, figs, grapes and bramble. Find them and help yourself.

Wandering through the Garden of Eden you may reach Nahal Ammud. If you cross a water channel, go left on the trail and descend to Sekhvee Pools of Nahal Ammud (there is a sign) shaded by tall plane trees (3). Note the flour mill and aqueduct crossing Nahal Sekhvee, 50 m. from Nahal Ammud. In this area there are many pools suitable for a dip.

From here begins an inner loop trip (about 3 km.), that covers most of the popular sites of Nahal Ammud. It is best to savor every step as these three kilometers are one of the lushest spots in Israel. Part of the loop can be done in the water.

To begin, retreat 50 m. to where you descended to Sekhvee Pools and continue north, along the eastern bank of Nahal Ammud. The wide trail is blue-marked and passes along the contact between water and regular Mediterranean vegetation. Pass a trail that heads left, across Nahal Ammud. Soon your trail drops to the stream and reaches an intersection with a green-marked trail. Here is the junction with Nahal Ammud, coming from the north, and Nahal Meron, coming from the west. Continue on the wide blue trail, ascending more steeply, north, on the eastern bank of the Ammud. Cross the small stream on a bridge by a pumping station and go right on the gravel road for 100 m. Here, on your left, is the source of Ein Po'em, below a large fig tree (4).

Retrace your steps on the gravel road and continue on it past all the pumping structures. The road bends around the N.R.A. ranger's home and runs on the northern bank of Nahal Meron. Two-hundred-fifty meters from the house, a clear path descends to the left on reinforced steps, past a stone building (5). This structure was used as an inn for people who came to grind their wheat in the mills.

You can quickly follow the road all the way to Ein Yakim (6). Alternatively, the path takes you across Nahal Meron (to the right) and then into an active water channel to Ein Yakim (6). The trail option offers more shade and sometimes more human activity, but takes a few more minutes. At Ein Yakim (6), the large tree is a walnut. The picnic area here is called Henyon Ha Shekedim—"The Almond Picnic Grounds."

From Ein Yakim, follow the red trail to the east, along the water channel. This channel has been recently restored. Reach a fenced-in pool used for fire salamander breeding. The pool may be inhabited by hungry carp (don't ask me why). Nearby is "the fruit garden" (*bustan*). Vegetables are grown by an ancient agricultural method: earthen water channels crisscross the entire lot between small crop patches. In Hebrew the method is known as *shelahin*—to send (the water among the patches).

At an intersection with the green-marked trail, go left and descend toward Nahal Ammud. From here there is a nice view of the Sekhvee Pools area downstream. The trail cuts through travertine and meets up with the black-marked trail arriving from Nahal Meron.

The building here is Tahunet el-Batan. Go right on the black trail, and after 200 m., reach the Iscandria flour mill. This is the most intact of the 12 mills in the area.

When the trail nears the stream it is possible to wade down to the Sekhvee Pools. In winter and spring the current tends to be strong! By land, follow the trail which crosses the stream to a T-intersection. Take a right onto the blue trail that you have already trodden and return to the Sekhvee pools.

From the Sekhvee Pools you have two options:

Option 1: Simply retrace your steps to the starting point via Nahal Sekhvee. This is the shorter option.

Option 2: Continue down Nahal Ammud for 2 km. and then return, above and beyond the canyon to the starting point.

Option 2: Follow the black trail south. Just after the Sekhvee Pools a sign points to a prehistoric cave on the left. At first the trail follows the Ammud's eastern bank. During dry years, the stream bed here dries up. Evidence of the fact is the decrease in plane trees. The trail follows a small avenue of pomegranate trees on your right and soon crosses the stream on an aqueduct by a mill.

Reach another flour mill. Right before the mill, note an aqueduct intersection. This allowed excess water to be channeled downstream to the next mill.

The trail again crosses over a bridge and recrosses twice. When you are back on the eastern bank, plane trees reappear and the trail continues to crisscross the stream.

After 2.5 km. from Sekhvee Pools, from the eastern bank by a sign, take a steep blue-marked trail up to the white monumental building known as Sheikh Koves (7). As you rest along the way, enjoy the view of Nahal Ammud and the Meron Mountains across the way.

From Sheikh Koves, follow the blue mark up the fire lane, to the right of a planted pine forest, until reaching a paved road. On your right, Ein Koves emerges from beneath the road.

Go left on the paved road (once a blue-marked gravel road). You will pass a small shooting range pit on your right. From Ein Koves it is only 1.5 km. to Lehi Street that descends to the industrial zone (8). Along the way you may catch whiffs of the Vered Hagalil chocolate factory nearby.

If you came by private transportation, cross the field ahead of you and climb up to the road above; go left, back to the starting point (1). A volunteer will be welcome to fetch the car while the rest of the tired hiking party waits or visits the chocolate factory, down the way.

Others can catch a bus from the industrial zone back to Safed.

14

See map on page 110

Parod Falls and Upper Nahal Tzalmon

Two Routes

Points of interest: *A stream full of falls beneath pine trees, continuing along a recreation site through large carobs and oaks. Further downstream it descends steeply in numerous falls, between remnants of a prolific Jewish community.*

Length and nature of hike: Option 1: Parod Falls: 1.5 kilometers, back-and-forth. Option 2: Upper Nahal Tzalmon: 2 kilometers, loop trip. The two routes can be combined.

Hiking time: Option 1) 1 hour. Option 2) 2 hours.

Preferred season: Winter and spring.

Suitable for: All.

Maps: Upper Galilee hiking and touring map.

Special preparation: Clothes for bathing in water.

Starting & ending point: Parod Recreation Grounds, off (Safed-Acre) Road 865 between kilometer posts 34 and 35, by a sharp curve.

To reach starting point:

Arrival by private transportation: Turn north (right, coming from Safed) off Road 865 to the Parod Recreation Grounds (1) and park the vehicle.

Arrival by public transportation: Take buslines that run between Safed and Haifa or Tel Aviv. Descend by the turnoff to Kibbutz Parod. For option 1, head up the road for 100 m. to the sharp curve. Cross the road to the Parod Recreation Grounds (1). For option 2, cross the road to Ein Parod (4).

Geography

Nahal Tzalmon begins at the national watershed along the Meron Range, at elevations exceeding 1,000 m. Its 30 km. course brings it to Lake Kinneret just south of Nahal Ammud, near Kibbutz Ginnosar.

The river changes direction a number of times along its winding course, due to geological faulting and karst phenomena (see Hike 15, 'Central Nahal Tzalmon').

The upper parts of the stream bed drop steeply from Har Hillel (1071 m.) to the Hanania Valley, creating three small canyonlike courses along the way. The first section is actually a number of dry tributaries that very steeply descend through thick vegetation to Shefer. The second section is the Parod Falls and the third is Eshed Hatahanot (Cascade of the Mills), where communities built around flour mills have survived for nearly two thousand years.

The slight change of stream steepness between Parod Falls and Eshed Hatahanot has been the passage way for centuries for the Safed-Acre Road. At 500 m. above sea level the location divides the Upper and Lower Galilee.

Plants and animals

Sabra (*Opuntia vulgaris*): Originating in the plateaus of Mexico, the sabra (also known as the prickly pear) was transferred by the Spaniards to tropical and subtropical countries such as Israel. Sabra cactuses are usually found by the outskirts of Arab villages; it was used to mark the borderline between properties. In Israel, the cactus is not found in the desert, but in Mediterranean regions.

The 3-meter cactus has oval leaves 20-40 cm. long containing 2-5 four-centimeter long thorns and hundreds of tiny hook-shaped thorns able to penetrate many surfaces (never relieve yourself near a sabra on a windy day...!). Every branch that breaks off is able to re-establish itself.

Today, the green-orange fruit is sold throughout the country. The thorns are removed and the skin is peeled off to reveal a succulent fruit. Its water-saturated leaves are edible, an important water source when the going is grim. The sabra is also used in herbal medicine to treat cuts and skin diseases. The flowers are used to cure dysentery.

Upper Nahal Tzalmon

History

Since the region has no surplus of agricultural lands, the water-powered mills had a big part in the economy of the Jewish villages of Parod and Beersheba that prospered in Mishnaic and Talmudic times. Beforehand, it seems, there was not much human activity in the region. Parod stood on both sides of Nahal Tzalmon. Beersheba was on the hilltop across the valley (also profiting from a roof tile industry). A third village, Kefar Hanania, was most likely the largest of these close-knit settlements. It prospered in the first century along the continuation of the ridge east of Nahal Tzalmon. Remains of a vast pottery industry have been revealed there.

Many aqueducts supplied water to Hanania Valley for vegetable crops. The slopes were covered with olives and vineyards. Parod is mentioned in the Talmud (Avoda Zara 31:a) regarding Rabbi Yohanan who reached the village to inquire about a Jewish viticulture law.

Based on documents from travellers, Jewish inhabitance continued in the three villages into the Middle Ages. As time passed, the villages became more Arabic. In 1948, the Arab village of Faradiya, named after Parod, which still ran one of the ancient mills, was deserted.

Upper Nahal Tzalmon's Arabic name is Wadi Rumileh.

Site description

Parod Falls: This stream is actually part of upper Nahal Tzalmon. The active stream originates at Ein Ramiel at the edge of Moshav Shefer. Ein Ramiel is usually a steady spring of 1,100 cubits per day. Its waters are used by nearby settlements. It is sometimes hyperactive in the winter and spring when the overflow is released to the stream bed, creating the Parod Falls.

To begin hike:

Option 1: Parod Falls is a short, scenic route. It is worthwhile only if the stream is flowing. The usefulness of the bridges at the Parod Recreation Grounds can indicate whether or not the stream is flowing.

From the recreation grounds (1), head up the wide dirt road to the northeast, alongside the shallow stream bed of upper Nahal Tzalmon. Half a kilometer from Road 865, the dirt road crosses the stream (2). The road heads eastward, up a tributary to the entrance of Moshav Shefer.

At this point (2), note the blue trail mark which you follow to the left, up the steep stream bed, the Parod Falls. The series of waterfalls descends upon thick coatings of travertine, a result of the large quantities of soluble material in the emerging waters and the large amount of contact of the waters with the air. The travertine surface is very slippery—be careful! The trail climbs the western bank up to Shefer

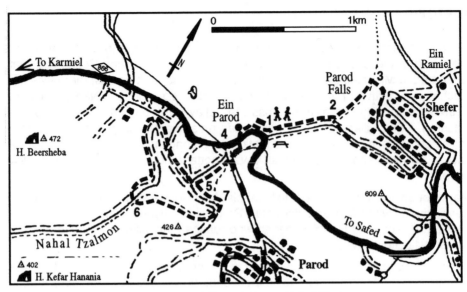

Hike 14, Parod Falls and Upper Nahal Tzalmon

(3) between pine and carob trees, and knee-high wild asparagus bushes. It is quickest to head back the same way ascended. It is also possible to follow the pipe along the eastern slope of the gushing stream back to the dirt road.

For a longer walk, ascend to the outside road of Shefer and follow it to the right. The road passes a few coops and offers a nice view. The forested hill to the south is topped with a British Tigart fort. Before the main entrance to the moshav, take a right onto a dirt road which descends back to Nahal Tzalmon (2).

Return to the Parod Recreation Grounds (1).

Option 2: From the Parod Recreation Grounds (1), head down Road 865 to the right. Just beyond the restaurant, Ein (Ma'ayan) Parod emerges into a small shallow pool (4). Note the wall to the left, covered with bramble, an aqueduct remnant. Notice the travertine coating it. More aqueduct remnants can be seen across the road.

Cross Road 865 and head right (south) on the dirt road. You should be in an open field parallel to upper Nahal Tzalmon, marked by a large carob tree. Note more remnants of the Ein Parod aqueduct. Reach the Parod access road. Cross it and continue south on the dirt road through a flat field which is marked by signs pointing to two tombs of Jewish sages. From here is a nice view of: Har Hazon, straight ahead past Hanania Valley; Hurbat Beersheba—the hill ahead on the right; ancient Parod and further ahead, Hurbat Kefar Hanania on the hills ahead to the left. Looking sharply to the right, (northwest) the sharp drop of the Meron Range clearly marks the geographic border between the Upper and Lower Galilee. To the left, note the relatively intact remains of the aqueduct. In March, groundsel and charlock coat the field in orange and yellow. Both suggest that the field has been used by humans. The fields, sabras and olive trees nearby were used by peasants of the Arab village of Faradiya until 1948.

Two hundred and fifty meters from the Parod road, reach a split (5). Down the slope toward the valley below are ruins of three flour mills, one after another. The builders took maximum advantage of the steep slope.

Here begins the main element of the loop trip. It is possible to descend the stream first by taking a left at this point. The text will follow the other option so that the tiring climb will be more exciting and shady. There are two choices: the shorter and rougher option is to head straight down the slope by the flour mills to the valley (6). The other option is to take a right to descend along the dirt road past orchards of different fruits.

Where the dirt road enters the valley (6), take a left and join a narrow, unmarked trail which hugs a trench—the stream bed of Nahal Tzalmon. Follow it to the left and begin to ascend. The trail stays loyal to the northern bank, sometimes touching the waterfall-full stream bed. The narrow gorge does not carry water year-round, hence the scarcity of water vegetation. On the other hand, travertine coating is evidence of times of flow. Furthermore, carob and oak trees, seem to be doing well along the stream.

After 250 m., the scenic stretch levels out. Either follow the trail a bit up the bank past tomb caves or continue along the stream bed to where the dirt road crosses Nahal Tzalmon (7). If you take the latter option, look across the stream below the dirt road at two tombs, of Nahamiah Ha'amsoni and Rabbi Yishmael Ba'al Habritot. The famous Rabbi Akiva was a disciple of Nahamiah Ha'amsoni that resided in the village of Emaus and Gimzo in the northern Judean Foothills.

On both sides of the dirt road, 50 m. west of the stream, are remnants of a large wine press. The rectangular trough upon the rock shelf to the north remains from the village of Faradiya.

Large bushes of the coarse leafed gum terebinth grow here. This bush grows in warm Mediterranean climates along with the carob. Its presence here hints toward the transition from the Upper Galilee upstream, to the Lower Galilee, downstream.

To return, it is possible to take a left on the dirt road back to the split (5) where a right turn retraces the arrival route. It is more interesting to continue up Nahal Tzalmon, across the Parod access road and Road 865, back to the starting point (1).

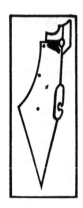

Lower Galilee

Geography

The Galilee is divided into two parts, the Upper Galilee and the Lower Galilee. The Lower Galilee is the southern part. Its borders are: Jezre'el, Harod and Bet She'an Valleys in the south; the Mediterranean Coast in the west; the Kinnarot and Jordan Valleys in the east. Its northern border with the Upper Galilee runs along the Bet Hakerem and Hanania Valleys.

The Lower Galilee does not have much in common with the Upper Galilee. Its peaks reach only 600 m. Its temperatures are substantially higher and snowfall is very rare. Its population composition is different and more plentiful. These factors make the Lower Galilee less rustic than its northern neighbor. The Lower Galilee has three subregions: western, central and eastern.

Western Lower Galilee has a gentle landscape of Eocenian chalk hills, rarely exceeding 300 m. above sea level. Most of the region is known as the Alonim-Shefar'am Hills. The wide valleys are used for agriculture and the wide ridges for settlements. During the 1960s and 1970s, Bedouins developed many small settlements in the region. The sparse settlement preceding this influx is evident by the presence of widely-spaced Tabor oak forests covering some of the slopes.

Central Lower Galilee is the most uplifted part of the region. A series of east-west faults lifted blocks of mountain ridges, creating a landscape of successive valleys and ridges. The various ridges all reach about 600 m. above sea level. The valleys average around 150 m. The ridges are of hard Turonian-Cenomanian sedimentary rock and the valleys hold fertile alluvial soil. The geology led to development of villages at the base of the ridges, adjacent to the agricultural land. Road 65 runs along the eastern edge of these ridges and divides the eastern and central subregions.

Eastern Lower Galilee is easily identified by its black basalt and dark brown soil. Its southwestern corner is Giv'at Hamoreh, rising to 515 m. above the town of Afula.

From here, a series of gentle basalt covered ridges run northeast. These ridges have moderate southwestern slopes, steep northeastern escarpments, and abrupt eastern drops to Kinnarot Valley. Perennial streams run east between the ridges. The topography of the region makes transportation comfortable, although water is only available in the streams.

The sharp drop to Kinnarot Valley, the deep ravines carrying fresh water and the relative sparsity of villages makes the eastern subregion a favorite springtime hiking region.

Climate

A semi-moist Mediterranean climate prevails in central and western Lower Galilee. The eastern subregion is semi-arid.

In the east, the low altitudes and the proximity to the Syrian-African Rift create hot air masses. In addition, the black basalt becomes very hot. Annual rainfall is only 350-400 mm. The southern parts of the subregion are even hotter than in the north.

Central Lower Galilee has more rain and lower temperatures. Average annual rainfall is 600 mm. in most of the Lower Galilee, over a period of only 40-50 days. In Nazareth, at 445 m., 626 mm. of rain falls. In Gazit, at the western edge of the eastern subregion, there is only 420 mm. The valleys have frost in the winter.

Western Lower Galilee is rich in dew, 200-250 nights per year, due to its high temperatures and proximity to the Mediterranean Sea.

Vegetation

The Lower Galilee landscape has permitted intensive settlement. Thus, the natural vegetation has remained only at a few sites.

The common Mediterranean maquis association of oak and terebinth is mainly found along the ridges of the central subregion, usually at elevations above 400 m. Growing on terra rossa soils, they are accompanied by other typical Mediterranean shrubs like the thorny calycotome, thorny burnet, sage and rockrose. The strawberry tree, Syrian pear, and buckthorn are additional trees in this association. The spurge bush, blooming in yellow, and the Crete germander are common dwarf shrubs. Pink patches of flax and tall purple flowering alknets are common flowers. Orchard grass and wild oat are the main grasses. They grow tall in spring, and brown and wilt towards June.

The carob and mastic terebinth association can be found along slopes throughout the region at elevations below 400 m. These trees grow both on rendzina and terra rossa soils. Buckthorn, calycotome and thorny burnet often join the group. Wild oat, blue eryngium, marjoram, clover and morning bride are common annuals that give green color to the carob and mastic terebinth landscape in late winter and spring.

Large Tabor oaks with snowbell trees create a plant association in the western Lower Galilee and along the western fringes of the eastern subregion. Technically, the association can be found anywhere above sea level, but today the jujube association dominates in low elevations. On shady northern slopes, the common oak joins the two and creates a thick forest rich in creepers. Common creepers (vines) are the clematis, thorny green brier and black bryony. Rockrose bushes sometimes manage to push their way in.

In the east, the lotus jujube and Christ thorn jujube association dominates below 200 m. Botanists think that the jujube-dotted regions were formerly covered with the Tabor oak association. Today the jujube association is present wherever people have cultivated or grazed in Tabor oak regions.

Three plant associations are found in the open fields. The gariggue of the calycotome and buckthorn association covers the eastern slopes overlooking Kinnarot Valley. The other two associations develop according to the soil. Marjoram association grows on brown rendzina, accompanied by plants that thrive in disturbed habitats, like the lagoecia, hare's ear (buplever), blue eryngium, asphodel and a number of types of clover.

Thorny burnet association is common on terra rossa soils, joined by wild oat, blue eryngium, phagnalon, clover and morning bride.

In the basaltic fields of eastern Lower Galilee there are neither trees nor bushes. This is probably due to three reasons: human interference, the lack of water-collecting conditions in the rock and the relatively poor water economy of the shallow grumosol soil. Therefore, grass batta is dominant. Two plant associations are common. Both associations include the jujube. One is the fennel and rest harrow association, found in several types of disturbed habitats. The other is the globe thistle and carline thistle, common in areas grazed by animals, since these two thistles are untouched by animals. A number of other associations are found on volcanic rock soils at specific locations determined by the slope, elevation and bedrock. Wild almond is common amongst cliffs in the subregion.

Desert plants from the Jordan Valley, such as the broom bush and sumac tree, have also penetrated into the eastern Lower Galilee.

Outstanding wildflowers include the mountain lupin that tints blue some of the open slopes and fields in February and March. Also common are poppy, buttercup and anemone, bright-red field flowers. Yellow asphodel, a protected wild flower, is also found in these basaltic soils.

Wildlife

Human settlement has ruptured the spontaneous ecological chain of the Lower Galilee. Though wildlife habitats remain, most are too small to sustain a natural ecological pattern. Sharp changes have taken place in the past century as some species have disappeared and others have adapted.

The western and central Lower Galilee's wildlife condition is similar to the situation in the Upper Galilee (see regional introduction). Amphibians and reptiles have had no problem with the living conditions and their distribution are as in other Mediterranean regions of Israel.

The situation in the arid eastern subregion is somewhat different. Its southern parts have been the least affected. The mountain gazelle, a protected animal, has done very well. They number in the thousands, thriving in the open fields along with herds of cattle. The large quantity of these herbivores has been good for carnivores like the striped hyena, golden jackal, wolf and red fox that were severely poisoned in the 1950s.

The Indian crested porcupine digs up bulbs. The Palestine mole rat is not common as the basaltic soil is too shallow for digging tunnels but other types of rodents thrive in the vast fields.

The cliffs in eastern Lower Galilee home Syrian hyraxes and raptors. Eagle owls have been seen among the cliffs and canyons. The short-toed eagle occasionally nests in a jujube tree. The kestrel is common here. Lower Nahal Ammud supplies homes for a wide variety of raptors like the Griffon vulture and Egyptian vulture.

The roller and bee-eater are two colorful birds that dwell in holes in soft rock such as marl and chalk. A number of species of warblers and Palestine (orange-tufted) sunbirds nest along streams. In the winter, flocks of chaffinches storm the stream bed valleys. In Nahal Tavor there are many nests of the Spanish sparrow on jujube trees.

In the east, desert birds have found new homes. Recent artificial sources of food and water along with the dry climate explain the expansion of desert bird habitats.

The great gray shrike has slowly spread northward along the Syrian-African Rift. Tristram's grackle, like the shrike, has moved into the subregion, from the desert. Thrushes may be seen along cliffs.

Human Involvement

Archaeologists have found prehistoric human remains along the outskirts of the Lower Galilee. Main finds were in Nahal Ammud, in Doves Cave by Ahihud, at Ubeidiya by the Jordan River (see Hike 18) and by Nazareth. Based on the finds, it seems that this creature preferred the valleys. During the Neolithic period (and surely during the Chalcolithic) the basaltic plateaus and ridges of eastern Lower Galilee became grazing lands.

Evidently, people began to settle the Lower Galilee only after reaching a certain degree of sophistication and after a population increase, since the regions to the east, west and south of Lower Galilee were always more suitable for settlement. In the Lower Galilee, the eastern subregion lagged behind, due to a number of water-related reasons: low precipitation and high temperatures, scanty and small springs, poor water economy of the soil, existence of flowing springs only in stream beds, lack of sedimentary rock suitable for water cisterns. The aridity did not keep main roads out of the subregion, as many branches of the famous Via Maris ran along southeastern streams. But only along the road did small settlements develop.

During the Bronze period the region was divided into small states. The Canaanites preferred the periphery of the Lower Galilee.

During the Israelite conquest a number of biblical events took place in the region (cf. the book of Judges). Following that period, the Lower Galilee disappeared from the headlines. During the end of the Second Temple period, the region was again in the center of things and many sects developed here, such as Jewish zealotry and Christianity. Josephus Flavius, who turned himself over to the Romans in Yodfat of the central Lower Galilee, writes of a sect organized by a Judah in order to boycott Roman taxes.

Historians have tried to create a stereotype of the typical ancient Galilean: a hard-working, uneducated farmer, who recognizes freedom and has no inhibitions in fighting for his beliefs. The farmers did not have time to devote themselves to

Jewish study as mentioned in the Jerusalem Talmud; Rabbi Yohanan ben Zakai spent eighteen years by the town of Arev (today Arabeh), during which only two religious cases were brought before him (Shabbat 16:8).

During Hasmonean times, the Lower Galilee was a single administrative region. The Romans divided it into five independent districts. But the region was still mainly Jewish. A hundred years later, during the Great Revolt (66-70 C.E.), the region had two rival districts, Tzipori and Tiberias. However, both were Jewish towns and were unified during the revolt—against it! These Jews were affluent and assimilated into foreign cultures and had much at stake. Naturally, there were hard feelings between the rural Jews and their brothers in Tiberias and Tzipori.

The picture changed after the destruction of the Second Temple; Priestly orders settled in the Galilee, mainly the Lower Galilee and the Sanhedrin (Jewish supreme court) moved to Usha in the western subregion. The Sanhedrin did not fare well in Usha: the Coastal Plain, not far from Usha, was not strictly Jewish. The Jews held lands in the Jezre'el Valley, near the south. It seemed that the Sanhedrin found its final location when it moved to the town of Tzipori. Tzipori thus became the world center for Judaism. Despite the transfer of the Sanhedrin to Tiberias in 234, the Lower Galilee continued to be a thriving Jewish center.

In 429, the Byzantine Caesar Theodosius canceled the position of the Jewish presidency and Jewish political power began to give way to Christianity. The Jews found themselves losing hold of the core of the Lower Galilee. A number of Christian remnants have been found adjacent to Jewish ones, representing the Christian conquest of villages. Consequently, the Jews had to settle in the problematic eastern Lower Galilee (a number of usually unimpressive synagogue remains have been found). These settlers did not live in the subregion for a long time and did not prosper, the materialistic evidence is therefore small. The Jews revolted against the Byzantine government at the beginning of the 7th century along with 20,000 Persian soldiers that invaded Israel in 614 (Jews were allied with Persians). Both Byzantines and Persians lost the land to the Moslems in 636.

The Moslems changed the administration and names. They made no distinction between Israel and Syria. The Upper Galilee belonged to Damascus while the Lower belonged to the district of Jordan, with its administrative center in Tiberias.

The Crusaders kept Tiberias as the capital of the Galilee. The land itself was divided between feudal estates. Belvoir (Kokhav Hayarden), overlooking the Yarmuk River-Jordan River merger, is the most impressive ruin from then. Nazareth did not gain any special status. Nor did Tzipori, which stood near large springs and at an important road junction. Due to the location of Tiberias, historians see the establishment of Tiberias as the Crusader capital as one of the contributing reasons to their fall to the Moslems at nearby Karnai Hittim in 1187.

Internal political battles in the Ottoman Empire (16th-17th century) kept a fluid administrative order in the Lower Galilee. A gifted Bedouin named Tahr el-Omar established an independent state here in 1710. He built fortresses and renovated other structures, like the wall of Tiberias, but his project only endured 30 years. The Ottoman Empire encouraged settlement in the eastern Lower Galilee. Circassians and Moroccan Arabs settled a couple of villages to counter Bedouin penetration. The Turks also freely gave out land to Arabs from villages in nearby regions. During the end of the Turkish period, the Lower Galilee was one of five districts belonging to Beirut.

At the end of the 19th century, Jewish resettlement began in the eastern subregion, possibly due to its small population. Nevertheless, they were harassed by Arabs and Bedouins. The harsh climate made things additionally tough. The settlements not only survived, but here the cores of later movements and institutions that were founded. Hashomer, beginning as Bar-Giora, was the first modern Jewish defense league, established at Kefar Tavor. Collective settlement also has roots here. The "Wall and Tower" defense program, during the Arab riots of 1936-1939, established a number of new settlements in the eastern Lower Galilee.

The British divided Israel into thirds. The Lower Galilee belonged to the northern section whose main city was Haifa. The British gave Nazareth and Tiberias a status of "regional" town in recognition of their Christian importance.

During the 1948 war the Jews were greatly outnumbered. The United Nations partition plan had designated the Lower Galilee for Palestinian control. The Arabs did not accept the plan and began to attack their neighbors in 1947. In April of 1948, after suffering hundreds of casualties, the Jews began to take the offensive, finally resulting in the total release of the Lower Galilee from hostile forces. During May 10-15 the Arab population by order of the Arab Command fled to Transjordan, in anticipation of invading Syrian, Iraqi, Jordanian and Lebanese forces. Altogether, two-thirds of the population fled. The group included the affluent leaders and professionals. During the first ten years of the State, the Arab community was confused and disorganized and remained under military control until the 1960s.

Since 1948, only a few new settlements have been established in the Lower Galilee. Only in the 1980s did the Jewish National Fund found small villages known as mitzpim at many Galilean hilltops. Each mitzpe was planned to have 10-50 families, but some never made the quota. Today, the Lower Galilee is part of the Galilee political district and is divided into two subdistricts centered in Nazareth and Tiberias.

Water

The watershed of the Lower Galilee runs between the eastern and central subregions. The many streams draining east are perennial and much shorter and steeper than those running west.

Considering its annual rainfall, the Lower Galilee is not rich in water sources. Eastern Lower Galilee has so little precipitation (400 mm. annually) that it is known as "the Negev of the North." The scarcity of water is evident in the enormous amounts of water cisterns surrounding ancient villages. Even during the British Mandate, Arab villagers would travel a few hours to a nearby spring to supply their home needs.

The Nahal Tzipori springs are the only plentiful ones in the central and western subregions. The central subregion's ridges also reveal small layer springs. By some of them, Arab villages developed, out-growing the natural supply long before the arrival of modern pipelines. In the eastern Lower Galilee a number of springs emerging in stream beds discharge over 100 cubits per hour.

In the 1950s the Israeli government invested in underground water searches. Geologists drilled in many places but had success only by Yavne'el, yielding 1,300 cubits per hour. Other drills in the eastern subregion yielded 600-700 cubits per hour. Central and western Lower Galilee enjoy water from the National Water Carrier.

Hiking in the Lower Galilee

Due to the widespread settlement of the region there are no problems reaching the vicinity of the hiking routes. For some, the Lower Galilee is too crowded to offer an outdoor experience.

Road 90, running at its eastern border through the Kinnarot Valley and Tiberias, reaches the eastern parts of the eastern subregion. Road 65 runs north-south across the eastern streams before they deepen to the east.

Three main roads leave Road 90 from Lake Kinneret and connect to Road 65. Road 77 from Tiberias to the Coastal Plain is the main road from east to west. Buses from Tel Aviv and Haifa run along Road 90 and Roads 77 and 65 towards Tiberias. Buses from Jerusalem also run up Road 90. Local buses can be picked up from Afula, Tiberias and Acre at their central bus stations.

Human intervention in the landscape has caused many political and natural problems in the Lower Galilee. Some of the streams are occasionally fed with sewage. Do not drink any natural source of water. In the summer the temperatures are high and an adequate supply of water is essential, even for a short hike.

The Lower Galilee is densely populated with Arabs and Bedouins. Their value system may be different to yours. Respect them and they will respect you. Hiking routes pass close to and possibly through private property. Please make sure to close all gates and do not disturb the surroundings.

Important Phone Numbers (area code 06)

S.P.N.I. Field Study Centers and Information

Alon Tavor F.S.C., Kurdani School:	767798, 766770
Kinnarot F.S.C. (no hostel), Bet Gordon, Deganya Aleph:	751088, 752340
Antiquities Authority, Afula:	527610
Tiberias Tourism Bureau, 8 Elhadaf:	720992

Safety Assistance

Police: 100	Ambulance: 101
Tiberias: 792444	Tiberias: 790111
Nazareth: 571444	Nazareth: 573333
Acre: 918111	Acre: 912333
Afula: 524444	Afula: 593334

Sites worth Visiting

Museums

Golani Museum, Golani Junction (Road 65 and 77).
Bet Alon, Kibbutz Ginnosar, off Road 90, by kilometer post 423.
Settlement Museum, Kibbutz Yif'at on Road 73.
Ein Dor Museum, Kibbutz Ein Dor off Road 65 at Gazit Junction
Bedouin Culture Museum, Shibli village, of Road 65, 200 m. west of Gazit
　　　Junction.
Farmer Museum, Kefar Tavor on Road 65.
Village Museum, Kefar Tavor on Road 65.

National Parks

Arbel, cliff and fortress, via Moshav Arbel or 1 km. along Road 807, 1 km. west
　　　of Road 90.
Tiberias Hot Baths, on Road 90, south of entrance to Tiberias
Karnai Hittim, volcanic mount and ruins, 2 km. north of Road 77. Turnoff by
　　　kilometer posts 73-74.
Belvoir (Kokhav Hayarden), 5 km. off Road 90, by kilometer post 390-391.
Mount Tabor, 7 km. of Road 65, 200 m. west of Gazit Junction.

Churches

There are numerous churches in Nazareth.
New Church of the Annunciation, street 603, Nazareth.
Church of Joseph, behind the New Church of the Annunciation, Nazareth.
The Synagogue-Church, at the end of Shuk St., Nazareth.
Gabriels Church and Mary's Well, northeastern Nazareth, north of Road 754.
Tabgha, 1 km. east Capernahum Junction (which is on Road 90).
Mt. of the Beatitudes, off Road 90 north of Capernahum Junction.

Others

Ein Nun pool, 500 m. on dirt road north of Migdal restaurant on Road 90.
Mitzpe Netofa lookout tower, 6 km. off Road 65 towards Mitzpe Netofa, by
　　　kilometer post 74.

Overnight Options

Indoors

S.P.N.I. F.S.C., see above.

Youth Hostels:

Tiberias, downtown.
Karai Deshe, off Road 90 by kilometer post 425-426.
Poriah, on local road off Road 90, 2 km. south of Tiberias Hot Springs.

Ginnosar, off Road 90, by kilometer post 423.
Many villages and kibbutzim offer places to stay. There are many organized
    campgrounds on the shores of Lake KInneret, north of Tiberias.

Outdoors

Many picnic sites along the shore of Lake Kinneret.
Parod Recreation Grounds, off Road 865, between kilometer posts 34 and 35, by
    a sharp curve.
Golani Junction Picnic Site, Golani Junction, (Road 65 and 77).
Lavee Forest picnic sites, off Road 77, by kilometer post 68 and by kilometer
    post 69-70.
Mitzpe Netofa Picnic Site, 1.5 km. off Road 65, towards Mitzpe Netofa, by
    kilometer post 74.
Giv'at Hamoreh picnic sites, off road exiting from Afula Illit.
Bet Hakerem Canyon Picnic Site, at junction to Gilon on Road 85, by kilometer
    post 14.

Gas Stations

Tzemah Junction, Tiberias, Ginnosar, on Road 90.
West of Golani Junction, east of Yiftah'el Junction, on Road 77.
In the settlements of Afula, Afula Illit, Davrat, Kefar Tavor, north of Golani Junction,
    on Road 65.
Karmiel, Rama, on Road 85.

Asphodel blooms in early winter

Central Nahal Tzalmon

See map on page 123

Points of interest: *A stream, containing small frog and fish pools running between the two highest peaks of the Lower Galilee, lined with relics from the past to the present.*

Length and nature of hike: 3 kilometers, back-and-forth.

Hiking time: 2-3 hours.

Preferred season: All year.

Suitable for: All.

Maps: "Lower Galilee, the Valley's and the Gilboa" hiking and touring map or Upper Galilee hiking and touring map.

Special preparation: Swimming gear.

Starting & ending point: Gravel parking lot by the bridge over Nahal Tzalmon, on (Arabeh-Rama) Road 804 just before the turnoff to the Bedouin town of Salameh. The parking lot is exactly 4 km. from Rama Junction.

To reach starting point:

Arrival by private transportation: Turn south off (Safed-Acre) Road 85 at Rama Junction onto Road 804. The road descends to Nahal Tzalmon beside an Arab village, where Ein Tzalmon emerges east of the road. The road runs above Nahal Tzalmon for two more kilometers, until it crosses the stream on a bridge. Here, park at the parking lot (1) to the right (north).

Arrival by public transportation: At the time of writing no public bus service was available to the town of Salameh.

Geography

This hike is along the upper middle section of Nahal Tzalmon. It runs between Har Kamon, at 602 m., and Har Hazon at 584 m. These two mountains, the highest in the Lower Galilee, mark the eastern section of the Shagor Ridge, which is the northern ridge of the Lower Galilee.

An east-west fault that runs along the southern base of these two mountains explains their origin. Underground pressure uplifted the two masses during the Miocene. As a result, the geological layers of both mountains slope towards the north where they disappear beneath the valley sediment of Bet Hakerem Valley. Thus, the mountains peak in the south, above the steep southern slope. An observant eye can note the northern dip of the rock layers when walking along Nahal Tzalmon.

The separation of these two mountains from one another by Nahal Tzalmon is due to two factors:

1) A short north-south fault.

2) The uplifting of these two blocks exposed thick layers of the marly-limy Tzalmon Formation. The soft lithology was easily eroded by Nahal Tzalmon, which incised itself deeply (over 400 m.) between the two mountains.

These soft rocks are also known for their capability to cause mud flows, a rare phenomenon in Israel: heavy rain causes the marls to swell. Upon reaching a certain point the marl begins to flow, collapsing whatever it holds above. During local mud flows, a number of houses have collapsed in the village of Maghar, on the other side of Har Hazon. Along the trail it is also possible to observe washed-out sections of the slope.

Nahal Tzalmon originally flowed west to the Mediterranean Sea along Bet Hakerem Valley. Today the stream runs in a east-west direction up to Ein Tzalmon. With the deepening of the Syrian-African Rift, the upper parts of the stream bed were 'captured' and diverted eastward towards Lake Kinneret. The section of Nahal Tzalmon between Har Hazon and Har Kamon is the westernmost part of the stream running north-south. Along this section, due to the soft lithology, the dramatic change in course took place.

Plants and animals

Egyptian Campion (*Silene aegyptiaca*): Also known as the catchfly; from the same family as the carnation. *Car-* in Latin means flesh, and here refers to the flower's color, which ranges from pink to purple. Its 5-petal flowers are easily distinguishable: each petal has an oval incision at the end. The plant rarely exceeds 40 cm. in height.

The campion usually grows upon terra rossa soil. It is very commonly found coating apple and olive orchards and vineyards in the Mediterranean parts of Israel in winter and early spring. During this period, it is one of the few annuals in bloom. It owes its abundance to the fact that it ripens and distributes its seeds before the Arab farmer finishes plowing his fields, while its competitors are destroyed by the spring plow before they can reproduce.

Goat (*Capra hirctus mambrica*): Archaeological finds show that the goat was domesticated 9,000 years ago, in southeastern Asia. Ancient goat remains found in Israel have been identified as the wild goat mentioned in Deuteronomy 14:5— one of the kosher animals.

The goat is in fact mentioned throughout the Bible, first in Genesis 15:9 as part of the covenant between Abraham and God. The Children of Israel kept goats and sheep together and used them for sacrifices and domestic purposes. In the Talmud, the black goat is often mentioned for the damages that it causes.

While most goats have beards, the male's is more distinctive. Strong legs are well-adapted to steep landscapes.

Israel has five races of goat, the most common (especially in the Galilee) being the Baladi, or Syrian (found both in Asia and Africa). Males reach 70 kg. while females rarely exceed 45. This goat is relatively non-productive, giving only 125 liters of milk a year. Swiss goats, in contrast, yield over 1,000 liters annually.

In 1985, 121,000 goats were counted in Israel, over 80% from the Arab sector. Many of the Arab goats are not counted as they are marketed internally as for family occasions.

Bedouins use the goat hair for tents and brushes. Goat skin is good for wallets, gloves and other leather items but is not popular in Israel. Goat milk, however, is used today for exotic cheeses.

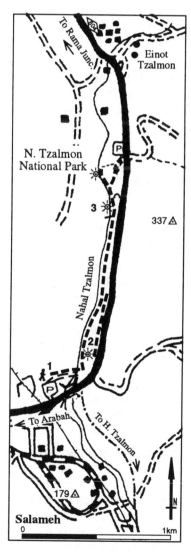

Hike 15, Central Nahal Tzalmon

History

This narrow part of Nahal Tzalmon has been an important route for many centuries. Just as it is today, the passage has always been used by locals traveling between villages and not as an international route. Some researchers see it as part of the main north-south travel axis in the Lower Galilee during certain historical periods.

The region is mentioned many times in the Talmudic literature. *Yoredet Hatzalmon* (Para 7:9) is an unclear term mentioned in the Tosefta, regarding the disappointment it caused during the Great Revolt. Most likely the term referred to Einot Tzalmon which dried up during that crucial period.

Central Nahal Tzalmon is known in Arabic as Wadi Salameh, after Hirbet Salameh, two kilometers south of the starting point. The 50-dunam hill is mentioned by Josephus Flavius as Tzalmin, one of the fortified Jewish settlements during the Great Revolt. Following the destruction of the Second Temple, the priestly orders of Delaya and Genaton settled there. In the Mishna, grape and vegetable farming is described as taking place "by Tzalmon." The last documentation of the Jewish settlement of priestly orders was during Byzantine and possibly Early Arab times. Roman pottery has been found on site.

Site description

<u>Kuradi Mills</u>: Since the 1930s, its use gradually declined because in its last few years only the family owning it used the mill. The lower flour mill was in use until 1955, possibly the last in Israel. Since then the structure has turned into living quarters. Inside the lower mill, the waterwheel and its axis still remain.

To begin hike:

From the parking lot (1), descend to the stream, cross it and pass the remains of the Mashra'ah (place of drink) Mill. Follow the blue-marked trail along the eastern stream bank. The dark purple flowers which bloom here in the spring are Egyptian campion. Along the stream many mint plants grow. The grassy stream banks visited often by local shepherds illustrate Psalm 23:2: "He maketh me lie down in green pastures; he leadeth me beside the restful waters." On a hot day it is fun to hike this stream in the water.

Three hundred meters upstream, reach Kuradi Mills (2). By the stream grow eucalyptus trees and a bit farther up on the western bank stand the rare ulmus tree, which sheds its leaves in winter. Heading upstream, look for remains of the aqueduct which led water to the mills on the slope above you. Walking along it on the way back makes the return more interesting.

Stick to the right (east) side of the stream, occasionally shaded by carob trees. One kilometer from the starting point reach the Rama waterfall (3). This is the largest fall and pool along the route, so savor it! Water falls over the aqueduct which carried surplus from Rama Mill (across the stream) to the Kuradi Mills. The aqueduct also dammed the stream bed in order to collect additional water. On the trail side of the stream stands a cliff with ancient burial caves.

Continue upstream on the wide path. The path ascends the slope back to Road 804. If time is not a problem, it is worthwhile ascending the wide, blue-marked path in order to visit a charcoal manufacturing site. Across Road 804 and 100 m. to the left is an open field full of earth-covered mounds where the wood is slowly burned into charcoal. Today, wood from uprooted citrus groves, eucalyptus and trimmed forests is the main charcoal source. Nevertheless, the Israeli charcoal business is in a decline due to the small inventory of trees.

From the place where the marked trail leaves the stream, continue on an un-marked path upstream for 150 m. The trail runs along remnants of an aqueduct. Reach a couple of large pools (4) near a couple of travertine-coated boulders. Cross the stream and take a few steps to the right, to another mill.

From here, begin to head back on the western bank, also along an aqueduct to the Rama Mill. Cross the stream. One hundred meters south of the Rama waterfall, leave the trail to the left and follow the ruined aqueduct. The aqueduct runs at a constant level on the eastern bank, but with the elevation drop of the stream bed, the aqueduct seems to run uphill. Along the way, note the round, thorny burnet bushes which have grown here since the 1950s. Pass by a clump of citrus tress and then reach the Kuradi Mills (2) from above. Descend back to the blue trail which returns to the staring point (1).

16 Lower Nahal Tzalmon

See map on page 129

Points of interest: *A semi-tropical stream decorated with flour mills and stream vegetation with travertine deposits in different shapes.*

Length and nature of hike: 4 kilometers, loop trip.

Hiking time: 2-3 hours.

Preferred season: Winter and spring.

Suitable for: All.

Maps: "Lower Galilee, the Valley's and the Gilboa" hiking and touring map or Upper Galilee hiking and touring map.

Special preparation: Clothes for walking in water (optional).

Starting & ending point: Hothouses of Livnim.

To reach starting point:

Arrival by private transportation: On Road 90, 10 km. north of Tiberias, turn towards Livnim and Kibbutz Hukuk. The road ascends, descends and crosses Nahal Ammud on a bridge (7). Here, looking upstream, you can catch a glimpse of the famous pillar, the Ammud (6), which gives the stream its Hebrew name. At the intersection, continue on road that curves across Nahal Hukuk and ascends to Livnim (1). For the continuing instructions see 'To begin hike.'

Arrival by public transportation: Take bus from Tiberias to the entrance of Livnim (1).

Geography

Nahal Tzalmon drains 110 sq. km. and drops over 1 km. along its 40 km. course from the Meron Range in the Upper Galilee to Lake Kinneret. Its tributaries in the Upper Galilee receive 800-900 mm. of annual rainfall while by Lake Kinneret rainfall is only 500 mm. a year.

Three streams of close proximity flow into Lake Kinneret: Nahal Arbel, Nahal Tzalmon and Nahal Ammud. The streams have deposited large amounts of sediment, creating Ginnosar Valley.

Nahal Tzalmon is geologically younger than the other two (see Hike 15, 'Central Nahal Tzalmon'). Thus, its morphology is distinct: while Nahal Arbel and Lower

Nahal Ammud cut deep canyons into Eocenian rock, Nahal Tzalmon makes its way to Lake Kinneret in a more subtle landscape, cutting a shallow valley through basalt fields.

Up until a few years ago, the perennial flow of Lower Nahal Tzalmon emerged at Ein Ravid. It then drops 110 m. to Lake Kinneret along a six-kilometer course. The stream bed most of the way cuts into travertine that was deposited by Nahal Tzalmon thousands of years ago. Among the regional streams, travertine appears only in Nahal Tzalmon. Before the travertine deposition, lava flows covered the area and Nahal Tzalmon cut through the basalt along its descent to Lake Kinneret.

Today the stream bed of Nahal Tzalmon cuts a narrow gorge, a few meters deep, into the valley above. This phenomenon is only thousands of years old, possibly due to a decrease in the level of Lake Kinneret.

Plants and animals

Sycamore (*Ficus sycomorus*): The sycamore and fig are the only representatives of the *Moaracae* family in Israel. The tree originated in tropical eastern Africa. Its intrusion to Israel is not yet understood. Today it is found along the coast and valleys.

The sycamore is an evergreen tree and sheds its leaves only during rough winters. It reaches 20 m. The round fruits, like the fig, are actually a covered cluster of flowers pollinated by a wasp. They appear along the branches and trunk in clusters.

The tree is mentioned in the Mishna a number of times. Its distribution used to define the Upper and Lower Galilee. Today, only a few specimens remain in the Lower Galilee. The tree's hard wood is used for construction and furniture.

Central Nahal Tzalmon (Hike 15)

History

The abundant, accessible water along Lower Nahal Tzalmon, has attracted humans for ages. The flour mills along the stream testify to human activity during the last centuries. It is possible that some of the mills were built on ancient ones.

In all, there are 14 mills which were active until the end of the 19th century and another 14 which previously fell to ruins.

Simon Berman, one of the first dreamers of renewed Jewish agriculture in Israel, planned in 1870 to found an agricultural settlement where Nahal Tzalmon enters Ginnosar Valley. He planned factories and a water-powered flour mill.

In 1856, Edward Robinson published *Biblical Researches in Palestine*, a journal of his 1838 and 1852 travels. Of Lower Nahal Tzalmon he wrote:

> Wady er Rubudiyeh coming down from the northwest from the plain of Ramah; where it bears the name of Wady Salameh. The hills are here low and gentle. The Wady brings down a very copious stream of pure water; which is scattered over the plain in all directions, by means of small canals and water-courses. Here is a deserted mill, which might easily be repaired; and also the remains of two or three others. Upon a slight eminence on the north side, are the remains of a village called Abu Shusheh . . .

Site description

Queen of the Mills: This large flour mill had two stories. Each one held two pairs of grinding stones. In the summer, only the lower ones worked, due to the decrease in stream water.

At the turn of the century, P.I.C.A. purchased the land and renovated the mill. They built a cement dam to block the narrow stream bed and an improved water channel to the mill. As with most mills in the Lower Galilee, it was rented. Soon afterwards, diesel-powered flour mills were introduced and the mill became unprofitable. The renters opened a shop on the spot which brought in the main income.

To begin hike:

From the entrance (1), take a right and pass between the homes of the settlement. At the T-intersection, go right and then left through an open gate. The straight gravel road descends towards hothouses, between bulldozed sections, some of them holding grapevines. The road curves left after 0.5 km. and dead-ends by two hothouses on the left (2). Park your vehicle here. To your right (west), straight below, is Nahal Tzalmon. (This starting point has been chosen in order to obtain easiest access to the highlights of lower Nahal Tzalmon).

Descend the steep slope freely toward the stream. Veer left (south) toward the palm tree in the valley. On your right should be a couple of ruins among eucalyptus, sabra and olive trees. Colorful anemones grow on the rocky slope in winter.

Lower Nahal Tzalmon

By the valley-slope contact take a left on an unmarked trail which passes jujube trees. Pass a couple more ruined structures and reach the buildings by the palm tree (3).

Here is a bridge which carried the excess water from the large flour mill across the stream. This mill was known by locals as 'Queen of the Mills.' The bridge's sides are decorated with travertine rock, deposited by water channel leakage.

From the bridge, pick up the blue-marked trail which runs along the remnants of the water channel. The trail is loyal to the contact of the slope and valley and thus leaves the channel (which reaches the second mill at the curve in the stream bed). By the trail's curve to the left, a channel leaves the trail to an impressive remnant of a third mill. Note the palm trees growing where excess water seeped from the channel. The palm trees probably sprouted from lunch-time deposits of the people coming to grind wheat at the mills. The slope exposes interesting travertine at this point.

From here the trail (among many) runs by jujube along the northern slope of Nahal Tzalmon. By a few boulders of travertine, the trail descends to the stream bed and crosses it (4). Here it is pleasant to continue in the oleander-filled stream bed.

The stream bed widens and a gentle slope appears on the northern side, rising to plantations. Cross the stream and follow the blue trail above. Many squills adorn the open slope here in the early fall. The trail descends to an olive grove, passing it from the left. At the edge of the grove grows a palm and a large sycamore, a rare specimen in the Lower Galilee. Here it is best for those walking in the water to join the blue trail. The wide trail leaves the grove and reaches another olive plantation. From here it is time to head back, either along the route taken or via plantations:

Ascend the blue-marked route along the dirt road on the northern bank.

Atop the low ridge take the first left (west) onto a dirt road, leaving the blue mark (5). Pass along a grapefruit orchard. The dirt road veers right and runs along the bottom of the basaltic slope of Livnim.

After 1.5 km., the dirt road curves left. Above you is the edge of the hothouse complex where the hiking route began. Find a comfortable place to manage the fence and ascend the short steep climb back to the parking area (2).

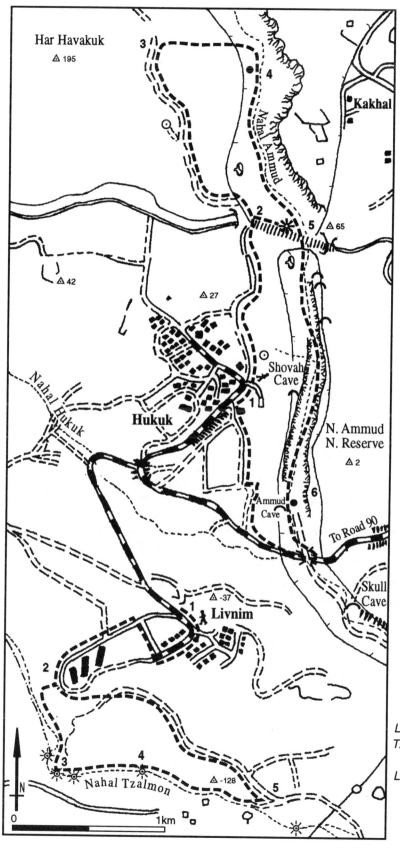

Har Havakuk
△ 195

Kakhal

Nahal Ammud

3

4

2

5

△ 65

△ 42

△ 27

Shovah
Cave

Nahal Hukuk

Hukuk

1

N. Ammud
N. Reserve
△ 2

6

Ammud
Cave

To Road 90

Skull
Cave

△ -37

Livnim

1

2

N

3

4

Nahal Tzalmon

△ -128

5

0

1km

*Hike 16,
Lower Nahal
Tzalmon and
Hike 17,
Lower Nahal
Ammud*

17 Lower Nahal Ammud

See map on page 129

Points of interest: *A stream cutting a steep canyon in cave-riddled limestone cliffs. Hovering raptors, local springs, hundreds of spring wildflowers and summer-blooming water plants add color to the festive route.*

Length and nature of hike: 8 kilometers, loop trip.

Hiking time: 4-6 hours.

Preferred season: Winter and spring. During these seasons the stream bed may carry sewage mixed with water! During other seasons the stream is usually dry.

Suitable for: All.

Maps: "Lower Galilee, the Valley's and the Gilboa" hiking and touring map or Upper Galilee hiking and touring map.

Special preparation: Shoes for walking in water (optional).

Starting & ending point: Entrance to Kibbutz Hukuk.

To reach starting point:

Arrival by private transportation: On Road 90, 10 km. north of Tiberias, turn off towards Kibbutz Hukuk. The road ascends, descends and crosses Nahal Ammud on a bridge (7). Here, looking upstream, you can catch a glimpse of the famous pillar, the Ammud (6), which gives the stream its Hebrew name. At the bridge, the hike officially ends. Drive another kilometer and take a right at the intersection to the entrance of Kibbutz Hukuk. Park the vehicle (1).

Arrival by public transportation: From Tiberias take a bus to Kibbutz Hukuk. Get off at the entrance to the kibbutz (1).

Geography

See Hike 13, 'Nahal Ammud.'

Plants and animals

Hyacinth Squill (*Scilla hyacinthoides*): The plant's name marks its resemblance to the squill and the hyacinth. It is indigenous to the northern Mediterranean Basin. In Israel it is found mainly in the north in open fields.

Cliffs of Eocenian limestone in Lower Nahal Ammud

The beautiful geophyte has ten long, two-centimeter-wide leaves sprouting from the base. The stem, up to 1 m. tall, holds more than 100 blue flowers. The flowers bloom gradually between February and April, after the appearance of the leaves.

The hyacinth squill is a protected wild-flower. It is also a garden plant. Its bulb can be made into glue.

Alpine Swift (*Apus melba*): A cosmopolitan bird. There are four species in Israel; they summer here from February to July. The swift superficially resembles the swallow: it has degenerate legs and does not stand straight, but clings to walls and tree branches.

The largest Israeli swift is the Alpine. Its body length reaches 20 cm. and its wing-span attains 50 cm. The lower body is white and the wings brown. Its tail is forked. It nests in flocks in crevices of canyons, uttering high-pitched trilling cries. Its wing movements, though powerful, are a rare sight as the swift is most often seen gliding with its wings swept backwards.

The swift builds its nest of grass and leaves, compacted into cone-shaped bricks. Look for them on vertical walls. Both parents incubate two eggs for 20 days in the spring.

History

Many caves dot the face of the canyon's cliffs. In four of them, archaeological digs uncovered important prehistoric relics. Ammud Cave was excavated by a Japanese mission in 1961-1964. They found a human skeleton of the Mid-Paleolithic, similar to ones found in the Carmel. The skeleton resembled Neanderthal man but had modern characteristics. This find helped change the theory regarding the Neanderthal man as the ancestor of modern man. Today the Neanderthal man is recognized as a different appearance of modern man and not as an ancestor.

For more information see Hike 13, 'Nahal Ammud.'

Site description

Hukuk: Founded in 1945, the kibbutz is named after a village in the tribal estate of Asher. The kibbutz earns a traditional livelihood, with cattle, orchards, fowl and an ostrich farm.

To begin hike:

The first part of the hike takes you north, along the western brink of the canyon of Lower Nahal Ammud. At the gate to Hukuk (1), you are standing at sea level. Follow the gravel road to the right (east) of the gate along the fence of the kibbutz. Almond trees dot the roadside. The road leads north. After 0.5 km., on the left beneath eucalyptus trees, is the kibbutz zoo. Continue on the dirt road.

Upon reaching a field, note Har Havakuk above you, 2 km. to the northwest. Follow the dirt road to the right and then curve left (to the north) running parallel to the deep gorge of Nahal Ammud. Along the dirt road grow single specimens of the jujube tree. In the spring, purple psoralea flowers of the clover family adorn the trail-sides. The flower's odor resembles tar.

Upon reaching the fence of the National Water Carrier (N.W.C.), take a right. At the closed gate ahead (leading to the siphon of the water carrier which crosses Nahal Ammud) take a left past a cattle gate (2). Here it is optional to leave the dirt road to the right (there is a small sign in Hebrew) and walk (gradually descending) 200 m. to the brim of the canyon which you will later descend. Note the pathway of the N.W.C. which crosses the gorge beneath an impressive array of over 500 steps. The open field boasts lanky asphodels and hundreds of the pink-purple cross-shaped ricotia. Return to the cattle gate (2).

Head along the dirt road, pass a cattle pen costing you two more gates and reach the slopes of Har Havakuk. Looking left (southwest), you can make out the ridges of the Lower Galilee and Upper Tiberias. After a thicket of yellow blooming (in the late winter) calycotome on the left, before a line of cypress trees, the dirt road splits. Take the right option and follow it over the small ridge.

The dirt road veers left and descends toward a valley. Note the steep slope of the eastern bank of Nahal Ammud in strong contrast with the other side. The cliffs on the east are Eocenian limestones while the gentle landscape on the west is carved into Senonian chalk and marl. Hawthorn trees grow on the left. Across Nahal Ammud, oak trees spread over the rocky slope.

Looking north, a grand view of the upper regions of Nahal Ammud is present: the lofty green ridge to the left of Nahal Ammud is the Meron Range and to the right is the Canaan Range crested by the town of Safed.

From the dirt road you are on, it is approximately 400 m. to the black-marked trail which runs along Nahal Ammud. There is no trail connecting the two. The best place to leave the dirt road is before reaching a large open meadow sloping toward you from the north. The local topography is of two small gullies descending east towards Nahal Ammud and merging some 200 m. east of the dirt road in a wide basin adorned by tall jujube trees. Take a right, leaving the dirt road at this point (3). You should pass anagyris bushes with clover-shaped leaves and yellow flowers. Pass a large, round almond tree and farther down, cross a fence. Continue towards the stream bed down the rockless slope.

Upon reaching the black-marked trail (you may reach the trail by a boulder with a black trail mark), take it to the right. Cross a small gully and enter a thicket of vegetation. Amidst the greenery of bramble and other plants emerges Ein

Shavshevet (4) — "weather vane spring." Head past the weather vane. In earlier times the wind was harnessed to pump water for grazing cattle.

The cliffs across Nahal Ammud are one of the few locations in Israel where vultures still nest. In early morning these raptors can be seen rising with the warming air.

Past Ein Shavshevet, the trail runs along the stream, crisscrossing many times. The stream holds oleander and chaste trees, both summer bloomers. On the right side of the stream are cliffs in alluvium, remnants of times thousands of years ago when Nahal Ammud flowed at a higher level up to a more elevated Lake Kinneret. Along the trail do not forget to look up, as you may catch a glimpse of a hovering raptor. Swifts often dart and glide across the canyon.

After about a kilometer, the trail passes beneath large oak and snowbell trees on the eastern bank. To the left of the trail rises a sheer cliff holding an interesting joint. The shaded area in the spring yields wild garlic blooming in white clusters atop tall green stalks. The next interesting feature is a gorge that the trail heads above from the left. In the summer it is possible to hike in the stream bed itself, to enjoy the cool shady atmosphere. Here, large carob trees appear, signifying the warm environment of Lower Nahal Ammud. Along the trail the I.N.T. mark is present.

One-and-a-half kilometers from Ein Shavshevet, the N.W.C. crosses the stream bed (5). A hundred meters downstream, the trail crosses to the eastern bank and passes by a fault beneath carob trees.

The stream bed opens up before entering the finale: the Ammud Canyon. Upon reaching it, look for an interesting chimney cave left of the trail. Across Nahal Ammud, note the cliff loaded with caves—the Shovakh Caves. Inside the caves, prehistoric artifacts have been found. From here, 0.5 km. downstream, reach the famous pillar, the Ammud (6). Along the way, left of the trail, dozens of wildflowers bloom in the spring. One of them is the distinctinve hyacinth squill, presenting blue flowers at the edge of lone stems.

Near the Ammud, next to the stream beneath a boulder, Ein Ammud emerges, especially refreshing in the summer when the stream bed is dry. Upon the cliff behind the Ammud and 100 m. to the east is Ammud Cave. It is possible to climb to the cave.

From the Ammud, follow the wide path across the stream for the last few times to the bridge over Nahal Ammud (7). Here the hike essentially ends.

To return to the entrance of Hukuk, head to the right up the paved road for 400 m. Note the outcrop on the right: white marl deposited during times that a larger Lake Kinneret covered this part. There are boulders on the marl, representing a shore or a stream. Above, the shallow basalt cover has slowly developed into soil. The source of the basalt flow may have been the protruding flat-top hill of Karnei Hittin, atop the ridge seen 8 km. to the south.

Take a right onto the dirt road and ascend the basaltic slope past the ostrich pens. The road veers left along the fence. At the intersection, go right and ascend (past citrus groves) to the Hukuk road. Upon reaching the road walk 100 m. (right) to the starting point (1).

18 Mitzpe Ela and Nahal Yavne'el

See map on page 140

Points of interest: *Spectacular vistas of Lake Kinneret and the Jordan Valley. Landscapes of basalt flows and dozens of crystal clear springs emerging along the slopes. A prehistoric human site near the Jordan River.*

Length and nature of hike: Option 1: A climb to Mitzpe Ela only! 10 kilometers, loop trip. Option 2: 14 kilometers, loop trip.

Hiking time: 7-9 hours.

Preferred season: Winter and spring.

Suitable for: Experienced hikers.

Maps: "Lower Galilee, the Valley's and the Gilboa" hiking and touring map.

Special preparation: Option 2: Clothes for walking in water.

Starting & ending point: Village of Menahamiya.

To reach starting point:

Arrival by private transportation: Turn off Road 90 by kilometer post 398, onto the road leading to Menahamiya. The turnoff is located between Tzemah Junction (by the southern tip of Lake Kinneret) and Bet She'an.

After 1 km. along the road, take a right turn into the village. Pass renovated buildings by a junction and continue past the shopping center on your right. There is an intersection by a memorial on your left. Park the vehicle here (1).

Arrival by public transportation: From Tiberias and Bet She'an take a bus to the village (make sure that the bus enters the village!). If you are coming from a more distant location, take a bus that runs along Road 90 between Tzemah Junction and Bet She'an. Get off at the turnoff to Menahamiya. Here, wait for either a bus or a cab that heads into the village. Descend by the memorial (1).

Geography

This hike will allow you to see a number of geological layers. On top, "cover basalt" is the youngest layer, that was deposited 3.5 million years ago. It covers the plateaus of the eastern Lower Galilee. Beneath the basalt are layers of volcanic ash. The ash covers layers of freshwater limestone and gypsum, representative of shallow water environments. The gypsum is extracted for commercial use at the Gesher quarries nearby. "Lower basalt" from the Neogene, creates the lower parts of the slopes above Menahamiya. At some places it is hundreds of meters thick.

All of these sediments were deposited on both sides of the Syrian-African Rift, before the rifting occured. The rifting created the steep slopes. Since then, erosion has pulled sediment into the Rift—conglomerate, salt and basalt piled over four kilometers deep. Some sediments are marl that were deposited just 15,000 years ago when this section of the Rift was covered with the Lashon Lake, which extended from here to the Dead Sea.

The streams which drain eastward into the Rift were created in the Pleistocene, when intense faulting dissected the eastern Lower Galilee into ridges and valleys such as Har Tavor, Yavne'el Ridge and Yavne'el Valley. These events were influenced by the opening of the Syrian-African Rift. Thus, the streams cut into the strata mentioned above. Where soft marls are exposed, springs emerge and the streams run in wide valleys. Where the stream beds cut into the lower Neogenian basalt, canyons are formed such as the basalt canyon of Nahal Tavor.

Nahal Yavne'el

Plants and animals

Jujube (*Ziziphus*): There are two jujubes in Israel. They are both common in their habitats. The lotus jujube grows up to 2 m. and is found only in the North, in elevations up to 500 m. The small yellow-green flowers of the bush-like tree bloom in spring. The 1 cm. fruit ripens through the summer. Its oval leaves shed.

The Christ-thorn jujube reaches 8 m. and does not shed its leaves. It blooms twice a year in the summer and spring. The tree is found throughout the warm Mediterranean areas of Israel. Its strong resistance to logging, fire and pasture makes it sometimes the only tree existing in the basaltic plains of the eastern Lower Galilee and Golan Heights.

With both varieties of jujube, the fruits are the only edible part (look out for a red dot on the fruit, a sign of infestation). They are eaten both fresh and as a preserve. Dried fruits can last a long time. The powder of the dried fruit with butter or oil was a common dish until this century. The fruits of the lotus keep better than those of its close relative, the Christ-thorn, whose fruits are only edible when fresh.

The Greek lotus tree is believed to be the lotus jujube. The tree is mentioned in the Odyssey: a few people tried the sweet fruits and forgot their mission and homeland, refusing to return to their vessel.

But jujubes are more than a simple food. They are used in Africa to treat diarrhea and other diseases. Sinai Bedouins prepare a tea from the leaves to treat heart condition. A leaf sauna is believed to be good for muscle aches. Finally, its bark is boiled into a mouthwash for toothaches.

The Koran tell that, due to sins, the jujube was turned into a bitter tasting fruit tree. In compensation the tree is seated by the 7th heaven. Due to this, Moslems treat the tree with respect, plant them a lot, and see them as a dwelling site for spirits. On the other hand, the Jewish settlers saw the jujube as an enemy of the land and made lengthy efforts to uproot the stubborn tree.

Chukar (*Alectoris chukar*): Commonly known as a partridge, the chukar often surprises hikers by noisily leaping into air from beneath ones feet. It is a common fowl in Israel, extending from the Hermon Range to the Central Negev. The bird can be found in nearly every open field, and its habitat usually coincides with the gazelle, also an open field animal. Worldwide, the chukar is found between China and Bulgaria.

Body length reaches 40 cm. Male and females are indistinguishable. Plumage colors are brown and grey. The chin and throat are white and ringed with a semicircular black border blending into the black eye-stripe, making identification simple. The legs and bill are red.

Chukars spend most of the year in mixed groups of 10-20 individuals. The adult males mark the flock's territory. The birds are active in the early morning and evening. In the middle of the day they rest in the shade of bushes. Upon being frightened, they fly a few meters and land.

The chukar feeds mainly on the seeds of plants such as onions and tubers, but also on insects. Only in the summer do they drink water. Pairs leave the flock in the winter and nest in a shallow depression in the ground, among bushes, or in the shade of a rock. Usually 8-15 eggs result, but as many as 50% of the vulnerable nests are destroyed during the 26-day incubation. The survivors usually hatch in May.

The chukar constitutes an important food for predators, including humans. This is, in fact, Israel's most hunted gamebird. Due to the poisoning of predators in the 1950s and early 1960s, the chukar proliferated to a remarkable degree. In the Negev, where food is more scarce, they are a nuisance to farmers.

History

Along this hike are human remains spanning a million years, the most ancient outside of Africa. The finds point towards a different climate in the region in those times. From the Chalcolithic period until today, the basaltic plains above Mitzpe Elot were pasture land due to the lack of water resources and the problem of sealing water cisterns in the cracked basalt. Grassy vegetation also induced the utilization of the plains for grazing.

Since the bountiful springs of eastern Lower Galilee only emerge at low elevations, their value is limited to low elevations. During the Canaanite period, large settlements developed along the fringes of the region, farming in valleys such as Yavne'el Valley. Along Nahal Yavne'el ran an international trade route, since it merges with the Jordan River close to where it hits the Yarmuk River.

Due to the region's proximity to the dense populations of the Syrian-African Rift and the Bet She'an Valley the slopes of the eastern Lower Galilee were relatively neglected throughout history. Only small settlements developed.

Site description

Menahamiya: The village was founded in 1902 by P.I.C.A. as an agricultural settlement, intended to grow grain. Progress was slow. The moshav suffered Bedouin and Arab attacks, causing many fatalities and merchandise loss. Before WWII, village residents opened a gypsum quarry to supply the Nesher cement works near Haifa.

After the War of Independence, North African and Romanian immigrants settled at the moshav. The moshav became a regional council and today supplies communal services to the settlements between Bet She'an and Tiberias. About 700 people reside at Menahamiya.

Mitzpe Ela (Hurbat Ela): *Ela* is a terebinth tree. There used to be two trees here, but careless visitors burned them in the 1960s. The two trees had stood for centuries as a holy site to Arabs. They believed that anyone swearing falsely beneath the tree would be doomed.

The nearby ruins are of a village which was founded in early Canaanite times prospering in the middle of the period. During the Israelite period there was a walled settlement; parts of the wall still stand up to 1 m. The site has been identified with a number of border towns of the tribe of Issakhar (Joshua 19:19-22). Blooming asphodels cover the area in late winter.

The view encompasses many sites and regions. In the south, there is Kokhav Hayarden (Belvoir) at the eastern crest of the Yissakhar Ridge. Jordan Valley below is vividly seen between Lake Kinneret in the north and the small lake of the dammed Yarmuk River by its joint with the Jordan River. This famous joint is known as Naharayim—the two rivers. The deep canyon of the Yarmuk, due east, is a cleft between the plateau of the Golan Heights to its north and the Gilead (today under Jordanian control) to its south. The volcanic mountains of the Golan are also visible. The ridge with a few settlements to the north is called the Poriya Ridge. Farther north stand the Canaan Mountains and the Meron Mountains, both in Upper Galilee. The valley to the northwest is called Yavne'el, with the village of Yavne'el at its southeastern end.

Ya'ala Grove: A 12 dunam nature reserve holding 9 ancient impressive jujube trees saved from the axe due to their holiness to the local Arabs. It is possible that this is the site of "the plain of Tza'ananim which is by Kedesh" (Judges 4:11) where Hever the Kenite posted his tent. The site is named after Yael, Hever's wife. The spring nearby is named Ein el-Kalb—the spring of the dog.

Nahal Yavne'el: Nahal Yavne'el drains Yavne'el Valley which lies between Yavne'el Ridge to its southwest and Alumot Ridge to the north. The wadi was formed by tectonic activity and was covered by a basalt flow during the Neogene. Many springs emerge along the lower part of the stream, between layers of basalt and tuff. The springs give 2,500 cubits of water per hour. The Arabic name Wadi Faigas is after the Greek *pegai*, meaning springs. In the 1950s, Yavne'el Wells were drilled reducing the stream's flow to 720 cubits per hour. Today Kibbutz Alumot uses its waters for irrigation.

In the first or second century, the Romans built an aqueduct to collect spring water from the stream's slopes and to channel it to Tiberias and Bet Yerah. Three flour mills were built near the upper section of the aqueduct. Today, one can barely make out remnants of these constructions along Nahal Yavne'el.

Ubeidiya Prehistoric Site: Here is the most ancient of all archaeological finds in Israel. Prehistoric human remains, evidently from 600,000-800,000 years ago (Early Acheulean) were first found in the fields of Kibbutz Afikim in 1959. Fifteen years of digging took place here. Findings included chopping tools, spheroids, bifaces and hand axes; and rich assemblages of mammalian remains, such as: elephant, rhinoceros, monkey and lion. The most common mammal was the hippopotamus due to the moist marshy environment which prevailed in those times. The stratum containing the finds is composed of Pleistocene lake sediments.

Tel Ubeidiya: Here, a small Arab village stood until 1948, whose residents often attacked the settlers of Menahamiya. They used the water-powered flour mill at the bottom of the slope to the east.

Two archaeological digs revealed a 10-meter-thick accumulation of settlement layers. Founded in the Early Bronze, the site was a walled town. The wall still stands 2-3 meters high. The site's importance lies in the fact that here by the merge of Nahal Yavne'el into the Jordan, it controlled a crossing of the Jordan and an intersection of an ancient seaway route that traversed Israel.

Remnants were found from all historical periods until the Mameluke period. The archaeologist Y. Aharoni sees Tel Ubeidiya as the Canaanite city of Ubeidiya mentioned in many Egyptian scrolls from those days.

To begin hike:

The memorial marks the sons of Menahamiya which fell in defence of Israel. Head up the street to the southwest for 150 m. to the old-fashioned gas station. Go right on to the dirt road which enters a forest and crosses a wadi. At the road split, head left, ascending a wide road parallel to Wadi el-Jarem and to a security fence.

After 350 m., the road exits through a gate on the right. Exit Menahamiya and immediately take a left toward the wadi. Head up the wadi along its northern bank. You will soon pick up some blue trail marks which will accompany you along this most difficult part of the hike. The clump of reeds marks Ein Abu Sidra. Farther up, the steep watercourse is canyon-like and the trail climbs up two small falls. The bedrock is basalt. The trail is usually loyal to the stream bed but sometimes runs alongside it. After the falls, the trail is on the northern bank of the wadi and here the waters of Ein el-Jarem sometimes appear in the narrow channel of Wadi el-Jarem.

The landscape widens and the trail crosses to the southern bank, leading you into a canyon which is a conjunction of two steep wadis. Stick to the right wadi, following the trail mark. Atop this canyon, the landscape again widens and runs along a planted cypress forest, part of the Levi Eshkol Forest. Levi Eshkol was Israel's third premier (and also minister of defense), succeeding David Ben Gurion in 1963. After WWI he helped found Deganiya Bet, 5 km. northeast of the forest.

Cross a dirt road and continue along the northern side of the wadi, passing a few jujube trees. The wadi curves north past a steep tributary coming from the left (west). At this point, water vegetation begins to color the stream and you should be able to hear a trickle below. The trail steeply ascends through trees to Ein Um Ze'it, which emerges next to a cattle pen marked by a tall palm tree (2). Nearby is an Arab cemetery called Um Ze'it.

At the pen take a right (north) and cross a dirt road. Heading up a slope now, you should pass a large boulder with a blue trail mark. Follow the trail up and along the slope to the north. The trail soon passes views, usually known only from Holy Land photograph albums. On clear winter days, the white crest of the Hermon Range stands out in the distance.

The trail reaches a huge pile of rocks adorned by small wild almond trees (3). The almond tree takes advantage of the fire-free spot. Hyrax dwell here, enjoying the cool spaces among the rocks. Along the trail you will pass colorful layers of sedimentary rock—shales, gypsum and chalk. The hard, cracked layer of basalt composing the cliff above is very sensitive to movements of these ductile sedimentary rocks. After rainfall, water seeps through the basalt and, upon reaching some of the more clay-like layers of the sedimentary rock, can trigger small-scale landslides which bring down the overhanging layer of basalt. Watch out!

The next stop is Mitzpe Ela (4), standing straight above the rock pile: follow the blue trail northwest for 200 m. to a fence along a dirt road. By the curve in the

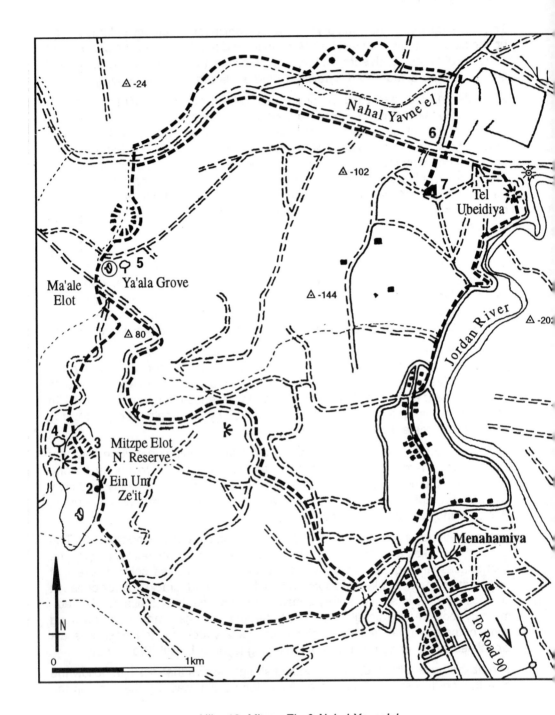

Hike 18, Mitzpe Ela & Nahal Yavne'el

road, a post marks a black-blue trail intersection. Take the black trail to the left (south) up the steepening slope to a lone terebinth tree at the edge of the basalt cliff, Mitzpe Ela (4). One kilometer to your west, atop the ridge, is Mitzpe Elot, 368 m. above sea level, the highest point on the Yavne'el Ridge. The site is named after the impressive terebinth trees which once covered the slopes along with the wild almond.

Return to the trail intersection. Here you have two parallel options to descend to the plain to the north. Either take the dirt road by the wheat field or follow the trail mark along the edge of the cliff which farther down becomes a steep slope. The dirt road zigzags down and is naturally a more comfortable track.

Upon reaching the bottom, cross through the gate and follow the black trail mark, which heads at first along the base of the slope. Here you can see an outcrop of rock and soil on your left. Note the thickness of the soil—this region is a bumper crop belt with sufficient rainfall.

The basalt here is undergoing spheroidal weathering, a common phenomenon in basaltic rock.

The trail cuts across the field to a wadi, a tributary of Nahal Yavne'el, reaching it where a dirt road crosses it by a medium-sized jujube tree. The wadi carries variable amounts of water, depending on annual rainfall.

For those following option 1: the dirt road is marked by a red trail mark. If you want to shorten your hike substantially and leave Nahal Yavne'el for another time, go right on the dirt road, heading east. After 0.5 km. the road reaches a watershed and descends in many curves and turnoffs, through the Levi Eshkol Forest back to the gate of Menahamiya and on to the starting point (1).

Option 2: head along the wadi, past a small canyon with almond trees to Ya'ala Grove (5). The site is surrounded by stones marked with white paint blotches.

Continue north along the ravine, which becomes a canyon. Before the dry fall, an interesting gully comes in from the east. The gully's shape suggests that it was once a dike where the more erodible rock was washed away.

The first fall can be taken from the east. The second fall is larger and you will find a steep slope of basalt boulders between the stream bed and yourself. Follow the trail down. Continue by the stream bed, which is incised in alluvium, to the dirt road. Continue to follow the trail mark down to the right, to Nahal Yavne'el.

Nahal Yavne'el

141

Hiking down Nahal Yavne'el can be done along three routes:

1) On a hot day it is refreshing to walk in the cool waters of the stream. The going is rough in some parts, making travel relatively slow. One and a half kilometers downstream, a dirt road crosses Nahal Yavne'el by a pumping station. Here, you can join either one of the other two options. Option 2: go right and ascend the dirt road for 250 m. until reaching a green marked dirt road. Take a left on it. Option 3: go left along the dirt road.

2) After resting by the waters of the Yavne'el, head back to the dirt road which you crossed. Go left and follow the stream from above. After about a kilometer, a dirt road descends to the stream. After another 1.5 km., reach an intersection with a black-marked dirt road coming in from the north (6).

3) This option follows the unclear black trail. Cross Nahal Yavne'el and head along the northern bank, where many springs emerge and flow through small marshes into the stream. The marked trail runs through these marshes. (It is possible to follow an unmarked trail that runs above the springs. It passes a fig tree which hovers above a spring, a palm and, further along, through a clump of jujubes. After 500 m., the stream veers east and it is possible to walk close to the waters following the black trail again.) Pass eucalyptus trees, a wonderful spot for a rest and dip. Not far from these tall trees, a dirt road runs through the stream past a pumping station. Here you can proceed as mentioned in options 1 and 2, or continue on the unclear dirt road eastward. (The latter option involves crossing a couple of bogs. They can be bypassed by heading up the northern slope for a couple hundred meters, up and past the bramble-covered spring source.) It is also possible to stick to Nahal Yavne'el itself.

After reaching a pen 800 m. later, make sure that you continue eastward on the dirt road for 400 m. This section runs parallel to the stream toward a couple of eucalyptus trees. Upon reaching a road take an immediate right across the clear stream waters. Four hundred meters further south you will reach another intersection (6).

At this black and green (trail mark) intersection (6) you can head southwest for 200 m. to the Ubeidiya prehistoric site (7). Return to the dirt road and head east for 0.5 km. Tel Ubeidiya protrudes to your southeast. Head to it. From the top, a scraggly trail descends the southern slope to the dirt road along the Jordan River. Follow it and then take a right.

On your left (across the river), behind some trees, stands a sheer marl cliff constantly being harassed by the Jordan. This incision creates a meander, a common phenomena along the Jordan. Eventually, the cliff will erode until the Jordan reconnects with its stream bed farther south, creating a straight section. The stream bed ahead will then become extinct. The straight stream bed will not last for long, as the Jordan will start working on a new curve.

Heading southwest along the west bank, pass a pumping station and reach a new power station. Circle the power station to the right and continue on the well-maintained road, which connects Menahamiya to the station. A kilometer from the power station brings you to the outskirts of Menahamiya. Go left and head 1 km. through the village back to the starting point (1).

19 Nahal Tavor

See map on page 146

Points of interest: *A hike through a basalt canyon decorated by a small stream supplemented with views of the wildest section of the Lower Galilee. Carpets of lupine and many wild flowers appear in spring and late winter.*

Length and nature of hike: 9 kilometers, loop trip.

Hiking time: 4-6 hours.

Preferred season: Winter and spring.

Suitable for: All

Maps: "Lower Galilee, the Valley's and the Gilboa" hiking and touring map.

Special preparation: Swimsuit, clothes for walking in water (optional).

Starting & ending point: Kibbutz Gazit.

To reach starting point:

Arrival by private transportation: From Road 65, turn off to the south onto Road 7276 (there is a sign for Gazit). The turnoff is by kilometer post 59, 1 km. south of Kefar Tavor. Follow the road for 8 km. to its end at the entrance to Gazit. Continue into the kibbutz, past a factory on your right, and take the second turn to the right past an old red-brick building to a (closed) gate along the fence of the settlement (1) where you park.

Arrival by public transportation: Take a bus to Gazit from the Afula central bus station. Get off at the main stop in Gazit and head back toward the kibbutz entrance. Take a left down a paved road past an old red-brick building to a gate in the settlement's fence (1).

Geography

Nahal Tavor is one of the largest streams in the Lower Galilee. It is 30 km. long and drains 220 sq. km. Part of the stream is a nature reserve of 9,378 dunams. The stream has two main tributaries, Nahal Keshet in the north and Nahal Tavor from the southern slopes of Har Tavor. Many springs join the stream, all along its length. The more significant of these emerge down-stream.

The basalt canyon in central Nahal Tavor is fed by two main springs, Ein Tavor Elyon and Ein Rekhesh. Their volumes are 162 and 28 cubits per hour, respectively.

For more information see Hike 18, 'Mitzpe Ela and Nahal Yavne'el.'

Plants and animals

Hawthorn (*Crataegus aronia*): The small tree has thorny branches, hence its name. It reaches 5 m. In the autumn, its leaves turn gray and fall. Before the leaves reappear in springtime, the tree blooms with small white blossoms. The flowers eventually turn into tiny yellow-orange fruits. The fruit resembles apples and is eaten by humans and birds, who disperse the seeds.

This tree is adapted to dry conditions, thus one finds it in low elevations such as the Lower Galilee and the Judean Foothills, and in the desert fringe. In less arid environments, the tree survives in open fields, exposed to full-day sunlight.

The fruits can be eaten when ripe. It is also possible to make hawthorn jam or syrup. Arab peasants add grape juice to cooked hawthorn juice to make hawthorn wine. They also graft pear to hawthorn trees. Before eating the fruit, it is important to check for infestation.

The hawthorn is traditionally believed to help strengthen the heart, open the arteries, relax the nerves and treat bloody urine and feces.

A relative, the red hawthorn, grows in the dark moist forests of Israel. This species bears bright red edible fruits.

Mountain Gazelle (*Gazella gazella*): The gazelle is often mistaken for deer (which was hunted to extinction at the turn of the century). The species is a native of the Middle East, though recently it has followed the deer into extinction in Jordan, Syria and Lebanon due to unrestricted hunting. In Israel, the mountain gazelle is found throughout the Mediterranean regions, while other species are found in the desert. It is commonly seen grazing during the day in open fields. During hot hours, it rests in the shade and at night it sleeps in the open.

The gazelle has a brown-grey body with a grey-black horizontal line along the contact between the torso and white belly. Males have S-shaped horns while the females either have non-symmetric shorter ones, or none.

Grasses make up the bulk of their food. In the winter they feed entirely on grass, but add leaves and jujube fruit in the summer.

In the 1950s, the gazelle was severely hunted by army units. Desert gazelles would die from heart failure after being chased for kilometers by jeeps. Since becoming a protected animal, it has proliferated in the absence of carnivores. The over-population turned to agriculture for food, causing serious damage. Today, the gazelle is hunted in a controlled manner where its population exceeds a given quota, such as around Nahal Yissakhar and in the Lower Golan.

History

See Hike 18, 'Mitzpe Ela and Nahal Yavne'el.'

Site description

Gazit: "Carved building stone" (Isaiah 9:9). This kibbutz was founded in 1947 by the Kibbutz Ha'artzi movement, specifically by immigrants from Argentina and Romania. Today the 500 residents have many fields: citrus and fruit orchards, cattle for meat and milk, poultry gardens, a plastic factory and a doll factory. The first Jews settled amidst the Arabs of Tira in 1943 who fled during the 1948 war. The group was known as the "Borokhov core" after D. B. Borokhov, Socialist-Zionist founder of "Po'alay Tzion," who died in 1917.

Tel Rekhesh: The largest tel in the eastern Lower Galilee. It is an elliptical, 40-dunam mound, 34 m. above sea level, overlooking Nahal Tavor in three directions. The tel has been surveyed but never dug.

Fortifications have been found on the tel along with an Egyptian victory plaque. The evidence indicates that it is the site of Anaharath, a Canaanite and Israelite city in the tribal estate of Issakhar. The city is mentioned in a list of cities captured by an Egyptian king in 1468 B.C.E. and as an important objective of a different pharaoh. In Joshua 19:19 the site is mentioned as a border with the tribe of Zevulun. After centuries of abandon, the settlement reestablished itself briefly during Byzantine times.

In ancient times, the broad valley of upper Nahal Tavor was a busy route: Tel Rekhesh is one of more than 10 settlement sites in the subregion.

To begin hike:

Head through (or beneath) the gate on a dirt road. Cross a wadi and 50 m. beyond, take the blue-marked trail to the left (along and above the wadi). The trail is clear, running along a fence on an unused dirt road. The steep wadi is a tributary of Nahal Tavor.

Half a kilometer along the trail, cross a small ravine coming down from the right. On the right you pass a lot of sage bushes. A kilometer later, after passing through (and closing) a gate, the dirt road steeply descends to the left to the stream bed (2). Here, the stream bed acquires a covering of denser vegetation suggesting water: Ein Dana. A steep tributary from the northwest also merges here, bringing sewage.

But do not head down, rather leave the dirt road, following the blue trail mark into the field ahead. The trail is not clear; stick to the same elevation if you lose track. You should pass to the left of a jujube tree. The trail crosses a ravine and heads between two trees on the slope. Nahal Tavor deepens to the left while the trail sticks to the relatively moderate part of the slope. Six hundred meters from the dirt road, the trail crosses a second ravine which is steep and shady. The ravine is cut into whitish-grey chalk, a sharp color change in the landscape. From the ravine, the trail gently descends through hawthorn trees to the wadi.

Where the trail hits the stream bed (3), continue on the southern bank for 100 m., between the jujube thicket and the fence. Before the merge with Nahal Tavor, cross the tributary (according to the trail mark) which now runs in a shallow trench.

At the blue trail, go right along a dirt road for 100 m. and then turn left (north) along the western bank of the Tavor on another dirt road.

Where the dirt road crosses the clear water of Nahal Tavor, stay with the blue-mark on the western bank. It is also possible to walk in the shallow waters of the stream all the way to the waterfalls (5). The stream is lined with summer-blooming oleander bushes and some willows. The area is full of blooming lupine in February and March.

Half a kilometer later the trail runs by a lone Atlantic terebinth tree (4). Note the large rock beneath the ancient tree. A flat surface has been sculpted onto the rock's top, a likely site of pagan worship. Here is a good spot to rest and enjoy the surroundings. Note the basalt wall across the stream. The wall is a dike. Another dike stands perpendicular on its left, parallel to the stream.

The trail descends to the stream bed, where thorny burnet bushes dot the steep shady southwestern slope. The trail crosses the stream and curves around a meander. The cliffs are speckled with wild almond trees, a common sight in the basalt canyons of Israel. On the way to the waterfalls (5), recross the stream a few times as it becomes more canyon-like, cutting into layers of hard basalt.

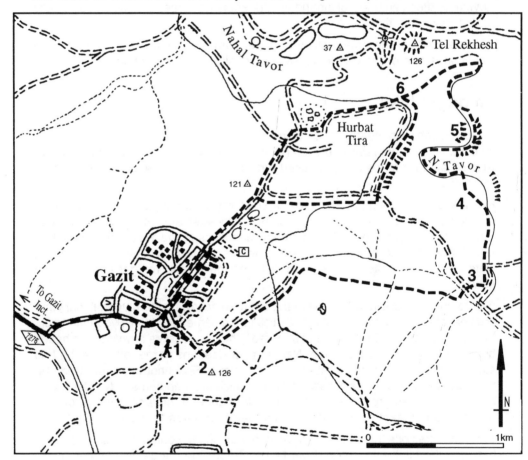

Hike 19, Nahal Tavor

Where the stream curves left, notice along the bottom of the western slope an exposure of dark red soil that was buried and burnt by the lava flow above it. The red color comes from the high iron content. The presence of soil between basalt indicates a period of time sufficient for soil development (thousands of years) between lava flows.

In the canyon are two small waterfalls with pools (5). A refreshing dip is highly recommended.

From the falls (5), follow the blue trail along the right side of the stream. Where the stream curves right (east), leave it, following the blue trail across the water and onto the ridge. While crossing, look to your left and note a steep trench running into the stream bed. This is possibly part of a negative dike.

The soft rock of the dike is more erodible than the surrounding rock. Consequently, the dike may have participated in the formation of the stream bed. As the watercourse found its way into the dike, the water cut deeply and later widened out of the dike's narrow confines.

Above the wadi, the trail takes a left and climbs a sharp, steep ridge. This type of ridge is known in Israel as *sawkeen,* a knife. Along this ridge many squills grow (in the spring, only their dark green leaves are seen), anemones of various colors and thousands of cyclamens.

At the top of the ascent (6), hard carbonate rock caps the canyon's top. The plants are different here than below. The aromatic grey-green stalks of margoram may ease your fatigue. Better yet, take in the magnificent view of Nahal Tavor and the eastern Lower Galilee.

At the end of the ridge (to the southeast), at 308 m., stands Kokhav Hayarden— the star of Jordan, a famous Crusader castle originally called Belvoir. To the northeast at the end of the ridge is Mitzpe Elot, at 368 m. Due north in the valley of Nahal Tavor is Tel Rekhesh. Note the ruins of a flour mill between the tel and the reservoir. Three kilometers northeast are the homes of Moshav Kefar-Kish and, in the distance, Har Tavor (588 m.) with the Nazareth Mountains behind.

To return to Gazit there are two options:

1) For a view westward, head west along the blue trail for less than a kilometer, to the right of the pamela grove. The road curves left and passes along the ruins of the village of Tira to a green-marked dirt road. The carved constructions in the limestone point to the site being substantially more ancient than the Arab village. The inhabitants of Tira fled from Israel during the war in 1948. Take a left onto the dirt road for 1 km. to Gazit.

2) For superb views of the hiked route and a visit with Gazit cattle, take a left onto the green trail. Follow the edge of the cliff to a gate. Enter the gate, and go right along the inside of the fence. After about 400 m., go onto the red-marked dirt road. The road exits the cattle enclosure and reaches a dirt road along a flat ridge. Go left on the dirt road to Gazit.

At the rear entrance to Gazit take the middle road to the left. Pass cattle and horse pens. The road becomes the access road of the kibbutz, reaching the bus stop and the turnoff to the starting point (1).

20

Nahal Tzipori

See map on
page 153

Points of interest: *A gentle stream running in a valley of
wheat fields and pomegranate groves, between green hills
dotted with Bedouin villages and modern Jewish settlements. Two impressive structures of inactive flour mills and
one bubbling spring.*

Length and nature of hike: 8 kilometers, loop trip.

Hiking time: 4-5 hours.

Preferred season: All year.

Suitable for: All.

Maps: Carmel hiking and touring map or Upper Galilee hiking
and touring map (even though Nahal Tzipori is in the Lower
Galilee).

Special preparation: Swimsuit.

Starting & ending point: Lower parking lot at the entrance
to Kibbutz Harduf.

To reach starting point:

Arrival by private transportation: Turn off Road 79 to the south toward Adi and
Harduf (an orange sign). Road 79 connects Movil and Sanhedrin Junctions (Road
70). At the entrance to Adi, take a left and continue for 3 km. until the dead-end
at Kibbutz Harduf. Park in the parking lot (1).

Arrival by public transportation: Public transportation is not frequent. A bus
runs from Haifa to Kibbutz Harduf (1) once or twice a day.

Geography

Nahal Tzipori flows through the southwestern corner of the Lower Galilee. The
region is known as the Alonim-Shefar'am Hills. The name is derived from the
Tabor oaks (*alonim*) which cover the region and Shefar'am, the urban center.

The Alonim-Shefar'am Hills are considered a separate geological entity. They are
round hills of soft Eocenian chalk, separated by wide valleys. Elevations range
from 200-300 m., rising gently towards the Nazareth Mountains in the east. The
hills drop sharply in the west and south to the Mediterranean coast and Jezre'el
Valley, respectively. The whole region, including Nahal Tzipori, drains into the
famous Kishon River.

The chalk slopes are covered with a hard, 0.5-5 meter-thick carbonate crust
known as nari or calcrete. The nari is often mistaken for limestone. Due to its
shallow depth, the nari is useful for carving cisterns in the soft chalk below.

Along Nahal Tzipori no substantial faulting has taken place. Small faults are visible
along the barren eastern slope of Giv'at Alil. The sharp meander of the stream
around Giv'at Alil was formed in a unique geomorphological sequence of events.

The ancient Tzipori flowed over the topographical saddle by Ras Ali, where a tributary merged from the north (covered with pine forest today). The saddle became plugged by debris from a landslide and a lake began to grow upstream and up the northern tributary. A fault north of Giv'at Alil (and similar to the ones seen on it today) allowed water to seep through the strata, reaching a soft layer of marl which gave way. The lake broke its way westward and then southward, reconnecting to the original stream bed below Ras Ali. Thus Nahal Tzipori nearly surrounded Giv'at Alil.

Plants and animals

Due to intense human involvement in the area, the landscape reveals little of its natural capability. The uncracked chalk of the Alonim-Shefar'am Hills create a poor water economy. Thus, the Tabor oak is the common tree as its root system is a wide shallow one. This explains why the trees usually create forests with open spaces between them. The oak has been used in the region for charcoal manufacture.

Large animals such as mammals are rare due to the human presence. Rodents, however, are abundant. The jay, blackbird and woodpecker are common songbirds in these hills.

Pomegranate (*Punica granatum*): Originally from Iran, the tree was introduced to Israel thousands of years ago. The spies brought back pomegranates as proof of the fertility of the land (Numbers 13:23). The fruit is one of the seven species with which Israel is blessed (Deuteronomy 8:8). During Talmudic times the fruit was a main crop in Israel and many localities are named for it (*Rimon*). The fruit was also used as an ornament and decoration, in synagogues, for example. Rimon is also an ancient personal name and was used to indicate beauty.

Today it can be found throughout the Mediterranean Basin and in Iran.

The pomegranate is a deciduous tree or bush, up to 6 m. During its first year the branches are thorny and pink. The leaves are shiny green, appearing in March. A month later the tree blooms for six weeks. There are two shapes of flowers: jar-shaped and bell-shaped. The latter do not produce fruit. Both are red with yellow pollen.

The fruit is ball-shaped with a thick rough crust. On top of it lays a crown, a remnant of the flower. Inside the fruit are hundreds of seeds coated with an edible, fleshy red transparent coating. Jewish tradition claims that there are 613 seeds in the fruit, equivalent to the number of commandments in the Five Books of Moses.

The tree is resistant to salinity and frost. Since the fruits develop on side branches, pruning initiates fruit production. In 1948 there were 3,000 dunams of orchards in Israel, mainly in the Arab sector, producing 1,500 annual tons. In the 1970s, due to the introduction of a wider variety of fruits into the market, pomegranate orchard area declined to 600 dunams.

Blackbird (*Turdus merula*): Common in all parts of Europe and southern Asia, the blackbird can even be found in the maquis of North Africa. The primary habitat of the bird is woodland. In Israel, since the 1950s, the blackbird has become one of the country's most common songbirds, extending its habitat from the green sections of northern Israel all the way to Beersheba.

The male bird is all black except for the bill and an orange-yellow ring around the eye. The female is greyish-brown on the upper parts and chestnut-brown below. Youngsters are dark brown with a mottled breast. Body length rarely reaches 30 cm. and wingspan rarely attains 50 cm.

Blackbirds stick to the same territory throughout their lifetime. In February, their song is often heard in the morning. By spring, they sing the mellow, flute-like song throughout the day. Egg laying takes place between March and May. They lay three eggs in woodlands and four in agricultural regions. Incubation lasts two weeks.

History

Throughout history, main transportation routes ran along the outskirts of the Alonim-Shefar'am Hills. The nearby fertile Jezre'el Valley was always higher priority farm country. The Hills were therefore always on the sidelines of development.

No villages from the region are mentioned in ancient Egyptian texts, nor in the Bible. The area most likely belonged to the tribe of Asher. The alienation from the center of Israel kept it from being in the headlines. Only following the Bar Kokhba Revolt did the region find the limelight: Jews immigrated and the Sanhedrin (Supreme Court) was transferred to Usha and Shefar'am and later to Bet She'arim and Tzipori.

The Jewish community slowly dwindled through the Byzantine period and no new settlements were founded. That is the reason why Bedouins infiltrated into the uninhabited area. Only Shefar'am remained an important center.

At the turn of the century, Christian German Templers settled in two agricultural settlements: Waldheim and Bethlehem. The German presence was severely cut during WWII and terminated in 1948. Jews moved into the abandoned settlements.

In the 1960s the Bedouins began to settle at permanent sites. In the 1980s, Jews established a number of small settlements, such as Harduf and Pee Haner, mostly populated by people looking for a countryside atmosphere close to Haifa.

C.R. Conder, who headed the P.E.F. survey in 1872-1875, described the Alonim-Shefar'am region as a dense oak forest, with thick underbrush:

> ...According to signs found all over the country, it is clear that considerable changes occurred in the natural vegetation by a reduction of trees. Now, with no laws to protect the forest, the *fellahin* (Arab peasants, J.R) cut trees and burn them for fuel (*hattab*). These activities undoubtly affect the appearance of the country for the worse. It is man—not nature—who has destroyed the good land.

Site description

Nahal Tzipori: The perennial stream is the largest in western Lower Galilee. Beginning in the Nazareth Mountains, Nahal Tzipori is 32 km. long and drains 270 sq. km. Running west, it cuts through the Alonim-Shefar'am Hills and drains into Nahal Kishon, east of Haifa by Nesher. Einot Tzipori and Ein Yivka are its main sources. Today, some of the water is pumped and sewage from Nazareth pig-pens mixes with the fresh water.

Harduf: Founded in 1982 by the Jewish Agency, this kibbutz specializes in organic agriculture, whose export products include milk, cheeses, grains and breads. There is an organic food grocery and restaurant on the premises. *Harduf* means oleander. Oleanders grow along streams. Today, however, no oleanders, grow in the polluted stream beneath Harduf.

Ras Ali Flour Mill: Actually two mills, ideally located where the aqueduct is of minimal length. The aqueduct, still partially intact, comes from Monk's Mill (see below) via the topographical saddle 100 m. east of Ras Ali.

The mill owners hired four workers who slept on site and were severely underpaid: they were allowed to collect the flour that accumulated at the grind's margins and grow vegetables nearby.

The elders of Shefar'am claim that the upper mill produced 85-100 kg. of wheat per hour in the winter and 25 kg. in the summer. During the mill's last years it was equally owned by three different entities: the Druze religious council (Wakf), the Catholic Church of Shefar'am and a private person. However, when someone filled the water chimney in the winter of 1930-1931, the owners decided that it was not profitable enough to un-clog it. The lower mill, owned by a Christian family from Shefar'am, continued working, as the water was diverted from the slope straight down to the lower mill (the diversion is visible today). A dispute between the owners brought the mill to a halt in 1946.

The upper mill's 12.3 m. chimney remains the tallest in Israel.

Monk's Mill: The original structure, not visible today, was constructed by Druze from Shefar'am. In the 19th century, Carmelite monks from Haifa bought the

Monk's Mill on Nahal Tzipori

site and built the impressive structure which still stands. The Carmelites, like most mill owners, leased the mill to local Arabs. In 1914, the wooden wheels were converted to steel ones for greater efficiency. In the 1920s, after electricity put the water-powered mills out of business, Monk's Mill became a storage building.

The structure is unique among the water-powered flour mills in Israel (and unusual in Israeli architecture): roofed with slanted red-tiles imported from Marseilles, it is more like a European chateau. The main entrance still has the niche where the Carmelite symbol was positioned. Many orange colored daisies bloom in the vicinity in April. A lone berry tree stands to the east. The water channel is visible atop the structure.

Ein Yivka: This spring supplied water to Monk's Mill and Ras Ali Mill. Its discharge runs between 860-4,850 cubits per day. The waters emerge into a large pool (35 x 10 m.). The pool was built during Jewish settlement of the area after the destruction of the Second Temple and Carmelite monks renovated it in the 19th century. The pool raises the level of the water in order to create a larger elevation drop to Monk's Mill, 2 km. downstream. Today, the main remnants of the aqueduct are found by the mill.

To begin hike:

Head west through the small kibbutz (at 220 m. above sea level). Exit Harduf and immediately descend along Harduf Ridge into Sawa'id, a Bedouin village. Hook up to the recently paved road which enters the village from the right (northeast) and curves west, downhill.

Looking west, enjoy a view of the valley of Nahal Tzipori and the Haifa Bay area. To the north is the Arab city of Shefar'am. Looking south, the Carmel Ridge towers above the close environs of the Alonim-Shefar'am Hills.

Descend through the village on the road to a topographical saddle. You will reach a junction (2), not far beneath a Bedouin home. Take a left and then a right (northwest) and descend steeply through planted evergreen forest to the valley of Nahal Tzipori (3). Along the way, you may hear the flute-like song of the blackbird, dashing between trees.

Take a left on the dirt road that runs along the contact of the fields and the forest. Across the valley stands Giv'at Alil holding the village of Ras Ali. Note the exposed chalk strata of Giv'at Alil, dotted by a few trees. To the southwest, ahead and above, stands the village of Pee Haner, 210 m. above seal level.

There is a split in the dirt road by a lone snowbell tree. Go right, toward the saddle to the left of Giv'at Alil. Reach Nahal Tzipori along abandoned fields of red poppies and white diplotaxis. Cross the stream (lined with watercress) and ascend via the dirt road back to the junction on the saddle. Take a trail which descends on the other side for 100 m. to the abandoned structure, the Ras Ali Flour Mill (4). Explore, enjoy the shade and view.

Return to the junction and follow the dirt road south, upstream (blue-marked, but poorly) along the bottom of the western slope. In April, yellow morning bride flowers bloom between the road and the stream bank. In fall, many squills bloom above the dirt road. After 400 m., the road curves east, parallel to the stream. Here, a second dirt road descends from Harduf Ridge and crosses the stream. Take a left onto that dirt road, cross the stream, and immediately go right on a

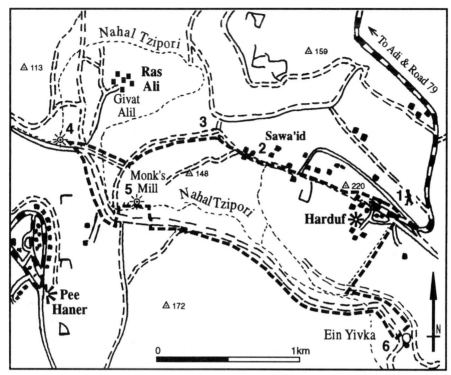

Hike 20, Nahal Tzipori

trail along the bank to Monk's Mill (5). Along the way, note a small spring emerging across stream.

From the mill, cross the bridge and go left on the dirt road. Head by the fringe of an oak forest. Eight hundred meters from the bridge, another road leaves the current one to the left and runs along the stream bank lined with bramble, reeds and single willow trees. Take it (it is the blue-marked way). Pomegranate groves grow here. Note the pipes that pump "water" from the stream for local irrigation. Also notice a gully across the stream, to the left and along the outskirts of the pine forest, on the northern slope. The gully initiates at Harduf and along it you will return to the starting point

The dirt road crosses the stream and heads up the northern slope alongside a pomegranate grove and a ditch carrying water from Ein Yivka. The road and ditch head to the large pool of Ein Yivka (6). Enjoy a dip.

Head straight upslope from Ein Yivka and connect to a dirt road running along the bottom of the pine forest. In March and April, the rare blue-colored hyacinth squill blooms by the road. Take a left on it, descending a bit and reaching a gully after 250 m. Head up the gully on a dirt road straight to Harduf between spring-blooming thorny calycotome bushes and small pink flax flowers. At Harduf, head to the right of the houses, across the road leading to the cowshed, back to the starting point (1).

Kinnarot Valley and the Bet She'an Valley

Geography

The Syrian-African Rift

Israel's most outstanding geographic feature is no doubt its section of the giant Syrian-East African Rift. Israel's section of the Syrian-African Rift, locally known as the Jordan or Dead Sea Rift is one of the largest and deepest scars in the earth's crust. It begins in Turkey, runs between the Alaoui Mountains and the Zaouie Hills of Syria, and further south, separates the Lebanon Mountains from the Anti-Lebanon Block.

The Israeli allotment of the Syrian-African Rift is divided into five sections:

1) The Upper Jordan Valley (Hula Valley).

2) The Kinnarot, Bet She'an and Central Jordan Valleys.

3) The Lower Jordan Valley.

4) The Dead Sea and Dead Sea Valley.

5) The Arava.

Eilat (Akaba) Gulf and the Red Sea continue the Rift southward. Near the southern outlet of the Red Sea, at Bab al Mandab Straits, the Rift splits; its eastern branch separates the Arabian Peninsula from the Horn of Africa, and its western branch enters Africa. Overall, the Syrian-African Rift stretches 6,500 km.

The Rift seperates Cisjordan from Transjordan. Cisjordan is the land, west of the Rift from the Negev through the Galilee. It is also known as the West Bank (of the Jordan). Transjordan is east of the Rift, mainly the kingdom of Jordan, the East Bank. The Rift is often accompanied by fault lines on both sides and is usually a valley. At some places, such as the Metulla Hills between Israel and Lebanon, it is hard to recognize the Rift's continuity. The Rift also sends out branches-the Harod and Jezre'el Valleys, west of the Bet She'an Valley, are good examples.

The Syrian-African Rift is a product of continental drift. It is the zone where the Arabian plate, to the east, rubs against the Sinai-Israel plate. Heavy geologic movement such as uplift, folding and horizontal displacement, began during the Miocene, creating shallow, broad, disconnected basins which held varying depths of water. In the late Miocene and early Pliocene a lake formed in the Central Jordan

Valley covering parts of Lower Galilee and Lower Golan. At certain times the Rift's waters were connected to the Mediterranean Sea via the Jezre'el Valley and possibly via the Arad region.

During the late Pliocene and Pleistocene, the Rift developed its present shape. The valley's bottom continued to subside while its rims were uplifted. At the Dead Sea, earth's most lowest point is revealed, usually around 400 m. below sea level (depending on Dead Sea level fluctuations). The Dead Sea itself is 400 m. deep. To its west, the backbone of Cisjordan was formed. Horst mountains, such as the Hermons, also appeared along its sidelines exposing ancient strata.

Since its initiation, the Arabian plate has moved about 105 km. north relative to the Sinai-Israel plate (as seen in relation to Cisjordan). Annually, the movement is 5-7 mm. This is scientifically proven by correlating geologic formations and members from both sides of the Rift, such as the sandstone formations at Timna, Israel and Hunon, Jordan. Large river beds that in pre-Rift times drained Transjordan into the Mediterranean Sea were split into two by the subsiding Rift. Geologists have found a correlation between large Transjordanian stream beds draining west into the Rift, with large Israeli stream beds draining west into the Mediterranean Sea. However, the horizontal difference between them is not 105 km. Since the river bed split, the sinking of the Rift has been accelerated by the weight of alluvium deposited by the streams that drain into it. At some places the alluvium has accumulated to a depth of 7 km.

Faulting movements are accompanied by earthquakes and volcanic eruptions. Yet, while volcanic activity has not been experienced since the Pleistocene, earthquakes often occur due to the friction that develops between the plates. Tectonic activity occurs more on the sides of the Rift than in the Rift itself.

Intense earthquakes usually take place every 100-150 years. It seems that the last strong quake was that which leveled Safed and damaged Tiberias and Jerusalem in 1837. A smaller quake affected both sides of the Rift in 1927, recently estimated at 6.1-6.75 on the Richter scale. At the end of 1995, an earthquake of 6.2 on the Richter Scale shook Israel. Miraculously, only Eilat suffered minor damage.

Kinnarot Valley and the Bet She'an Valley

Kinnarot Valley consists of Lake Kinneret and its shores, several adjacent valleys and the surrounding slopes. The most prominent valleys are Bethsaida Valley on the lake's northeastern shore and Ginnosar Valley to the northwest. The valley along the Jordan River to the south, down to Nahal Tavor's merge with the Jordan, is also part of the Kinnarot Valley. It is known as Negev (south) Kinnarot.

The slopes on both sides of the lake are of Neogenian sedimentary rock and basalt.

Kinnarot Valley is part of the Syrian-African Rift. The present form of the Valley, is recent—only 12,000 years old. That is when the Lashon Lake—which ran from today's Kinneret to Hatzeva, south of the Dead Sea—dried up. The Dead Sea and Lake Kinneret were the remaining bodies of water.

Bet She'an Valley is actually a merge of the Jordan Valley, running north-south, with the Jezre'el and Harod Valleys, running northwest-southeast. North of the Bet

She'an, stand the gentle slopes of the Lower Galilee, and (further east) Negev Kinnarot. To its south hovers the Gilboa Ridge, which is the northeastern edge of Samaria and further east, the Central Jordan Valley.

The Bet She'an Valley widens into a fan shape as it approaches the Central Jordan Valley. It descends from -115 m. in the west to -275 m. close to the Jordan River. The descent has three natural terraces formed by the Lashon Lake. The town of Bet She'an at -160 m., lies near the scarp between two terraces. Here, being a former lake bottom, the soils are mostly carbonates. In the east, the soils are relics from the marl that was deposited in the Lashon Lake, and from Bet She'an westward, they are spring and lake deposits.

Part of the Bet She'an Valley, from Bet She'an northward, was covered by a lava flow during the Pleistocene. The lava blocked Nahal Harod that drains large parts of the valley and probably caused a lake to form west of town.

A series of small faults run along the valley's contact with the Gilboa Ridge. These faults release a number of springs whose waters originate from the Samaria aquifer. The bountiful springs begin as crystal clear pools and then feed small streams such as Nahals Hakibbutzim and Amal. Some of the springs are warm. Elsewhere in the valley, layer springs emerge upon marl.

Climate

The Syrian-African Rift

Its climate is considerably warmer than the hills west and east of it; for every drop of 100 m. in altitude, the annual average temperature decreases 0.67°C. Israel's highest temperatures have been measured in the Bet She'an Valley. On June 22, 1942, a temperature of 54° (129°F) was measured at Kibbutz Tirat Tzvi in the eastern Bet She'an Valley.

Rainfall is also substantially lower along the Rift compared to areas east and west of it. This causes the desert characteristics which are prevalent in southern Israel to creep north up the Rift, all the way to the slopes of the Golan.

Kinnarot Valley

At -200 m., Kinnarot Valley is the northern-most section of the Syrian-African Rift below sea level; high barometric pressure prevails. Air, descending 500-1000 m. from the surrounding ridges into the valley, is compressed and warmed by friction. Thus temperatures are high during most of the year, averaging at 22.2° (72°F). August's mean is 31° (87°F). Lake Kinneret mitigates winter temperatures; the January mean does not drop below 14° (57°F).

Lake Kinneret creates a breeze circulation of its own; during the late hours of the night, especially in summer, weak winds blow from the shores toward the lake's center. In the morning the direction is reversed. In the early afternoon, the stronger breeze from the Mediterranean overrides the local microclimate: compressed in its descent into the valley, it increases the oppressive heat and dryness. Since it hits the eastern shore more sharply, there is a temperature difference between the eastern and western shores causing strong winds which kick up high waves; in the west they cause swimmers to be swept into the lake, in the east they create discomfort.

Violent winter winds trapped in the Kinnarot Valley also raise high waves and create thunder storms with torrential rain. In general, the region is very sunny. The annual average of 350-500 mm. of precipitation often arrives in short, concentrated showers, so there are never more than 50 rainy days per year.

Humidity averages approximately 65%.

Bet She'an Valley

Although topographically lower than the Kinnarot Valley and south of it, the Bet She'an has a continental climate: very hot summers and moderate winters (January averages 13°/55°F). On clear winter nights, cold air rolls down, dropping temperatures close to freezing. On these winter mornings, a sheet of fog and dew gracefully blanket the valley. This excludes banana cultivation but permits date palms.

Annual rainfall is only 350 mm. It is quite capricious, so drought is common. Relative humidity is low and dewfall sparse. Since the 1950s, dew has been on a rise, possibly because of the installation of fish ponds.

Vegetation

The Syrian-African Rift

The special climatic characteristics of the Syrian-African Rift have a pronounced effect upon the botany and zoology. In Israel, the Rift has four phytogeographic zones:

1) The Mediterranean Zone begins north of the southern tip of Lake Kinneret.

2) The Irano-Turanian Zone lies along the Central Jordan Valley and overlaps with the Mediterranean Zone in the north. In the Lower Jordan Valley this zone overlaps the Saharo-Arabian Zone.

3) Saharo-Arabian species dominate south of the northern tip of the Dead Sea, with enclaves of Sudanian species (mainly around oases).

4) Sudanian species dominate near Eilat, mixed with Saharo-Arabian species.

Kinnarot Valley and the Bet She'an Valley

Both regions have been intensely influenced by humans. Subsequently, its flora is meager. Bethsaida Valley in northeast Kinnarot Valley, is an exception.

Kinnarot Valley contains Irano-Turanian flora despite its mild winter. Tall grasses and perennials sprout every winter and brown and wilt with summer. The hot, dry summer yields no growth away from the lake. Jujube and white acacia are occasionally found upon the slopes. Tabor oak and wild almond trees are found here, just like in the Lower Galilee. There are also small pockets of Mediterranean vegetation, such as the calycotome, thorny burnet and marjoram.

Three plant associations line Lake Kinneret's shores: the common reed, chaste tree and *Myriophyllum spicatum*. The common reed often grows alone in shallow waters with clayish bottoms. The chaste tree association is common along the gravel northern shores of Lake Kinneret. Tamarisk, oleander and willow accompany it. The *Myriophyllum spicatum* was common along the lake's shores until the 1960s. The intense lake shore development and the increase in bathers, along with the fluctuations of the lake level, has surrendered the fern-like plant to sewage sites.

Bet She'an Valley has very few enclaves of natural vegetation. Even the stream banks have been manipulated. People have diverted water, planted eucalyptus trees and grown crops right along the stream banks. Nonetheless, the region is unique, for all four of Israel's phytogeographic zones meet here. The Sudanese Egyptian balanites tree reaches its most northern point along the Rift by Kefar Rupin. Sudanese white acacia is found here. The open fields are covered with small, scraggly mezquit bushes from the acacia family. Roadsides are often lined with mallow. Lone jujube trees shade field sides.

Wildlife

The Syrian-African Rift

Zoographic regions tend to resemble vegetation regions, in their extent and, to a certain degree, their borders. The blurred and often transient character of these borders is strikingly demonstrated along the Syrian-African Rift due to anthropological and geographical phenomena, such as the connection and disconnection of the Rift to the Mediterranean Sea, volcanic eruptions, climate change, etc. A series of Pliocene sea invasions most affected aquatic animals. It led to an abundance of new species along the Rift. After the invasions terminated, some species died and some survived in specific enclaves. Others adapted to their changing surroundings and became new (endemic) species.

Kinnarot Valley and the Bet She'an Valley

The strong human impact upon the region is least felt by migrating birds. The birds migrate between the three continents, using the Syrian-African Rift as a detour around large bodies of water such as the Mediterranean Sea. Flying along the Rift suits the physical characteristics of many birds. Rising hot air currents (thermals) enable them to soar. Over one million birds of prey have been counted migrating along the Rift, via Eilat, in a single season.

Surprisingly, Lake Kinneret does not attract many waterbirds. Grebes, ducks, gulls and the pied kingfisher are about the only ones seen. The surrounding environs hold many land birds, especially around the Ginnosar and Bethsaida Valleys and their tributaries. Black francolin, little swift, long-billed pipit, blue rock thrush and the great grey shrike are common species.

Many birds migrating through the Rift stop to rest and feed at the fishponds and pools of the Bet She'an Valley. Flocks of white storks are a common sight. In spring, up to ten ospreys can be seen standing together in the open fields, between excursions to the fishponds.

Human Involvement

Kinnarot Valley

Abundant water and fish, a rare phenomena in the Middle East, have attracted people to Lake Kinneret in its different phases since prehistory. Most of the prehistoric remains have been found in Negev Kinnarot. Here, archaeologists have uncovered Israel's most ancient of finds, by Tel Ubeidiya (see Hike 18, 'Mitzpe Ela and Nahal Yavne'el'). A number of Neolithic remains have been found, such as at Hamadia and Hurbat Minha—first evidence of permanent settlement.

The region became more popular during the Chalcolithic and Bronze periods, when Tel Yerah was a city of close to 10,000. Then the region's population declined for hundreds of years. Settlement picked up only in the Persian-Helle-nistic times, accelerating during the Second Temple period. Tiberias was established and the Romans built water systems sustaining settlement on both sides of Lake Kinneret. Many events described in the New Testament took place on the shores of Lake Kinneret, also known as the Sea of Galilee.

During the Moslem period, in contrast to other parts of Israel, the lake shores continued to develop, for they were crossroads to Moslem regions in the east.

The Crusaders brought on an agricultural regression, causing a slow but steady, population decrease. The Mamelukes operated a postal route through Kinnarot Valley. This slowly began to bring in new residents. The pattern ceased when the Ottoman Empire lost control over Bedouin tribes which raided the region, wreaking havoc and destruction.

At the beginning of the 20th century, Jewish settlement began by the southern shores and slopes of the Kinneret. The first communal settlement was established in 1910 on the lands of Um Juni. The ten men and two women named the settlement Degany, after the five cereals (*dagan*) which grow in the region. Malaria, Arab attacks, drought and diseases made the going tough.

Jewish settlement began to prosper following WWI. In 1932, a dam was built at the head of the Jordan where it leaves Lake Kinneret (today's bridge on Road 90). This was done in order to control discharge for the hydroelectric plant, Naharayim, 15 km. downstream at the merger with Yarmuk River. In 1948, Jordan destroyed the plant and left the dam neglected. In 1963, with the opening of the National Water Carrier, the dam turned Lake Kinneret into Israel's national reservoir.

Bet She'an Valley

At the point of the Syrian-African Rift's largest ramification, the Bet She'an Valley's function in human history and settlement is explained. The Jezre'el-Harod-Bet She'an Valley are a corridor connecting the Mediterranean Coast with the Rift. As the most comfortable route, it was traversed throughout the centuries by travelers heading from Egypt towards Mesopotamia, Anatolia Turkey and Lebanon.

Throughout history, many battles took place in the vicinity of Bet She'an. These include Biblical battles, such as the one between Gideon and the Midianites (Judges 7-8) and between Saul and the Philistines (I Samuel 31). Many others were fought west of Bet She'an in the Harod and Jezre'el Valleys.

East of Bet She'an are a number of shallow sections of the Jordan River. These parts, known as *ma'abarot* (crossings), have been used throughout time for crossing the Jordan. The *ma'abarot* are often mentioned in the Bible (Judges 12:5). Romans and Mamelukes built bridges over a number of them. Today, Israel's border runs along the Jordan and the crossings are occasionally used by smugglers and terrorists.

Bet She'an, founded in the 4th millennium B.C.E., accelerated agricultural development. Thousands of years earlier, the valley was frequented by nomads and hunters. During the Israelite period, the tribes were unsuccessful at first in conquering the strong Canaanite cities in the valleys. By the time of King Solomon (960 B.C.E.), Bet She'an was one of his governorships.

Eventually, Israelite Bet She'an dwindled, as Megiddo and Jezre'el further west became commercial centers. Nevertheless, the valleys were still known as fertile enclaves and were settled by Babylonian Jews returning to Israel. During Hasmonean times the region grew in importance, peaking during the Roman-Byzantine period.

The Talmud often mentions Bet She'an; Raish Lakish of the third century says: "(The) Garden of Eden, if it is in Israel—opens at Bet She'an" (Eruvin 19a). In those days, linen was the bumper crop. In 421, the town became the capital of northern Israel.

Following the Moslem conquest, the region declined after an initial production boom of sugar cane, rice, indigo and dates. Bet She'an became a Crusader feudal estate during the years 1172-1183. In 1183 it was captured by Saladin. In 1268 it was destroyed by the Crusaders defending themselves against the Mamelukes.

From then until the 19th century, the whole region was neglected by all but Bedouin tribes. Their herds decimated the remaining forests and fields. Passageway through the Bet She'an Valley involved protection money paid to the Bedouins. The only Turkish achievement in the region was the Valley Railroad, part of the Haifa-Damascus line. It ran through the Jezre'el-Harod-Bet She'an Valley heading north through Negev Kinnarot and then up along Yarmuk River. It was finished in 1912. Remnants of the railroad can be seen upon an embankment west of and parallel to Road 90 north of Bet She'an.

Jewish settlement began during the violent Arab revolt against the British and Jews in 1936-1939. Kibbutz Nir David was established in 1936 as a "fort and tower" settlement. In 1937 a chain of settlements sprang up on land bought by the Jewish National Fund from Arabs who had recently received land from the British. Since 1948, fishponds and date groves have been introduced here. Cotton and sugar beet have also been successful.

Water

Kinnarot Valley and Bet She'an Valley are one of Israel's most water-rich regions. Here lies Lake Kinneret, one of the few lakes in the Middle East. South of Lake Kinneret, the Yarmuk River, draining large sections of Jordan and Syria, flows into the Jordan River. Furthermore, as part of the Syrian-African Rift, the region drains many perennial streams and has many abundant springs. It is no wonder that people consider the Jordan River south of Lake Kinneret to be one of the possible locations of the Garden of Eden.

Lake Kinneret's area is 168 sq. km. It holds 4 billion cubits of water and has a drainage basin of 2,735 sq. km. By Western standards, its dimensions are nothing extraordinary. Its main source is the Jordan River, although 15 other streams drain into it. The name Kinneret is believed to be from the word *kinor*, the biblical harp, similar to the lake's shape.

Since the 1960s, Lake Kinneret has been Israel's national reservoir. From its northwest corner, water is pumped to the center and southern parts of the country via the National Water Carrier. In order to control water input and output, the lake has a "red line" of maximum and minimum capacity. If the level surpasses the upper red line of -204 m., beaches and the promenade of Tiberias will be flooded. If the lake falls below the lower red line at -209 m., it is possible that saline springs would be released, causing water-quality damage. Altogether, 600 million cubits can be stored, about 30% of Israel's current annual consumption.

The region's aquatic importance extends to thermal mineral springs—nearly all of Israel's emerge along the Syrian-African Rift. The Hot Baths of Tiberias are the regional representitives. These springs are defined as fault springs rising through rock crevices from great depth. The deeper the water originates, the warmer it tends to be. The rising water becomes enriched along the way with dissolved sulfur, magnesia, bromine, iodine and other salts.

In the Bet She'an Valley, some springs are mildly warm but none are truly hot springs. Because they are relatively salty, Israel has built a purification plant producing irrigation water for agriculture. A high underground water table exists in 13% of the valley, only a meter below the surface. The springs in the eastern section of the valley emerge off this water.

A large proportion of the spring water was not channeled before this century, creating extensive marshes along the slow flow, eastward to the Jordan. The swamps were challenged by the Jewish settlers who arrived in the 1940s. At first they thought that fishponds could solve the "problem." Later, they built channels to divert the swamp waters to the Jordan. Today's drainage and water purification system, which has sharply affected the landscape, is a result of a 1968 plan.

Hiking in the Kinnarot Valley and Bet She'an Valley

The valleys, rich in springs and streams, make it an ideal place for water-lovers. There are many water attractions and sites beyond the hiking routes described.

The region is less than 3 hours by car from the center of Israel. Access to the Kinnarot Valley from the north or south is via Road 90, along the Jordan Valley. Coming from the west, three regional roads drop to the shores of Lake Kinneret: Road 757 from Kefar Tavor, north of Afula; Road 77 from Golani Junction; and Road 807 from Tzalmon Junction. These three roads all come off Road 65 that runs from the town of Afula through the eastern Lower Galilee. Five roads also descend from the Golan Heights to the Kinnarot Valley.

Access to the Bet She'an Valley is via two main roads: Roads 90 and 71 connect Afula with Bet She'an. Road 669 runs between some of the settlements of the Bet She'an Valley, and connects to Bet She'an and Road 90.

Public transportation is available from the Tiberias and Bet She'an central bus station Both stations have many connections to the cities of Israel.

The intense summer heat makes water-walking great fun. Serious hiking outside of water is outstanding in the winter and early spring when the slopes are a pastoral green and the sun is kind. In both cases, drinking water is always necessary for a safe hike. The waterscapes of the region are heavily visited by all types. Upon immersion it is wise to don a pair of sandals or used shoes.

Swimming in Lake Kinneret is not advisable after 3 p.m. due to strong winds. Fishing can be fun but do not expect big fish (the large type of tilapia feed on plankton).

The scenic Gilboa Ridge, climbing 500 m. above the southern Bet She'an Valley is dissected with marked hiking trails and dirt roads.

Important Phone Numbers (area code 06)

S.P.N.I. Field Study Centers and Information

Alon Tavor F.S.C., by Kaduri School on Road 65:	06-766770, 767798
Kinnarot F.S.C. at Bet Gordon, Kibbutz Deganya Aleph, west of Tzemah Junction:	751088, 752340
Antiquities Authority, Afula:	527610
Tiberias Tourism Bureau, 8 Elhadaf:	20992

Safety Assistance

Police: 100
Lake Kinneret: 792444
Tiberias: 792444
Afula: 524444

Ambulance: 101
Tiberias: 790111, 798211
Tiberias Poriah Hospital: 798211
Afula: 593334

Sites Worth Visiting

Kinnarot Valley

Museums:

Bet Harofeh, Menehemiyya, 2.5 km. off Road 90, 6 km. south of Tzemah Junction.
Bet Gordon, Deganya Aleph, 1 km. west of Tzemah Junction.
Regional Prehistory Museum, Sha'ar Hagolan, 2 km. east of Road 90, 3 km. south
      of Tzemah Junction.
Bet Alon, Kibbutz Ginnosar, off Road 90, by kilometer post 423.

National Parks:

Kursi, Samar Junction, Road 82.
Capernahum, Road 87, 3 km. east of Capernahum Junction with Road 90.
Korazim, on Road 4277, 3 km. east of Road 90, north of Lake Kinneret.
Tiberias Hot Baths, Road 90, 2 km. south of Tiberias.
Park Hayarden, off Road 888, 1.5 km. north of Bethsaida Junction on Road 87.
Ein Sheva Churches, Road 87, 0.5 km. east of Capernahum Junction.
Yardenit, 0.5 km. off Road 90, along the road to Kibbutz Kinneret.
Mitzpe Gadot Memorial, Road 91, kilometer post 10 (in Golan).
Mishmar Hayarden, Road 91, kilometer post 7, by Mishmar Hayarden Junction.

Bet She'an Valley

National Parks:

Bet She'an, downtown Bet She'an.
Gan Hashlosha, off Road 669, by kilometer posts 6-7.
Bet Alfa Ancient Synagogue, Kibbutz Bet Alfa, Road 669.

Sites:

Maoz Ha'im Mosaic Floor, Kibbutz Maoz Ha'im, 5 km. east of Bet She'an.
Nir David Archaeological Museum, Kibbutz Nir David, Road 669.
Ein Hoga Park, off Road 90 by the Roman bridge, 2 km. north of Bet She'an.
Ein Moda, 2 km. on dirt road south of starting point for Hike 26.

Overnight Options

Indoors

Youth Hostels

Karei Deshe, off Road 90, by kilometer post 425-426.

Tiberias, by Road 90 downtown.

Poriah, on local road off Road 90, 2 km. south of Tiberias Hot Springs.

Kibbutz Guest Houses: Ginnosar, off Road 90 by kilometer post 423.

Eastern and western Kinneret beaches have numerous picnic sites which are good for camping. Eastern and northwestern Kinneret beaches offer overnight camping facilities (entrance fee).

Jordan Park (Park Hayarden), see Hike 22.
Olive Picnic Site, see Hike 23, 'Bethsaida Valley.'
Ein Hoga Park, off Road 90 by the Roman bridge, 2 km. north of Bet She'an.

Gas Stations

Kinnarot Valley

At Tzemah Junction, in Tiberias, and by Ginnosar, all on Road 90.

Bet She'an Valley

At Mehola, Sdeh Terumot, and Bet She'an, all on Road 90.

Looking south, down the Jordan River Canyon towards Lake Kinneret

Jordan River Canyon

*See map on
page 170*

Points of interest: *A rushing river between green vegetation, and steep basalt walls. The hike begins at a Crusader
fort.*

Length and nature of hike: Option 1: 1 kilometer, loop trip.
Option 2: 4 kilometers, loop trip.

Hiking time: Option 1: 1 hour. Option 2: 2-4 hours.

Preferred season: All year.

Suitable for: All.

Maps: Golan and Hermon hiking and touring map.

Special preparation: Clothes for a dip. In winter and spring
the strong currents make swimming dangerous!

Starting & ending point: Metzad Ateret by Gesher Benot
Ya'akov.

To reach starting point:

Arrival by private transportation: Gesher Benot Ya'akov (Bridge) crosses the
Jordan River and is part of Road 91, connecting Mahanayim Junction (near Rosh
Pina) on Road 90 to Nafah in Central Golan.

For traffic heading east, at the sharp curve on Road 91 before the bridge turn
south onto the gravel road (1). There is a sign. For vehicles coming from the
Golan, turn left at the T-junction, 300 m. after crossing the Jordan River, and at
the sharp curve, turn right onto the gravel road (1).

Arrival by public transportation: At the time of writing this book, no bus stops
at the starting point. It is possible, however, that buses heading from Mahanayim
Junction to the Golan via Gesher Benot Ya'akov will stop (if the bus driver is kindly
asked) at the sharp curve by the gravel road turnoff.

Geography

The Jordan River Canyon is geologically recent. Following the basaltic flow of the
Rosh Pina Sill which filled in the Syrian-African Rift and connected the Golan to
the Galilee hundreds of thousands of years ago, the Jordan River has cut into the
hard, dark rock in order to reach Lake Kinneret, which is at a lower elevation. Along
this 13-kilometer section, the Jordan descends 275 m. to Lake Kinneret, from
around 70 m. above sea level to -200 m.

This part of the Jordan is its most wild section. It is known in Hebrew as the
"mountainous Jordan." It is also part of Jordan Park (Park Hayarden) which
continues to the river's mouth at Lake Kinneret.

Until recently, the canyon has been well preserved due to the tough access to it, and the fact that it often was a border. The torrential waters are quite unclean as they drain the Hula Valley fishponds and agricultural fields. Annual average discharge is 560 million cubits, a third of Israel's annual consumption.

The hot climate beyond the shady river banks is intensified by the black basalt which absorb solar rays. Small layer springs emerge along the slopes between layers of ancient (fossilized) clayish soil.

Plants and animals

Smyrna or White-Breasted Kingfisher (*Halcyon smyrnensis*): This colorful bird can be easily distinguished by its long, pointed red bill which stands out from its brown and white body and its red legs. When flying, the bird flashes blue wings and a tail with a turquoise tint. Its wingspan is around 40 cm. and its body length about 30 cm.

The kingfisher is found between southwestern Turkey and the Philippines. In Israel the bird has expanded its distribution considerably due to the development of artificial bodies of water in the last 50 years. In the 1930s, it bred only in the Kinnarot and Jordan Valley. Today it can be found in the Arava and also along the coast, near various bodies of water. It does not migrate.

Most of the day the Smyrna kingfisher perches at a fixed vantage point in its territory, uttering high-pitched and trilling calls resembling laughter. It repeats the very loud, two-second call at short intervals. The call is intensified during spring-time, mating and whenever threatened. When changing vantage points the bird makes a different call in flight.

The bird is useful to humans as it devours hordes of mole-crickets, an agricultural nuisance. Crabs, beetles, tadpoles, frogs, amphibians, reptiles and even small birds and partridge chicks are also on the menu.

Nesting begins at the end of March when both partners dig a one-meter horizontal hole in an earth wall, usually 1.5-2 m. above ground level and 7 cm. wide at the opening. The nesting chamber is larger, about 15 cm. wide. Nests can easily be identified by remnants of food and footprints at the opening. After the 4-6 eggs hatch, the young stay home for nearly a month. After this time, the accumulated dung and food remains emit a pungent odor from the nesting hole.

History

Like many canyons, the Jordan River Canyon was never a core for historical events. There were a few flour mills which utilized the strong river flow. Along the springs that emerge in the canyon slopes, small settlements were established during different periods. More consistently, the canyon has been an international border line. It divided the Crusaders from the Moslems, the French from the British prior to 1948, and Israel from Syria until 1967.

People have built expansive settlements at both ends of the canyon, by Gesher Benot Ya'akov and by the Jordan River delta (part of the Bethsaida Valley).

Gesher Benot Ya'akov has for 5,000 years been an important crossing of the Jordan, since it was the only feasible crossing place between Banias and Lake Kinneret. Here ran the ancient route between Egypt and Damascus. The site itself is not mentioned before Crusader times. Today, extensive archaeological digs are taking place by the bridge, exposing rich prehistoric remains.

The current bridge is Israeli. Many bridges have been built and destroyed here. During Turkish renovation of the Mameluke bridge in 1887, a Napoleonic cannon was found, marking the northernmost spot he reached in Israel. In 1934 the British constructed a new bridge and dynamited the old one. The new bridge was blown up by Palmach sappers on the "Night of the Bridges" in June, 1946. The British rebuilt the bridge on its cement pillars.

The Palmach destroyed it again two years later in order to slow the Syrian invasion. The Syrians nevertheless managed to cross the river with two brigades and capture the village of Mishmar Hayarden. Since then, the bridge has been rebuilt. The bridge and Road 91 were crucial during the Yom Kippur War; military reinforcements to the Golan were led along the road as Syrian forces reached Nafah, only 10 km. east of the bridge.

The Jordan River Canyon is unique in its large quantities of perennial water which drop 270 m. along its short course. Many engineering plans have focused these two factors. The National Water Carrier was at first planned to draw from the canyon's headwaters, thus drying the canyon. In the 1970s, the Almagor Project proposed a canal to divert the water to a reservoir in the Almagor region above Jordan Park and there to release it into the Kinnarot Valley through a hydroelectric complex. The Society for Protection of Nature organized public protest against the plan and succeeded in postponing it. In 1985 Kibbutz Kefar Hanasee proposed a small-scale operation based on the Almagor Project, in order to create electricity for themselves. The S.P.N.I. launched one of their most aggressive campaigns against the proposal, arguing that local electricity production is not worth disturbing a natural treasure, which has no counterpart in Israel. During demonstrations, nature lovers chained themselves to tractors, but in vain. S.P.N.I.'s dedicated supervision at least kept environmental damage to a minimum.

Edward Robinson traveled in Palestine in the years 1838 and 1852 and published his journal under the title, *Biblical Researches in Palestine* (1856). He writes of the region:

> The portion of the Jordan between the lake of Tiberias and that of el-Huleh, was to us a matter of no little interest; and becomes perhaps the more important, in connection with the varying and inconsistent accounts of the elevation between the two lakes. Yet I am not aware that any traveler except Pococke had then passed along this part of the river... Schubert speaks also of the rapid current and gives the breadth at about eighty feet, the depth being about four feet... We naturally felt a strong desire to pass up through this valley; but our muleteers were averse to it, and the Arabs described the path as neglected and difficult, on account of the many thorny shrubs.

Tristram, traveling a few years later, also saw the canyon:

> The lake Huleh at the south end contracts to a point and concentrates its waters in a dull heavy rush into the narrow bed of the Jordan, which rapidly

pours a deep impetuous stream between green treeless banks to the Sea of Galilee. But the whole plains, the western side of which is here four miles wide, is fully tilled and this was the height of the harvest season.

Site description

Gesher Benot Ya'akov: "Bridge of Jacob's Daughters." Since Jacob had only one daughter, the name is most likely from the Crusader period. The bridge toll helped support the St. James (in Hebrew, Jacob) Convent in Safed.

Stories tell of Jacob crossing the Jordan here, hearing the news of the death of his favorite son Joseph and grieving by the bridge. This legend corresponds to the Moslem tradition that the cistern where Joseph's brothers threw him is a few kilometers south of Rosh Pina (Dotan, where Joseph was abandoned, is actually in northern Samaria). Another story tells of Jacob's daughters entering western Israel via the bridge, but again, the Bible mentions only one daughter.

Many stories and historical events are located at this site.

Metzad Ateret: Remnants of a Crusader fort from 1179. The site is a small tel built on remains from the Hellinistic period and possibly from Roman times. The fort offered protection from Moslems who were positioned east of the Jordan. The Templar order of knights from Safed constructed the fort in six months and called it Chastellet. Before they had even finished construction, Saladin recognized the fort's strategic value. It was a barrier against Moslem attacks into northern Israel and a point of departure for Crusader attacks in the opposite direction. Saladin tried unsuccessfully to buy the property for 100,000 gold dinars.

The fort held over 1,000 men, who were prepared for a long siege. After three months, Saladin's men set about capturing it. In five days they dug a tunnel beneath Chastellet's only tower. They burned its supporting beams. When it collapsed, they attacked. They slaughtered the Crusaders and demolished the fort.

Recent archaeological digs have revealed surprising finds due to the fact that the fortress had stood for only 11 months. The structure, 15x70 m., was essentially a double wall, eight meters high. Parts of the wall are still fully intact, disproving the Moslem report that the fort was totally ruined. The inner wall is of limestone plates brought from the Galilee. It is unusual to have only one tower; this is further evidence that the Crusaders were pressed for time.

The main gate is on the southern side—two doors of metal-plated wood locked inside with a beam. There was also a secret exit in the east, to the river. A skeleton was found in this passageway.

This river front was supposed to protect the eastern side; moats ran along the northern and southern walls. However, historical documents mention that the fort was taken from the southeast. Excavations there have uncovered 200 iron arrowheads, spearheads, hatchets, axes and other weapons.

Inside Chastellet, archaeologists exposed a series of vaults. These included storage rooms, a flour mill and quarters for horses and men. They also found a knight's personal equipment (dagger, arrowheads and whetstone).

A plane tree branch upon the Jordan

North of the fort, rare Nazareth irises bloom in March. The iris is black and white with dark spots. It is possible that a Moslem cemetery was once here and the flowers were planted for it.

Tahanat Ateret: A ruined flour grinding mill (*tahana*) right next to the Cataraft rafting center. The mill is a bit different than the usual; it is powered by slide rather than by chimney. Though a slide is less efficient, the large quantity of water flowing here did the job. The mill is one of the largest in Israel—it has four slides and many mills. The water arrived via a riverside channel which followed the riverside trail.

Siara Mill: Located at the merger of the Jordan River with Nahal Rosh Pina. Clerks of Baron de Rothschild purchased it and leased it to the inhabitants of Mishmar Hayarden (founded in 1890). In the 1930s, a unique pumping device supplied them with water. Arabs sabotaged the mill during the 1936 riots and destroyed it in 1948.

The name comes from the nearby tomb of Sheikh Ibrahim e-Sir. The mill structure is visible from afar by the clump of tall eucalyptus trees. Remnants of the water channel are still intact.

To begin hike:

Follow the red-marked dirt road south. Pass a graveyard for Syrian soldiers and immediately take a left down to the Cataraft parking lot (2). Two seperate loop trips begin here:

Option 1: Leave the parking lot on the dirt road to the east (not down to the river). Leave it to the north and ascend on a trail to Metzad Ateret (3). Enter the fort through the remains of its gate. Explore the flat top. The elevation of the hill above its surroundings is artificial. Part of the impressive eastern wall can be seen.

Descend north from the fort on a clear black-marked path. Along the descent, pass a lone terebinth tree. Note the moat along the northern slope. The trail winds through an open field. Two hundred meters from the fort, a dirt road arrives from the west. Take a right (east) and descend toward the Jordan River. The wide trail ends above the river; there is no descent to the water! On your left stands a plane tree, easily recognized by its palm-shaped leaves.

Go right, following the black mark. Note the chiseled rock at trail level. This was possibly the site of the Crusader-era bridge over the Jordan. Heading along the trail to the south, there are a number of possible descents to the river. After 200 m., by an open area, a dirt road ascends to Metzad Ateret. A large berry tree marks the spot. Here, the trail is flooded during rainy periods.

Continue west to Tahanat Ateret (4). To finish option 1, go right for 100 m. on the dirt road back to the parking lot (2).

Option 2: Across the road, there is a modern, red pumping station and the rafting office. A dam is at a sharp curve in the river where the canyon begins, and is the cause of the widening of the river here. The dam was built in the 1950s for the National Water Carrier project. Military and political Syrian involvement halted the development. Today, a channel diverts water to the Kefar Hanasee power plant reservoir.

From here, traverse the channel and head along the gravel road. After 200 m., descend left on a clear trail to the riverbank (the gravel road you just left runs parallel to the trail along the river). Where the curve of the river straightens out, across the stream stands the "Star of the Morning Mill."

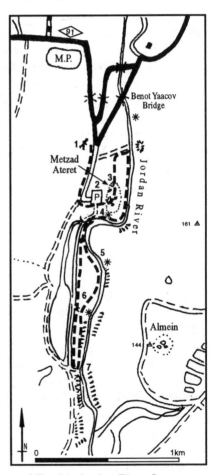

Continue along the Jordan on the marked trail. Four main plants line the banks: reed, willow, oleander and purple loosestrife. Other common plants are grapevine, fig, poplar and plane.

Half a kilometer from the dam, in a grove of eucalyptus trees, reach Siara Mill (6). The trail splits into two, meets after 50 m. and crosses Nahal Rosh Pina. The stream is lined with bramble which enjoy the trickle of spring water. Half a kilometer downstream, a steep basalt cliff blocks the trail (7). Follow the steep ascent, lined with wire railings, up to the gravel road.

To the left (south), is a nice lookout spot, known as jujube lookout. Look west to see the slopes of Ramat Korazim and south for the deepening Jordan Canyon. To the east are the slopes of the Golan. Jujube lookout is a good spot to note the main components of the slope vegetation—mainly jujube with almond trees in rocky sections.

Head back (north) on the gravel road, along the reservoir, to the parking lot (2).

Hike 21, Jordan River Canyon

22 Jordan Park

See map on page 175

Points of interest: *The beginning of the Jordan River delta. Views, vegetation, water channels and water mills, plus a recreation park with facilities.*

Length and nature of hike: Option 1: 1 kilometer, loop trip. Option 2: 500 meters, loop trip.

Hiking time: Option 1: 1-2 hours. Option 2: 1 hour.

Preferred season: All year.

Suitable for: All.

Maps: Golan and Hermon hiking and touring map.

Special preparation: Swimsuit. Park entrance fee.

Starting & ending point: Restaurant in Jordan Park.

To reach starting point:

Arrival by private transportation: At Bethsaida Junction on Road 87 (by kilometer post 10) head north onto Road 888. After 1.5 km., turn left at the orange sign (1) onto a poorly paved road towards Jordan Park. After the entrance booth continue straight (south) on wide gravel road. Four hundred meters from the booth, the road undiscernibly descends into the Kinnarot Valley. Go right and park by the restaurant (2).

Arrival by public transportation: Take bus from Tiberias central bus station to the village of Had-Ness. Get off at the turnoff to Jordan Park (in Hebrew, Park Hayarden) (1). Follow directions by foot as described in "Arrival by private transportation."

Geography

The famous historical geographer G. A. Smith called the Jordan "the river most spoken about by mankind" as the Jordan is mentioned numerously in the Bible, New Testament and travelers diaries. Its geography is certainly not the most researched.

The hikable part of Jordan Park is part of the Jordan River delta. The delta can be divided into three. Its upper part is from the opening of the Jordan River Canyon by Gesher Hadodot to A-Tawahin, by the hikes' starting point. Large boulders are deposited here, due to the decrease in the waters' energy. The river bed often changes here. The central part is roughly between A-Tawahin and Gesher Arik on Road 87. Here, small sediments are deposited and the river runs in a number of branches.

South of Gesher Arik, the Jordan merges with Lake Kinneret forming a delta. The exact location depends on the lake's level. Here, only small clay particles settle, creating mud flats. Since its death in the 1950s, Lake Hula has failed to serve as a sedimentation bowl for Lake Kinneret, and the sediments running down the Jordan have increased six-fold; from 20,000 annual tons to 120,000 tons. The increased quantity of sediment settles by the mouth of the Jordan. This has caused the delta to increase its length by one kilometer.

In contrast to the upper and lower parts of the delta, the section along the two walks has not undergone serious landscape change in the past 40 years.

Plants and animals

Yellow-Vented Bulbul (*Pycnootus xanthopygos*): H. B. Tristram identified the bird with verse 12 of Psalm 104, which reads: "By them shall the fowls of heaven have their habitation, which sing along the branches." Tristram writes:

> In this passage ... speaking of the trees which overhang the water courses ... the singing of the different species...is perhaps pointed to, and especially the bulbul and nightingale, both of which throng the trees that fringe the Jordan, and abound in all the wooded valleys, filling the air in early spring with the rich cadence of their notes.

The bird is easily distinguishable. Its head, cheeks, throat and tail are black. The undertail is bright yellow.

It is common throughout the Middle East. It is often seen in the parks and gardens of towns and villages. In Israel, it can be found anywhere in which bushes and trees are found. Bulbuls rarely visit cultivated fields.

The species feeds on fruit and insects. It devours small fruits and nibbles others, such as dates, pears and tomatoes, causing great damage to agriculture. Sometimes hundreds of young birds gather together and attack one plantation or orchard. They are therefore not protected by law. It also feeds on leaves and petals of some flowers like the iris. In winter, when supply is short, it will eat snails and even carrion.

The bulbul has a very varied vocal range. Its territorial song between March and April, which begins before sunrise, consists of a series of fluty notes arranged in four to six syllables, constantly separated. It also imitates its neighbor, the blackbird. An approach of humans and when partners meet are other times of song.

The birds live in pairs (not necessarily a male and female). Their territory, which they guard and defend vigorously, is quite small—only a few hundred square meters—and usually not large enough to provide all their food.

Nesting begins in March, peaks in late spring and ends in mid-August, following three broods. The female builds the nest 1-2.5 m. above ground in a seclusion among thin branches. She lays two to four eggs, whitish-lilac in color and speckled in purple-brown. The female incubates but leaves the nest sporadically in search of food.

History

This part of the Jordan Park was ideal for human settlement because the river supplies water year-round. In the A-Tawahin area, suspended sediment settles in flood plains, creating fertile earth. The decrease of the river's energy encourages the construction of water channels. To prevent them from being wiped out during flooding, they are erected along the contact of the slope and valley.

By A-Tawahin the valley widens to the east, leaving elevated areas to the east and to the north. The topography easily accommodated at least two ancient settlements right above A-Tawahin: Hurbat Daka to the north and Tel el-Amaria (also known as Et-Tell and Hurbat Betaiha) to the east. The water channels and mills of A-Tawahin are a result of many stages of renovation and reconstruction. It seems that some of them are from Talmudic times, a fact that correlates with historical and archaeological evidence regarding Hurbat Betaiha. Most of what is seen today is part of the small Arab settlement which began in the Middle Ages. A few buildings from this period topped Hurbat Betaiha.

Oleander and pools at Jordan Park

At the time of this writing, archaeological digs were taking place at Hurbat Betaiha. The Antiquities Authority plans to renovate the site. Hurbat Betaiha has just been identified as the ancient Jewish village of Bethsaida. It is a large tel of 80 dunams, standing 25 m. above its surroundings. It was first established during the Early Bronze when a sturdy wall encircled the town. Rich Roman remains have been found among the ruins, including fishing equipment. This find points toward the fact that previously Lake Kinneret was at a higher level than today, its shores reaching the village. The Jewish village of Bethsaida is mentioned numerously in the New Testament. The messengers Patrus and Andrianus were born here. At Bethsaida, according to Christian belief, Jesus performed a number of miracles, such as feeding 5,000 men with 5 loaves of bread and 2 fish.

Herod Phillip made Bethsaida his secondary capital and called it Julias, after Caesar Augustus's daughter (his capital was at Banias—Caesarea of Phillip). Josephus mentions that Julias is where Argrippa confronted his forces. Josephus blames his failure in the fact that his horse fell into a swamp, knocking him off and injuring him.

Midrash Raba on the Song of Songs tells of a couple from Bethsaida. The husband wanted to leave his wife due to fertility problems. The couple consulted Rabbi Shimon bar Yohai (Rashbi) who instructed them to hold a party. During the party the woman asked her husband what items she should take to her new home. He replied—take your most valuable possession. She intoxicated him, had him carried home and they made up. Rashbi prayed for them and she later gave birth.

Between 1948 and 1967, Syrian troops held fort at Hurbat Betaiha. They often advanced and opened fire on Israelis across the Jordan. In 1951, Syrians crossed the border and tried to establish positions atop the ridge where Almagor stands today. The Israel Defense Forces retaliated, suffering dozens of casualties. Almagor was established in 1961, manned by NAHAL soldiers. A couple of them where shot by Syrians from across the river. Later, civilian settlers moved to Almagor and at least five of them found their death on mines laid at night by infiltrating Syrians. The Six Day War brought an end to Syrian harassment in the region.

For more information, see Hike 23, 'Bethsaida Valley.'

Site description

Jordan Park (Park Hayarden): A park of 20,000 dunams, beginning at Gesher Benot Ya'akov. It is 20 km. long and includes the Jordan River Canyon, its slopes and the delta of the river. Today, the developed part of the park is at the delta of the Jordan River in the Kinnarot Valley. The park was organized by the Jewish National Fund and the Nature Reserves Authority and has been under smalls-cale development since 1975. Today the J.N.F. still owns it, but allows a private manager to run it. They have recently built a gravel road from Gesher Benot Ya'akov to the Jordan River delta.

At the delta's eastern side, (along the hike route) there are over 12 flour mills. This is the largest concentration of water-powered mills in the country. The cluster is known by its Arabic name, A-Tawahin—The Mills. Local Arabs grew pomegranates, figs, grapes, olives, sycamores and date palms. They also planted eucalyptus trees. They fled in 1967, following the Six Day War.

To begin hike:

From the restaurant, head on the wide trail lined with basalt rock through the open field for 150 m. to A-Tawahin, adorned by a few palm trees (3). Looking back (east), stands Hurbat Betaiha, beyond the retaurant. From here begin both options:

Option 1 (blue arrow route): Cross the pools and head north (right) along the complex. Cross over the active aqueduct and reach a dirt road running east-west. Go left (west). After 50 m., a road ascends to the right. Continue straight for 35 m. and reach a V-intersection. Take the right option, following the blue arrow. Here, cross a gate and head uphill (north) on a dirt road. The basalt slope is covered with jujube trees and hyraxes live among the basalt rock piles. Pass a neglected olive plantation.

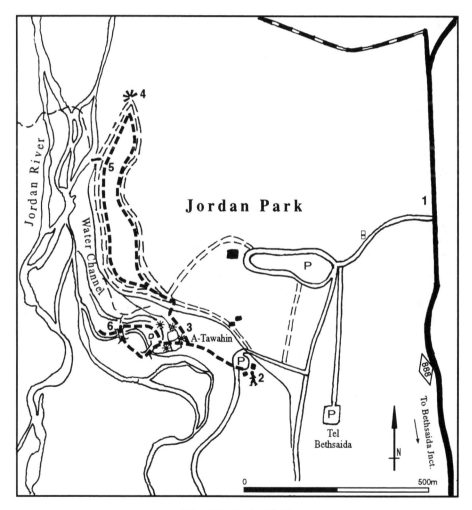

Hike 22, Jordan Park

After 400 m. reach an intersection. Go left following the blue arrow. On your right was a Syrian bunker until 1967. Do not stray from the path—there is an opinion that a few mines are still scattered in the area. Reach a viewpoint at an intersection (4). Across the way, atop the ridge, stand Moshavs Almagor and Karkom.

Look north to make out the opening of the Jordan River Canyon where the powerful winter floods cover vast parts of the upper valley. The annual floods deposit coarse gravel, making plant stability difficult. Below flows the Jordan River in a braided pattern, the only place in Israel where this phenomenon (common in glacier-fed rivers) is seen year-round. To the south is Lake Kinneret with Tiberias on its western shore and slope (Poriya Ridge).

Go left and descend on the dirt road toward the Jordan. The waters are surrounded with typical water vegetation: oleander, willow, bramble and reeds. In the valley cross a gate, and after 50 m. follow the blue arrow to the right, to the water channel (5). Take a left along the channel. (It is also possible to continue on the dirt road.) Along the way, note remnants of more channels. The white clam shells along the trail are evidence of water flow in the channel between the path and dirt road. As the path curves east, notice how the neglected channels crisscross. Here also stands a deserted water-powered flour mill. The loop trip ends by the bridge over the channel.

Option 2 (red arrow route): Begin by the J.N.F. sign (3). Here, the water is channeled out of the complex. A canopy of vegetation shades the short route which passes by numerous flour mills. This is a good place to get acquainted with the process of wheat grinding which was in practice until this century. Note the two channels; they end at chimneys which dropped the water onto the mill to turn the wheat grinds. The grinds were in the lower part of the structure, beyond the arched entrance.

The short loop trip section begins by a bridge and picnic bench. Cross over the bridge and continue into a thicket of reeds. Here you cross over a branch of the Jordan running in the "wrong" direction (north)—it is most likely an artificial diversion ditch still intact. At the end of the bramble and reed tunnel, to the left, there is an open area along the stream beneath tall eucalyptus trees, a nice rest stop (6). From here, take the continuation of the red arrow trail back through a thicket and back to the picnic bench where the loop part ends. Return along the same trail.

23 Bethsaida Valley

*See map on
page 179*

Points of interest: *A peaceful stream of warm, waist-deep
water, packed with aquatic wildlife and shaded by water
vegetation.*
Length and nature of hike: 1 kilometer, loop trip.
Hiking time: 1-2 hours.
Preferred season: All year.
Suitable for: Swimmers only!
Maps: Golan and Hermon hiking and touring map.
Special preparation: Equipment and clothes for walking in
water. An innertube or water mattress is recommended.
Starting & ending point: Olive Picnic Site.

To reach starting point:

Arrival by private transportation: Turn west (left, when coming from the south)
off Road 92 (Kinneret eastern shore road) at Ma'ale Gamla Junction (1). Follow
the poorly paved road by banana plantations for 500 m. By a lone eucalyptus tree
at a T-intersection, go right onto the basalt cobble road lined with lone jujube trees,
(north) along a water pipe. After 1 km., turn left (there is a green sign) onto a gravel
road, between grape-entwined bramble and an open field. The low green bushes
growing along the road are mezquit. Nahal Daliyot is behind the brush on your
right. After 1 km., take a right at the V-intersection and immediately reach Olive
Picnic Site on your right (2). Park.

Arrival by public transportation: Take the bus from Tiberias to Ma'ale Gamla
Junction (it is often a long ride, possibly 90 minutes). Follow directions by foot as
described in "Arrival by private transportation."

Geography

Bethsaida Valley (*Betaiha* in Arabic) contains a lagoon waterscape, of no comparison in Israel. It is actually a delta of five streams flowing at close proximity into
the northeastern corner of Lake Kinneret. The streams are well known: Jordan
River, Nahal Meshushim, Nahal Yehudiya, Nahal Daliyot and Nahal Shefamnun.
(The mid-three are popular Central Golan hiking routes described in *A Guide to
Hiking in Israel with 40 selected one-day Hikes.*) The valley is 6 km. long and about
2.5 km. wide. Its width depends on the fluctuating lake shore. The valley sometimes floods after rainy winters. Its eastern border is the contour of -190 m.

Upon reaching Kinnarot Valley, the streams of Bethsaida spread into fifteen small
rivulets. Closer to the lake they unite into two main lagoons. The northern is the
Za'aki and the southern, the Majrasa. The region is a nature reserve of 8,400
dunams. The hike is along Nahal Daliyot, which runs into the Majrasa.

Plants and animals

Oleander (*Nerium oleander*): The oleander is a bush found along most of Israel's warm Mediterranean streams, and along the Syrian-African Rift north of the Arava. Its scientific name relates to its warm moist habitat and it resembles the olive (*olea*). It is also mentioned in the Talmud.

The tree-like bush grows up to 4 m. high. It has a branched trunk. The hard leaves are similar to olive leaves, in shape and color. Three sprout out of each joint. Both the leaves and stems contain a toxic milky substance. The aromatic flowers are pink and bloom in bunches.

Being a water plant in Mediterranean conditions, it is not dependent on winter rain to bloom and so blooms in the summer. Oleander-shaded streams turn into pink boulevards. In such streams there is no underbrush.

The toxic substance of the plant is harmful to animals and humans and thus it is not used for grazing. The substance has been found to help heart disease. The oleander's beauty has made it a popular public garden plant.

The wildlife in Bethsaida Valley is diverse. After the Six Day War, 12 new insects were defined by an Israeli scientist. While Syrian hunters cleared the valley of all mammals but the wild boar, since then dozens of types have found their way back. The reserve is a favorite breeding place for many fish and twenty-three types have been found. Until 1967 it was dangerous to fish the lagoons and the aquatic life boomed. Following the Six Day War, fishermen began to raid the region.

Lake Kinneret's waterfowl concentrates at Bethsaida. Winter bird watchers will see three types of gulls, nine types of ducks, four types of terns, seven types of sandpipers and many more. The open fields host the black francolin. Bethsaida is also a northern distribution line for a number of desert birds such as the sand partridge, the sandgrouse and the desert lark.

Jordan Tilapia (*Tilapia aurca*): Also known as St. Peter's fish. This plankton-eater grows up to 40 cm. In May when mating, the males turn deep blue and their fins turn red. The male digs a one-meter-wide hole in shallow water where the female deposits 400-1,000 eggs. After fertilization, the female takes the eggs into her mouth and fasts for a month. She spits them out and watches them during the last two weeks and during the first two weeks of life the young find refuge back in the mother's mouth.

The plate size fish is a delicacy. Today its popularity has decreased due to hybrids of the Jordan tilapia and another tilapia that are grown in fishponds.

History

History usually took place at the northern end of the Bethsaida Valley. A number of ruins stand there. Sir Lawrence Olifant observed in 1885 that human involvement succeeded in the region when people channeled the water and dried the marsh.

Before the Israelite period, people chose not to cope with the difficult marsh conditions. The region flourished only during Second Temple times, with villages of fishermen and farmers. The settlers did well. In the Jerusalem Talmud (Shekalim 6), Bethsaida, called Tzaidan, was visited by Raban Shimon ben Gamliel who received over 300 fish. The region is also mentioned in connection to its fowl.

The port of Julias is believed to be in Bethsaida, and the town is mentioned many times in the New Testament. Since Jesus cursed the Jewish settlers for not following him (Matthew 11:21), researchers surmise that the Jews of Bethsaida were pious. Here also is the site of the bread miracle (tradition inaccurately transferred the site to Ein Sheva (Tabgha) on Lake Kinneret's northwestern shore).

Jews from Crimea resettled Bethsaida in 1904. They chose the valley for its bounty in water and fertile land. The Kurdish-Moslem land-owner, "Mr. Bek," refused to sell but was willing to let them settle as tenant-farmers, paying one-third of the produce to him. They signed a nine-year agreement. This practice was already current among some Arab peasants and fishermen. Bek, residing in Damascus, hoped that the Jews would raise the land value. The Jews hoped that in time he would be willing to sell.

Sixteen highly motivated families moved into small shacks and Bek's house (Bet Habek) at the northern part of the valley and immediately planted eucalyptus trees and sowed vegetable gardens. Some fished.

After initial success, conditions worsened; in the winter the region flooded and the settlers were cut off. They became dependent on the Arab fishers to get to Tiberias to purchase rations. Malaria hit them, some died and many working hands were immobilized. Bek, who promised to build strong homes for the settlers, failed to stand by his word. The difficulties brought social disputes, eventually terminating the settlement in less than two years.

H.B. Tristram describes the region not long before the Jewish settlement.

> About two miles up was the ford to the "tell" of the ancient Bethsaida, not very deep, but across a rapid stream with muddy bottom. On a rising ground, a mile back from the river, stood, at the edge of a low spur from the northward, a miserable Ghawarineh village, worse than that of Er Riha, among heaps of shapeless stones,—the ancient Julias; but no traces of sarcophagi or carved stones were to be seen, probably because the ancient buildings had all been constructed of the hard black basalt (hammer-dressed), of which the heaps were composed.

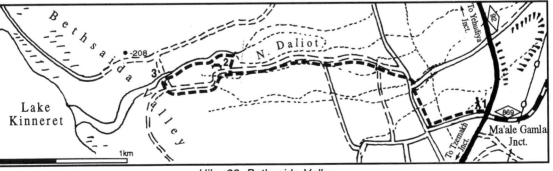

Hike 23, Bethsaida Valley

E. Robinson also visited the region, a few years before Tristram. Its interesting to compare the two descriptions. He wrote:

> It is perfectly level, a more fertile tract can scarcely be imagined. There is a striking resemblance between it and the Ghuweir north of Mejdel; yet the Batihah appears if anything, to be superior. Like the other, it is given up to the Ghawarineh, who cultivate upon it wheat, barley, millet, maize and rice...

> The excellent honey, which according to travellers is produced here, we did not hear of. The Ghawarineh have also large herds of horned cattle, among which are many buffalos... The plain is owned by the government, which receives a share of the produce from the Ghawarineh, it isonly cultivators...[Bedouins] were encamped all along the shore, mostly in small huts made of reeds and rushes; though a few had tents of black cloth. They never live in houses. There may have been in all not far from a hundred and fifty of these temporary dwellings.

> The people for the most part, were sitting listless in and around their open tents and huts; exposing themselves fully to the strong lake breeze under the temperatures of 90° F. and apparently enjoying themselves in their indolent mode of life.

Following the Independence War, Syria established a fort by Bet Habek. The Syrians fired on Israeli fishermen. Israel destroyed the fort in 1955. Until 1967, the Syrian border ran 10 m. from the lake shore. Soon after the Six Day War, Israelis from nearby settlements turned the open areas of the Bethsaida Valley into bumper crop belts. The use of insecticides was feared to injure the nature reserve, so agricultural fields are not allowed to come within 50 m. of the streams.

To begin hike:

Looking north, upon entering Olive Picnic Site (2), descend to the right, through an opening in the stream brush to Nahal Daliyot. In the summer, the stream is shallow and in the winter it reaches the brim of the ditch. Note the mosaic of black and white rock—the black basalt from the plateau of the Golan and white sedimentary rock from Nahal Daliyot's lower canyon walls.

Head left downstream. Willows and oleander create a canopy. Purple loosestrife, bramble and chaste trees grow along the banks. After a few meters the shady stream widens and deepens.

Catfish lurk in the deep, dark waters. You may feel them and some of the 22 other types of fish tickling your legs. Freshwater crabs scuttle through the shallow waters while swamp turtles sunbathe on logs.

The watercourse widens after passing through a line of willows .Note green leaves of pond weed floating on the water. At the edges of the pool are tall eucalyptus trees and a dirt road crosses the stream (3).

Here the wet trip ends. Go left onto the dirt road, pass a lone palm and reach another dirt road which runs parallel to the brush. Take a left for 0.5 km. and reach Olive Picnic Site (2).

24

See map on
page 183

Jordan River

Points of interest: *A wide, peaceful, slow-moving body of*
water, shaded by tall eucalyptus trees.
Length and nature of hike: 2 kilometers, back-and-forth or
2.5 kilometers, loop trip.
Hiking time: 1-2 hours.
Preferred season: All year.
Suitable for: All.
Maps: "Lower Galilee, Valleys and the Gilboa" hiking and
touring map.
Special preparation: Swimsuit.
Starting & ending point: Yardenit, on the Kibbutz Kinneret
access road off of Road 90.

To reach starting point:

Arrival by private transportation: Two kilometers west of Tzemah Junction, by
the southern tip of Lake Kinneret, turn off Road 90 towards Kibbutz Kinneret. The
junction is beside Deganya Dam, which serves as a bridge for Road 90. After 250
m., turn into the Yardenit parking lot where the hike begins (1).

Arrival by public transportation: Take the local buses which leave from Tiberias
central bus station heading south along the lake. Descend at the turnoff to Kibbutz
Kinneret. Walk the road for 250 m. to the Yardenit parking lot (1) where the hike
begins.

Geography

This section of the Jordan River is geographically, and possibly historically, recent.
Lake Kinneret's southern shore was created by the alluvial fan of Yarmuk River
which drained into the Lashon Lake. The sea shrank to today's size 12,000 years
ago, leaving Lake Kinneret behind. The Yarmuk then veered south to merge with
the newly formed Jordan River. The Jordan exited Lake Kinneret 1.5 km. north
of today's location, just north of the ancient tel/settlement of Bet Yerah. Maps from
the 19th century show a channel occasionally filled with water along the Jordan's
previous route. The small valley can still be made out.

The formation of the new outlet has been postulated by many researchers. Some
see it as a result of tectonic activity, but no faults have been found. Another
explanation is that the present-day channel is artificial, dug during the Byzantine
period to protect Bet Yerah from the south. As years went by, lake shore currents
deposited sediments which blocked the northern exit.

The hike runs along the banks of the Jordan and along a saltwater channel. The channel drains saline springs which emerge on the northwestern shores of Lake Kinneret. In order to control the lake's salinity, an elevated channel conducts these waters along the western shore of the lake. Along the way, the sewage of Tiberias drains into the system. The mixture is deposited into the river bed of the Jordan at the far point of the hike. Downstream, along its southern course, the water is naturally purified and is used for irrigation in the Bet She'an Valley.

The Jordan River of this hike is actually a dammed continuation of Lake Kinneret (Israel's national reservoir). At this point, the Jordan River system has drained 2,735 sq. km., only 17% of its total drainage area.

When hydrologists fear that the lake is nearing the upper red line level, they release water down the Jordan. Before human intervention, between 250 and 1,000 million cubits flowed down the Jordan annually. Following the rainy winter of 1991-1992, water managers released 1,500 million cubits from Deganya Dam, a quantity nearly equal to Israel's annual consumption.

Plants and animals

Eucalyptus (*Eucalyptus camaldulensis*): The eucalyptus is from the same family as the myrtle. The first specimens arrived in Israel in the 1880s. Two people introduced them. Carl Neter, founder of the Mikve Yisrael agricultural school (today in Holon) brought seeds from Algeria. An Englishman brought seeds from Australia. Different types were introduced through the years but only the *E. Camaldulensis* made true aliya. Hadera was the first place where large planting took place. Shortly after, they were planted at many of the new Jewish settlements, in order to dry the swamps and exterminate malaria mosquitoes. Later research found that the tree was not a main factor in the effort.

The eucalyptus is a tall tree, reaching 40 m. Its trunk's girth reaches 2 m. The peeling bark has many hues as many photographers have enjoyed this display. The tree's green-grey leaves are brittle and scalpel-shaped. The tree flowers year-round, mainly in spring.

Today the tree is found throughout Israel due to its high adaptability to many different types of hazards. Its wood is second in importance among the trees of Israel, even though it is not considered a good wood. Its trunk quickly rejuvenates after being cut and the lumber can be used for many simple uses. The tree is also used as a wind-breaker for roads and orchards. Its sap is used in the paint and medical industries and its flowers support the honey business.

Catfish (*Clarias lazera*): This eel-like fish is the largest of all freshwater fish in Israel. It reaches 1 m. in length, sometimes even 1.5 m. It can surpass 20 kg. Its long, black, slippery body has no scales, rendering it unkosher. Its head is flat with four barbels around the mouth.

This type of catfish lives in all of the warm waters of the Middle East, Africa and southeast Asia. In Israel, they live in all of the slow-moving waters. When bodies of water dry up, the catfish has the ability to bury itself in mud and breathe air until the habitat becomes aquatic again for a number of months.

The catfish is an omnivore and carrion eater. Reproduction takes place in spring and summer. This is when it is a common sight to observe many specimens in shallow water rubbing upon each other. In the Hula Valley they breed in streams which feed into the Jordan River and Lake Hula.

Catfish eaters claim that the tender white meat tastes like chicken.

To begin hike:

From the Yardenit parking lot (1), head south onto a dirt road. At the fork, take the left option which is marked with a blue mark and an Israel National Trail mark (orange and blue). The trail runs between the Jordan on your left and the saltwater channel on your right.

The trail curves west and heads onto a dirt road in order to get around a pumping station. The sewage channel is re-exposed and the marked trail leaves the dirt road to run again between the two bodies of water. Quietly peeping at the sewage flow, catch a glimpse of turtles sunbathing on objects before they become aware of your presence and dash into the artificial stream.

At a number of spots along the way there are swimming spots marked by hanging ropes for jumping into the water. Before jumping in, make sure that the depth is adequate!

The trail reaches a pipe bridge crossing both bodies of water (2). Here, a view west displays the Poriya Ridge. Between you and the ridge stand the desolate buildings of Bitaniya, amidst tall palm trees.

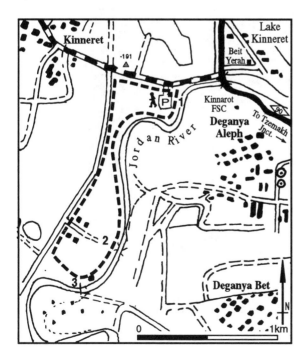

Hike 24, Jordan River

The next pumping section is the end of the walk (3). Follow the trail mark to the right around the fence to the Alumot Dam. Here, one discovers the sad secret of the modern Jordan River. The dam blocks the portion of the Jordan River from Deganya Dam. Deganya Dam is the bridge on Road 90. Thus, the portion you have walked is actually an artificial lake, not a river. The semi-stagnant water is an ideal place for catfish. Sometimes they lurk in shallow water, such as around the Yardenit.

Just beyond the dam, the sewage channel merges into the trickling river bed, creating a "modern," i.e., polluted Jordan River. Along the river's 300 km. course to the Dead Sea, the sewage is naturally purified to some extent by numerous freshwater streams which merge along the way. The long distance of friction with air and land also contributes to the effort.

From here you can head back the same way you came. To see new sights on a different route back, cross over the sewage at the small bridge by the pumping station, head west through the field past Bitaniya and connect to the dirt road. Go right on the dirt road. After one kilometer reach the Kibbutz Kinneret road, 350 m. west of the starting point (1). Go right along the line of olive trees back to Yardenit (1).

A eucalyptus tree beside the Jordan River

Nahal Harod and Bet She'an

See map on
page 189

Points of interest: *A canyon, shaded by eucalyptus trees
and surrounded by impressive archaeological finds: Tel
Bet She'an and ancient Bet She'an; roads, bridges, churches
and more.*

Length and nature of hike: 2.5 kilometers, loop trip.

Hiking time: 2-3 hours. Visiting the Bet She'an National Park
can take up to half a day.

Preferred season: Winter and spring.

Suitable for: All.

Maps: "Lower Galilee, Valleys and the Gilboa" hiking and
touring map

Special preparation: Entrance to the Bet She'an National
Park costs a fee.

Starting & ending point: Bet She'an National Park. Detailed
discussion of the excavations is beyond the scope of this
book.

To reach starting point:

Arrival by private transportation: Park at the entrance to the Bet She'an
National Park. Enter, visit the lower city, and begin the hike at the dirt road (1)
which leads to Amputated Bridge, not far from the central monument.

Arrival by public transportation: Take bus to the Bet She'an central bus station.
From there it is a short walk to the Bet She'an National Park. Head west on Herzl
street towards Sha'ul Hamelekh street. Along the way, pass the Roman amphitheater on your right. Cross Sha'ul Hamelekh street and go left on it. Your first right
descends to the entrance of the National Park. Pay, visit the lower city, and begin
the hike from the dirt road (1) which leads to Amputated Bridge.

Geography

Nahal Harod begins 65 m. above sea level, east of Afula at the national watershed
between the Harod and Jezre'el Valley. It drains 163 sq. km. The stream runs
southeast for 35 km. and drains into the Jordan River east of Bet She'an. This is
the main drainage route of the Harod and Bet She'an Valleys. Along its way, it
picks up a number of springs which emerge at the base of the Gilboa Ridge such
as Ein Yizre'el and Ma'ayan Harod. Perennial streams like Nahal Amal and Nahal
Hakibbutzim also merge into Nahal Harod.

If one opens a map and looks at the course of Nahal Harod, its straight shape hits
the eye. The British channeled its waters between fields and fishponds. At Bet

She'an, the stream enters a basalt and limestone canyon and descends 60 m. over 2.5 km.—a steep, 2.4% gradient.

There were three main stages in the formation of this gorge:

1) With the opening of the Syrian-African Rift, a stream drained the Bet She'an Valley along the course of this section of Nahal Harod.

2) Flowing lava filled up part of this ancient stream's valley, cooling to basalt.

3) Stream water continued to flow along the route. The steep change in elevation gave the flow a lot of energy, allowing incision into the hard basalt.

During the British Mandate this section was planted with fruit trees, vegetable gardens and scrub. Recently, the stream began to drain regional sewage.

Plants and animals

Charlock (*Sinapis arvensis*): This common plant grows in disturbed habitats in all Mediterranean regions of Israel. Originating here, the plant has spread to agricultural lands worldwide. Ancient ruins create a habitat favored by the charlock, which in springtime paint the ruins in bright yellow.

It is mistakenly known in Hebrew to be the mustard plant, even though poor-mans mustard can be extracted from its seeds. Its height reaches 60 cm. This annual can be identified among similar-looking plants by the many small, hairy stems breaking off from the main one. The leaves at the base of the plant are violin-shaped while those on the stem are thin and short. Four yellow petals, up to 1 cm. long, compose the flower, which blooms in bunches in early spring. The fruit is a 3-4 cm. pod.

The leaves, young sprouts, seeds and buds are all edible. It is best to soften them by boiling in water, changing the water once. Add salt and spices. The buds can be eaten raw and young leaves can be added to salads.

History

Although Neoliths lived sporadically in Bet She'an, the first settlement's remains—grey ceramics—are from the Early Bronze. Egyptian records from ca. 2000 B.C.E. mention "Ashan," possibly referring to Bet She'an.

During the Late Bronze, the settlement developed. Archaeologists revealed a large temple from then. Late Bronze Bet She'an was also mentioned in Egyptian documents. Egyptian influence is apparent in the archaeological finds, for their troops resided there during part of that period. Two memorial monuments were found, one describing battles in the region and the other mentioning the invasion of a tribe from nearby Lower Galilee.

Archaeological finds support biblical accounts of Bet She'an Philistines. Two temples from then differ distinctly from the Egyptian ones.

The tribe of Menasheh did not succeed in capturing the city (Judges 1:27), most likely due to a strong Egyptian force. The Philistine-Egyptian city became Israelite only after King Saul. During the reign of King Rehav'am, in 924, the city fell to Egyptian King Shishak.

Alexander the Great named Bet She'an Scithopolis, probably after Scithian knights who served in the Ptolemaic army and settled here. The Greeks brought the cult of Dyonysus, the god of wine, and they erected a temple on top of the tel. When the Seleucids captured Bet She'an, Zeus had become the principle god, worshipped at the same temple.

During Hasmonean times, Jews living in the polis were neutral toward the Maccabean Revolt. In 108 the Maccabees captured Bet She'an, tried unsuccessfully to convert its non-Jewish inhabitants, and expelled them. When Pompey took over, he returned the exiles and reestablished the pagan status of the city. During the Great Revolt (66-70 C.E.), the Jews of Bet She'an fought along with the pagans against their fellow Jews. Nevertheless, the pagans did not trust the assimilated Jews and afterwards slaughtered 13,000 of them in a nearby forest.

By Hellinistic times, the city had expanded beyond the tel. Its climax, in terms of size, came during the Byzantine period, when the surrounding wall covered both sides of Nahal Harod. In the west and east, impressive bridges were laid over Nahal Harod. The city, rich in culture, had a theater, amphitheater and a horse racing arena. In the Hellinistic and Roman eras, Bet She'an joined other cities in the Gilead and Golan to form the *Dekapolis,* the Ten Cities association, to promote Greek civilization.

Bet She'an eventually became a Christian center. It was the capital of the province of *Palestina Secunda* and the episcopacy sat here. Four churches and a number of monasteries were built. At this time Jews were a minority. The city by Jewish law, was not considered part of the Land of Israel in regard to certain laws such as tithes.

The Moslem invasion was slowed down when the inhabitants destroyed the aqueducts and turned the Bet She'an Valley into muck. The Moslems reached an agreement with the city, leaving them half of their homes. The conquerors then transferred the regional administration to Tiberias. This transfer, along with the ruined aqueducts, brought the decline of Bet She'an and the local villages.

The Crusaders reached the town. A family settled in and built a fort. By the 14th century, Bet She'an had become a horse-exchange stop on the Cairo-Damascus way and a khan was built. The remote town changed little until the 1920s, when a few Jewish families arrived. They fled for their lives during the 1936 Arab revolt. In 1948 the Bet She'an Arabs launched attacks on nearby kibbutzim. Finally, the Jews captured the town and its inhabitants fled. Shortly after the war, Jews rebuilt the city and by 1978 the town had 15,000 inhabitants.

Site description

Nahal Amal: Along this wadi, on its northwestern side, ran a second-century thoroughfare which came from Amputated Bridge to the northeast. The road is known as "Column Road" or "Valley Street." The road builders filled the street with earth on its lower southeastern side. On the northwestern side, they carved into the soft limestone and travertine at the base of Tel Bet She'an to create room for shops. They decorated the road with columns all the way to the bridge. The middle part of the road is not excavated.

Kyra Maria Monastery: Founded in 567 along the city wall and named for one of its benefactors. American archaeologists discovered it in the 1920s. The structure includes rooms decorated with mosaic floors, a common style in monasteries. Some of the mosaics have interesting decorations of plants and animals. A fortune wheel mosaic is one of the most interesting finds. The Antiquities Authority has installed a protective roof.

Tel Itztabba: Remnants from the Early Bronze and Roman periods were discovered on the mound. The Byzantine wall on Bet She'an is the most impressive find. East of the main road leading to Amputated Bridge is Tel Hammam, part of the huge cemetery which surrounded the city on three sides.

To begin hike:

By the central monument in the excavations (1), a dirt road heads on the northeastern side of the small wadi called Nahal Amal. Take it to the northeast. The wadi widens, and jujube trees appear. Along the dirt road grow bushes of the silver-grey, pointed-leafed saltbush. A building stands in the middle of the valley. There seem to have been many stages of use for the structure until this century.

Continuing along the dirt road, reach a heavily excavated area above the bridge known as "Amputated Bridge." Descend to the bridge's impressive foundations and cross Nahal Harod on a wooden bridge to the left (2). Note the ancient stream channel.

Measuring the channel can give us an estimate of how much water ran here 1,800 years ago. This can help with an understanding of the hydrological regime of the time. Note the steps heading down to the stream, most likely a service for people who did not want to transverse along the bustling main road.

Ascend to the continuation of the dirt road, to an intersection. One road heads west and the other heads north between Tel Hammam on the right (east) and Tel Itztabba. This northern road is the continuation of the ancient column road. It exits the Byzantine city through a gate at the northern tip of the bridge. Along this road a small synagogue was found (today there is nothing to see).

Take a left and gradually ascend on the dirt road, along the steep slope of Tel Itztabba. Parallel to the road runs the wall of the Byzantine city, dotted with ruined towers. After 400 m., a dirt road arrives from the right, along a ravine. By a split, continue west on the upper dirt road along the Byzantine wall, which soon leads you to the remnants of the Kyra Maria monastery (3), built by one of the tower remnants of the city wall. Return to the split, take a right descending a bit. The dirt road winds through the eucalyptus forest and reaches a bustling road which leads into Bet She'an. The modern road follows an ancient one, which crosses

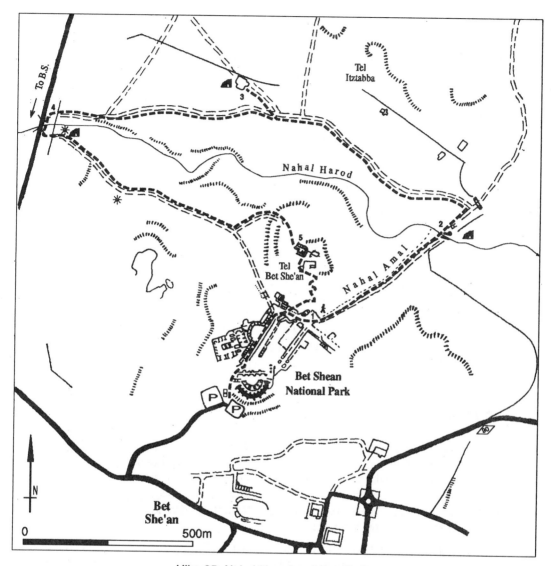

Hike 25, Nahal Harod and Bet She'an

Nahal Harod over a bridge (4), known as the "Western Bridge." Later, Arabs called it Khan Bridge after a khan was built to the south. Note the structure beneath the bridge, a flour mill.

Cross to the southern side of Nahal Harod. Here was one of the main entrances to the Byzantine city. Follow the dirt road toward Tel Bet She'an between euca-lyptus trees and unexcavated ruins. In late winter, charlock adorn the disturbed countryside. Note that you are walking on a Byzantine basalt cobble road which leads to Tel Bet She'an. Here ran a cardo (shopping mall), decorated with pillars, and a few still remain by the sides of the road. Follow the road up to the tel (ignore a left turnoff) and through its northern gate (5). Explore the tel and descend on its southern side back to the lower city (1) and excavation entrance.

26 Nahal Hakibbutzim and Ein Shokek

See map on page 192

Points of interest: *A view of the region, water channels, ruins of a flour mill, pools and an easy-moving stream.*
Length and nature of hike: Option 1: 3 kilometers, loop trip. Option 2: 1 kilometer, loop trip.
Hiking time: Option 1: 3-4 hours. Option 2: 1-2 hours.
Preferred season: All year.
Suitable for: All, if done alongside the water, but *swimmers only in the water!*
Maps: "Lower Galilee, Valleys and the Gilboa" hiking and touring map.
Special preparation: Clothes for walking in water. An innertube or water mattress is recommended.
Starting & ending point: Pool beneath Tel Shokha.

To reach starting point:

Arrival by private transportation: The dirt road leading to the starting point leaves a paved road (1), 100 m. south of the paved road's junction with Road 669, 1 km. east of Nir David. At this spot (1), two channels of water run beneath the paved road. Take the dirt road west for 350 m. to a walled pool in front of a eucalyptus grove (2). Tel Shokha is to the left (south) and is dominated by a three-story tower (3). Park by the pool.

Arrival by public transportation: Take a bus from Bet She'an central bus station toward Nir David. Descend before the kibbutz at the junction on Road 669. Walk 100 m. south on paved road past a bus stop and telephone to the dirt road turnoff (1). Follow as described above in 'Arrival by private transportation.'

Geography

The geography of Nahal Hakibbutzim is probably a result of human intervention. Nahal Hakibbutzim, at -80 m., drains three springs and is 1 km. long. The natural stream ends where the water is led in channels to a purification plant. Excess flow is channeled into Nahal Harod.

The basic form of today's landscape in the Bet She'an Valley was put down 12,000 years ago when the Lashon Lake which covered the eastern sections of the Bet She'an, significantly dropped in level.

Spring-deposited friable limestone, known as carbonate tuff, began to accumulate quickly in the western parts of the valley. This occured due to carbonate saturation in the water that slowly moved eastward. The process continues today. Spring water created small lakes and marshes. In some places, streams cut a shallow trench into the tuff creating stream beds. People have used the waters for at least 5,000 years and it is not clear whether today's stream beds are natural or really ancient ditches.

Plants and animals

Hollyhock (*Alcea setosa*): The most striking flower in Israel that represents the beginning of summer. It blooms between April and June, depending on the season and region. Its large, purple-pink flowers stand out among the newly browning vegetation in open and disturbed Mediterranean areas.

The buds, young fruits and internal parts of the upper stalks are edible when fresh. In Arabic, the plant is known as camel's tongue, due to its rough leaves used for bandaging wounds. The flowers are used for healing open cuts. The leaves and roots are used as pain killers, especially for burns and leg pain.

The hollyhock has been cultivated and is a common garden plant.

White Stork (*Ciconia ciconia*): This large bird has a 1.8 m. wingspan and a bill of up to 20 cm. Its color is white with a number of black spots. The bills and legs are red. Young white storks have a browner tint until 3.5 months.

The white stork breeds in Europe, the Middle East and North Africa. Migration begins after the nesting season in late July-early August. Young storks migrate before the adults. Migrating flocks hold hundreds and thousands of individuals. Most of the journey is done by climbing warm air thermals and then gliding. Hence, they prefer flying over land. In Israel they mainly travel through the Syrian-African Rift and are most commonly seen in the Bet She'an Valley, Dead Sea Valley and Eilat. White storks pass through between late July and October, peaking in early September. A majority of them continue to Zambia and South Africa.

From the end of February they return to Israel. Traveling north, they sometimes are swept westward by strong easterly winds. But more than half pass through the Bet She'an Valley.

Today, the storks winter and occasionally breed here. The number of wintering storks has risen from hundreds to thousands since the 1950s. This is due to the creation of fish ponds and open agricultural fields. In Psalms (104:17), the stork was known to breed in Israel, "Where the bird make their nests; as for the stork, the cypresses are her house."

Although it traditionally nests in trees and sometimes on rock-piles, the white stork today enjoys artificial structures such as silos, towers, chimneys and electricity pylons. Pairs return year after year to the same spot. Three to five eggs are laid and incubated for 33-34 days. The chicks are fed with semi-digested food. Snakes, mice and frogs are their favorite Israeli cuisine. After 60 days the young leave the nest.

History

Based on finds at a number of tels, but mainly at nearby Tel Amal, it seems that this part of the Bet She'an Valley was developed only during certain periods. Metropolitan remnants still remain in the shape of tels. There was a Bronze period settlement and a few hundred years later King David captured the region. Israelites settled the valley and prospered. Commerce flourished with Egypt and Phoenecia. Phoenecian- and Cyprus-made tools were found on the tels. The primary industries were weaving and dyeing. The settlements were burnt with the invasion of King Shishak of Egypt in 925 B.C.E. During the 8th and 9th centuries B.C.E. the villages made a short-lived comeback effort.

To begin hike:

Among the eucalyptus trees you might sight a white stork. To increase your perspective and for a panoramic view of the Bet She'an Valley and the Gilboa Ridge, ascend to Tel Shokha (3). Head further along the dirt road and 100 m. on reach a junction. Go left and ascend the wide steep trail to the tel. Climb up the ladder to the second story of the tower. Descend the same way. Hollyhocks bloom here in April, representing spring's end.

Option 1: From the bottom of Tel Shokha, head left on the dirt road, circling the tel from the west. In the spring, dark pink, five-petal mallow bushes bloom along the dirt road. The mallow's very edible fruit is ripe in April when its close relative, the hollyhock, blooms.

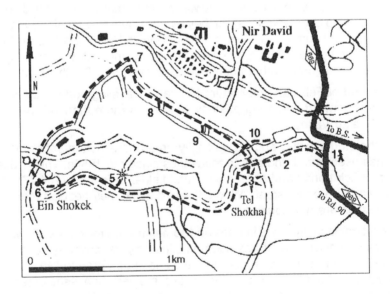

Hike 26, Nahal Hakibutzim and Ein Shokek

Another dirt road approaches from behind the tel. Continue on the main route, heading east. To the right of the road a small rivulet runs: Nahal Shokek. Cross a reedy Shokek tributary and reach a T-junction. Take a left and, after 100 m., reach the water channel of Ein Shokek (3). The snails in the water are evidence that the water is probably potable.

Go right, heading upstream along the channel. It is fun to walk in the water! The channel veers left. After 300 m., a dirt road descends to Nahal Shokek, which is parallel to the channel to the north. A bit upstream from the dirt road, a ruined flour mill stands among trees (5). It is worth a look, for the mill still offers important shade.

Continue up the channel until reaching the colorful pool of Ein Shokek (6). Ein Shokek is the largest and most important of the fault springs emerging along the base of the Gilboa.

Head up the dirt road from Ein Shokek to the northeast. Pass by turkey coops and, after 750 m., cross the wadi of Nahal Hakibbutzim. The crossing is just upstream from Ein Migdal, the stream's main source. Immediately after crossing, go right at the junction, and pass the water management building at Ein Migdal where the watercourse emerges (7). The stream is beautiful here. Continue along the dirt road, parallel to the water. Here and there it is possible to peak through the shrubs and view the waters.

Three hundred meters from Ein Migdal, a dirt road crosses the stream. Take it to the right and enter the waters of Nahal Hakibbutzim by a lone palm tree (8). From here until the next dirt road (200 m.), you will be immersed between waist and shoulder height. This is the place to inflate the air mattress.

After 200 m. another dirt road crosses the stream (9). Cross it and continue downstream to the pipe bridge (10). It is usually possible to slide through the pipe on the right but first check the waters on the other end! Continue downstream to the starting point (2).

Option 2: From the bottom of Tel Shokha, head east and cross Nahal Hakibbutzim over the pipe bridge. Go left on the dirt road and head northwest, parallel to the stream. After 150 m. and 350 m. (by a palm tree), there are dirt roads that cross the stream and give access to it (9, 8). At either place, begin the aquatic route. The first bridge—the shorter option—is suitable for youngsters, while the longer option includes water over a meter deep.

Head downstream, between thick vegetation, back to the starting point by the swimmable pool (2).

Jerusalem Hills

Geography

The term Jerusalem Hills, describes more than a geographical region. It is a geopolitical entity, for its borders were shaped by the 1949 cease-fire agreement with Jordan. In fact, most of the cease-fire lines follow the geography of the Jerusalem Hills. Politically, the region is known as the Jerusalem Corridor, connecting the heart of the Jewish Israeli population along the Mediterranean Coast, to the capital, Jerusalem. The region covers only 250 sq. km. It partially overlaps with metropolitan Jerusalem, whose area is 100 sq. km.

The Jerusalem Hills form the lowest of the three subregions of the Judean Hills. Saddled between the Bet El Hills to the north and the Hebron Hills to the south, the highest crests in the Jerusalem Hills reach only 840 m.

The elevation difference exemplifies the geology of the Judean Hills. The Hebron Hills are based on one main anticline running north-south, ending by the slopes of Gilo in southern Jerusalem. Along the backbone of this anticline axis, which is also the national watershed, runs the Jerusalem-Hebron road. The Ramallah Anticline axis runs in a similar direction but more westerly as its southern tip runs through the central section of the Jerusalem Hills. This means that the dip of the strata changes along this line: the western flanks rock layers dip sharply west and the eastern Jerusalem Hills have a gentle eastward dip.

The Jerusalem Hills is actually a syncline standing between these two anticlines. Thus, the Hills do not attain the heights that the other two sub-regions achieve. Their elevated spots are usually hills that have withstood erosion.

The geographical borders of the Jerusalem Hills are:

In the west: the series of narrow valleys running in a north-south direction clearly differentiate the steep slopes of the Jerusalem Hills from the Judean Foothills to the west. A road runs along these valleys.

In the east: eastern Jerusalem marks the border; here runs the national watershed, further east, the Judean Desert Fringe begins.

In the north: the elevated ridge of Shu'afat-Nebi Samuel-Giv'at Haradar continuing via Nahal Kefira is known as the northern boundary. North of this line are the Bet El Hills.

To the south: Upper Nahal Refa'im, from the northern slopes of Gilo down the wide wadi to the Arab village of Batir. From Batir the line continues along the western flanks of the Hebron Anticline via Nahal Hama'ayanot (Wadi G'ama'a) and down Wadi Phukhin to Emek Ha'ela.

The Jerusalem Hills have three main wadis practically draining the whole region to the west with finger-like ridges between them:

1) Nahal Kesalon drains the northern section of the area and by the Sha'ar Hagai-Bet Shemesh road drains into Nahal Sorek. To the north of Nahal Kesalon runs the Shoresh Ridge.

2) Nahal Sorek drops into the Jerusalem Hills from the north by Ramot and then winds westward, north of the Sorek Ridge upon which Jerusalem sits. Further west after the merge with Nahal Refa'im, the Ya'ala Ridge runs to the south of the sewage-fed stream. Between Nahal Sorek and Nahal Kesalon runs the Tzova Ridge, upon which the Kastel (Mevasseret)- Eshtaol road runs.

3) Nahal Refa'im begins at Jerusalem's train station and runs south of the Sorek Ridge. The sewage-laden stream drains into Nahal Sorek in the middle of the Jerusalem Hills, at the tip of the ridge. South of the upper parts of the wadi, the northern tip of the Hebron Anticline, stand Gilo and Har Gilo.

The southwestern Jerusalem Hills do not belong to these drainage systems. West of Batir, a number of ridges descend from south of Nahal Refa'im to the west, such as the Sansan Ridge and the Matta Ridge.

The geological strata of the Jerusalem Hills are composed of sedimentary rock only. The main rock types are limestone, dolomite, marl, chalk and chert. All of the exposed formations belong to the Judea Group except the Menuha (chalk) and Mishash Formations (chert), exposed at the eastern crests, which belong to the Mt. Scopus Group.

Climate

Since the Judean Hills' southern and eastern border is along a desert, it has a semi-humid Mediterranean climate. The western Jerusalem Hills, above the sharp drop to the Judean Foothills, receive 600 mm. of rainfall. The amount of annual rainfall recedes heading east. Similarly, in the city of Jerusalem, annual rainfall averages 500 mm. with the western communities receiving more precipitation than the eastern side. The core of the rainy season of the Judean Hills has been found to be later than the coastal area. Most of the rain falls in the months of January, February and March. All of the yearly rainfall is between October and May. For all of its rain, Jerusalem has an average of only 47 rainy days per year. Per total amount of precipitation, it is the sunniest city on earth.

Temperatures are closely correlated to elevation. High in Jerusalem, winter temperatures reach freezing and a few days of snowfall are common. In elevations below 650 m. snow usually does not stick to the ground. The annual average temperature span in the Hills is 15°C (compared to 12° in the Coastal Plain). The January average temperature is around 10° while in August it is 25. Temperatures rarely exceed 35°. The annual average temperature in Jerusalem is 17.1°. An important difference between the hills and the coast is the daily temperature span. In the hills, the temperature drops significantly at night, and even during the summer one usually needs a jacket for an evening stroll.

Jerusalem has an average humidity of 62%. Humidity fluctuates daily. It is low in the morning and rises in early evening; the daily sunlight evaporates moisture and the dusk air quickly cools and condenses.

Vegetation

There are four primary environmental factors affecting vegetation in the Israeli Mediterranean landscape:

1) The climate and the surrounding climates. Total annual precipitation is the most important factor of the climate for plant growth.

2) The lithology, as it determines the water economy and the subsequent soil which in turn are major determinants of plant growth.

3) The microclimate, which is mainly determined by the face of the slope. The southern-facing slope, which is the southern slope of a ridge, is exposed throughout the day to sunlight. The high evaporation rates, radiation and temperatures (7-10 degrees more than the northern face) limits the development of dense, variated flora.

4) The human factor. Deforestation, agriculture and grazing have significantly changed the botanic appearance of the Jerusalem Hills landscape in the last 5,000 years.

The main modes of vegetation of the Jerusalem Hills are maquis, garrigues or battas. Only at a few spots are remnants of forests that once covered the whole region. The whole Jerusalem Hills is in the Mediterranean phytogeographic zone.

In the maquis, the most prominent plant association is the evergreen common oak and Palestinian terebinth. This maquis is found mainly on terra rossa soil. Relatively few other trees and creepers grow beneath and among this maquis. The few trees found are the olive, hawthorn, snowbell, buckthorn and carob. In marly soils the strawberry tree is also common.

In the high spots and northerly slopes one can find the Syrian pear and the Boissier oak that are common in the Upper Galilee and Carmel. These shady forests will also hold a number of creepers, the most common of which are the green brier (smilax) and madder. The honeysuckle, common in Jerusalem gardens, appears in small shady patches throughout the Hills. The drooping white flowers of the winter blooming clematis creeper, cover exposed piles of rock in the elevated regions. On the dry southerly slopes the carob and mastic terebinth commonly appear together. The carob and mastic terebinth plant association becomes more prevalent near the warmer Judean Foothills.

The Aleppo pine is found growing naturally at two spots in the Jerusalem Hills; the Masrek Nature Reserve by Bet Meir and on Har Pitulim in the Sorek Nature Reserve. At both spots the pine grows in rendzina soil (see Upper Galilee vegetation introduction).

Battas of dwarf shrubs cover large sections of the Hills. This has been caused by human involvement which created open fields. In the last 150 years the flora cover has undergone dramatic changes with the Turkish deforestation, the abandonment of fields in 1948 and the later declaration of nature reserves.

While most of the population of fields are Mediterranean species, a number of plants have invaded the Hills from the Judean Desert Fringe. The round, brown, knee-high thorny burnet, which covers fields abandoned in 1948, most likely came from the Fringe. The thorny burnet represents one of the three main batta associations in the Hills. The thorny burnet and oat association is mainly found on terra rossa soil. The other two associations are the *Hyparrhenia hirta* grass with oat grass and the thyme association, found on marly soils (rendzina).

Today in the nature reserves we witness the comeback of harassed vegetation. Experts estimate that the green glory of the Jerusalem Hills will return to Zion in about 200 undisturbed years.

Over 1,000 species of wildflowers can be found in the Jerusalem vicinity. Throughout the centuries, many of them have been domesticated worldwide. Wild cyclamen, iris, daisy, poppy, narcissus and orchid are some of the leading wildflowers. This extraordinary diversity is due to the proximity of the Jerusalem region to both the Judean Desert and the Mediterranean region.

Jerusalem is one of the few cities to have 7 plants named after it.

Wildlife

Today's green landscape of the Jerusalem Hills is a new scene among the Judean Hills. The Turks, during their last decades of control, totally decimated the forests of Judea. The destruction of shady habitats along with the introduction of firing weapons and the influx of Arab peasants, brought down the quantity and diversity of the mammal population in Judea. These changes naturally damaged the whole ecological chain.

Biblical sources can help us picture the wildlife situation 3,000 years ago. King David boasts, "Thy servant slew both the lion and the bear." (I Samuel 17:36) Most of the biblical wildlife nearly survived until the 20th century. Nineteenth century travellers documented heavy hunting in the region, especially of raptors and deer.

Today's green landscape is mainly pine forests planted in this century which were not the natural foliage in earlier times. Also today, the Jerusalem Hills are significantly more inhabited by humans. Thus, even today things are quite different than before and the idea of a complete wildlife comeback is out of the question.

Animal species in Israel originate on all three surrounding continents: the chukar, rabbit, agama and the great tit are Mediterranean species. The Palestine sunbird, bulbul, badger and mongoose are Sudanese species from tropical Africa. The Indian crested porcupine and the bunting are from tropical Asia. The marbled polecat comes from an Irano-Turanian steppe environment.

Of the mammals today, the most impressive is the mountain gazelle found in open fields, even in Jerusalem. The most common predator is the fox, which is a nuisance to moshav members for it raids chicken coops. A rare mammal is the honey badger. The sleek, dark marten is sometimes seen, often residing near homes. Wild cats live among thickets and copulate with alley cats. Jackals were poisoned to near extinction in the 1950s but today their howling is a common noise toward dusk. A variety of rodents, such as the common field mouse and the shrew, thrive throughout the Hills in different environments. The Egyptian fruit-bat is common. They sometimes migrate between the Jerusalem Hills and Judean

Foothills. Three types of insect-eating bats are also found in the Jerusalem Hills, the most common being the Kuhl's pipistrell which resides in roofs and trees.

The Palestinian viper is the only venomous snake in the Hills. Its bite can be deadly. The triangular-headed nocturnal snake frequently appears near chicken coops and human settlements. A variety of shapes and colors characterize the other snakes of the Hills. The coin-marked snake is often mistaken for the Palestinian viper. The Syrian black snake lurks in trees and can attain a length of 2 m. Common lizards are the swift agama and chameleon. Geckos are common night time sights on walls, in their search for insects.

No salamanders have been spotted in the Hills. The green toad appears everywhere at night and lays its eggs in every type of water. The stream frog lives in stable water sources while the lemon tree frog travels between sources of water, even into Jerusalem gardens.

Of the common fowl, the wooded landscape of the Jerusalem Hills houses Sardinian warblers, Syrian warblers and jays. The wider wadis that contain fruit orchards like Nahal Sorek and Nahal Hama'ara hold many migrants as well as large numbers of wintering finches and buntings. Of particular interest are the wintering flocks of yellowhammers, which often include small numbers of pine buntings. The bare rocky hillsides are home to longbilled pipits, and many migrant passerines drop in to rest during spring and fall. Short-toed eagles soar close to Jerusalem and lesser kestrels even nest in the city. Recently cuckoos have been observed in Nahal Refa'im, dwelling in long-billed pipit nests.

Human Involvement

The importance of the Jerusalem Hills in the history of the Holy Land and the whole world surpasses the limits of this essay. Jerusalem, which sits at the eastern corner of the Hills, holds many values and traditions of the Jewish people which were shaped throughout the last 3,000 years. Here also the Christian Messiah preached and was executed. Later, the Moslems developed a tradition of importance to Jerusalem. Interestingly, the Jerusalem Hills outside of Jerusalem have always been in the shadow of events that occurred nearby, in the Hebron and Bet El Hills.

Due to the dense floral cover, the Hills were lightly inhabited in prehistoric times. During the Mid-Bronze, humans began to infiltrate the mountainous regions. This is when the city of Jerusalem first appeared. Jerusalem and other cities of Judea and Samaria developed adjacent to the watershed.

With the Israelite settlement of the land, changes began to take place as the whole region was divided into tribal estates. Each estate was subdivided into regions controlled by prominent families—similar to the Arab *hamula* of today. This political development coincided with forest clearing in order to adapt the landscape to settlement. Only with King David's conquest of Jerusalem, a few hundred years later, did the Jerusalem Hills begin to develop. Small villages multiplied tenfold. The Bible mentions settlements such as Kiryat Ye'arim, where the ark rested on its way back to Jerusalem. Remnants of smaller settlements that dotted the Jerusalem Hills have recently been uncovered. Hirbet Tura above Nahal Sorek and Hirbet Livnim by Mevo Betar are good examples. The region belonged to the northwestern corner of the tribe of Judah. The Jerusalem Hills-Bet El Hills border today is equivalent to the biblical tribal border between Judah and Benjamin. The Bet El Hills are still known as the Benjamin region.

During this period the Jerusalem Hills were dotted with small family-sized farms and no towns. The average farm had about 1-2 sq. km. of land. Larger settlements most likely consisted of a few families living together. This type of settlement continued into the Persian period.

With the return from the Babylonian exile and the establishment of the Second Temple, the area near Jerusalem became the center of Jewish settlement. This state continued up until the destruction of the Temple in 70 C.E.

This period of 600 years can be divided into a few time periods. When Jews began to return in 538 B.C.E., an effort was made around Jerusalem to rebuild the city and Temple. There are not many detailed sources about this period.

A hundred years later, Ezra the Scribe and Nehemia describe in detail the rebuilding of a Jewish Jerusalem and of all the villages that were resettled by Jews in the area (known as the Yehud province). This province was divided into 7 districts. It seems that there was not a strong Jewish settlement block west of Jerusalem but rather north and south of Jerusalem. The towns of Kefira, Kiryat Ye'arim and Be'erot are mentioned together (Ezra 2:26); we believe them to have been along the northern border of the Hills. For the next two hundred years, the simple Jews of the Yehud province led peaceful lives.

After the quiet Greek invasion in 332 B.C.E., no major sudden demographic changes occurred for 170 years. But in 166 B.C.E., the Maccabean Revolt broke out. The battles took place in Jerusalem, in the Hebron and Bet El Hills, in the Judean Foothills, but not in the Jerusalem Hills. It is possible that Simeon the Maccabee fortified the way from Gezer to Jerusalem via the northern Jerusalem Hills. Hirbet Metzad, west of Neve Ilan (later along a Roman road), may have been one of the forts.

The Roman period, beginning in 63 B.C.E., ended the independent Jewish rule. The Judean province was reduced to the Jewish settlements only. The Jews lost control over the Mediterranean coast, but the Jerusalem Hills, still less developed than the areas to its north and south, remained a Jewish region. The Romans constructed two main roads through the region, remnants of which survive today:

1) Emaus (Latrun)-Jerusalem via Hirbet Metzad—Neve Ilan-Abu Gosh—Kastel—Motza—Giv'at Sha'ul—Binyanei Ha'uma (one of the remnants is the sturdy fort wall along the sharp curve of Highway 1 at Motza).

2) Ashkelon-Jerusalem via Bet Guvrin—Emek Ha'ela—Matta Ridge—Mevo Betar—Bethlehem.

A smaller road through Nahal Refa'im connected Jerusalem to Batir (ancient Betar) and continued through Nahal Dolev to the Bet Shemesh region. This road stands out among Roman roads that usually tended to be on top of ridges for tactical superiority.

Despite the blow to the Jews of Judea, King Herod brought economic prosperity to the region between 37 and 4 B.C.E. Possibly for the first time, organized clusters of villages developed in the Jerusalem Hills — such as Betar, Kobi and Kefar Tzoom.

After the destruction of the Temple, Jewish settlements continued in the area. Sixty-two years later the Bar Kokhba Revolt erupted, lasted for three years and crumbled with the fall of Simeon Bar Kokhba (Koziba) at Betar in the Jerusalem Hills. This revolt really unnerved the Romans, who responded with a rampage, destroying villages and making significant political reforms, including name changes: Jerusalem was razed and called *Aelia Capitolina*. Judea was called *Provincia Syria Palestina*. This is the source of the word Palestine. Jews were barred from the vicinity.

Sixty years later, the Jewish situation improved and many settlements began to prosper. This scenario repeated cyclically until the Roman Empire declared Christianity its official religion, beginning the Byzantine period. During Byzantine times, the population of the land increased, most likely also in the Jerusalem Hills. This is when the serious infrastructure of terraces took over 60% of the region's landscape. This period has left its signs upon the natural rock: on every ridge, wine presses can be found carved into the rock.

After the Moslem conquest in the 7th century, the population gradually became Moslem. There was an influx of Arabs and Bedouins. Judea prospered as an agricultural region. Jerusalem underwent a momentous change with the construction of the Dome of the Rock, the El Aksa mosque and a palace to their south.

With a government change in the 11th century, accompanied by widespread internal fighting, Judea in all aspects declined. The number of settlements declined from 65 to 23. Government centers were established in the coast; the main economic push was given there and in the Judean Foothills.

With the arrival of the Crusaders, the Jerusalem Hills were spared of battles and destruction. Between 1099 and 1187, the Crusaders invested in fortifying the access to Jerusalem. Thus a number of fortresses, as well as Christian settlements, were established. With the fall of the Crusaders they became Moslem villages. Abu Gosh, Bet Atab, Tzuba and Kastel are examples. Some of the sites of Christian settlements today retain the Arabic title of *dir*, meaning monastery.

In 1283 the Mamelukes took over Judea as a county in the Damascus district. These zealous Moslems built up religious institutions in Jerusalem while neglecting the countryside. The Christian and Jewish population was oppressed and Judea became inhabited by Moslems only. The Hills suffered from frequent clashes between peasants and Bedouins. The village scene deteriorated.

The arrival of the Ottoman Empire in 1516 brought positive changes to Judea. The population doubled and agricultural villages and farms expanded. The prosperity lasted for a hundred years. Many remnants from then have been found along the local springs. Then, from the 17th century until the short Egyptian conquest in 1831, the stability in Judea slowly disintegrated. The government was weak and suffered raids from both Bedouins and non-regular Turkish soldiers. During these years, the first *hamulas* crystalized, which are still influential today. These clans fought each other and competed for positions in the Ottoman government.

In 1831, the Egyptian Ibrahim Peha took advantage of the weak Turkish position and the internal family feuds, and conquered the region. Peha was educated in France and brought modern government to the region for the first time. People emigrated from Egypt and desolate villages sprung up again. The conquest united the local *hamulas* against Peha and in 1834 the Peasant's Revolt erupted. By 1840 the peasants succeeded in kicking every Egyptian soldier out of Palestine. The Turks returned with their corrupt ways but with a new international flair. Foreigners toured the land and many documented their travels. Jerusalem was flooded with consulates and charity organizations. In the second half of the 19th century, Jews began to immigrate. Yet even then, the Jerusalem Hills were overlooked.

In 1869, the introduction of the buggy led to the opening of the Jaffa-Jerusalem road via the Jerusalem Hills. Today, Highway 1 follows the same general route. In 1892, the Jaffa-Jerusalem railroad was completed. The route winds through the core of the Jerusalem Hills, along Nahal Sorek and Nahal Refa'im. Even today, the slow train ride is a spectacle for nature lovers.

In the early 20th century, the land seemed to remain in the 19th. Christian and Jewish settlement attempts, mainly in the Hebron and Bet El Hills, did not succeed. The impoverished Moslem population showed little interest in any type of change.

World War I brought an economic disaster to Judea. A locust plague intensified the near-famine situation. This, along with the British introduction of western government and technology, brought sharp social changes. The villages strengthened their connection with the cities and young men began to find jobs outside the village. Modern medicine saved many lives that would have previously been lost and the village population increased dramatically, a process still occurring today. The modernized atmosphere broadened the Arab world-views and nationalistic feelings were aroused among some. Three periods of Arab rioting, in many ways similar to the Intifada, broke out against the British and the Jews during the British Mandate, in 1920, 1929 and 1936-1939. The rioting was accompanied by internal feuds and murder among the Arabs themselves. The British army sometimes used very severe methods to subdue the disorder, killing hundreds of Arabs in the process.

The 1947 partition plan endorsed by the United Nations allocated to the Arabs all of Judea including the Jerusalem Hills. Jerusalem was to be an international city. The Arabs did not accept any type of partition and began severely assaulting the entire Jewish population. All of the Jewish villages in the Jerusalem Hills were along the main road to Jerusalem. For the next year many bloody battles were fought along this road and in its environs in order to control access to Jerusalem. The fighting created what is known as the Jerusalem Corridor. Most of the Moslem villages were deserted. Two remained and one was relocated: Abu Gosh, Ein Rafeh and Ein Nekoba, respectively.

After the War of Independence, the Jerusalem Corridor was mainly settled by Jews from Oriental countries. The type of village created for this was known as a moshav *olim* or a 'labor moshav.' Each member received a chicken coop and land for agriculture, mainly fruit trees. The lack of land suitable for farming brought many men to work for the Jewish National Fund in afforestation and reclamation programs. Today, the evergreen pine forests covering the Judean Hills are the fruits of this effort.

A few communal moshavim and kibbutzim were also formed in the Jerusalem Hills in the echo of the bloody battles such as Shoresh, Ramat Raziel and Tzuba. Being in proximity to the Jordanian border, some settlements suffered from occasional security problems. After the Six Day War in 1967 the villages of the Jerusalem Corridor were relatively neglected. With the political changes in the 1990s and the possibility that developing Jerusalem will be blocked in three directions, it seems that the area west of Jerusalem faces many changes. Many moshavim have begun to allocate land for expansion.

Water

The Jerusalem Hills contain a respectable amount of underground water due to the climate and geology. Winter is the rainy season and rainfall is highly concentrated. Cold weather rainfall is common—more here than world-wide. Thus, evaporation is minimal. The hard, cracked carbonate rocks of the Hills create terra rossa soils that absorb rainfall. Thus, runoff is practically nil as most of the water sinks underground. The water is stored amidst the cracked limestones and dolomites, upon impermeable marl layers.

The geologic watershed is not in coordination with the topographical one. The topographical watershed runs in a north-south direction through Jerusalem. The geologic watershed follows the axis of the Ramallah Anticline in a north-south direction via Shoeva-Ramat Raziel-Ness Harim-Sansan Ridge. Thus, infiltrating rainfall east of this line runs underground to the east and emerges along the Syrian-African Rift in the springs of the Jericho region and along the northwestern shores of the Dead Sea. These springs are much more plentiful than those in the Jerusalem Hills.

A majority of the 102 springs of the Jerusalem Hills are layer (strata) springs emerging upon layers of marl rock. The rest are karstic springs such as the Gihon spring in the City of David and the Te'omim Cave spring. Although the ratio of springs per area is high in the Hills, their average discharge is not impressive. The largest springs release only 10-12 cubits per hour. The spring water is relatively fresh—70-100 mg. chlorine per liter on average. Annual rainfall does increase spring discharge for short periods, sometimes tenfold.

Among 87 of the springs are relics of human harnessing, beginning during First Temple times. Most of the springs have gone through a typical discharge dismissal construction. The natural crack where the water emerged was widened into a cave shape. From there a tunnel was made with a water channel at its bottom. The tunnel fed a storage pool. Beneath the pool were agriculture compounds for vegetables. This type of spring is mentioned in the book of Song of Songs 4:12: "A garden enclosed is my sister, my spouse; a spring shut up, a fountain sealed."

Flowing streams are not typical of the Jerusalem Hills landscape. A few wadis have springs which create a short rivulet of water such as Nahal Ketalav and Nahal Matta. During periods of intense rain, the wadis will flow for a day or two but usually not more than that.

Wells are not common either. A shallow pool of water above Ein Kerem known as Mary's Well is one of the few wells in the Jerusalem Hills.

Water cisterns can be found throughout the Hills, usually by ruins of villages. The water cistern, more than the small springs, has been for thousands of years the main water source for civilization in the region. Due to the cracked rock, cisterns were always plastered. Usually they were constructed in a bell shape to minimize evaporation and infection. Jerusalem sustained itself on cisterns until the British Mandate introduced pumped water to the city. Even today, Jerusalem's water supply consists mainly of water pumped from the Rosh Ha'ayin springs, the source of the Yarkon River.

Across Nahal Sorek, west of Moshav Bet Zayit, stands the Ein Kerem Dam. It was known that the artificial lake would only be seasonal, due to swift percolation into the cracked, porous rock beneath it. The goal was to enrich the aquifer. What was not known was the geological structure. The dam is east of the axis of the Ramallah Anticline and the aquifer water drains eastward to the Syrian-African Rift. In pre-1967 days that area was under Jordanian control and the utility of the dam was minute. After rainy winters, the dam creates a one-kilometer long lake which lasts until June. Throughout the spring, the lake hosts an assortment of water fowl and is a popular recreation site for Jerusalemites. The muddy bottom of the lake has caused a few casualties. Swimming is forbidden.

Hiking in the Jerusalem Hills

Jerusalem has been rated as the number one city in Israel for cohabitance with nature. Jerusalem is the center of access to hiking routes in the Jerusalem Hills only a few minutes out of town (and in town). Three main roads leave the city and dissect the Hills: Tel Aviv-Jerusalem Highway 1, Kastel-Eshtaol Road 395 and Bar Giora Road 386 which begins at Ein Kerem. On all roads public transportation is operated, allowing walking-access to any spot in the Hills. This makes the Jerusalem Hills an easy place for short family trips when only a few hours can be spared. Due to the intense development of forests and recreation sites, the J.N.F. has created hundreds of kilometers of dirt roads, some of them suitable for cars.

The best place to catch public transportation is the Jerusalem central bus station where buses, cabs and *sherut* cabs are always available. Many of the bus lines that head to the Corridor settlements begin at the Davidka Square in downtown Jerusalem.

Even in the middle of winter a clear sunny day can make the temperature very pleasant. Two liters of water is necessary on winter outings. In summer, at least four liters of water should be consumed on a strenuous hike, and a hat is a must. Off-trail, the thorny calycotome bushes require long sleeves and pants. In winter, water seeps through the soil and is exposed upon layers of rock making things slippery.

The moderate weather, the abundance of trails and dirt roads and the proximity to Jerusalem and settlements makes the Jerusalem Hills one of the safest and most pleasant places for a one-day hike. For orientation purposes it is a helpful hint to know that all of the large wadis run in an east-west direction.

Important Phone Numbers

S.P.N.I. Field Study Centers and Information

Jerusalem S.P.N.I. complex, 13 Queen Helena Street: 02-252357, 244605
Sha'ar Hagai, Moshav Bet Meir, Jerusalem Hills: 02-913291
Har Gilo: 02-742586

Safety Assistance

Police: 100
Jerusalem: 02-24444
Bet Shemesh: 02-91444

Ambulance: 101
M.D.A. Jerusalem: 02-523133
M.D.A. Bet Shemesh: 02-911288

Sites Worth Visiting

Nature Reserves and National Parks:
Ein Hemed (Aqua Bella) National Park off Ein Hemed Junction on Highway 1.
Kastel National Park on Highway 1.
Avshalom Stalactite Cave Nature Reserve at end of Bar Giora-Ness Harim road.
Har Tayasim I.A.F. Memorial, picnic site and nature reserve off Road 395.
Masrek Nature Reserve off Highway 1, by Bet Meir.
Pillars of Fire Monument off Road 395 by Moshav Kesalon.
Monument of the Jerusalem road, by Shoeva Junction on Highway 1.
Kiryat Ye'arim Church, by Abu Gosh on old Tel Aviv-Jerusalem road.
Bet Zayit Reservoir, behind Moshav Bet Zayit, access from entrance to Ein Kerem
      Agricultural School on Road 395.

Overnight Options

Indoors

Camping: Mevo Betar; Bet Zayit
Youth Hostels: Bar Giora; Bayit Vegan, Ein Kerem and downtown Jerusalem
Kibbutz Guest Houses: Ma'ale Hahamisha; Kiryat Anavim; Shoresh

Outdoors

Many picnic sites with tables, some with running water
Jerusalem Forest, western Jerusalem (water)
Salamon Forest, (Hurbat Sa'adim, see Hike 27) (water)
Nahal Sorek, on Road 386
Har Haruah, by road to the village of Nataf
Ness Harim, off the access road (water)
Bar Giora, across Road 386 from the moshav
Ein Kobi (water)

Gas Stations

Sha'ar Hagai, Shoeva, Neve Ilan, Mevasseret, Kastel all along Highway 1.

Springs Trail

Points of interest: *A scenic mountaintop monument amidst Jerusalem Hills scenery, ruins, pine forest and five springs.*

Length and nature of hike: 4.5 kilometers, one-way. 5.5 kilometers, loop trip (for those with one vehicle). The hike can be continued with Hike 28, 'Ein Hindak to Sattaf Springs.'

Hiking time: 3-4 hours.

Preferred season: All year.

Suitable for: All.

Maps: Jerusalem Outskirts hiking and touring map.

Special preparation: Flashlight, swimsuit, binoculars.

Starting point: Yad Kennedy/Hurbat Sa'adim for hikers with private transportation; Moshav Aminadav for hikers arriving by bus.

Ending point: Moshav Evn Sapir (for one-way route).

See map on page 211

To reach starting point:

Arrival by private transportation: Drive through Jerusalem towards Ein Kerem Hadassah Hospital. At Ora Junction take a left and follow road that leads to Yad Kennedy. After 5 km., following a sharp left curve, (where a road heads right, to Aminadav) right before the ascent to Yad Kennedy, note the turnoff to the right towards Hurbat Sa'adim. Follow the road up to Yad Kennedy (2).

For loop trip: After visiting Yad Kennedy drive down to Hurbat Sa'adim and park the vehicle at the parking lot (3). It is possible to hike down to Hurbat Sa'adim while one member of the party drives the vehicle down to the parking lot (3).

Arrival by public transportation: Take bus from Jerusalem's central bus station to Aminadav. Get off at the last stop (1).

Geography

This hike heads along the Aminadav Ridge, also known as the Sorek Ridge, since it rises south of the winding Nahal Sorek. The ridge attains the highest elevations in the Jerusalem Hills, around 840 m. Aminadav Ridge is relatively short as it ends where Nahal Refa'im to the south merges with Nahal Sorek, 5 km. west of Aminadav. From Aminadav Ridge, grand vistas of the Hebron Hills and Jerusalem Hills are open from many different spots.

Being between two ends of the Hebron and Ramallah Anticline, the ridge is part of a syncline. Thus the geological formations exposed are recent in comparison with the other main ridges of the Jerusalem Hills. The crest of the ridge and the peaks, such as the western communities of Jerusalem, Yad Kennedy and Har Ora consist of soft rock of the Kefar Sha'ul Formation that have withstood erosion. Aminadav Formation is the most exposed formation along the slopes. Motza Marl (Formation) forms a ring around the ridge and upon this layer 10 springs emerge. The lower parts of the ridge's slopes are of the Bet Meir and Sorek Formations.

Plants and animals

Aleppo pine (*Pinus halepensis*): Named after the Syrian city. In Hebrew known as the Jerusalem pine, after the verse in Isaiah 44:14 "He heweth them down cedars, and taketh the cypress and the oak, which he strengtheneth for himself among the trees of the forest: he planteth a pine and the rain doth nourish it." The tree is also mentioned in the Mishna, tractate Para. The tree may have been known as the oil tree in the scriptures.

The Aleppo pine covers large sections of the Jerusalem Hills and was once the popular tree planted by the Jewish National Fund— most likely due to J.N.F. leaders' European conception of a green landscape and the fact that the pine grows quickly. Some 80% of Israel's planted forests are pine forests.

The pine can attain a height of 15 m. The trunk has a tendency to twist, the bark is thick and cracked. The leaves are needles up to 10 cm. long, arranged in pairs on short limbs that branch out from larger ones. The easily flammable needles create a mat beneath the tree, inhibiting new growth. In the spring, male pine cones with pollen appear at the base of young branches. The female cones appear at the end of each branch. These pine cones develop in two years into hard brown cones that open and release the seeds.

Symbiotic mushrooms grow off the tree's roots as they supply the tree with materials that are not common in rendzina soils such as iron and phosphorus. The roots do not dig deep, rather they spread along the subsurface. (This type of root pattern is adapted to soils with a poor water economy such as rendzina.) Planted saplings are able to grow off terra rossa soil. The root depth offers low stability to the tall tree as heavy snow or strong wind sometimes topples pines.

The tree grows for only 150 years, in contrast to the oak and terebinth which can surpass 500 years of age. Pines need sunlight to grow, oak and terebinth do not. Due to these facts, botanists think that the pine was never a main component of the Mediterranean forest, rather a pioneer in open lands, preparing the earth for the stabler forest of oak and terebinth. For example, following a fire in an open area, the pine, enjoying the available sunlight, flourish, creating a dense shady forest which inhibit new pine growth. Slowly but steadily, oak and terebinth trees sprout, and with the death of the pine tree generation, take over.

Today in Israel there are only a few spots with a natural pine forest, mainly in the Carmel Mountains and at a few sites in the Jerusalem Hills and Galilee. In the Mediterranean Basin the Aleppo pine is found in relatively arid regions. This is the only native pine in Israel. In Israel six other pines have been planted. Pine wood is used as lumber.

History

Historical issues are connected naturally to the people of the relevant period. People in historical contexts are usually connected either to settlements, roads or battlefields. The western Aminadav Ridge region and Har Eitan is a relatively desolate place in terms of historical events. The reason may have to do with its geographical location. Both ridges end abruptly in the middle of the Jerusalem Hills by the Nahal Sorek-Nahal Refa'im merger. This means that these two ridges do not reach the Judean Foothills. The next ridge south of the Aminadav Ridge, is the topographically higher backbone of the Hebron Hills that has for centuries carried the main road from Hebron to Jerusalem. These facts kept the Aminadav Ridge and Har Eitan strategically unimportant and neglected. As no main roads were built in the area, intense development has never taken place, and only small villages have occupied the ridges. Thus this area, sitting between three main roads to Jerusalem to the north, and the Hebron-Jerusalem road to the south, was always on the sidelines.

Only the summit of the ridge at Har Ora, 839 m. above sea level, has been utilized for observation and communication purposes for generations. From Har Ora on a clear day one can see the Mediterranean. The village of Ein Kerem has been identified by some as the biblical Bet Hakerem. Following this assumption, Har Ora, standing high above the village, was used for lighting bonfires to announce incoming danger as mentioned by Jeremiah (6:1) and for holiday declarations. Later, Har Ora was used for similar purposes by the Crusaders who called it *Montana*. The Turks, before the telegraph, also used the hilltop to transfer messages. Today the Israel Defense Force has a base there with tall antennae on the peak.

Another security installation, the Crusader fort of Belmont, was built atop Tel Tzuba, 1.5 km. north of the Sattaf. It was the southernmost of a series of fortresses around the Bet Horon road to Jerusalem. This Tzuba may have been the Tzova mentioned in the book of II Samuel, 23:36.

Sometime after the Ottoman conquest, Tza'ataf (Sattaf) and Tzuba developed from farm estates into central villages. With the laying of the railroad along Nahal Sorek and Nahal Refa'im, the first route of transportation passed by the Aminadav Ridge (from the south). The train station at Batir may have brought some modernization to the area dotted by small Arab villages. During WWI, General Sir Edmond Allenby attacked Jerusalem from many fronts, including Har Ora, by the village of El-G'ora. From Har Ora the force split into three groups. Two of the forces advanced along the ridge toward Jerusalem while the third took the village of Ein Kerem.

During the War of Independence the region was further ignored. One significant battle was the twelve-day Nahshon Operation fought by the Har'el Brigade under the command of Yitzhak Rabin, in early April 1948, which opened the siege to Jerusalem along the Sha'ar Hagai road. The farthest south that the forces reached was Tzuba, where they twice failed to capture the protruding hill.

Between the Nahshon Operation and the declaration of the State in May, soldiers of the the Har'el Brigade made two more attempts to capture Tzuba, but to no avail. During the battle of Ten Days in July the narrow Jerusalem Corridor was widened. This is when, during the Dani Operation, the I.D.F. finally took control of Tzuba and Tza'ataf and reached Nahal Sorek. The village of El-G'ora on Har Ora was taken by a youth force coming from Jerusalem. The I.D.F. kept an observation force on the hill. In October a cease fire seemed imminent. Between October 19-20 the Har Operation took place against the Egyptian Army and local Arabs in order to widen the Jerusalem Corridor. The forces coming from the captured village of Hussan (by Mevo Betar) made an attempt to capture the dominating Har Gilo (Bet Jalla) Ridge and failed, but the western parts of the Aminadav Ridge were secured by the Etzioni Brigade.

With the signing of the Rhodes cease fire treaty with Jordan, Israel gained official control of the whole Aminadav Ridge and received permission to operate the train freely via Nahal Refa'im which coincided with the border. Unfortunately, the train issue, like other agreements, was not respected by the Jordanians.

In the years after the war, with the influx of Jewish immigrants from the Oriental countries, a number of working moshavs were quickly established and roads constructed between them and Jerusalem.

Ein Yogad (Uzi) in the Judean Hills

Site description

Aminadav: The moshav was established by the Moshavim Movement. Founded in 1950 along with many other moshavs in the Jerusalem Hills, this one was settled by Jews from Kurdistan. The settlement is named for the father of Nahshon, one of the heads of the tribe of Judah during the exodus from Egypt. The moshav at first supported itself from fowl, crops and fruit orchards. Today its population is a more mixed group. It is a suburb of Jerusalem, where many of its members work.

Yad Kennedy: The memorial to J. F. Kennedy stands on a topographic high, 840 m. above sea level. The structure is shaped as a chopped tree trunk, symbolizing the tragic death of the American president. The 50 cement rails creating the trunk-shaped building represent the 50 states of the U.S.A. Inside on each cement rail is a plaque for each state and in the center a burning torch. The memorial was built with the support of American Jews and opened on July 4, 1966. Yad Kennedy is a very popular tourist site.

From the forested hill there is an outstanding view of the Jerusalem Hills and northwestern Hebron Hills. Here between 1948 and 1967 uprooted settlers of the Etzion Bloc in the Hebron Hills would come to look over the border at their destroyed settlements, 15 km. to the south.

Hurbat Sa'adim: In Arabic is known as *Hirbet Sa'ida*, either meaning happy or lucky. The ruins of the settlement include terraces, walls, broken pillars, olive press pieces and the tomb monument of Sheikh Ahmed. The latter is found, ruined, on the northern side of the open field, amidst the tall trees. Sheikh Ahmed, according to Moslem custom, had healing power. He had an ability to heal barren women to fertility, making them happy, and thus the name. The Moslem settlement here was preceded by Byzantine Christians. A Greek inscription was found on a lintel saying "This is the institute of the Priest Maruanus." This implies that a church or monastery was part of the agricultural settlement. About 15 years ago the inscription disappeared (like many other archaeological relics in the country).

The tall carob, terebinth and oak trees have survived due to the speciality of the tomb of Sheikh Ahmed. Some botanists look at the size of the trees at Hurbat Sa'adim as representing the natural potential of the Mediterranean forest. Intense human involvement has injured the development of such tree size in todays 'natural' forests of the region.

To the north of the low hill there is a memorial for the officer Shlomo Malakhi who was killed in the Six Day War. Northwest of the ruins by a road intersection begins the planted Salamon Forest, which is planned to be the future cemetery of Jerusalem. Right off the road is a picnic ground with water facilities, dedicated to the three Jewish Egyptian members of an Israeli underground movement in Cairo. Trying to uproot the government, they were caught and sentenced to death.

Hurbat Sa'adim is a nature reserve.

Ein Sa'adim: The spring was the main source of water for the people of Hurbat Sa'adim. The site is a beautiful example of the traditional structures built around a spring. Throughout the years the remnants have slowly deteriorated and were recently partially restored. This layer spring flows to surface from three points at 715 m. above sea level off a layer of Motza Marl. The main structures, including the tunnels, are Byzantine. The Moslem inhabitants kept up the basic structure that they found. Two hundred meters east of the spring is a small building that was once the home of the spring keeper. East of the spring are terraces that once held gardens fed with spring water.

Einot Aminadav: A series of three springs with chiseled source tunnels along Springs Trail. The water flows off Motza Marl. There is an individual spring, 200 m. east of two more adjacent ones (the western springs). It is plugged by falling debris from its tunnel's sides. All of the springs emerge a few meters south of the trail.

The two western springs which are 100 m. apart from each other are more interesting. The eastern of the two is the larger one with a tall cave-like tunnel reaching the source. After rainy seasons water makes its way from the tunnel, through the blocked man-made tunnel into the large storage pool. With flashlights it is possible to explore the tunnels. The tunnel of the western spring drops below the original level of the man-made tunnel, which leads to the pool. On the upper terrace is a chiseled water basin.

The eastern spring emerges in a man-made cave. From the cave the water runs along a 16 m. tunnel to a small storage pool. Below the storage pool and inside the cliff by the eastern spring is a burial cave, most likely Roman-Byzantine. During the years 1992-1994 I led a field crafts and navigation club of the Society for the Protection of Nature in Israel. We restored the spring's structures, cleared the tunnel of debris and found a chiseled water channel at the bottom of the tunnel, reaching the pool. We cleaned and restored the pool, which consequently refilled with water.

Einot Uzi: Named after the Arabic Abu Azi. Also known as Einot Yogad. Two springs flowing off Motza Marl, 680 m. above sea level, 250 m. above Evn Sapir. The springs are 150 m. apart, and here begins Springs Trail. Today, these two springs have the largest output of those along the hike. On the trail to the west of the springs is a ruin of a small Arab structure, most likely of the spring guardian. Like most of the traditional spring architecture, both springs have four main sections: 1) The source, in a chiseled-out cave. 2) Artificial tunnel. 3) Storage pool. 4) Agricultural terraces.

The northwestern spring's waters trickle down the terraced slope and feed a thicket of reeds, bramble and willow trees. Unfortunately, the hydrophylic vegetation is hidden by pine trees. The southeastern spring boasts a very interesting water channel hewed into the natural rock, running along and above the agricultural terrace. Along the channel's sides are openings for water release at different sections of the garden below. This type of ancient irrigation was used in the City of David with the Gihon Spring waters, feeding the gardens of Nahal Kidron during the time of the First Temple.

Today, both springs are being restored by field crafts and navigation clubs of the S.P.N.I.

To begin hike:

From the bus stop walk back 60 m. and take the road to your left. Sometimes the bus stops before the bus stop, at the intersection. The street heads between houses. Sixty meters down the street take a left, past a white gate. From this road you can see Yad Kennedy straight ahead. The road exits Aminadav, heads along cypress trees and then joins the road that heads up to the memorial. Follow the road down a bit and then up to Yad Kennedy (2). Along the way to the right note the outcrops of the soft chalk of the Kefar Sha'ul Formation. Enjoy the scenic spot.

From Yad Kennedy (2) a trail descends steeply from the paved road just after the wide parking lot. The trailhead is marked by a wooden sign. Be careful as the steep trail passes by a large bramble bush. The trail goes by a pine forest and then descends among the rough rocky terrain known as lapies formations, here occurring among the Aminadav Formation. The trail hits a paved road. Take the road to the left, to the parking lot of Hurbat Sa'adim (3).

Note the dirt road marked with a green trail mark that heads to the right (east), right before Hurbat Sa'adim. You will later connect to this trail.

Enter the ruins via the wide trail which heads through some almond trees. After visiting the special site, continue along the wide trail to the north, passing the memorial rock to your left. The trail drops to a dirt road. Take a left to the nearby intersection with the paved road which ends. By the intersection is a memorial plaque for three martyrs in Egypt. Take a right onto the gradually-descending dirt road. The way runs along the Salamon Picnic Site. After 300 m. take a right down a trail to Ein Sa'adim (4). In the spring cave a lot of maidenhair ferns grow and on the southern side of the channel a couple of anagyris trees have yellow blossoms in early winter.

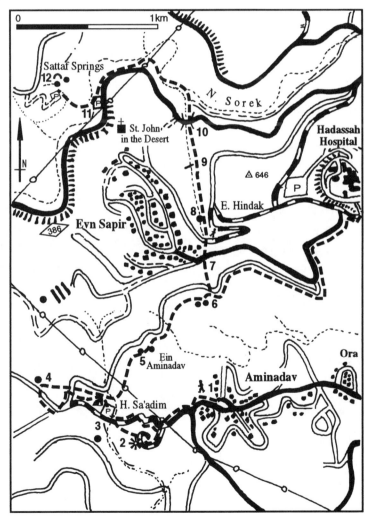

Hike 27, Springs Trail, and Hike 28, Ein Hindak to Sattaf Springs

From Ein Sa'adim, a wide trail heads toward Hurbat Sa'adim through an open field. Take it. The trail runs along a marly terrace covered with thorny calycotome that has yellow blossoms in late winter and knee-high, round, thorny burnet bushes. The trail brings you back, just about to where you were before, on the dirt road. Cross the dirt road and follow unmarked trail which begins by a lone post and a few small pine trees. The trail runs upon a marly terrace. As the trail passes a number of oaks, note the terrace wall on your right. This wall is recent, from the pre-1948 period, made by local Arab peasants. The trail reaches the green marked dirt road. This green-marked trail is known as Springs Trail.

Take a left, following the trail marker which immediately breaks off from the dirt road and leads you on a trail down a couple of terraces and across a gully into the pine forest. Looking back at the terrace you descended, note parts of it that in the last few years have collapsed. Soon after entering the forest reach Einot Aminadav which are along a few hundred meters of the clear trail (5). Explore. Unfortunately, the forest has covered the beauty of the interesting relics.

The green trail continues through pine and cypress and crosses a small gully. From the trail are nice views of Har Eitan and the Tzova Ridge. After crossing the dry gully, the trail drops a couple of terraces, rounds the ridge and after 350 m., reaches Einot Uzi (6). Explore <u>both</u> springs and enjoy a refreshing swim!

Between the two springs, the green trail (also bearing an I.N.T. mark) descends very steeply to the dirt road. Please be careful! For the loop trip, either return via Springs Trail or take the dirt road to the left back to Hurbat Sa'adim (3).

To get to Evn Sapir, cross the dirt road and follow the marked trail down through an olive grove, growing among rock of the Bet Meir Formation, to the entrance of Evn Sapir (7) where you can catch a bus back to Jerusalem.

Tulips bloom in March in the Judean Hills and Galilee

28 Ein Hindak to Sattaf Springs

*See map on
page 211*

Points of interest: *Human-improved springs and ancient
agriculture, ancient dam, Mediterranean scrub and pine
forest.*

Length and nature of hike: 2.5 kilometers, one-way. 4.5
kilometers back and forth. This hike can be continued after
Hike 27, 'Springs Trail.'

Hiking time: 2-3 hours.

Preferred season: All year.

Suitable for: All

Maps: Jerusalem Outskirts hiking and touring map.

Special preparation: Flashlight, swimsuit.

Starting point: Moshav Evn Sapir.

Ending point: Sattaf Springs.

To reach starting point:

Arrival by private transportation: From the Ein Kerem Hadassah Hospital head
toward Moshav Evn Sapir by taking a left, before the main entrance. At the
intersection below the hospital, take a right (not to Evn Sapir) and follow the road
all the way to the bottom of the wadi. This is the old road to Evn Sapir. Along the
way you will pass a turnoff to Road 386 on the right; further down, the road will
curve to the right and then to the left. Turn right upon reaching the parking lot by
Ein Hindak (8) in Wadi Yussuf. There is a brown sign in Hebrew on the right side
of the road marking Ein Hindak.

Arrival by public transportation: Take bus from Jerusalem to Evn Sapir. Get off
at the entrance (7). Just beyond the booth by the gate follow a trail that descends
one level below, it passes between two rectangular buildings (that once were chicken
coops). The unmarked trail leads you to Ein Hindak (8) 200 m. below, in the valley
of Wadi Yussuf.

It is also possible to take more frequent city bus lines to the Ein Kerem Hadassah
Hospital. This will cost you an extra 1.5 km. of scenic road walking. Get off by the
entrance and follow instructions above in 'Arrival by private transportation.'

Geography

The hike runs along the lower slopes of both sides of Nahal Sorek. The whole hike
is upon the Sorek Formation of alternating hard sedimentary rock and marl which
gives the landscape a terraced shape. The hard dolomite or limestone layer create

a short cliff which is separated from the next hard rock layer by a thin layer of soft marl which creates a very gradual slope. In the dolomites of the Sorek Formation, one can find round quartz geodes (balls) and chert nodules.

This natural phenomenon of terraces was easily utilized for agriculture. At the top of the small cliffs, small stone walls were created during different periods to hold the marl layer in place and to collect debris from above. Over time, a thick layer of soil accumulated, ideal for agriculture. With the continued soil accumulation and formation, the retaining wall was built higher. Today's landscape is a symbiosis of humans and their natural surroundings that has been going on for thousands of years.

Nahal Sorek is the largest of the wadis of the Jerusalem Hills. It drains 220 sq. km., 180 of them in the Jerusalem Hills. Nahal Sorek's two main tributaries, Nahal Refa'im and Nahal Kesalon, merge further downstream from the area of the hike. Between Jerusalem and the Nahal Refa'im-Nahal Sorek merge, Nahal Sorek flows in a relatively wide valley that narrows toward the west. The wide valley can be clearly viewed from Highway 1 between Motza and Jerusalem.

West of the Nahal Refa'im-Nahal Sorek junction, Nahal Sorek is a winding wadi with a number of sharp incised meanders. Geomorphologists explain the sharp turns of the stream bed with the theory that Nahal Sorek was once a large river, possibly 150 km. long! Before the Syrian-African Rift dissected the whole region, Nahal Sorek began somewhere in Transjordan. The power of such a stream is the only logical explanation for Nahal Sorek's strong impact on the landscape.

East of the junction with Nahal Refa'im, in the area of the hike, you can see a series of hills that were possibly the stream bed level of the ancient Nahal Sorek. Notice the elevation of Evn Sapir and the ridge to its southwest, holding three rectangular buildings, the slope west of the Hadassah Hospital, and further east, the Ein Kerem Agricultural School and Moshav Bet Zayit. All have a similar elevation, possibly representing the level of ancient Nahal Sorek. Since the rifting, Nahal Sorek has cut into the Sorek Formation in the vicinity of the hike, creating small tributaries like Wadi Yussuf.

Plants and animals

Grape Vine (*Vitis vinifera*): From the dawn of human history the vine and its fruit were widely cultivated in the Old Testament world: "Noah began to be an husband-man, and he planted a vineyard." (Genesis 9:20). The high standard of viticulture in Canaan prior to the Israelite conquest is evident from the story of the spies sent by Moses to explore the land, returning with "a cluster of grapes" (Numbers 13:23). In those days a courteous host offered wine, the choicest drink, to honored guests: "Malkhitzedek King of Salem (Jerusalem) brought out bread and wine to Abram" (Genesis 14:18).

The importance of viticulture in the Land of Israel during biblical times was manifest in the vintage season. The late-summer days were recognized as the most joyous. Young men would disperse in the vineyard where the girls of

Jerusalem danced in white gowns. The men would then select their spouses. This festival is mentioned in detail in the Mishna (tractate Ta'anit 4:5).

The wine became a symbol of bounty and of God's blessing for the future (Amos 9:13). The vine was one of the 'seven species' with which the Holy Land was blessed, and was regarded as a national emblem. It appeared on mosaic floors, murals and portals of houses of worship, on pottery, furniture, tombs and coins. Even in exile the Jews cultivated the memory of the grapes of Judah, chiseling their shape on tombstones in foreign lands.

In the New Testament, spiritual meanings are attributed to the vine, and the most significant of them is recorded in John when Jesus identifies himself with this plant.

The grape vine is a climbing shrub from whose base numerous slender woody branches sprout, spreading along the ground or climbing with long entwined tendrils. The plant holds sterile and fertile branches, the latter growing so fast that they sometimes increase by 4 m. in a single season.

Cultivators prop up the vine with sticks to keep the heavy fruit off the ground. The fruit, whose color comes from the membranous skin but whose flesh itself is colorless, is a berry containing two seeds. In the wild species the berries are dispersed by birds. The five-toothed lobe leaves unfold in early spring and drop in the fall.

The vine is one of 50 species, all of temperate regions. The species in Israel is a native of southern Europe, established in the Levant in the Early Bronze. In the Byzantine period there were vineyards even in the Negev. Today the wine industry is bubbling again in Israel while throughout the Mediterranean parts of the country, wild grape vines can still be found.

Horn-leaved sage (*Salvia fruticosa*): This small plant has fuzzy pale green leaves that are tri-lobed, with one leaflet on each side of the main leaf. The aromatic plant makes a good tea (a little sugar can overcome the bitterness).

History

See Hike 27, 'Springs Trail.'

Site description

Evn Sapir: Founded in 1961, it is mainly inhabited by immigrants from Kurdistan. The moshav is named after the book "Evn Sapir" written by the Lithuanian rabbi and traveller, Ya'akov Halevi Sapir. The mid-19th century book describes his 5 year fund-raising mission in Yemen, Australia, India and New Zealand. Evn Sapir is situated on the ruins of the small Arab village of Katra. In 1978, 500 people lived in the moshav, making a living from the traditional moshav occupations; orchards, chicken coops and working outside of the moshav.

Ein Hindak: In Arabic the spring's name, En el-Handak, means gouged-out trench, an apt description. The spring is 580 m. above sea level and is one of the more interesting water sources in the Jerusalem Hills. It emerges on marl and the three tunnels are chiseled into limestone of the Sorek Formation. The three plastered tunnels are full of waist-deep fresh water which emerges at their end. Dams at the mouth of the tunnels elevate the water table in order to allow irrigation at an additional terrace level. All three tunnels drain into a large storage pool which today is usually full of litter and (aside from a puddle or two) devoid of water. The storage pool drains via a narrow tunnel and from there a water channel runs along the eastern bank of the valley.

The southern tunnel is the longest—53 m.—and along it rises a manhole with a ladder installed. The eastern tunnel splits into two tunnels inside as the right tunnel (southern) is 31 m. long.

Descending the ladder to the tunnels and wading through these dark tunnels is an exciting, cool experience.

Dam in Wadi Yussuf: The wall was constructed when the wadi to its south still looked like the continuation of the wadi further north; i.e., relatively narrow. The builders of the dam had two goals: to utilize the waters of Ein Hindak for agriculture and to create an area which can support such crops. Thus, they built the dam higher than the field level. During agricultural periods, the vegetation cover on the slopes was sparse and runoff carried a lot of earth particles that were deposited in the wadi bed. Many years of this process created the landscape of today—a wide valley of rich earth that, with the presence of a dam, abruptly becomes a narrow wadi downstream.

The dam is 43 m. long and 9.5 m. high. The blocks, held together by cement, are arranged in eleven rows. The longest block is 3 m. long. Note the openings at different spots along the wall to allow water seepage.

Since the wall resembles the famous Western Wall in Jerusalem, some think that this wall is from the same period, around the year 0. Today, sometimes, the dam is referred to as *Hakotel Hakatan*—"the Little (Western) Wall," and Wadi Yussuf is known as Wadi Kotel. The Western Wall was built without cement and the blocks have a very typical Herodian masonry, differing from the wall of Wadi Yussuf. The wall was probably built during the Early Arab period, although it is likely that the wadi was utilized before. The reason for such an effort at this unique site is still baffling.

Today the dam supports interesting cliff vegetation.

Nahal Sorek: The 42 km. long wadi begins along Israel's watershed in the Bet El Hills, and enters the Mediterranean Sea by Palmahim, between Ashdod and Tel Aviv. Nahal Sorek is the most winding wadi in Israel. *Sorek* or *soreka* is a type of excellent grape vine as mentioned in Isaiah 5:1-2:

> Now I will sing to my well-beloved a song of my beloved touching his vineyard. My well-beloved had a vineyard in a very fruitful hill and he fenced it and gathered out the stones thereof and planted it with the choicest vine (*sorek*) and built a tower (*shomera*) in the midst of it and also made a wine press therein and he looked that it should bring forth grapes and it brought forth wild grapes.

We also read of the *sorek* when Jacob blesses Judah in Genesis 49:11:

> Binding his foal unto the vine, and his ass's colt unto the choice vine; he washed his garments in wine and his clothes in the blood of grapes.

Along its route, Nahal Sorek has at least five Arabic names. In the section of the hike it is known as Wadi Kolonia, after the Roman fort and later the small Arab village of Kolonia at Motza. For generations, Christians identified the wadi as Emek Ha'ela where David battled Goliath, as many *ela* (terebinth) trees grow in the vicinity. The Crusaders saw the valley of Nahal Sorek as being a holy valley. The story of John the Baptist from the village of Ein Kerem, secluding himself in the crannies of the cliffs of Nahal Sorek, strengthened their mistaken conclusion. In the 19th century the monastery of "St. John in the Desert" was established by a small spring on the southern slope of Nahal Sorek, across from Sattaf. The chosen site was by a cave and spring where by tradition, John the Baptist meditated.

Sattaf Springs: The springs emerge from the southern slope of Har Eitan. The site is unknown from written sources. The root of the word is used in the Mishna in tractate Damai 1:1, referring to a cut in the sycamore fruit which increases its ripening speed.

Archaeological survey has found pottery from the Chalcolithic period and the First Temple period (6th-8th century B.C.E.), but the main finds are from Roman-Byzantine times. The lower parts of the Ein Bikura pool appear to be Roman-Byzantine. During the last few centuries an Arab village existed known as Tza'ataf. A 19th century traveller writes of Tza'ataf as having 180 residents. The seventy families abandoned their village in 1948 and until today continue to live in refugee camps.

After 1948, Sattaf was settled for a short while by a group of ex-Lohmei Herut Israel (Lehi) fighters who called it Bikura. The settlement did not last and the site was abandoned. During the 1950s the site was used as a training camp for soldiers of the famous I.D.F. Unit 101, commanded by Ariel Sharon. Ever since, the site has gradually deteriorated. In 1970 the structures were destroyed during a 'project' of the Labor government directed at all of the abandoned Arab villages in the Jerusalem Corridor. In 1983, the J.N.F. in association with the Jewish Agency and the Regional Council of the Judean Hills began site renovations. These renovations were undertaken in conjunction with two families who live by the site and take care of it. Volunteers also maintain small garden sections beneath the springs. The vegetables and herbs of the gardens are organically grown and sold locally. The aim of the renovations is to turn the site into an educational center relating to ancient and traditional agriculture, as well as make the site an attractive place to visit. Today there is also a kiosk and on Fridays a shepherd who lives nearby sells goat cheese. Future plans call on creating a traditional produce processing workshop such as an olive press, wine press, flour mill and more.

Sattaf Springs are among the largest and most detailed water systems in the Jerusalem Hills. The two springs of the site, Ein Sattaf and Ein Bikura, emerge

The tunnel and pool of the eastern Sattaf Spring

at 580 m. above sea level from a marl-limestone contact in the Sorek Formation: they have water systems which were built to exploit the natural spring aquifer. Horizontal tunnels were cut into the slope of the hill in order to increase the spring outflow. The springs give 4-12 cubits per hour of fresh water. The water collects in plastered storage pools and then overflows into terraces.

The western spring, Ein Sattaf, is known in Arabic as En el-Balad, "spring of the village." The name is a common one for an Arab village's main source of fresh water. The pool can hold up to 170 cubits and is great for swimming.

Ein Bikura is known in Arabic as the eastern spring, a common Arab name. The spring's short tunnel ends at a stalactite-adorned source room. The two rows of holes at the base of the plastered pools may have been used for breeding fish. Today the pool contains fish. The holes date to the Roman-Byzantine period. A fruitful lemon tree stands above the pool.

To begin hike:

Twenty m. from the paved road, find the manhole with a ladder descending to the northern tunnel of Ein Hindak (8). Single almond and olive trees grow in the restored park where the manhole is found. Head to the manhole, which is to the right of the main trail, between two one-meter-high walls that encompass it. Descend with water walking attire and a flashlight. Leave your belongings above with somebody. The tunnel to the right dead-ends at the source. To the left, the tunnel drains out into the main (empty) storage pool. From the storage pool it is worthwhile exploring the eastern tunnel as well.

From the storage pool follow the green-marked trail along the eastern side of the valley of Wadi Yussuf. Note the difference in composition between the rock wall on your left and the more ancient one on your right. The wide field on the left is full of common fennel. The fennel is easily recognized by its long green stem and small yellow flowers.

The trail after 100 m. passes a *shomera*, a guardhouse. The *shomera* was used by peasants to rest by their fields and to store tools and crops during the harvest season. The *sorek* fable of Isaiah (5:1-2), begins in such a place:

218

My well-beloved had a vineyard in a very fruitful hill. And he fenced it and he built a tower (*shomera*) in the midst of it.

The thick stone walls keep the insides of the *shomera* at a very stable, cool temperature during the hot summer days. Even today in the hills north and south of Jerusalem the *shomera* is still used. Most *shomerot* have two floors and an accessible roof deck. The roof was used for sleeping, socializing and drying produce.

It seems that this guardhouse is a result of at least two building stages. The impressive entrance posts contrast sharply with the small rocks of the domed roof.

Note the unkempt water channel from Ein Hindak which runs parallel to the trail. At this section the trail heads along a terrace. In better days, the water was diverted at a number of spots into the now deserted field below where vegetables were grown. A short cliff is exposed on the right. Many oriental podonosma plants dot its face. Looking closely you can see tennis ball-size holes in the rock, from which quartz geodes have fallen out. If you are lucky you may see one along the trail or in the wadi.

The trail descends some carved stairs along the water channel. At the bottom of the stairs to your left there is an interesting set of stairs dropping to the field, built into the rock terrace. Growing along the water channel by the bottom of the stairs is a small line of inulas. The inula bush grows year-round, with yellow blossoms in the fall. In winter also look for the gracefully blooming narcissus.

Continue on the trail to the impressive dam wall (9). It is worthwhile exploring the construction from above and then follow the trail (on the right) to the bottom.

From the dam, for the next 300 m., you have two options: 1) the green-marked trail continues along the lushly adorned dry stream bed and drops down a few small falls. 2) An unmarked trail, indicated at first by two rows of stones, also heads out from the bottom of the dam along the eastern bank. This trail heads through the pine forest and follows the wadi from about 20 m. above.

Both trails meet before Road 386. Just before it you can find the horn-leaved sage. Follow the trail marker beneath the road (10) and merge with the dirt road.

Descend on the dirt road, marked both blue and green, and soon it heads to the left parallel to Nahal Sorek, which is on your right. Beneath the dirt road runs one of Jerusalem's sewage lines. A few kilometers downstream the pipe ends and Nahal Sorek becomes a flowing stream of sewage.

The fields nearby were once olive orchards. Today, the natural oak is on the comeback and the J.N.F. recently planted trees there. The open landscape here is a good place to catch a sight of gazelles, a hovering bird of prey such as a kestrel or chukars—partridge-like fowls. The open landscape in summertime is colored by blue, yellow and purple thorny thistle flowers. In the winter, hundreds of red anemones dot the countryside.

The dirt road follows the stream bed for 1 km. until reaching the asphalt-covered parking lot below the Sattaf Springs (11). From the parking lot, head up the steep clear trail to the Sattaf complex. Along the way up, enjoy the expanding view behind you of the St. John in the Desert monastery, Evn Sapir, Hadassah Hospital and western Jerusalem. In winter and spring, white to pink cyclamens and yellow groundsels adorn the trails' sides.

Note how along the ascent, the geological pattern is of rock ledges, 1-2 m. high. These ledges, typical of the Sorek Formation, give the landscape its terraced shape.

Upon reaching the pool of Ein Sattaf, explore the complex. From the pool a trail leads to the right and after 200 m. descends to Ein Bikura. With a flashlight it is worthwhile exploring the spring's tunnel to its source room.

Return to Ein Sattaf via the agricultural compound, beneath mulberry and other trees. Descend to the parking lot (11) the same way you came. On Road 386 by the parking lot is a bus stop where you can catch a bus back to Jerusalem via Ein Kerem.

29 Ein Kobi to Ein Yoel

See map on
page 226

Points of interest: *Springs with pools surrounded by fruit gardens amidst a pine forested landscape.*

Length and nature of hike: 7 kilometers, loop trip, can be done by vehicle.

Hiking time: 4-6 hours.

Preferred season: All year.

Suitable for: All.

Maps: Jerusalem Outskirts hiking and touring map.

Special preparation: Swimsuit, flashlight.

Starting & ending point: Moshav Mevo Betar.

To reach starting point:

Arrival by private transportation: Road 375 from Emek Ha'ela or Road 386 from Ein Kerem (by Jerusalem) meet 1.5 km. west of Mevo Betar. From here follow Road 376 past the village of Tzur Hadassah to Mevo Betar. Enter the moshav and follow the main road which curves to the right. Park by the minimarket on the right (1).

For those who want to drive the hike, pass the main entrance to Mevo Betar and 750 m. later take a left off Road 376 on to a gravel road. The turnoff is marked by a number of signs. Stick to the right as the gravel road descends along the eastern side of the valley which is the beginning of Nahal Kobi. After 1.5 km., turn to the left onto a dirt road and immediately reach the Ein Kobi complex (3).

Arrival by public transportation: Take bus from Jerusalem to Mevo Betar. Get off in Mevo Betar at the minimarket (1).

Geography

The Mevo Betar, or Ya'alah Ridge, is one of the five ridges of the Jerusalem Hills. It is a relatively flat area which comprises a watershed between the sharp drop to the deep valley of Nahal Refa'im and Nahal Sorek to the North and a series of shorter wadis that drain southwest into the Emek Ha'ela region.

Along the watershed (which coincides with Road 386) runs a geological fault, the southwestern section being the lower block. The eastern side of the watershed is covered with dolomites and limestones of the Aminadav Formation. Deeper strata are exposed along the slopes dropping to wadis. The layer below the Aminadav Formation is the well-known Motza Formation of yellowish marl (Motza

Marl). Due to its unique lithology and appearance in the landscape, Motza Marl is defined as a key horizon. In the Mevo Betar region this point is accentuated.

Since Motza Marl is revealed at the upper, gentler parts of the slope, it creates a wide flat terrace. It is an aquiclude; springs emerge all along it. In the Mevo Betar area, small springs emerge along the slopes. This is due to the meager dip of the strata and the thinness of the Aminadav Formation, the only formation lying above. Livelier springs (such as Ein Kobi and Ein Yoel) gush out in the wadis (Nahal Kobi and Nahal Yoel). Both of these wadis drop steeply to Nahal Refa'im.

Plants and animals

Quince (*Cydonia vulgaris*): Quince originates in central to western Asia. The tree was known in Babylonia 6,000 years ago. Not much later it became common in the Middle East. It is mentioned in the Mishna. Today, the tree can be found as far afield as California and South America.

Known in Hebrew as *Havoosh*, the quince is a deciduous tree. The tree has round leaves and boasts a large, five-petal white or pink flower, one per branch. Thus, cultivated trees demand much pruning to induce new branches. The yellowish fruit has a wrinkled texture and ripens in October. One hundred grams of fruit flesh contain 84 grams of water, 7.6 grams of available carbohydrates, 0.5 grams of protein, 200 mg. of potassium, and 34 calories.

In 1948 there were 600 dunams of quince orchards in Israel, expanding to 2,800 dunams in the 1960s. This created a surplus and orchards were uprooted. Today only 800 dunams of quince orchards are known.

The quince is not eaten ripe, but used for jams, canned fruit and jellies. Maimonides writes that the juice is good for curing a hangover and for finishing off a meal. He also recommends eating broiled quince to induce merriness.

Snake eagle (*Circaetus gallicus*): A large reptile-eating raptor. Its length is 62-70 cm. and its wingspan reaches 2 m. The bird has a large wide head with large yellow eyes resembling a night raptor. Its upper body is brown-grey while its lower body is lighter, dotted with dark brown spots and a brown throat.

The snake eagle lives in North Africa and southern Europe. Wintering takes place in the Sahel, south of the Sahara. In Israel the bird is usually found in summer in the non-desert hilly regions. Migration peaks in early October and March, in small groups of 3-5 members. Sometimes the bird will fly in a flock of twenty or thirty. The route to Africa is over northern Sinai, rather than the well-known migration route of the Syrian-African Rift.

Snake eagles usually nest in pairs in Israel. The nests are generally atop trees and sometimes cliffs, in regions that have open fields in close proximity. The nest is about 1 m. across, constructed of twigs and leaves. Two to three kilometers is the average distance between nests, as each couple has 1–9 km. of territory. Territorial feuds can occur, although usually the dominant couple will allow another snake eagle to hunt their grounds once in a while.

Reeds

The raptor can hover in the air but usually glides to scan the area. Sometimes it will watch the hunting grounds from a treetop or cliff. Its diet consists mainly of snakes, giving it the Hebrew name *hivya'ee*, from the Aramaic *hivviya* (snake). It kills a snake with the brute force of its feet and beak. Another way it kills is to drop the prey from the sky. In this manner, the raptor can consume snakes up to 2 m. long and even venomous ones (although the bird is not immune).

The phenomena of a snake turning the tables and choking a snake eagle to death has been observed. With this possibility, the eagle sometimes turns to other prey, such as lizards, rodents and small birds. Poisoning of field rodents by farmers in the 1960s caused a severe decrease in Israel's raptor population. As die-hard reptile eaters, the snake eagles kept their number steady.

The mating season begins upon their return to summer nesting. The male performs dives and other acrobatics. During this time the snake eagle is one of the most vocal raptors with a loud whine. In early April the female lays one white, 135 gram egg which incubates for 45 days. Both parents tend the chick. At 75 days or so the young one leaves the nest. It returns to its parents the following spring and remains there until a younger sibling is born.

History

The Arabs called Kobi, Kabo, meaning a sealed—ceiling basement. This name describes the underground pool at Ein Kobi. Some researchers have tried identifying Kobi with the village of Kabon of the land of Judea mentioned in Joshua

15:40. This interpretation is a stretch, for the neighboring towns mentioned are in the Judean Foothills. Kabo is mentioned in the description of Sennacherib's (King of Assyria) approach to Jerusalem from Lakhish in the Judean Foothills.

A tale connects Kobi with King David. Goliath's brothers caught David in the land of the Philistines and tried to kill him by smashing his head in an olive press. A miracle occurred—the rocks became soft. Avishai, David's brother, rescued him and they escaped from the Philistines (in the southern Judean Foothills) with Goliath's brother in pursuit. When reaching the village of Kobi, David and Avishai said: "*Kub bey*"—we will avenge. When they reached Betar they said: Can "*batri*" (two) cubs kill the lion? And they got up and killed Goliath's brother.

The area was intensively settled during Talmudic times. Kobi and Kefar Tzoom, which lies above Nahal Yoel, is mentioned along with Betar in the tractate of Sanhedrin (95a). No information about Kobi is given. Betar was most likely the larger village of the area as many Talmudic sayings mention it. According to tractate Sanhedrin (17b), Betar was home to three people who each knew 70 languages, thus qualifying the town as a seat for the Supreme Court. Finally, Betar was the place where Bar Kokhba found his death after withstanding the lengthy Roman siege.

Mevo Betar coincides with the Roman Jerusalem-Ashkelon road. The road is based upon an Israelite one. The Roman road came from Emek Ha'ela up the Matta Ridge and then ran along the ridge of Mevo Betar, eastward, up to the Hebron Hills by Solomon's Pools. From the pools, the road ran via Bethlehem to Jerusalem. This lengthy route follows ridges in order to protect against ambush.

For details of the area's events during the 1948 war, see Hike 30, 'Nahal Hama'ara.'

Site description

Mevo Betar: Founded by the Herut-Betar movement in 1950 as a communal moshav. At the time it was a frontier settlement, being less than 1 km. from the Jordanian border. The name derives from the ancient Jewish village of Betar where the Arab village of Batir stands today. The moshav at first invested in field crops and chickens. Today they have a swimming pool, overnight facilities and other tourism facilities. Some of the members work in Jerusalem.

Ein Kobi: The spring lies at the edge of a broad alluvial valley. The permeability of the valley's strata, along with the fact that it lies on the Motza Formation, gives it a relatively decent output. From Ein Kobi, Nahal Kobi begins its steep descent to Nahal Refa'im.

The spring is sealed, like the one mentioned in the Song of Songs (4:12): "A garden enclosed is my sister, my spouse; a spring shut up, a fountain sealed."

The spring's structures include two tunnels, an underground reservoir, two vertical shafts and two fountains—for drinking and to supply the garden outside. The underground pool shows Roman or Byzantine hewed rocks at the base of its walls. The cement ceiling is from this century. The building beside the trough and external pool was first constructed in Roman-Byzantine times. Later, when Moslems arrived, they converted the building to a place of prayer. Evidence of the fact is the *makhrab*, the niche in the southern wall. A 19th century traveller writes of this site being known as Sheikh Mahmid el-Ajami.

Around the spring grow fruits of the "seven species" and many others such as almonds, bramble, pear and quince. Some of the nearby terraces also date back nearly 2,000 years. The J.N.F. has turned the site into a place for picnics and recreation.

At the peak of the ridge to the east stand the ruins of the village Kabu. Ein Kobi was the water source for the village that was a thriving Jewish settlement during the Roman and Byzantine period. The site was also home for Arab peasants who fled in 1948 to the Hebron Hills. Today, survivors and their descendants are probably still in refugee camps.

Ein Yoel: A group of springs with a neglected terraced garden. The terraces hold bramble, almonds, pears and figs. The spring was formerly used by the villagers of Ras Abu Amar which is located further down the above ridge.

The springs emerge below a limestone cliff upon Motza Marl. The main spring's water collects in a round cement tank which once served Mevo Betar. There is a recent accumulation of travertine on the tank's sides. It is usually full of clear water. On the pump building by the trail is a memorial placard: "Yoel, son of Yehudah Potopovitz, was murdered here in 1950 by terrorists" coming from across the then nearby border.

Along the terrace of springs leads a trail among bramble, which ripen in late summer-fall. The trail passes many interesting sites, such as the ancient spring tunnels, pools and burial caves, edible grape vines descending from the cliff and other plants and trees.

To begin hike:

From the minimarket (1) continue along the external road of the moshav, passing a section of new houses. As the road curves to the right, exit the moshav through a gate in the fence (2).

If the gate is closed continue on the external road and soon on your left is a gate leading to an adjacent A.T.V. rental site. Exit Mevo Betar on road that goes through gate and go through the gravel parking lot. Continue on clear dirt road that goes through young pine forest. At blue gate, turn left. At triple intersection take left along pine trees. The dirt road descends, curves left and after 200 m. meets a paved road coming from the closed gate (2) of Mevo Betar.

Follow old paved road that descends between planted pine forest on the left and wide valley on the right, the beginning of Nahal Kobi. Across the valley is a gravel road which was once the I.D.F. patrol road along the Jordanian border. Today, the gravel road is the access road to Ein Kobi. As the road curves to the left you can see the pine-topped summit of Yad Kennedy (see Hike 27) 4 km. to the northeast. At the top of the pine forest across the valley a bit further north, stands Hurbat Kobi where the Arab village of Kabu stood until 1948.

One kilometer down, the paved road ends. Descend ahead to the edge of the plum orchard. Cross through the natural forest tussled with grape vines to the Ein Kobi complex (3).

From Ein Kobi follow the dirt road that heads up between the picnic sites. The black-marked dirt road levels off, heading 500 m. to the north through pine forest. The dirt road more or less follows a layer of soft yellow Motza Marl, ideal for road construction.

After a sharp curve to the left there is a small spring cave and a fig tree on your left. The cave has collapsed since the man-made cut in soft marl eventually caused the dolomite on top to crumble. The plugged spring is known as Ein Tasit (*Tooz* in Arabic), named after a small ruin to the south. Continue on comfortable dirt road. Here, through the trees, you have a view of Nahal Refa'im far below, where the railroad passes to Jerusalem, and of Aminadav Ridge on the other side. Here, in the summer, you may spot the snake eagle.

Follow dirt road around a gully and reach a turnoff to the left. Take left following the black trail mark. After 200 m. at the ridge top, take the second right where a carob tree stands between two parallel dirt roads. Descend on dirt road into the drainage basin of Nahal Yoel. Along the way, a number of dirt roads merge from

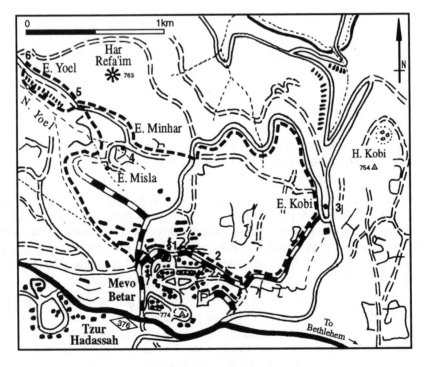

Hike 29, Ein Kobi to Ein Yoel

the left. Four hundred meters from the carob tree intersection, Ein Minhar (4) emerges into a pool 75 m. to the left of the dirt road, above the open field in the valley. A bit further down the valley, the western tributary of Nahal Yoel merges.

There is no sign or clear trail leading to Ein Minhar. The descent to the spring begins where a large fig tree stands on your right and a fence and black pipe on your left. The (usually dry) pool of the spring is just beyond an overgrown dirt road that runs parallel and 75 m. southwest of the one you came on.

Return to main dirt road and continue for 1 km. from Ein Minhar as Nahal Yoel deepens on your left and a pine forest hugs your right. (For those coming by car, it is best to park 500 m. after Ein Minhar where a dirt road comes in from the left (5). Here continue on foot as described.) After reaching a clear turnoff to the right continue straight and begin to look for an unmarked steep descent to the left. Do not take the dirt road's curve to the right, rather find a descent to the left. There seems to be a mediocre way down through almond trees, where the dirt road runoff veers left of the road and cuts a path down (6). Twenty m. below is a clear trail upon which the Ein Yoel springs emerge.

Warning: Descent to this unmarked and unclear trail is very steep! On rainy days the descent can be very slippery! The descent is *not* to the wadi of Nahal Yoel!

When hitting a wide terrace with relatively minute vegetation, go left on the clear trail. You should pass the dwelling quarters of Nahman Farkash, Israel's number one boxer in the 1950s who lives off nature and uses Ein Yoel's water for many purposes. The trail drops and continues left to the water tank where the most plentiful spring emerges. It is a great swim inside!

Continue along the trail past two more springs. Explore! The Ein Yoel area is one of the relatively unknown natural recreation sites in the Jerusalem Hills. Pass poplar trees on right and caves on left and ascend stairs by burnt-out area on your left to dirt road intersection where you have previously been (and parked private transportation) (5). Take a right on the dirt road and veer gently to the right by the open area where the two wide tributaries of Nahal Yoel coincide.

Along the current dirt road runs a ditch which drains the water of Ein Misla. Ein Misla will interest die-hard hikers only. It emerges among the thick vegetation between this dirt road and that which ascends to the left between the two valleys. One of the sources of Ein Misla is just to the right of the dirt road that turns off to the left, some 40 m. from the intersection. At the source, a couple of deep niches have been cut in the small cliff and below them runs a channel through the vegetation into the roadside ditch.

Continue on dirt road through gate and take sharp left onto a paved red-marked road. Follow the road past Mevo Betar's cemetery on the left. At intersection, follow the red marking to the right, past chicken coops, and reach the external Mevo Betar road. Take left to the starting point (1).

Nahal Hama'ara

See map on
page 235

Points of interest: *Springs of different types, an impressive karstic cave, ruins, grand view of the western Judean Hills and eastern Judean Foothills.*

Length and nature of hike: 9 kilometers, one-way. A 4-kilometer loop trip by private transportation access can be done, omitting the Te'omim Cave.

Hiking time: 5-8 hours.

Preferred season: All year.

Suitable for: All.

Maps: Jerusalem Outskirts hiking and touring map.

Special preparation: Flashlight, change of clothes and/or clothes suitable for getting very dirty (for (optional) entrance to Ein Soofla).

Starting point: Moshav Bar Giora.

Ending point: Moshav Zanoah or Giv'at Sharet by Bet Shemesh where there is public transportation to Jerusalem.

To reach starting point:

Arrival by private transportation: Coming from Jerusalem, exit the city through Ein Kerem and follow Road 386 to Bar Giora. Coming from the west (from Bet Shemesh, no road number), head to the Ness Harim road where you turn right to Bar Giora (1). The moshav's entrance has a sign. Turn into the moshav (1). For the loop trip follow the hike description from here on.

Arrival by public transportation: Take bus from Jerusalem central bus station to Bar Giora. Get off by the entrance (1).

Geography

Nahal Hama'ara begins at the divide with Nahal Sorek, near Bar Giora. It drains westward into Nahal Zanoah, which in turn drains the valley between the Jerusalem Hills and Judean Foothills. Nahal Hama'ara is named for the large Te'omim Cave on its northern bank.

Nahal Hama'ara is only 6 km. long and drops 400 m. The wadi is one of eight that run westward from the divide with the basin of Nahal Sorek, to the Judean Foothills. The wadi is wide at its upper parts since the geological layers have no tilt. This is because the axis of the Ramallah anticline passes in a north-south direction. Further down, the wadi keeps its width as it cuts the soft Motza Marl. Upon this formation the wadi springs emerge.

Further west, the dry stream bed narrows as it cuts deeper into the hard sedimentary rock of the Bet Meir Formation. The last two kilometers of Nahal Hama'ara cut through the heavily-tilted strata. The sharp tilt gives the stream a steep drop, which causes the formation of small potholes in the exposed rock. The stream is short and runoff in the area minute, due to intense vegetational cover and deep soil. Hence, the bedrock denudation is not sharp and the stream bed runs along layers of rock—an interesting phenomenon. Due to the dip, the lower parts of Nahal Hama'ara cross a number of geological formations. The sharp dip of the strata, being exposed, gives the opening of the wadi a rugged landscape. Along here the Te'omim Cave is exposed.

Nahal Hama'ara opens into a valley which marks the beginning of the Judean Foothills. The (one-way) hike passes the Jerusalem Hills-Judean Foothills contact. This topographical contact represents a geological and geographical change as well. The field is composed of conglomerate of the Bet Nir Formation from the geologically-recent Miocene epoch. The eastern slope is chalk of the Ghareb Formation from the late Senonian. The formations do not lie upon each other in succession; this is known as an unconformity.

Geographically, the slope is the edge of the Jerusalem Hill section of the Judean Hills. The field belongs to the valley where the Judean Foothills begin. The wide valley follows the Judean Hill-Judean Foothill contact. It was formed by a sharp geological change. The sharply-tilted rock layers of the Judean Hills dive underground and are covered in the Foothills by more recent formations that were deposited millions of years after the deposition of the Judean Hill strata. The softer Judean Foothill rock was hardly influenced by the serious tilting that occurred earlier to the Judean Hill rock.

Plants and animals

Lemon (*Citrus limon*): Originally from tropical Asia, it is mentioned in 4th century B.C.E. texts of the Near East. In the Mediterranean region, the lemon has been around for only hundreds of years. It was a common fruit for sea-goers as its high vitamin C content (40-60 mg. per deciliter of lemon juice) prevents gum disease and scurvy. It is a common tree in Arab villages and is found in every Israeli church or monastery garden.

The lemon has two subspecies: the egg-shaped, rough-rinded Eureca and the Lisbon. The Lisbon is common and has many local varieties. The leaves are light colored and sharp at the end. The branches contain many thorns. The purple flowers bloom throughout the season, thus at any given moment, the fruits will be of different sizes.

In contrast to other citrus trees, the lemon grows quickly and often needs pruning. All Mediterranean species have recently been decimated by Mal-secco disease. Today, lemons grow on 20,000 dunams of land in Israel, 5% of the total citrus crop.

The lemon has uses beyond vitamin supplementation. Lemon juice has been found effective against infectious illnesses such as the flu, pneumonia and arthritis. The perfume industry extracts an ether oil from the rind.

<u>Egyptian Fruit-Bat</u> (*Rousettus aegyptiacus*): Largest of bats found in Israel, it reaches 14.5 cm., and weighs over 100 grams. It is covered with short, dark, brown-grey fur.

The bat is found in all of Africa (except in the Sahara), through the Middle East all the way to India. In Israel, the bat prefers the Mediterranean region, but also lives in the desert, adjacent to cultivated fields. Some think that this bat found its way to Israel following the sycamore tree, which was introduced by humans thousands of years ago. The sycamore's fruits are a main constituent of the bat's summer diet. Before the fruit tree trend which began in the mid-20th century in Israel, the fruit-bat lived mainly off of sycamore in summer and carob in the winter.

With the agricultural development of Israel, the fruit-bat population has severely increased and has had to adapt to the shortage of living quarters. Fruit-bats prefer dark, moist places: caves, wells and ruins. Thousands of bats can dwell in a suitable cave. Today in Israel, due to cave shortage, we also find the bats in unused buildings and underground parking lots. For example, before the Diaspora Museum in Tel Aviv was completed, fruit-bats were found in the structure.

In caves, sometimes all-male, all-female, or all-juvenile groups are found. These groups leave their homes at dusk to look for food. It has been found that the fruit-bats do not necessarily return every night to their main dwellings. Distance between their 'work' home and main home can be up to 80 km., but distance between the feeding grounds and dwelling does not exceed 13 km.

Fruit-bats can give birth throughout the year, allowing the species to multiply quickly. There are two main birth seasons, April and September. Most females give birth in each, after a 16-week pregnancy. Life expectancy is 20 years.

In the last two decades, unknowledgeable farmers have waged war on fruit-bats by poisoning and blocking off caves. Insect-eating bats are killed while the fruit bats, being more flexible than their counterparts, quickly flee and find a new place of dwelling. The poisoned caves become hazardous to humans also.

Research has found that fruit-bats eat only ripe fruit and most fruit is picked unripe. Therefore in most orchards the bats enjoy no more than the few pieces of fruit left on the tree. This consumption of leftover fruit destroys the habitat of the Mediterranean fly which damages crops. The fruit-bat has thus become an economically useful mammal.

History

In biblical times, the area of Nahal Hama'ara, like most of the Jerusalem Hills, belonged to the tribe of Judea. Few impressive remnants have been found in the vicinity, for then the area was densely covered by forest. Other areas were more inhabited, especially the Judean Foothills, and the region to the east, closer to Jerusalem. During Hasmonean times, this area was part of the small region first to be liberated by the Maccabees.

By Roman times, the area had become more densely populated. A heavily-used road ran from Ashkelon to Jerusalem two ridges south of Nahal Hama'ara, by today's Moshav Matta. This Roman road was based on a biblical one. A secondary road ran from Jerusalem via Betar, Bar Giora and Nahal Dolev to the Bet Shemesh region. (Nahal Dolev is the wadi north of the Bet Atab ridge.) The Crusaders probably used this route also. Though Bet Atab yields no Roman remnants and definitely dates back to the Crusaders, it is possible that the strategic site was also a Roman fort or road stop for the Nahal Dolev route.

Robinson describes the Bet Atab vicinity in the mid-19th century:

> As we advanced, the hills became more covered and green with shrubs and bushes, chiefly the prickly oak mingled with arbutus [strawberry tree]. The country, however, was little cultivated and most of the villages were deserted or in ruins.....Bet Atab has several high square, tower-like houses of two stories; the rest are small and low; but all are of stone, solidly built. In the center is a ruined tower or castle; but so dilapidated as to be nearly lost among the houses. The place contains perhaps one hundred and fifty men... It is the chief town of the district *Arkub* belonging to the province of Jerusalem. We found several of the chief men sitting on carpets under a fig tree in the middle of the village, smoking and holding converse with each other. The Sheikh himself soon came, a good looking man; coffee was served for us.... the guide spoke of a very large cavern with a fountain in it capable of containing hundreds of people; it is called *el-Tuweimeh*..."

During the War of Independence, the region was captured in late October 1948, in what was called "the Mountain Mission." The goal of the operation was to widen the passageway from the Judean Foothills to Jerusalem, in order to reduce Jerusalem's vulnerability to siege. On the evening of October 20th, two separate Har'el forces left Hartov (north of Bet Shemesh). One battalion took points along the eastern Foothills while the other advanced by foot and controlled the whole Bar Giora-Ness Harim-Matta-Mevo Betar area. By October 22nd, the forces had taken the village of Hussan, east of Mevo Betar. From Hussan, they were in position to take the Hebron Hills. Political decisions led them to evacuate Hussan and cancel plans to capture the vulnerable populated Hebron Hills. Thus, the cease-fire line prior to the Six Day War ran between Hussan and Mevo Betar.

Site description

Bar Giora: Founded in 1950 as a communal moshav by the Herut-Betar movement for new immigrants. The name is after Shimon Bar Giora, one of the prominent leaders of the great anti-Roman revolt in the years 66-70. There is no connection between the geographic location of Bar Giora and its name. The basic income of this moshav came from orchards and chickens. Today, many of the members work outside of the moshav, most of whom commute to Jerusalem. The youth hostel that was once here reopened recently as a guest house.

Ein Hood: *Hood* in Arabic means trough. The spring, like Ein el-Birkeh, flows off Motza Marl. Ein Hood was the main water source of Bet Atab. The spring may have been a water stop for the users of the Roman Nahal Dolev road that runs just below. The tunnel is 40 m. long with three manholes. The broken arched building and the manholes are quite recent, from this century. Note the English writing on the street sewer case which holds the top of the manhole. These were evidently installed during the British Mandate.

Bramble grows beneath the spring. A large oak tree and fig tree shade the spring's environs. The lemon tree to the left of the bramble bears much fruit. Behind the lemons is a roof of a building that was most likely the spring keeper's home.

Bet Atab: Ruins of an Arab village built upon a Crusader fortress. The site is located upon a lone hill, 678 m. above sea level. In 1962, the Crusader fortress was revealed, including remnants of an olive press and a secret tunnel, which leaves the northwestern corner of the ruin to the columbarium on the eastern slope below.

The Bet Atab Ridge

Most of the remnants of the main structure are likely from the Peasants Revolt against the Egyptian Ibrahim Feha, who ruled Palestine between the years 1830-1840. During this period many peasant villages were fortified.

The British P.E.F. documents of 1873 record the Abu-Lahm family as residents of the village. James Finn, the American Consul in Jerusalem a few years later, writes that the Arab villagers of Abu Gosh raided Bet Atab and wiped out the Abu-Lahm clan.

The tomb caves on the southern slope date before the Crusaders. These may have been used by a Jewish settlement here during Talmudic times.

Forest: The fifty-tree forest is dominated by tall Aleppo pines with a few cypress and celtis trees, two *schinus* trees and two eucalyptuses. Around the clump of trees are small quarries used for building Bet Atab.

Hurbat Soofla: Remains of a small village lie on a low saddle between Nahal Hama'ara and Nahal Dolev. The village was last inhabited in 1948. Today, walled-in caves remain. They were once used as animal pens or storage rooms. A nice olive orchard remains along with sabra cacti and almond and fig trees nearby. An old building is still standing, out of quarried rocks, which are larger than the simple village home masonry. It probably dates to earlier periods. Beside it is a clogged water cistern. By the eastern section of the village is a carved wine press with a round basin. These artifacts, along with others, hint that the Arab village was not the first settlement of the site

Ein Soofla: Known as En el-Mahpoora, meaning in Arabic the dug spring. It served the village of Soofla. The spring emerges along the contact of the two prominent geologic formations in the area. The water drips into a karstic cavern from the ceiling of dolomite rock into a one meter-deep pool with a marly bottom. The dripping water has caused precipitation of calcium carbonate into small stalactites. The water troughs outside suggest that at one time the water table was higher and the spring's water was accessible from the outside. Today, between the boulders, a short narrow passage leads into the source. Large oak and carob trees shade this special place. The short crawl to the waters is exciting. A change of clothes is essential.

Te'omim Cave: This large and impressive cave was once the most popular cave in the Jerusalem Hills, before the discovery and opening of the Avshalom-Sorek Stalactite Cave. Te'omim Cave is in limestone of the Veradim Formation. The cave is about 50x70 m. in size but seems more spacious. Quarried rock by the entrance and by the spring at the far end of the cave, along with flint artifacts, indicate different stages of human involvement.

Looking back toward the entrance from the spring, a thick stalagmite stands out, known as Hamadan's pillar. Different Arab folk tales recount the courageous and handsome Hamadan of the nearby village Jeresh. He was eyed by Latifa, the village beauty. Latifa had to test her desired man: she told Hamadan to descend, alone and at night, to the bottom of the cave. He took a metal post in order to prove that he completed the mission, but as he descended he heard the squeaking noises of the many ghosts, demons and spirits that dwell in the cave and his fear grew. Only the thought of Latifa kept him moving. Reaching the bottom, he noisily hammered the post into the ground, to the chagrin of the demons. Hamadan tried to straighten up and to race out but then he felt his clothing being pulled by a demon, holding him in place. From stark fear, he froze on the spot. By morning, when he hadn't returned, his friends went into the cave and found that Hamadan, who in haste had hammered the post into the floor through his clothing, was transformed into a stone pillar.

Te'omim is Hebrew for twins. The name comes from the Arabic Marat Um e-Teumin, the cave of the mother of the twins. According to the legend, the spring water not only heals infertility, it also causes the birth of twins. The story is of a barren woman from the village of Jeresh, who tried everything to conceive. An elderly lady told her of the cave and its waters. The young woman tried the magical waters and a year later gave birth to twins. Years later the army (most likely the Turks) came to recruit young men. The mother of the twins hid her children in the cave. The army trailed them, and the cave filled with soldiers looking for the fugitives. The moment the twins and their mother were discovered, they froze on the spot. All three still stand together, fossilized—three stalagmites with a human shape.

Hirbet el-Omadan: In Arabic it means the ruins of the columns. It is one of a series of ancient settlements along the slopes of the Jerusalem Hills, right above the Judean Foothills. This archaeological site lies upon the low ridge between Nahal Azan and Nahal Hama'ara. Many interesting remnants are above ground while many more wait to be revealed. Mosaic stones and a large flat structure supported by a rock wall hint that this place held large public buildings, possibly a Byzantine church. The two large posts still standing held the piece used for the secondary process of olive crushing (oil extraction).

Zanoah: This moshav was founded in 1950 by the Po'alei Agudat Yisrael movement. The first settlers were Yemenite Jews followed by Moroccan immigrants,
who are the dominant population today. In 1978 there where 400 residents who
worked in the traditional jobs of these types of settlements. It was first named Dir
Aban Bet (II) after the large hostile Arab village that stood nearby until 1948.
Zanoah was an ancient Judean town, mentioned in Joshua 15:34.

To begin hike:

Head into Bar Giora (1) for 100 m. and turn right at the intersection. Follow the
paved street through the moshav to the last house. Here take a right along the
blue-marked dirt road. Fifty meters later, take a left at the intersection following
the blue trail mark. The dirt road descends Nahal Hama'ara.

Here stand orchards once expected to be main contributors to the moshav's
economy. Note, on the southern facing slope, oak and terebinth tree growth out
of the piles of rocks. This is due to the fact that among the piles of rock there is
more shade and moisture making it easier for a new sapling to start life. The rock
around here is dolomite of the Aminadav Formation.

One kilometer from the moshav's exit, the blue trail takes a right at a split. Leave
the marked way, taking the dirt road which continues to follow the terraced wadi
bed. Note the small cliff ahead, lying above a wide terrace. This terrace, the
parallel terrace across the wadi and the wadi itself are of the soft Motza Marl upon
which Ein el-Birkeh emerges.

As the dirt road veers slightly to the left, and a stone wall begins to the right, leave
the road and head onto the terrace that the wall holds. (If you are doing the short
loop trip, park your car here.) Here, small Autumn crocuses bloom in September.

Follow the cliff to your left until reaching a fig tree growing outside the small cave
of Ein el-Birkeh (2). *Birkeh* is Arabic for pool. There are no signs of a pool in the
spring's vicinity, nor does the spring's discharge seem sufficient for a pool. The
name is not understood.

Ascend the trail to the right of the small spring. The trail is unclear. Head up and
to the right (northeast), toward the saddle of the ridge. Along the way, you might
come across a series of clogged burial caves carved in the rock. These caves may
date back to the Roman-Byzantine period. Half-way up, to the right (east) of the
caves, the trail appears again, running between a line of rock piles and standing
rocks. A lot of marjoram grows here. At the ridge crest you will come upon the blue
marked dirt road. Cross it and head down the gully on the left side on a wide
unmarked path. Note the disturbed graves, mainly on your left.

Two hundred yards down the gully you will notice a couple of round manholes of
Ein Hood in the middle of the open wadi. Descend to them and reach Ein Hood
(3) just beyond the third manhole which is beneath a fig tree. From Ein Hood,
follow the red-marked trail which climbs the hilltop to your east up toward the ruins
of Bet Atab. The trail ascends, eventually looping to the northern slope.

234

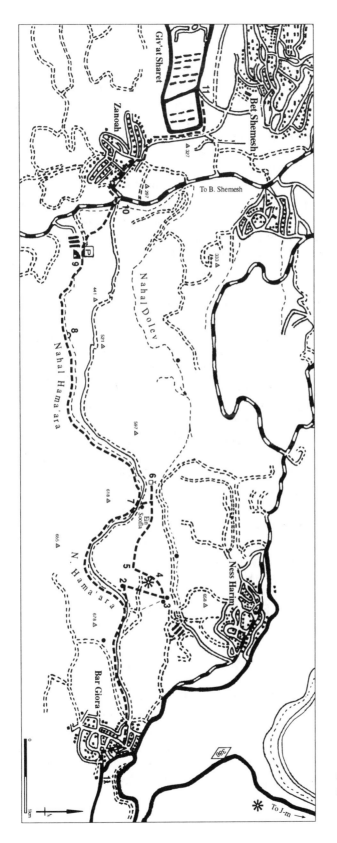

Hike 30,
Nahal Hama'ara

235

The artificial caves seen along the way were used for storage and animal pens by the villagers of Bet Atab (4). Along the way you may pass a columbarium cave by some terebinth trees, which was most likely opened later from the bottom. From here a secret tunnel led into the fortress of Bet Atab. Further up, the trail passes a lone cypress tree, surrounded by almonds, and afterwards goes along a pile of rocks. Leave the marked trail to climb to the top of the hill. Cross debris of the destroyed houses of Bet Atab and its outer wall. Enter Bet Atab through its northern gate in a double wall and explore the site. From the *unstable* rooftops savor an encompassing view. Try to view the continuation of the hike.

Your next stop is the small forest 500 m. to your southwest. Head there, again passing graves (this time more impressive ones). Along the way, pass a uniquely-shaped pine tree. This flattened pine is found at a number of sites in Israel and has no firm explanation. The common theory is that its shape is wind induced.

From the forest (5), follow the dirt road along the fringe of the ridge. As a small ravine drops to Nahal Hama'ara on your left, note the change in vegetation on the slope. This correlates to the lithology change between the Motza Formation below and the Aminadav Formation above. Naturally, each type of rock creates a different type of soil. The dolomite creates the terra rossa while the marl creates a rendzina soil that has a poor water economy. Herb plants thrive on rendzina.

The dirt road curves right and at the ridge crest the red-marked trail arrives from the right, from an open forest of small oaks and buckthorns. Continue on the dirt road as it runs along the exposed crest of the ridge. At the electricity pole you can follow the red mark down to the left. It is also possible to continue along the ridge to visit the ruins of the village of Soofla (6) and then return to the electricity pole. Down the red trail there is an open area with a few rock drinking troughs. Amidst the shaded boulders, Ein Soofla (7) emerges in a small cave. From the hidden spring, drop down to the dirt road in Nahal Hama'ara.

For those who left their vehicle farther up, take a left (east) on the dirt road, up Nahal Hama'ara for 1.5 km., back to your vehicle.

For the one-way route, follow the red mark down Nahal Hama'ara to the right (west). Soon, the marked trail leaves the dirt road and descends along the dry but vegetated stream bed. Follow it. Here, many daisies bloom in early winter. The trail crosses the stream bed a number of times and eventually parallels it. Nahal Hama'ara here runs along the Bet Meir Formation as the soft marls of the Motza Formation are exposed above, along the slopes.

The vegetation here is a typical Mediterranean type with evergreen oak trees and late spring blooming rockroses. After 1.5 km. along the forested wadi bed, the landscape widens as the wadi crosses the Motza Formation. Here, the western dip of the strata steepens, signifying the edge of the Judean Hills.

The wadi begins to cut into hard rock, creating a series of slides and pools. Here, the wadi enters the dipping Aminadav Formation at an angle. This section, like the previous one, lasts for only 250 m. Through the next overlying strata, the Veradim Formation, the wadi continues its semi-canyon-like appearance. Here, the incision of the wadi has exposed the Te'omim Cave (8).

Being well-visited, the cave's location is indicated by both official and unofficial human markings. After resting and preparing flashlights (no candles, please) climb up the northern bank to the hewed entrance. Outside the cave, yellow-white narcissuses bloom in early winter. Drop into the mouth and descend along the railing. Do not fear or disturb the shrieking Egyptian fruit-bats. Where the railing ends, follow the unclear level path to the right, where a railing leads you to the left, up to the spring pool. Another railing leads down the lowest section of the cave. Return the way you came. Beam the flashlight to all directions to discover the natural treasures of this karstic cave.

Follow the well-trodden trail for about 1 km. Just before the parking lot, a small unmarked trail climbs the low ridge to your left (south), the site of Hirbet el-Omadan (9). Explore. Return to the parking lot and follow the dirt road for about 250 m. Where the road curves left, follow the clear trail off the dirt road to the right and up to the field. Walk north along the contact between the field and the slope.

Looking north-northwest, you can see the forested Tzorah Hills in the far distance and the water tower of the town of Bet Shemesh, 2 km. ahead. Left of the water tower stand the eastern buildings of Giv'at Sharet, which is a developing Bet Shemesh suburb. The settlement to your left on the facing slope is Zanoah.

At next wadi, take a left onto the dirt road to the entrance of Zanoah (10). From here there is a nice view of the sharp drop of the Jerusalem Hills. At the bus stops in Zanoah you can catch a bus to Bet Shemesh. For other public transportation options, continue for 2 km. to Giv'at Sharet: head up the main road in Zanoah, taking the first right. By park of pine trees on your left, cross over to a parallel gravel road which runs behind the houses on your right. Go left on the gravel road, and then take a right past the coops and follow the dirt road into the circumference road of the Kirya Haredit, the ultra-orthodox section of Giv'at Sharet. Follow the boulevard to the end where it curves left. Three hundred meters down the street is a bus stop (11), served by many lines. It is also possible to pick up a *sherut* cab here.

Judean Desert

Geography

The deserts of Israel comprise the Samaria Desert, the Negev, the Arava, the Eilat Mountains, the Sinai and the Judean Desert. Of all the deserts, the Judean Desert is the most exciting: Biblical stories, Byzantine monasteries, Bedouin folklore, deep canyons, rich waterscapes, towering cliffs and the Dead Sea, the lowest place on earth.

The Judean Desert is a long and narrow strip between the eastern flanks of the Judean Hills in the west and the Syrian-African Rift in the east. It is only 20-30 km. wide, less than a day's walk. Its northern and southern boundaries are less defined. In the south, the Desert merges with the Negev in an undefined manner. The line is usually drawn between Arad and the southern tip of the Dead Sea.

The northern boundary is most complicated. "Judean Desert" is a mixture of a historical term (Judea) and a geographic one (desert). The Desert used to be the eastern part of the estate of the Israelite tribe of Judea. North of (Jerusalem-Jericho) Road 1, the desert narrows, though desert-like features continue north all the way to the Gilboa Ridge, which is the northeastern tip of Samaria. Thus, the official line is drawn between the desert east of the Judean Hills (Judea) and the desert east of Samaria, known as the Samaria Desert. This line runs along the canyon of Wadi Auja, 16 km. north of Road 1.

Along its narrow width, the landscape drops 1,400 meters hosting striking geographic and climatic changes, such as a decrease in rainfall. Despite its unclear borders, the Judean Desert can be clearly divided into five thin north-south strips. From west to east:

1) The Desert Fringe: east of the national watershed, along the eastern flanks of the Judean Hills, annual rainfall is about 300-400 mm. The eastward slopes consist of hard Turonian sedimentary strata, occasionally capped with bright white Senonian chalk. Vegetation is grassy with single trees. The town of Ma'ale Adumim lies at the Fringe's eastern edge.

2) The Desert Plateau: this is the heart of the Judean Desert and is sometimes over 10 km. wide. Geologically it is along the axis of a syncline. The Turonian strata of the Desert Fringe runs underground the Plateau. Geologically more recent Senonian chalk lying above it is widely exposed, creating a landscape of high hills often capped by hard, dark layers of chert (Mishash Fm.). Wide shallow wadis wind between these hills. In the north and south, even younger colorful metamorphic rock is exposed above the chert.

The Desert Plateau receives only 100-200 mm. of annual rainfall. The impermeable chalk enhances the aridity, as much of the precipitation is carried away in the wadis, creating flash floods in the canyons to the east. The dry conditions intensify in the southern Judean Desert. Thus, while in the south it has plants only in its wadis, the northern Desert Plateau has a dotted plant cover on the slopes. Following rainy winters, in February and March the northern Desert Plateau is carpeted with grass and hundreds of colorful wildflowers which are fed on by flocks of sheep and goats.

3) The Plateau Fringe: the eastern end of the Desert Plateau is defined by the appearance of the same strata found in the Desert Fringe. Here, the wadis cut deeply into the hard strata and create canyons. The decrease in rainfall and lithological change make the vegetation here different than that of the chalk cover to the west.

4) The Fault Escarpments: these impressive cliffs of hard (Cenomanian and Turonian) sedimentary rock are 300-600 m. high, dropping to the Syrian-African Rift. Great canyons break through the cliffs and many springs emerge along them. It is an arid section of the Desert, although the shade among the crags creates niches of varied vegetation. The presence of water, shade and vegetation make these cliffs an ideal spot for rich fauna.

5) Jordan Valley and Dead Sea Valley: these famous landmarks are part of the Syrian-African Rift. The Valley is an array of alluvial fans, accumulations of escarpment debris and Lisan Marl moon-landscapes (such as below Masada). Lisan Marl is the calcium carbonate and clay deposit of the Lashon Lake (sea) which covered the Rift between Lake Kinneret in the north and Hatzeva in the northern Arava. Its water line was over 200 m. higher than it is today. The lake quickly receded to today's Dead Sea about 12,000 years ago.

The width of the Dead Sea Valley fluctuates depending on the Dead Sea level. Today vast expanses spread eastward due to the sharp drop since the 1960s. In the northwest, by Einot Tzukim, the Dead Sea still reached the Fault Escarpments at the turn of the 20th century.

The intense climate and salinity of the Dead Sea make the flat open areas an adaptive challenge. Vegetation is symbolically ruled by the acacia tree, which lines large wadis and is a source of food for many animals

The hikes in this book go where water is bountiful, at the eastern part of the Judean Desert—the Plateau Fringe, Fault Escarpments and Dead Sea Valley.

Climate

The Judean Desert is a rainshadow desert. This means that the desert results from its local situation rather than its global one. It lies "behind" the mass of the Judean Hills which "face" the Mediterranean Sea in the west. When moist air masses reach the Hills from the Mediterranean, their temperature decreases and rainfall occurs. Crossing over the watershed, these now-empty clouds descend along the topographical drop to the Syrian-African Rift. Due to the sharp topographical drop, the clouds are at a higher relative elevation. The actual elevation has indeed dropped, which raises the atmospheric pressure and the temperature, thus substantially decreasing the chance of rain.

Each drop in 100 m. of altitude means an increase of two thirds of a degree (centigrade) in the average annual temperature and 40 mm. less yearly rainfall. Moreover, as in most of Israel, the farther south the site, the lower the precipitation and the higher the temperature.

For example, the average annual rainfall in Jericho is close to 100 mm. Ein Gedi, 50 km. south of Jericho, receives 70 mm. and in Sedom, at the southern tip of the Dead Sea, only 47 mm. falls. Along the Judean Hills, 25 km. to the west and 1,200 m. higher, annual precipitation is 500-700 mm. while the annual temperature is approximately 17°. The Dead Sea Valley tends to be 8°C warmer in the day and 6° warmer at night, than in Jerusalem.

Vegetation

The sharp changes in altitude, rainfall, lithology and consequent soil salinity make for fascinating plant life in the Judean Desert. Each different desert strip has its own dominant plant associations. Thus, along the Plateau Fringe, the bean caper is most common. South of Mitzpe Shalem the jointed anabasis (which looks similar to the bean caper) and the halogeton grass join the club.

Many species, even Mediterranean ones, home in the cracks of the Fault Escarpments. The cracks drain cliff faces and sometimes accumulate water quantities similar to those found in Mediterranean regions. For example, in the Northern Judean Desert, cyclamens and great fennel grow. In the canyon cliffs grow podonosma, caper and desert broom bushes. Vegetation is more variated along small ravines where one finds henbane, horehound, lavender, blepharis and many more. The globe thistle is one of the few thorns found in the Desert.

Among the oases of the Dead Sea Valley grow over 50 species representative of the Sudanese phytogeographic zone. In Israel, only along the Syrian-African Rift are there Sudanese representatives. The most common species is the Sedom apple. Another common Sudanese tree is the moringa that grows along water seepages.

Palms grow in saline water environments. Along wadis with high underground water, a jujube tree may find root. In the alluvial fans, common acacias suck up water that has percolated in the alluvium. South of Ein Gedi another type of acacia and orchadenus bushes are common.

For information regarding plant and animal adaptation to desert conditions, see the Negev regional introduction.

Wildlife

The proximity of the Judean Desert to both non-desert regions and the Syrian-African Rift as well as its own climatic variations, has brought a wide assortment of animals to the region. Wildlife in the Desert can be divided into two groups: oasis animals and desert animals. Most are of Saharo-Arabian and Sudanese origin.

Sudanese species found their way up the Rift from tropical Africa, settling in the oasis. Half of Israel's venomous snakes are Sudanese: Burton's carpet viper, the black Ein Gedi viper and the black cobra. The Dead Sea area is the main stronghold for the fan-tailed raven seen diving in the open areas in front of the Fault Escarpments. Tristram's grackle is found mainly at Masada and Ein Gedi. The striped hyena, leopard and caracal are the most outstanding Sudanese mammals in the Desert.

Saharo-Arabian wildlife is a collection of animals adapted to desert conditions (see same section in the Negev regional introduction). Both the desert coin-marked snake (often mistaken for the carpet viper), and geckos are common Saharo-Arabian reptiles. Look for the sand partridge, blackstart and the desert lark—typical Saharo-Arabian birds found here. Scrub warblers and black wheatears are also common. The golden spiny mouse and the fat sand rat (fat jird) are the only two rodents active during the day. The Cairo spiny mouse and Wagner's gerbil are common nocturnal rodents.

The oases also have Oriental animals that have penetrated the region from India and tropical Asia. You may see, for example, the Indian crested porcupine, Israel's largest rodent. The short-tailed bandicoot rat is harder to spot, for it lives in tunnels cut into Lisan Marl by moist areas. Ein Gedi is famous for being the place to see Hume's tawny owl.

Two amphibians are found by water, the stream frog and the green toad which utilize water for reproduction. A number of fish live in the springwater of the northern Desert such as the *capoeta* (*Hafaf*) and, at Ein Fashkha, a few species of the tilapia (St. Peters fish).

In the spring, the cliffs house migrating raptors searching for thermals. Hundreds, if not thousands, of birds can be seen passing north each morning. Lesser spotted eagles pass the desert en route from across the Negev and the Sinai. Today the Judean Desert is an ideal place for raptors; it is relatively far from man and pesticide-laden agricultural fields.

Human Involvement

Human settlement in the Judean Desert naturally concentrated around water sources. Since most of them are in the northern part, a majority of the archaeo-logical relics are found there. Sporadic human settlement has taken place throughout history along the Desert Fringe. Prehistoric remains were found only here, among caves and niches of the hard Turonian strata.

The Desert Plateau has rarely held human settlement, other than monasteries. The water cisterns that dot the Plateau serve nomadic goatherds who penetrate deep (east) into the Judean Desert during the winter.

Along the Plateau Fringe there is not much to be found other than Murba'at Caves in Nahal Darga. Here and there, round structures stand by wadis. They most likely date to the Chalcolithic period, though they were used later on. Chalcolithic remains have been found in a number of caves. In Nahal Mishmar, 429 beautifully sculpted bronze, hematite and ivory pieces were found from then. Ein Gedi was used by the Chalcoliths for worship. By far the most common human relics in the Plateau Fringe are the niches and caves, blackened by fire and covered with dung. These solid shelters have been used by nomads for centuries.

In contrast, many remains of human settlement are found at the base of the Fault Escarpments on soft Lisan Marl, or near the Dead Sea shore. The Fault Escarpments are crossed with many trails "ascents" (ma'ale), evidence of thousands of years of human use. These trails connected the Judean Hills with the Dead Sea and Transjordan. On a more local scale, the trails offered access to the sources of water by the Dead Sea shore and in the canyons. About 20 small forts, Chalcolithic to Roman-Byzantine, stand at Fault Escarpment crests overlooking the ascents. They guarded the trailheads and offered primitive rest stop facilities. King Uzziah of Judah pushed the effort: "Also he built towers in the desert" (II Chronicles 26:10). Also in this case, humans invested most of their effort in the Desert north of Mitzpe Shalem, where water is more available. The Fault Escarpments are lower and the Dead Sea offers a shore.

Five ancient roads connect the Judean Hills with the Syrian-African Rift via the Judean Desert: Tekoa-Ein Gedi, Herodian-Murba'at Caves-Mitzpe Shalem, Nahal Kidron (from Jerusalem and Bethlehem), Jerusalem-Jericho, and Bet El-Jericho. One ancient way runs north-south through the desolate Desert Plateau. It was mainly used by nomads. The Dead Sea shore was also used as a travel route.

The Judean Desert, being in the backyard of the heavily populated Judean Hills, has hosted an assortment of biblical and historical events, and is possibly the most famously documented desert after the Sinai. Being in close quarters with the villages of the Judean Hills, the Desert was divided into smaller deserts in biblical times. Each desert was named after the large village nearby, usually to its west. Saul went after David to the Desert of Ma'on (I Samuel 23:24) and later heard that he was in the Desert of Ein Gedi (I Samuel 24:2).

David was one of many who used the Desert for refuge while keeping the distance from the administration only a day's walk away. Other famous refugees include Tzedekiah, Elijah, Jonathan the Hasmonean (fleeing but continuing the armed battle against the Seleucids), and Shimon ben Shetah (fleeing Alexander Janneus). During the end of the Second Temple period, the famous Essenes sect settled in the northern Judean Desert, where they cut themselves off from mainstream society but kept open the option to make contact when needed. Palmach military units used the Desert for illegal practice during the British Mandate in the 1940s.

The Jewish return to Zion from Babylonia which began at the end of the 6th century B.C.E. did not reach the Judean Desert. The region was redeveloped by the Hasmonean dynasty in the 2nd century B.C.E. Forts were established with roads running between them. Agricultural centers bloomed by oases. In Jericho the Hasmoneans built a palace. This process continued with the reign of King Herod.

Jewish refugees from the Great Revolt (66-70 C.E.) and the Bar Kokhba Revolt settled in the Desert but were finally subdued by the Romans. Masada was the last Jewish stronghold, falling to the Romans in 73.

During the Roman-Byzantine period, many footholds were established in the deserts of Israel. While many were military forts, between the 5th and 7th century over 50 monasteries flourished in the northern Judean Desert (since it was relatively compatible and near Jerusalem). With the Moslem conquest in 636-640, interest in the Desert decreased (except Jericho and its environs where a new palace was built). The monasteries, lacking a supportive government, eventually sublimated. Only one monastery has continued to the present day: Mar Saba, in central Nahal Kidron. The Crusaders did not step into the Desert, other than visiting a few monasteries.

Since the 13th century there has been a constant influx of Bedouins from all directions. Some tribes have slowly assimilated into the villages of the Judean Hills. About 10 tribes still roam in the Judean Desert. Following the War of Independence, the Desert north of Ein Gedi fell to Jordan. This pushed the Bedouins to settle down, mainly along the Desert Fringe, as a number of tribes lost access to their traditional grazing lands. Today a majority of the Desert Plateau is an I.D.F. firing zone.

Jewish settlement has kept mainly to the Dead Sea Valley. In 1927 the Dead Sea Works were established by the northern tip of the sea. They extracted potash. In 1934 the industry found its way to Sedom. Kibbutz Bet Ha'arava was founded by the northern branch of the Dead Sea Works in 1939, only to be captured by the Jordanians and destroyed and looted by Jericho residents in 1948. Later, Kibbutz Ein Gedi was established, followed by the first field study center of the S.P.N.I.

After the Six Day War, a road was constructed for the first time along the western shore of the Dead Sea (part of Road 90). Three kibbutzim were established in the northern Judean Desert along Road 90.

Water

The two main natural sources of water in the Judean Desert are springs and potholes. Springs are most plentiful in the northeastern part of the Desert. Potholes are found in deep canyons. Shaded narrow canyons create a microclimate, comfortable for humans. If the pothole is deep enough it will hold year round.

Water cisterns are common on the Desert Plateau. The overlying chalk is easily carved and is impermeable.

The springs release water from aquifers of the Cenomanian and Turonian strata that composes the Judean Hills, where 500-700 mm. of rain falls each winter. Recently, signs of decrease in spring output have appeared; sites known as springs no longer yield water and trees are dying where underground water used to be. Deposits of travertine and ancient relics at Ein Gedi point towards a more plentiful waterscape than today. It is possible that modern wells are depleting the aquifers of the Desert.

The springs in the southern Judean Desert are more saline than their counterparts in the north. This is due to the longer underground route of the waters.

Thermal mineral springs emerge at a number of sites along the Dead Sea shore. They have medicinal qualities and a majority of them are utilized for that purpose. Water temperature rises with aquifer depth. Minerals slowly seep into the water with time, in conjunction with depth and lithology. The sulfuric smell of some of the springs is due to bacterial activity.

Hiking in the Judean Desert

The Judean Desert was known by Byzantine monks as the Jerusalem Desert, simply due to its proximity to the city. Today, it is only a matter of minutes between downtown Jerusalem and the steep drop via the Judean Desert into the Dead Sea Valley. Ein Gedi is only a 75 minute drive from Jerusalem. Many bus lines head from the Jerusalem central bus station to (Dead Sea) Road 90. From Eilat, Beersheba and Arad, bus lines run to Ein Gedi.

The Judean Desert is a desert of contrasts: the quick change between the urban environment and the harsh conditions of the desert have many times caused serious injury and even death due to lack of adequate preparation. It can be a cold rainy day in Jerusalem, while the Judean Desert is bathing in hot sun. An intense rain in this situation can suddenly create a flash flood wave down the large canyons. Unalert hikers have been washed away.

Hikers along a freshwater stream in the Desert may see no reason to take much water. But if the party decides to change the route a bit and climb a cliff, the hot weather along with the effort can quickly bring on dehydration.

Hiking along the relatively flat Desert Plateau seems a nonchalant thing to do. Leaving a marked trail is hazardous. The lack of familiar sites, and the strenuous heat can easily mislead hikers' judgement causing them to get lost (usually without an adequate supply of water) or try to overcome steep cliffs.

In order to safely absorb the uniqueness of the Judean Desert, strictly follow all of the precautions. Proper water consumption (large quantities!), head covering, and remaining on the trails are basic musts.

Leopards may be seen, but they do not attack humans. In any case, upon meeting one, retreat slowly and do not block its way. Finally, if darkness happens to fall, do not try to negotiate your way. Stay put until the morning or until a rescue team finds you. On days that rain is expected in Jerusalem, do not hike in the wadis.

Important Phone Numbers

S.P.N.I. Field Study Centers and Information (area code 07)

Ein Gedi F.S.C.:	584288, 584350; fax: 584257
Ein Gedi Nature Reserve:	584285
Metzokai Deragot:	02-964501
Dead Sea Works:	465111

Safety Assistance

Ein Gedi Rescue Team: 594711, 594736, 594705
Arad Police: 100

Ambulance: 101	Arad: 101, 957222
Ein Gedi: 584348	Neve Zohar: 584181, 584191 (night)

Sites Worth Visiting

<u>On Road 90</u>

Atraktzia Water Park, kilometer post 283.
Kumran National Park, kilometer post 278.
Einot Tzukim Nature Reserve, kilometer post 275.
Dead Sea Beach at Ein Gedi, kilometer post 244 by gas station.
Hami Mazor Mineral Springs, kilometer post 239.
Masada National Park 2.5 km. west, off kilometer post 227.
Dead Sea Works, kilometer post 192.
Arubotayim Cave, at base of Sedom Mt., between kilometer posts 199 and 200.

<u>By Arad</u>

Arad Visitors Center, at the Arad Community Center.
Kefar Hanokdim 8 km. from Arad, on Arad-Masada Road 3199.
Masada National Park (ramp ascent), end of Road 3199.

Overnight Options

<u>Indoors</u>

Hostels

Metzokai Deragot
Ein Gedi Field Study Center
Ein Gedi Youth Hostel
Masada Youth Hostel

Others

Ein Gedi Guest House
Ein Bokek Hotels
Arad Hotels

<u>Outdoors</u>

Ein Gedi Campground
Masada (picnic site)
Neve Zohar (picnic site)

Nahal David, Ein Gedi

Gas Stations

Mishor Edumim (Road 1), Ein Gedi, Neve Zohar (Road 90), Arad.

31 Nahal Darga

See map on
page 250

Points of interest: *A narrow gorge, hundreds of meters deep, containing many falls and deep pools, visited by a variety of wildlife.*

Length and nature of hike: 12.5 kilometers, loop trip, including 6 km. on a road up to the trailhead of Nahal Darga, 5 km. in Nahal Darga and 1.5 km. on Road 90 back to the starting point.

Hiking time: 6-8 hours. A large group can significantly lengthen the hiking time.

Preferred season: Spring. Ropes are usually installed at the end of April. Do not take this hike if there is a slight chance of rain in the Judean Desert and/or Jerusalem area. Being caught in a flash flood in Nahal Darga means instant death. In summer the temperature is comfortable in the canyon but unbearable out of it.

Suitable for: Experienced hikers only! The hike involves descending falls via ropes and swimming across deep pools of water.

Maps: Judean Desert (north) hiking and touring map.

Special preparation: If coming by private transportation, it's best to have two vehicles. Prepare equipment for total immersion in water. Photocopy from the book, this hike. Check with the Ein Gedi F.S.C. that ropes are installed. It's best to take one in any case. Leave information regarding your party at Metzokai Deragot.

Starting & ending point: Turnoff to Metzokai Deragot on Road 90, between kilometer post 258 and 259 (15 km. north of Eín Gedi) (1).

To reach starting point:

Arrival by private transportation: Park the vehicle by the turnoff to Metzokai Deragot (1). It is also possible to drive up to Metzokai Deragot (4 km.) and park there or by the trailhead (4).

If two vehicles are available, park one at the trailhead (4) (follow description in 'To begin hike'), and the other where Nahal Darga crosses Road 90, 1.5 km. south of the starting point.

Arrival by public transportation: Take the Jerusalem-Ein Gedi/Neve Zohar/Eilat bus to the starting point (1). It is possible that once a day a bus ascends to Metzokai Deragot.

Geography

Nahal Darga is among the five largest canyons of the Judean Desert and is the largest one in the northern Judean Desert. It is 43 km. long and drains about 230 sq. km. The wadi begins along the national watershed between the southern outskirts of Jerusalem and the Etzion Bloc.

The morphology of the lower canyon is unique among those of the Judean Desert that cut into the steep Fault Escarpments. While the other canyons begin abruptly with a grand fall of 100 m., Nahal Darga drops in a series of short falls, each less than 10 m. At the bottom of each fall is a pothole holding water year-round. This is mainly due to the remarkable narrow shape of the canyon, obstructing sunlight throughout most of the day. These pools are the most reliable sources of annual water north of Ein Gedi.

The Hebrew name of the canyon, *Darga* or *Deragot,* is based on the Arabic *Darageh. Darga* means steps, thus describing the canyon's morphology. The Arabic name, however, relates to an upper portion of the canyon where steps do not appear in the stream bed. The Arabic name results from a feud between two Bedouin tribes. While being advanced on, the tribe in fleet cut a deep step (*darga*) along the road descending to the wadi, slowing down the advancing tribe.

Plants and animals

Blackstart (*Cercomela melanura*): This non-timid bird is often seen by Judean Desert hikers. Most of its time is spent maintaining its territory, perched on a rock or other vantage point.

The bird originates in Africa and is found in the deserts of Israel. It has expanded northward along the Syrian-African Rift up to the slopes of the Lower Galilee and Golan. Its habitats are mainly oases and wadis with acacia trees.

The blackstart is a grey songbird with a black tail, slightly smaller than a sparrow. It feeds on insects and fast-moving ground creatures. It also eats organic garbage.

During mating season, the male warbles melodiously. Partners seek out a nest site in late February, beneath a boulder or in a burrow. The basket-shaped nest is of soft materials, usually plants, roots and twigs. In March, 3-4 eggs are laid. Incubation lasts about two weeks. Both parents feed the chicks for two weeks.

Nubian Ibex (*Capra ibex nubiana*): "The high hills are a refuge for the wild goats..." (Psalms 104:18).

The graceful Nubian ibex can be easily seen during the day throughout the cliffs of the Judean Desert. Their weakness is their dependence on water. In the winter and spring, when potholes in the canyons are full, they disperse along the Fault Escarpments and even graze on the Plateau Fringe, not far from the protective cliffs. One member will always be on guard. When danger approaches, a sharp whistle will be heard and immediately the herd races to the cliffs. In the summer, they cluster around the sources of water in the canyons.

The ibex is a mountain goat, found only in or beside cliffs. It is muscular, with short, strong legs, adapted for steep climbs and leaps over deep crevices. The animal's most outstanding feature is the horns of the male, bent back and pointed at the ends. At age ten, the horns are over a meter long. The male at age three also begins to sport a goatee that lengthens and darkens with time. The horns of the female are short and erect.

The horns grow at a rate of one to three ridges per year. During mating season, horn growth halts and a growth ring appears. Horns are used as an adornment and as a fighting tool. During mating season (autumn) the clamor of clashing horns between rival males echo among the towering cliffs.

Ibex only eat greenery.

Kids live in herds with adult females. Males mature at age six, whereupon they join small herds of mature males. During mating, the males grow dark and coo females in a low, bent position. Females give birth during early spring when the grasses are at their peak. Births are in private among the clefts of the cliffs. A few days later, the female returns to the herd with her newborn.

History

Humans have long recognized the high probability of water in Nahal Darga. To the north and south of the canyon run ancient ascents from the Dead Sea shore to the Desert Plateau. For travellers heading south along the Dead Sea shore, the wadi was a main stop between the oases of the northwestern Dead Sea shore and Ein Gedi.

Another ancient route runs along the Darga from Herodian (east of Bethlehem) all the way to the Dead Sea, via the Nakb Hamar ascent to Mitzpe Shalem. This route was most likely used by Romans during their siege on the Jews in Murba'at Caves. Today most of it is a gravel road. Its continuation is the access road to Metzokai Deragot, the only road descending from the Fault Escarpments between (Neve Zohar-Arad) Road 31 in the south and Road 1 in the north.

Canon H.B. Tristram did not miss Nahal Darga:

> Now and then the lower portions of the cliffs pushed into the sea in broken masses over which we had to climb. Close to the Wady Deregeh we found another wady: a fork separating from it just at its embouchure, forming a tremendous fissure of surpassing grandeur, but the grandeur of terrific desolation where the cliffs gape and open upon the shore.

Since 1967, Nahal Darga has become a favorite hiking route. In 1971, Kibbutz Mitzpe Shalem was founded where the Metzokai Deragot touring center stands today. The kibbutz moved to its present location on the southern bank of lower Nahal Darga. In the early 1970s, Ein Gedi F.S.C. prepared the wadi for hikers, installing stakes along the falls. In April of 1976, six hikers were killed as a flash flood swept them into the Dead Sea.

Site description

Murba'at Caves: The caves have sheltered people since Chalcolithic times. Archaeological finds date up to the Early Arab period. In 1952, Bedouins looted this cave, selling the finds in the market of Bethlehem. Nearby, Kumran was under excavation; the archaeologist there realized that the Hebrew scrolls being marketed in Bethlehem must have come from Murba'at.

The name means "square," describing their opening.

The scrolls found in the caves included several signed by Bar Kokhba (Simeon Ben-Kosiba) himself, the first archaeological evidence of the famous rebel leader.

The scrolls shed light on the personality of Bar Kokhba: tough and unmerciful. It is understood that the last of the rebels held out here, hoping in vain that the rough terrain would save them from the Romans.

The large caves can be explored. Note the plastered pool by the middle cave's opening. It most likely collected water from the slope above.

To begin hike:

Head up the paved road. The road is based on an ancient ascent that was damaged during road construction. Along the shoulders are plants that enjoy road runoff, such as the saltbush. The lower parts of the road are built on Lisan Marl. The marl contains many rocks deposited from the cliffs above.

Where the road curves to the left (south), the ancient trail (now a dirt road, coming from the north) merges with the paved road. Continue along the base of a cliff (along a fault line). The cliff is negotiated right above Nahal Darga (to the south). The road then curves around a ravine. By the sharp right turn where the road levels, take a minute to leave the road to the left and view the canyon of Nahal Darga (2).

Continue on the road and soon reach Metzokai Deragot (upon the Plateau Fringe). Head to the office on the right and leave information regarding your route. Drinking water is available here.

From Metzokai Deragot follow the paved road, soon becoming gravel, westward into the Desert Plateau. One-and-a-half kilometers from Metzokai Deragot, a wide trail veers to the south, reaching a hill and vista (3) after 400 m. There is a monument on the hill in memory of those killed in the canyon.

Continue on the gravel road for another 400 m. Here a small wadi descends to the left, towards Nahal Darga and on the right there is a place to park. The black-marked trail begins (there is a sign) just across the wadi (4).

Follow the black trail south along the wadi, which quickly deepens. Along the way, note the Arabian box thorn bush, blooming in small purple flowers throughout most of the year. After 300 m., the wadi drops sharply to Nahal Darga, which is 200 m. deep and 500 m. wide here. The trail descends and runs west, above Nahal

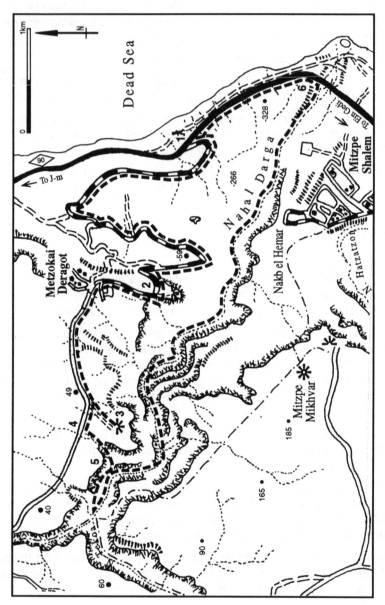

Hike 31, Nahal Darga

Darga. After a few hundred meters a white-marked trail ascends to the right to Murba'at Caves (5). The caves offer great shade.

Continue on the black trail, which gradually descends to the merger of the two main tributaries of Nahal Darga. If you have time, it is worthwhile exploring these two canyons.

Follow the black mark downstream, in the wadi. After 200 m. a red-marked trail ascends the southern bank to Nakb Hamar. Continue in the wadi and soon reach the first fall of 7 m. The adventurous part of the canyon begins here! The descent is via a crack to the right of the fall where stakes are installed.

If there are no stakes or rope there is no way (without ropes) to continue! Prepare yourself for swimming.

From here the going is simple; continue in the wadi bed—all the way to Road 90.

The following text denotes a number of locations along the wadi to assist you in orientation and how to return to the starting point:

After 50 m. the wadi turns sharply to the south due to a north-south fault. The crack of the fault is visible. Along the way, note the cliffs. The smooth white walls represent the section occasionally engulfed with flash flood water. In narrow parts of the canyon, flash flood water can attain a depth of 20 m. Above that part, the rock is coated with a brown-colored surface, known as patina.

The most common plant seen on the walls is the thorny caper. The round fleshy grey-green leaves and large pink-white flowers cannot be mistaken. Due to flash flood intensity, nothing grows in the wadi itself.

The wadi runs straight southeast for 500 m. through 10 pools, as the gorge becomes 60 m. deep. The next 200 m. are in an easterly direction. The gorge is deeper, holding about 20 pools. A couple of the falls have ropes. The canyon keeps its direction as a gully comes in from the north where the canyon widens a bit. The canyon narrows, sometimes to one meter!

The canyon hits another fault and widens for 300 m. Then another gorge begins dropping 9 m. into a deep pool. It is short and narrow, but soon changes as shear cliffs, 100 m. high, tower above the wadi, which widens to 25 m. and is full of boulders. Plants begin to appear, such as the chaste tree (hemp tree) which is actually a bush of hand-shaped leaves that blooms in clusters of blue flowers in summer. The chaste tree grows along water. Here, deep in the gravel, water is stored year-round.

Further downstream, along the cliffs, white rock appears—the Lisan Marl stuck upon the dolomite cliffs. Erosion has created interesting shapes in the rocky marl. Flash flood water has cut under the marl, creating shaded sections (an important feature for hikers).

The canyon narrows again into a gorge, 400 m. long and up to 20 m. deep. Enter it. The three falls create deep pools at their bases. This is the last gorge of Nahal Darga. After the canyon widens, chaste trees and tamarisks appear. Conglomerate occupies the wadi walls for a while.

The last kilometer before Road 90 is east of the Fault Escarpment. The wadi runs in a wide fashion between hills of marl and conglomerate of the ancient alluvial fan of Nahal Darga.

Upon reaching Road 90 (6), there are two options back to the starting point (1):

1) The short option: take a left and carefully walk along Road 90 for 1.5 km.

2) Follow Nahal Darga to the Dead Sea. Take a left along the beach, and after 2 km. look above for the starting point (1), marked by a bus stop and a couple of signs.

Beneath a dry fall in a Judean Desert Canyon

32

Dead Sea Shore
from Nahal Hatzatzon to Ein Gedi

See map on page 260

Points of interest: *Scenic views of the Amon and Moav Mountains, the Dead Sea and the highest cliffs above the western Dead Sea shore. Periodical lagoons, unique shore landscape and thermal sulphur springs dot the route. This hike is especially for beach lovers and scavengers.*

Length and nature of hike: 12 kilometers, one-way. The bus runs past the starting and ending point.

Hiking time: 8 hours, one-way.

Preferred season: Winter and spring.

Suitable for: All, but it is a long hike.

Maps: Judean Desert (north) hiking and touring map.

Special preparation: Swimsuit and change of clothes.

Starting point: Turnoff to Kibbutz Mitzpe Shalem on Road 90.

Ending point: Ein Gedi, by the turnoff to the Nahal David Nature Reserve entrance.

To reach starting point:

Arrival by private transportation: Take Road 90 to the Mitzpe Shalem turnoff. Park the vehicle at the lot (1) on the eastern side of Road 90, opposite the road heading to Mitzpe Shalem, between the two bus stops.

Arrival by public transportation: Take the Jerusalem-Neve Zohar/Ein Gedi/Eilat bus. Get off at the bus stop by the turnoff to Mitzpe Shalem. Cross Road 90 (1).

Geography

The Dead Sea shore and the nearby towering cliffs are lively and dynamic places. Earthquakes and faulting, fault springs, wave and water currents, change of sea level, flash floods, debris/gravel flow and sea spray are some of the phenomena. Plant development reflects some of these factors. For example, only certain types of plants can adapt to the saline sea spray and the saline soil exposed by the retreating waters.

Faulting: The faulting of the Syrian-African Rift is still occurring and earthquakes are intense in the Dead Sea vicinity. Earthquake tremor initiates different geomorphological reactions such as debris or gravel flow and high waves. Small faults from the last 12,000 years are apparent at some alluvial fans where they are seen cutting through vertical walls of wadi banks. These prove that the landscape is being affected by earthquakes during historical periods.

Thermal springs: Along some of the faults, close to Dead Sea level, thermal fault springs emerge from deep down. The warm waters are heated deep in the crust. Salinity of the springs is usually higher than normal strata springs along the Fault Escarpments.

Waves, wind and water: Waves have a strong effect on the formation of the Dead Sea beach. Although wave height is not colossal, its high specific weight (due to the high salinity) contains a lot more energy than its seawater counterpart. Strong winds in the winter tear apart beaches built in summer. Winter winds begin at midnight. Towards noon the waves calm down. During storms, waves achieve maximum height after 8 hours of wind. Strong winds of 20-30 mps (45-65 mph) have created waves of up to 2.5 m. high in a 2-3 second cycle.

Along the northwestern beach the waves come from the southeast. Fault Escarpments dropping to the sea block wind effects. Waves drop various things on the beach, such as driftwood mainly from the Jordan River, flash flood water deposits, rocks and garbage.

Along certain parts of the beach, small cliffs are formed in the compact gravel. This is usually a symbiosis of wave power and the declining sea level. These gravel cliffs are cemented by saline solution spray from the waves.

The waves naturally induce the creation of sand, by friction with the rocks along the shore. Since the Dead Sea is young in geological terms, there is not much sand yet.

The general water current direction in the Dead Sea is counter clockwise, around the shores. This is caused by heavy, more saline water from the south flowing north into the deep parts of the sea's northern basin. Due to Coriolis force the water is deflected to the eastern side. The rotational rhythm continues as the water, displaced by the southern current, flows south along the western shore. This process explains the remains of Jordanian debris found on Israel's beaches. The large amount of small particles coming in from the Jordan River is also deposited on the western shores.

Dead Sea level: The Dead Sea has gone through severe level fluctuations of hundreds of meters. Climatic change has been the main cause, but recently human activity has become the main culprit, as Israel, Jordan and Syria have intensively harnessed the Jordan River. Since the Dead Sea drains variated geographic regions, it is hard to pinpoint a specific climatic change that has induced base level fluctuation. Many people have researched evidence of changes. The research combines geological, geographical and botanical aspects with historical and archaeological material.

One of the peaks in the fluctuations seems to be 2,000 years ago. A minority opinion claims that then, the Dead Sea was 70 m. higher than today. An old photograph of the ruins of Kumran showing the lower parts of the walls encrusted with aragonite coatings, hints that it was submerged for some time. Other opinions see a somewhat more modest sea level rise taking place then.

In the 1920s the Dead Sea was 390 m. below sea level. Since then, the water level has fallen intermittently. Since the 1960s when the level was 395 m., the process has been accelerated by enhanced pumping of waters from the Jordan River Basin and intensified evaporation of the Dead Sea by the Dead Sea Works. In the 1980s the water level fell about 40 cm. annually.

Clear evidence of changes in sea level, mainly in the receding direction, is the beach shore-lines known as 'relic beaches.' Relic beaches can be found along the moderate slopes between the Fault Escarpments and the present sea. They appear as continuous mounds of rocks parallel to the present seashore, marked by driftwood and bushes.

Flash floods and their consequences: Flash floods have a strong impact on the beach in the vicinity of the wadi mouth. This is where water, small particles such as clay, and floating material are disposed into the Dead Sea. The clay particles accumulate in bays along the shore, where water currents are meager. The bottom of the sea is covered by a 100-meter layer of clay that has accumulated over 12,000 years.

An outcrop of rock by the shore will yield the same pattern as one deep in the sea: an interchanging of a dark layer and a light colored layer. The dark layer is clay that came from flash floods. The light colored layer is the mineral aragonite (calcium carbonate) that precipitates in the summer when water salinity rises. The uniformity and small size of the accumulated particles create an environment depleted of oxygen. Oxygen reduction, in turn, causes the formation of iron solutions that give the mud a dark color. This "black mud" is known for its medicinal qualities.

Plants and animals

Jointed Anabasis (*Anabasis articulata*): The jointed anabasis is known in Hebrew as *yafruk hamidbar* and in Arabic as *ushnan, shenan* or *agram*. According to the famous botanist Michael Zohary, the Arabic names are cognate with the biblical names Shuni (Genesis 46:16) and Hagarmi (Chronicles 4:19).

The 25 species of the genus *Anabasis* are found in deserts of Northern Africa and Central Asia. In Israel, the jointed anabasis is found throughout all the deserts, while other species are found only in extremely arid deserts.

This dwarf-shrub, 20-40 cm. tall, is intricately branched with a leafless stem and branches consisting of very fleshy, cylindrical joints. These joints are green at first, but become woody and dry after a year or two. Small green flowers growing from the upper joints appear in early winter and often produce small fruits. The fruits are in a wing-like case that pinkens when winter begins. Towards the summer, it is carried away by the wind.

Some of the species contain alkaloid anabasine, a medicinal substance.

Tristram's Grackle (*Onychognathus tristramii*): If a black bird joins your rest stop near cliffs, you have probably met a Tristram's grackle as they are one of the most common birds along the Fault Escarpments. These birds socialize in small flocks. They tend to pass above and make a flute-like sound. In winter they gather in large flocks. The grackle was first classified by Henry Baker Tristram, an English canon who toured and documented Israel in the 1860s.

The bird is a resident of tropical climates. Of its genus, this species is the only one of ten that have left the bounds of Africa. In Israel it was once found only along the Syrian-African Rift all the way to Jericho. With the establishment of settlements in the Israeli deserts, it has expanded considerably, from 20 species in Ein Gedi during the 1930s, to several hundred species counted in the 1980s. Today, the grackle's distribution has expanded beyond the Rift, reaching the towns of Arad and Dimona in the northeastern Negev.

Tristram's grackle is well adapted to the desert: its metabolic rate is lower than normal for its size. Water storage enables toleration of both high and low temperatures, characteristic of the desert.

The bird is black and similar in size to the blackbird, 25-30 cm. long with a 40 cm. wingspan. The male exhibits a tint of purple-blue, with some rust-colored feathers. The female is similar but more grey.

Favorite foods include fruits of desert plants such as the nitraria and the salvadora. Grapes and dates are on the menu, enough to cause damage to agriculture. It also eats insects, ticks and bees.

Nests are built in crevices and rocky ravines, usually inside a cave. They lay three to five eggs at a time, sometimes twice in the same year, in the spring.

History

The sea shore served as a passageway but was never settled along the hike route for a few reasons. First, the Fault Escarpments along this section are at their highest, causing additional access difficulty between the Desert Plateau and the seashore. Second, the close proximity of the cliffs to the seashore does not offer room for development and agriculture. Third, there is a lack of fresh water sources.

It seems that this section was always travelled in one day's time, as Ein Gedi and the Mitzpe Shalem region always offered better conditions for rest and development.

H.B. Tristram's journey is an example:

> The next wady, Hasasah, is faced by another spit, running out into the sea ... More than one interesting discovery rewarded our long walk from Ain Terabeh to Ain Jidy. In a little bay, just before reaching the Wady Shukif, we were struck by a powerful sulphurous odor, and, after some search, found hot water bubbling through the gravel at a temperature of 95 degrees Fahr. only six inches from the sea.

> The smell of sulphur and rotten eggs was very strong, and while scooping in the gravel, my hands became quite black, and my boots were covered with a yellow incrustation. Pebbles thrown in became incrusted with sulphur in a few minutes and all the rocks in the sea, which was here quite hot of the temperature of 80 degrees Fahr. were covered with it, as well as in a less degree the boulders on the shore, probably from its fumes. There must be an enormous discharge of this mineral water under the sea as the heat of the water extended for 200 yards...

From the sulphur spring we rounded by a difficult track or rather by forcing a way where there was no track, the headland of Ras Mersed, where it appears from his journal, we had been preceded by the indefatigable Seetzan at the beginning of this century. There we descended to the beach, along which a walk of a mile and a half round a lesser headland brought us to the sloping plain of Engedi across the gravelly bed of Wady Sudeir which forms its northern boundary.

Here the stream of the Sudeir sends down a trickling rill of pure water, at which we gratefully slaked our thirst, as it was our first fresh water since leaving Ain Tarabeh.

A natural jacuzzi on the Dead Sea Shore

Site description

Dead Sea: Also known as the Salt Sea, it is 830 sq. km., with a drainage area measuring over 40,000 sq. km., draining parts of Sinai, Jordan, Syria, Lebanon and approximately half of Israel. Its length is 75 km. and maximum width 17 km. It is divided into a shallow (2 m.) southern basin and a deep (400 m.) northern basin. The northern basin contains 95% of the sea's waters. Today, the entire southern basin has been transformed into the evaporation ponds of the Dead Sea Works who extract a number of elements such as bromine and potassium.

Throughout geological times, the body of water in the Dead Sea Basin has changed in many properties. The Dead Sea of today was created about 12,000 years ago; the previous (Lashon) lake level was over 200 m. higher. Today the Dead Sea Valley is the lowest place on earth, more than 400 m. below sea level.

Thousands of meters of sediments lie on the sea bottom, including a layer of salt nearly 4,000 m. thick. The waters contain over 40 billion tons of minerals.

Nahal Salvadora: A small wadi that drains about 5 sq. km. By the base of the sheer part of the Fault Escarpment, some 800 m. from the seashore and 180 m. below sea level, a small layer spring known as Ein Salvadora emerges. Access to the spring can be made via the wadi from Road 90. The wadi is named after the spring which is in turn named for the large salvadora tree that towers over it.

Lower Nahal Salvadora cuts a canyon in the Lisan Marl and its lowest part cuts into hard sedimentary rock of the Hevyon Formation. The Hevyon Formation composes the bottom formation of the Judea Group and is the oldest strata exposed in the region. The outcrop of this formation is exposed as a cliff that runs

257

for about two km. beside the seashore. The phenomenon of an "extra" cliff, one kilometer east of the main Fault Escarpments, only appears here. The geologist who studied the region was unable to correlate this outcrop to anywhere else in the region.

The bottom fall in the canyon creates a cool microclimate that supports many purple flower podonosma plants. Tristram's grackles are often found in the vicinity. In Nahal Salvadora you have the only chance along the hike to meet up with the grey-leaved saltbush and the aromatic white broom.

Nahal Kedem: In Arabic known as Wadi Shukif or Wadi Mookadem. It drains 12 sq. km., mainly along the Desert Plateau and boasts the largest fall in the Judean Desert—300 m. The horseshoe-shaped canyon decorated by the impressive fall can be seen from the seashore. Although the steep canyon looks unfit for human passage, one can scale the northern slope via an unclear, unmarked trail. South of the wadi is Mitzpe Kedem. At 369 m., it is the highest point closely overlooking the Dead Sea, nearly 800 m. below.

To begin hike:

Standing at the Mitzpe Shalem junction (1), you are 365 m. below sea level. Looking toward the Dead Sea, on your right, 300 m. to the south, the wadi of Nahal Hatzatzon (*Wadi Hasasah*) runs, marked by three large green acacia trees not far from Road 90. Head down to Nahal Hatzatzon to the left of the trees. The gradual descent is upon ancient shores of the Dead Sea. The brown coatings of the rock, similar to the color of the Fault Escarpments towering above you, is proof that this open area has been exposed to air for a considerable amount of time.

The first flowers of winter are the desert bellevalia, blooming at grass level. The light-colored flower blooms on a spike and has pointed, fleshy green leaves. The bushes growing here are mainly the anabasis and the saltwort.

Upon reaching the wadi bed, go left and follow it down to the Dead Sea (2). Note how the bed is devoid of vegetation, evidence of strong flash floods. The two bushes that have hold here, mostly by the banks, are the strongly rooted, round-leafed, thorny caper and the ropey-leafed, yellow-flowered orchadenus. The rapid drop of the Dead Sea level in the past 20 years has created a relatively steep drop of the bed right before reaching the sea. The small cliffs, cut into shore gravel on both sides of the bed, make the point. Note how the patrol dirt road, although lowered, is cut by the wadi.

Take a right along the shore; your direction is southwest. Here is one of the few places where the shore does not run north-south. The shore here is also relatively far from the Fault Escarpments. The whole route from the junction to your current location, and for the next kilometer, is in the alluvial fan of Nahal Hatzazton.

On your right, you may notice that some rocks have a white coating of salt. This comes from the evaporation of large amounts of sea spray and wave water. The salts remain on site and, with the evaporating water, usually flow and drip downwards. The formations resemble icicles or stalactites.

After 1 km., reach the fringe of the alluvial fan near a bay (3). The shore is now composed of uniform small pebbles and soon you will reach, beside the quiet waters, a mud flat. The mud is composed of clays that have settled in this environment, protected from currents. If you are thinking about a mud-bath, be patient: the best spot isn't far ahead.

From the bay, follow the shore straight south. The towering Fault Escarpments close in and the shore becomes rocky again—rocks tumble down straight from the cliffs to the shore. In earlier times, when the sea level was higher, the debris ran into the water. The continuous wave movement has moved the fragments back and forth, thus rounding and/or flattening them, and has deposited them in layers. Along the way, you may begin to notice sulphurous puddles of water at the water's edge.

Half a kilometer from the bay, a wadi enters the Dead Sea; one kilometer further, a second wadi merges. Both wadis come down a short, steep canyon which you can see to the west. By the second wadi's merger with the sea, right by the water's edge, a thermal fault spring emerges (4). The spring is known as Hami Shalem. Its waters are the warmest of all springs along the western Dead Sea shore, 44.5° Celsius (112° F). Visitors have built two pools for bathing, a shallow pool and a deep, jacuzzi-stye pit. The pit is dug into the mud, a great place for a few minutes of pure relaxation, especially on a cool day.

Continue along the shore. After 1 km., a lone cliff begins to follow you on your right. Along the shore itself, another spring emerges and runs into the sea. As a second cliff begins to close in on the shore, ascend to the sloping ground between the two cliffs. Here runs a dirt road which you can follow to the south. Two kilometers from the bathing springs, a narrow canyon cuts into the cliff about 200 m. to your west. This is Nahal Salvadora and it is one of the few shady spots along the route. Climb up into the gorge.

Note how the vegetation on the alluvial fan plain becomes denser near the canyon. Here bloom the pink flowers of the dock (sorrel) from late winter to spring. The plant, up to 35 cm. tall, has edible, semi-fleshy triangular leaves. They have a mild tangy taste.

It is possible to climb the first set of huge boulders in the wadi and then take the 5-meter fall from the right. Reach the bottom of an unclimbable 15-meter fall, a beautiful cool and shady dead end (5).

From Nahal Salvadora, descend via the wadi to the dirt road which you take to the south (right). Passing a quiet bay, you reach the alluvial fan of Nahal Kedem. On your left, note beautiful examples of relic beaches. Some still have a row of driftwood and some have a uniform line of plants.

The bridge over Nahal Kedem on Road 90 and the lone acacia nearby offer shade for weary hikers. At the dry stream bed of Nahal Kedem take a left back to the seashore and from there you do not have far to go (south, of course) to reach the series of pools known as Ein Kedem (6).

From Ein Kedem continue down the coast where there may be piles of rocks with many layers of coatings. Head back up to the dirt road and continue south. The road rides upon relic beaches, between the shore cliff and the Fault Escarpments.

Three kilometers from Ein Kedem, pass through the alluvial fan of Nahal Yishai (7). Nahal Yishai is a 1.5-km. canyon that ends at Road 90. It is an effort but worthwhile entering the canyon (cross Road 90 carefully!) and enjoy the shade, atmosphere and view.

Continue south on the dirt road, past a peaceful bay, until you merge with Road 90. Stay on the platform between the road and the sharp drop to the seashore, or if you prefer, walk by the seashore. The platform is conglomerate— gravel cemented by sea solutions. The inner part of the platform is not cemented, leaving this formation easily erodible. Be careful!

Two hundred meters from the road merger, a small wadi drops to Road 90. A family of hyraxes lives here, along the cliffs. From here, it is possible to see the outskirts of Ein Gedi. The current way is dotted by tamarisk trees. Tamarisks grow where there is fresh water, although no springs emerge here.

Where the cliff ends, look up to the west and note patches of vegetation on the steep slope. This is where the outermost spring of the Ein Gedi oasis emerges. The spring is small and not marked on the maps. The local people call it Ein Kiyor, meaning sink, as the water accumulates in a sink-shaped basin. A clear trail leads to the spring from the Ein Gedi F.S.C.

Follow the shore until reaching the mouth of Nahal David (*Wadi Sudeir*). This part of the shore has a few laminated layers of the lower Lisan Marl exposed as a small step. The exposure is of dark laminated clay-like marl, similar to what you saw at the beginning of the route by the mud flats.

Head up the stream bed to Road 90. Here is the turnoff to the Ein Gedi Nahal David Nature Reserve. Here also is the bus stop (8) to take you home or back to the starting point.

For those who have strength or who desperately need to wash, it is also possible to continue into the Nature Reserve (250 m.) and bathe in the cool freshwater springs and pools of Nahal David. Details are described in Hike 33, 'Nahal David and Ein Gedi.'

260

33 Nahal David and Ein Gedi

See map on page 273

Three options

Points of interest: *The most luxuriant desert oasis in Israel of springs, waterfalls and pools, a grotto, a gorge and relics; amongst a canyon sustaining unique vegetation and wildlife.*

Length and nature of hike: 2 kilometers to Ein Shulamit, loop trip, where there are 3 options: 1) 1 kilometer. 2) 2 kilometers. 3) 800 meters.

Hiking time: 4-6 hours.

Preferred season: All year.

Suitable for: All, experienced hikers to the Dry Canyon.

Maps: Judean Desert (north or south) hiking and touring map.

Special preparation: Swimsuit, binoculars. No food is allowed in the nature reserve. Clothes for walking in water (for the Dry Canyon option).

Starting & ending point: Entrance to the Nahal David Nature Reserve. A fee is required that covers entrance to Nahal Arugot on the same day. Entrance is between 8 a.m.-1:30 p.m. for the described route!

To reach starting point:

Arrival by private transportation: Ein Gedi Nahal David Nature Reserve is located east of Road 90. A sign directs you (250 m.) to the parking lot. After parking, head to the reserve entrance (1).

Arrival by public transportation: Buses from Beersheba, Jerusalem and Eilat run to Ein Gedi. Get off at the Nahal David stop (the first stop coming from the north). Head (250 m.) to the reserve entrance (1).

Geography

Four perennial springs make Ein Gedi an oasis: Ein Arugot, in Nahal Arugot, Ein David in Nahal David, Ein Gedi and Ein Shulamit south of Nahal David. Altogether, they yield 46 million cubits per year.

All of the springs emerge from upon marl of the Ein Yorke'am Formation. The same marl layer in the Judean Hills (there known as Motza Formation) is also the source of abundant springs. It is soft and creates a gentle landscape; this helps explain the level area south of Nahal David, where the Ein Gedi and Shulamit springs emerge.

Spring water originates as rain in the Hebron Hills 25 km. west of Ein Gedi. The rainwater seeps through cracked limestone and flows eastward to the Fault Escarpments and downwards to the Ein Yorke'am Formation. The water emerges by a low spot along the Escarpment.

Years ago, before the advent of modern drilled wells which pumped up underground water, a number of smaller springs emerged in the area along this same formation. Today, all that remains are travertine accumulations and water-collection pools from 2,000 years ago. At some places, although no water emerges, high underground water sustains thick vegetation.

The two streams of Ein Gedi, Nahal Arugot and Nahal David, have deposited a large quantity of alluvial soil at their mouths creating rich agricultural land. This is where the crops of Kibbutz Ein Gedi are grown today.

Ein Gedi is one of twelve nature reserves in Israel to be recognized by the International Union of Conservation of Nature. It is also listed in the United Nations List of National Parks and Equivalent Reserves.

Plants and animals

Sedom apple (great calotropis) (*Calotropis procera*): The name is derived from Sedom and Gomorrah which were at the southern tip of the Dead Sea. Josephus Flavius explains that the fruit represents what is left of the cities: "If you pluck them with your hands they dissolve into smoke and ashes."

This tropical (Sudanese) tree is also known as the Dead Sea apple. It reaches a height of 5 m. and is found throughout the plains of Ein Gedi (especially at the parking lots). The trunks are coated with distinctive cracked white cork. The green-greyish leaves, purple white flowers and hollow green ball of a fruit also stand out. The unique fruit is 10 cm. in diameter with a soft peel, small black seeds and silken hairs inside.

These hairs have many uses. They are mentioned in the Mishna (Shabbat 2:1), as forbidden material for Sabbath candle use. Even today, the Bedouins use the hairs as a wick, hence its Hebrew name, *petila* ("wick"). Arabs have used the hairs to accelerate combustion in gunpowder. Since it was also used as part of the *akal*, the headband that holds the *kaffiyeh* (Arab head garment) calotropis plantations were once in the region.

The fruit contains a poisonous milky liquid that can burn the skin and inflame the digestive system. Arrows can be poisoned with the substance.

Sand partridge (*Ammoperdix heyi*): The common bird is often mistaken for the chukar, which is common in the Mediterranean regions of Israel. The sand partridge is common in Israel's deserts (which are not sandy).

The camouflage-colored female differs from the more flamboyant male who has black and reddish brown stripes on the sides of its belly and a white spot behind each eye. The bird drinks water in the summer and after eating dry seeds. It can also drink salt water (not Dead Sea brine). Its diet includes seeds, buds and leaves, and occasionally fruit and insects. Usually the bird is active during the cool hours and rests in shade during mid-day.

The birds cluster in flocks of ten to twenty specimens. In spring the flock breaks into pairs with the male spending large amounts of time singing and calling from observation points. Hence the Hebrew name—*koreh* ("call").

The female digs a nest hole and lays eight to fourteen eggs. Sometimes two females share a hole. This restrains many eggs from hatching. Prophet Jeremiah (17:11) refers to this phenomenon: "As the sand partridge sits on eggs and does not hatch them, so he who obtains riches unjustly, will leave them in the midst of his day's ..."

History

"Gedi" is not a modern Hebrew word. It possibly means a young goat referring to the Nubian ibex, which thrives in the region.

People have been attracted to Ein Gedi for thousands of years. Throughout history, the central administration of Judea, whatever its nationality or religion, was interested in maintaining a friendly population in the adjacent Judean Desert. The desert-dwellers would guard important trade routes from the Dead Sea, convey taxes and possibly deal with the fierce nomads. Ein Gedi's importance was primarily economic. From King Josiah (8th century B.C.E.) to the Roman-Byzantine period, profitable crops were grown in Ein Gedi. Remains of the central settlement of Ein Gedi are found at Tel Goren between Nahal David and Nahal Arugot.

There are no remnants of distant prehistoric times. The Lashon Lake, reaching 150-180 m. below sea level only 12,000 years ago, washed away whatever was left.

The Chalcolites left rich remains; a 5,500-year-old temple, the only one from that period found in southern Israel. Strangely, no tools or other artifacts were found on site.

Ein Gedi is mentioned as a city in the book of Joshua (15:61), but only later is Israelite settlement described. It most likely was a small community before King Josiah's era.

Israelite Ein Gedi lasted for only two hundred years, until it was destroyed by Nebuchadnezzar. In the fifth century, a small settlement was renewed. Further development came during the Hasmonean dynasty, expanding significantly during the reign of King Herod.

The Great Revolt (66-73 C.E. (here)) caused much agony to the local Jews. As described by Josephus, the Sicarii of Masada raided, killing 700. During their siege of Masada, the Romans also cleaned out Ein Gedi. The secluded population during the Bar Kokhba Revolt 60 years later, were quite apathetic toward the revolt.

After the fall of Bar Kokhba, the Romans expropriated the land and leased it back to the residents. The community prospered nonetheless. Artifacts from these times were found 300 m. northeast of Tel Goren, highlighted by a synagogue with beautiful mosaic floors and inscriptions.

Salt and asphalt from the Dead Sea enhanced the economic importance of the area. Date palms were another product, important enough to earn Ein Gedi the biblical name Hatzatzon-Tamar (II Chronicles 20:2) (*Tamar* is Hebrew for date). Jericho and Ein Bokek were other oases that supported similar occupations. Ancient Jewish farmers in the region cultivated plants for the extraction of spices, perfumes and medicinal substances. These products were in high demand. A mosaic inscription from the 6th century synagogue of Ein Gedi promises a cruel fate to anyone who reveals the "secret of the town," referring to details of the spice industry.

It is still unclear what plants were grown. It seems that the two main crops were balm and henna. Balm, the biblical *bossem* or *afarsemon,* was used mainly by Greek and Roman society. Josephus claims that the Queen of Sheba brought *afarsemon* seedlings to Israel. The resin of the plant, the "balsam," was used as a holy oil, a medicine, an antidote for snake bites and an ingredient of perfume. The resin was extracted from the bottom of the tree, three times a summer. It took a whole day to collect a cupful.

The henna, from the Arabic *hina*, was the biblical *kofer.* A yellowish-red aromatic dye was prepared from its leaf. The dye, besides coloring uses, helps treat urinary tract ailments.

"My beloved is unto me as a cluster of henna flowers in the vineyards of Ein Gedi" (Song of Songs 1:14). According to the verse, wine was also a product of Ein Gedi. The grapes of Ein Gedi are the first to ripen in Israel.

*David Falls in Nahal
David, Ein Gedi*

During the Great Revolt, a battle was held over every balsam plant. The Jews tried to destroy them. Titus and Vespian displayed the prized plants during their victory procession in Rome.

During these historical times, it seems that there were more springs in the region. We make this inference from water-collection pools found far from springs on dry slopes. Fourteen plastered pools have been found along the lower section of the Fault Escarpments from south of Nahal Arugot to north of Nahal David. The pools average 3 m. in depth with a capacity of 12-100 cubits. From each pool, a channel led water to terraces below. Pools filled from emerging spring water during the night. In the morning, the farmers diverted the water by force of gravity along an elaborate network of channels and ditches, to the plots.

With the Moslem conquest, there was a small settlement at Ein Gedi. It survived the Crusader period. But the oasis seems to have been neglected from then until the establishment of an I.D.F. base in 1949, by all but Bedouins of the Ar-Rashadiye tribe.

In 1953, a Nahal unit prepared the site for civilian settlement, Kibbutz Ein Gedi, which was first located in 1956 beside the ruins of the ancient settlement at Tel Goren. In 1960, the S.P.N.I. built its first field study center there and in 1968 moved to the marl hill above Nahal David. Until 1967, the border with Jordan ran nearby, from the Dead Sea shore north of Ein Gedi in a southwesterly direction.

H.B. Tristram documents Ein Gedi:

> About a mile and a half from the shore is the true Ain Jidy, midway between the two wadys. Its little silver thread of a streamlet dashes down lofty, but (in volume) pigmy cataracts to the sea. Below the falls, in the center of the plain is a group of ruins of some extent, built of unbevelled square stones of fair size ...

> The plain around is now as desolate as the old city of the Amorites though once a forest of palms. Not less deserted of their fruitful vines are the slopes above, once the farmed vineyards of Judah, though the old terraces remain distinct, from the foot of the hills to the pass above the fountain and also on the enclosing mountains beyond. The "cluster of camphire is the vineyards of Eingedi" is withered and gone. Not a palm or a vine remains: their place is occupied by scattered acacia-trees, a tamarisk, the Nubik and a few straggling bushes ...

> The fertility of Engedi lies only in the immediate neighborhood of the fountains, or is enclosed in the narrow gorges of the two boundary streams, choked with canes and great fig trees, and so deep that they are not perceived until the traveller has entered them ...

> We went up the Wady Sudeir to trace its source, when we soon came upon a faity grotto of vast size under a trickling waterfall with a great flat ledge of rock overhanging it, dripping with stalactites and draped with maiden-hair fern. Its luxuriance was wonderful. The sides of the cliffs, as well as the edges of the grotto, were clothed with great fig-trees hanging about and springing forth in every direction, covered with luxuriant foliage ... It is said that this wady is the home of the leopard ... we saw none here ... No pen

can give an adequate description of the beauties of this hidden grot which surpasses anything Claude Lorraine ever dreamt.

Site description

Nahal David (*Wadi Sudeir*): Named after King David, who found refuge in the cliffs from King Saul.

> And David went on from thence, and dwelt in strong holds at Ein Gedi. And it came to pass, when Saul ... it was told him saying, Behold, David is in the wilderness of Ein Gedi" (I Samuel 24:1-2).

Nahal David is a small canyon in Judean Desert terms. Whereas a big canyon might drain the eastern flanks of the Judean Hills, Nahal David only begins in the Desert Plateau. It is 8 km. long and drains only 18 sq. km. The stream's canyon is close to 500 m. deep and less than 2 km. long. It has four sections:

1) The upper canyon, where the dry stream bed runs beneath sheer cliffs, beginning at a fall of over 100 m. In one of the adjacent ravines is Pool Cave— a cave with a rainwater-collection pool where Jews hid from Roman soldiers during the Bar Kokhba Revolt.

2) The Dry Canyon, a gorge cut into hard sedimentary rock of the Tzafit Formation, full of small falls and potholes. The canyon ends at the 15-meter Window Fall, overlooking the source of Nahal David, Ein David.

3) Central Nahal David. This section includes Ein David, where the stream begins. Its discharge is 72-216 cubits per hour, and salinity 70 mg. per liter. A leopard resides in the nearby thicket. The section descends along small falls and ends atop David Falls, by the lush Dodim Cave.

4) Lower Nahal David, highlighted by David Falls where the section begins. Downstream, water rushes down a few falls and trickles to an end near the reserve entrance. From there to the Dead Sea, the stream resembles other Judean Desert wadis.

Ein Gedi: The spring emerges beneath a canopy of jujube and acacia trees.

Beside the spring grow thickets of reeds, home to families of friendly hyrax. Head through the tunnels, which open to a view of ancient agricultural terraces: Tel Goren, by the tall thick trees at the bottom of the slope ahead, and Kibbutz Ein Gedi, on the Lisan Marl ridge south of Nahal Arugot.

A ruined flour mill stands nearby to the left beside the steep ravine. It utilized the waters of Ein Gedi for grinding wheat of local Bedouins. The mill was closed in 1948, probably because the new Israel-Jordan border which ran above Ein Gedi gave territorial problems to the Ar-Rashadiye tribe.

The spring yields 36-70 cubits of water per hour. Some of it is transferred to the fields below. Its salinity is quite low, 70 mg. per liter.

Ein Shulamit: It closely resembles Ein Gedi in discharge, salinity and location, as both emerge on the flat plateau. Today a majority of its waters are captured. A small trickle is still released, just enough to maintain the vegetation.

To begin hike:

From the entrance (1), head up the wide path lined with jujube and acacia trees. A number of nightshade stalks (solanum) grow on the right. The greyish-leafed plant blooms in purple and has colorful but toxic fruit. The nightshades flowers are evidence that it belongs to the same family that includes tobacco, tomatoes and potatoes.

It is interesting to peek through the tree canopy to the right, toward Nahal David and the white Lisan Marl cliffs. The sharp vegetational change illustrates the impact of water in the desert.

After 200 m., a trail ascends to an ibex observation point. Take it. It is possible that you may see ibex throughout the day. Toward late afternoon, herds of these mountain goats descend to Nahal David to eat and drink. At the same time, hyrax also gather. Return to the main path.

At the entrance to the lower canyon, the path splits into two parallel routes. Take the northern option, crossing the stream. An extremely torrential flood in late 1993 wreaked havoc in the reserve, notably to this area. The water uprooted all of the vegetation in the stream bed, exposed waterfalls and damaged the trail. Until then, the stream between the trail split and David Falls was totally hidden by reeds.

The trail passes to the left of two boulders containing a matrix of cobbles and pebbles—what is known as conglomerate. Nearby, pass by a lone balanites tree, a rarity in Israel. Before the stairs, a short pathway veers off to the bottom of a waterfall, a nice place to cool off (2). This waterfall also was exposed in 1993.

Continue up the trail and reach David Falls (3). The waters fall down a massive accumulation of travertine coated with moss and maidenhair fern. David Falls is the main attraction of Ein Gedi.

Head east on the trail along the southern bank. Note on your right, flattened plant debris marking flash flood flow at this point, far from the stream. One hundred meters from David Falls, ascend the trail to the right. (If the climb seems too much, continue on the wide trail back to the entrance gate (1) to end the walk.)

Along the ascent, note the black earth, a rare phenomena in Israel. The dark earth is residue of organic material—reeds that have covered the slope for centuries. As the trail reaches a cliff-bottom, note a large water-collection pool, 20 m. left of the trail. Here is a nice place to get a good scope of lower Nahal David. Looking straight across, note the bright white rock stuck onto the northern slope, from the stream bed all the way up to your elevation. This Lisan Marl is reminiscent of the Lashon Lake that only 12,000 years ago was 200 m. higher than today's Dead Sea.

As the trail becomes a stairway, note the interesting rocks on the left, including travertine (evidence of water flow), fossils embedded in the rock and slightly off-trail, layers of rock representative of an ancient seashore.

The trail ascends and straightens, running west along the brink of lower Nahal David. Note a trail arriving from the left. This is the return trail from Ein Gedi. Reach the reed tunnel of Ein Shulamit which emerges today as a fountain (4). Here is a good spot to recharge and decide what options to choose. There are three:

1) Back-and-forth to the Dodim Cave, which is above David Falls in central Nahal David, one hour (1 km.).

2) A semi back-and-forth route to Dry Canyon via the Chalcolithic Temple, returning past Ein Gedi, two hours (2 km.). For experienced hikers.

3) Back-and-forth to the Chalcolithic Temple and Ein Gedi, one hour (800 m.).

Option 1: Take a right at the trail junction 60 m. ahead and descend through reeds to central Nahal David. Along the descent, look upstream and note Window Fall, the termination of Dry Canyon. At the stream, a left turn leads to the source, but access is closed to the public. A leopard dwells among the reeds and it is the only part of Nahal David (only 250 m.) left to the wilds.

Follow the path across the stream and head east (to the right) past a lone moringa tree on the left. Reach a cliff over lower Nahal David. At this point descend to the right via stakes to Dodim Cave (5). You are now right above David Falls. There is no access at all from this point to lower Nahal David! Retrace your steps to Ein Shulamit, and continue on another option or head back the same way to lower Nahal David where you exit the reserve to the right, described at the end of option 3.

Option 2: Take a left (south) at the junction by Ein Shulamit. After 100 m. ascend a trail to the right (there is a sign) where a rocky cliff separates between the two trails. Atop the cliff in a flat area stands the Chalcolithic Temple (6). Looking toward the Dead Sea (east), note the clump of trees 200 m. to the right, marking the spring of Ein Gedi.

Above you, to the west is another cliff-like slope. Head to the left of it and connect to a green-marked trail (there is a sign, down the trail to the left). Go right. After crossing the topographical saddle, head west along the brink of the central Nahal David canyon.

The dry rocky slope is dotted with bean-caper bushes. Squills bloom in the fall, the fleshy dark green squill leaves are visible in other seasons. The leaves are not edible for the ibex who uproot them in order to dry the leaves. A yellowish color signifies their edible condition. The small ravines dissecting the rocky slope are often visited by sand partridges, that fly off in a clutter when approached.

A nice vista of Window Fall opens up as the trail heads past and above Dry Canyon. At a point about 150 m. after Window Fall, the trail splits (7). Continue on the left option which stays loyal to the contour.

The trail here runs by the contact of two geological members; the Tzafit Member of hard limestone and dolomite and the Avnon Member, out of soft marl. Tzafit Member creates a protruding cliff in the landscape and through it Dry Canyon cuts itself. Avnon creates a slope above Tzafit. The marl is hidden beneath the rocky debris that has fallen from the cliffs above.

Where Dry Canyon begins in Nahal David (8), drop along the trail to the wadi. A nice view of the upper canyon of Nahal David and the grand fall initiating it, is to the west.

Go right and descend Dry Canyon. Note the white, smooth appearance of the canyon's walls caused by friction with flash flood debris. Pass a lone acacia tree. It is able to stay put, due to the curve in the wadi and its deep roots. A more common plant in the gorge is the caper with grey-blue leaves and large pink-white flowers.

By a funnel shaped fall, before the canyon takes a sharp left turn, there is an ascent to the right. It is marked by a series of stakes 4 m. above wadi level and leads to the green trail. Continue down the canyon.

The morphology of the wadi bed is dependant on the nature of the previous flash flood. Sometimes all the potholes will fill with debris and the canyon's name is accurate. Usually, there are many potholes around 1 m. deep that one has to wade through, making the going exciting. Reach the end of the gorge at Window Fall (9), by a huge pool of water. While resting, look for the leopard that dwells below the fall. Tristram's grackle is a more common sight. Be careful not to get to close to the slippery edge!

Head back up the gorge to the stakes on the left wall, where you ascend the short but steep flank of Dry Canyon, back to the green trail. Retrace your steps on that trail and descend to the right of the Chalcolithic Temple past a trail-mark sign to Ein Gedi (10). From the spring, continue as described in option 3.

Option 3: Reach the Chalcolithic Temple as described in option 1. Descend from the temple to the other side, (west) to a trail-mark sign where you take a left for 200 m. to the pool of Ein Gedi (10).

From the spring, head north between a couple of ruined buildings. Two trails run parallel here: the wide path reaches Ein Shulamit (4). Another path runs to the right (east) of it and is marked by two lines of rocks. It runs along the edge of the plateau, passes a water-collection pool full of greenery and merges with the trail ascending from lower Nahal David by a Sedom apple tree.

Take either trail and retrace steps taken earlier, down to lower Nahal David. At Nahal David take a right and descend along the stream toward the entrance (1). If it is almost closing time, the wide part of the path may be teeming with timidless ibex and hyrax. Exit the main entrance (1), to end the hike.

The fault in Lower Nahal Bokek (Hike 35)

Nahal Arugot
Two options

Points of interest: *A deep canyon carrying a freshwater stream of pools and waterfalls, gorges and exotic tropical plant life upon which feed herds of ibex and clusters of hyrax.*

Length and nature of hike: 6 kilometers, back-and-forth or loop trip: It is best to hike up the canyon in the pleasant refreshing water and return along the trail. It is 4 kilometers round-trip to Hidden Falls.

Hiking time: 3-5 hours.

Preferred season: All year.

Suitable for: All.

Maps: Judean Desert (north or south) hiking and touring map.

Special preparation: Clothes and shoes for water walking and swimming. No food is allowed in the nature reserve.

Starting & ending point: Nahal Arugot Nature Reserve main entrance (1 km. from Road 90). Entrance costs a fee which covers entrance to the Nahal David Nature Reserve on the same day. Open 8 a.m.-3 p.m. every day.

To reach starting point:

Arrival by private transportation: At Ein Gedi, turn off Road 90 south of kilometer post 244. There is an orange sign announcing Wadi Arugot. The paved road heads west between palm groves and the northern bank of Nahal Arugot. Five hundred meters from Road 90, reach a split (there is a sign).

Before turning left, look across the field on your right. There, two hundred meters away, are the ruins of Roman-Byzantine Ein Gedi, including a renovated synagogue with colorful mosaic floors (1). It is well worth a visit. Return to the road split.

Turn left on the paved road. On the right, you will see the bare Tel Goren—the ancient settlement of Ein Gedi. Pass through an unmarked gate into the Nahal Arugot Nature Reserve. The road winds left and is bordered on the right by gravel full light-colored marl of the Lisan Formation (Marl). The road curves right and after a few hundred meters ends at the Nahal Arugot Nature Reserve parking lot (2). Here are picnic tables, water, restrooms and even a kiosk. Since Nahal Arugot is heavily visited by all types of people, you are requested to eat here and not in the reserve.

Arrival by public transportation: Get off the Jerusalem-Eilat/Ein Gedi/Neve Zohar or Beersheba-Ein Gedi bus by the Ein Gedi gas station and head north along Road 90. Cross Nahal Arugot on the bridge. Note the large boulders in the dry wadi of Nahal Arugot. Take a left by the orange sign announcing 'Wadi Arugot.' Follow as described in 'Arrival by private transportation.'

Geography

Nahal Arugot (*Wadi Aregeh*) means in Hebrew and Arabic, "Wadi of Garden Beds." It is one of the largest and longest wadis in the Judean Desert. Beginning south of the Etzion Bloc in the Hebron Hills at an elevation of 1,000 m., the wadi drops 1,400 m. along its 46-km. length. Its drainage area is 280 sq. km.

Eight kilometers west of the Dead Sea, the stream bed begins to deepen, and after 4 km., it climaxes at a grand dry fall of 100 m. heading a grand canyon at some places close to 500 m. deep.

Ein Arugot emerges 500 m. downstream from the fall, initiating the perennial flow along the canyon. Smaller springs emerge downstream, altogether amounting to 140 cubits per hour.

Nahal Arugot is the second-longest oasis in the Judean Desert, after Wadi Kelt. The stream is the official boundary between northern and southern Judean Desert.

Along the southern cliff of the canyon ascends Ma'ale Isi'im (Essenes), built during Roman times. Above and a bit downstream from Hidden Falls is Ma'ale Benai Hamoshavim ascending the northern slope towards Mitzpe Ein Gedi.

The large alluvial fan of Nahal Arugot absorbs the running water. It is used for agriculture and recreation.

Plants and animals

Leopard (*Panthera pardus*): Leopards, once common throughout Israel, made a comeback in the Judean Desert during the late 1960s. In 1994 their future became uncertain due to two killings of leopards by man during a natural, periodic dwindling of the population.

These leopards are among the smallest in the world. The mature male rarely surpasses 30 kg.

The cats are mainly nocturnal, feeding upon hyrax, ibex and porcupines. They often visit the Ein Gedi settlements, hunting down house pets, even cats! Leopards have been found enjoying carcasses. During the day each leopard rests at fixed spots in its territory.

Each animal, male and female, has its own territory. A male territory may encompass a number of female territories. Biologists have found that each female has at least 150 sq. km. of territory.

The Ein Gedi leopards can usually be seen only during the hours that the reserve is closed to the public. But leopard signs are visible everywhere. Claw diggings with feces or urine along trails or by water and lacerated tree bark are common markings.

Since the leopard has no mating season, births are scattered throughout the year. Gestation lasts three months, yielding 1-3 cubs. Mothers tend the young alone. Usually only one survives the harsh desert conditions.

Nature Reserves Authority rangers will be happy to supply you with more information.

History

Chalcolithic tools have been found in the caves west of the grand fall (these caves are still used by Bedouin shepherds). East of the fall, atop the cliffs, stand remnants of twelve structures littered with Byzantine potsherds. The site is known as Mitzpe Arugot. An ancient trail leads from the site, down to Ein Arugot. Three other trails meet at the site, two from the Hebron Hills and one from Ma'ale Ein Gedi, 2 km. to the east. Experienced hikers can reach the site from Nahal Arugot via Ma'ale Benai Hamoshavim.

The oldest known ascent from the canyon is Ma'ale Isi'im. In the cliff caves of Nahal Hever, (the canyon south of Nahal Arugot) Bar Kokhba rebels hid. The Romans camped above and laid siege until the rebels ran out of supplies. Ma'ale Isi'im connected the Romans to their main base at Ein Gedi.

A water collection pool stands at the mouth of the canyon. It was used for irrigation of nearby crops. Northeast of the canyon's mouth stand ruins of a small fort known as Metzad Arugot. The fort most likely was a guard post for the fields.

It seems that substantial human activity never took place in the canyon, rather in the plains between it and the Dead Sea. Nomads throughout the centuries utilized the caves and the canyon's perennial water. Although a large Byzantine monastery thrived in central Nahal Arugot, no remnants of monasteries have been found in the canyon vicinity.

H. B. Tristram in the late 19th century writes:

> I started early after a bathe at sunrise in the sweet pool below our camp to explore the Wady Aregeh. Here we found a perennial stream in a romantic glen, but not a deep gorge like Sudeir, and with canebrakes, bulrushes, and a species of willow new to us ...

To begin hike:

From the entrance booth (2) head along the clear trail. Nahal Arugot is cut into gravel that has collected here by the mouth of the canyon, due to the decrease in energy of the flash flood torrent. The Dead Sea level has sharply dropped this century. In order to keep up (down) with it, Nahal Arugot has easily incised itself in the alluvium.

Pass a couple of acacia trees near a clogged pool on your left. The ancient pool was part of an irrigation system on the northern stream bank.

The trail passes an impressive green bush adorning the steep bare northern slope on your right. This is the tropical Persian salvadora.

Two hundred meters from the pool, reach the opening of a gorge (3). Leave the trail and enter the stream. This first contact with the running stream, the dripping maidenhair-decorated travertine rocks and the sleek canyon walls, makes this excursion already worthwhile. The canyon's northern wall sometimes has a strong flow of water gushing forth from a horizontal crack. The short canyon ends and the stream bed is aligned with the trail, but not for long. Continue along the running water!

The wadi opens a bit and curves right. A small, dry tributary merges from the left. A few Euphrates poplar trees appear on the right. On the left, about 5 m. above

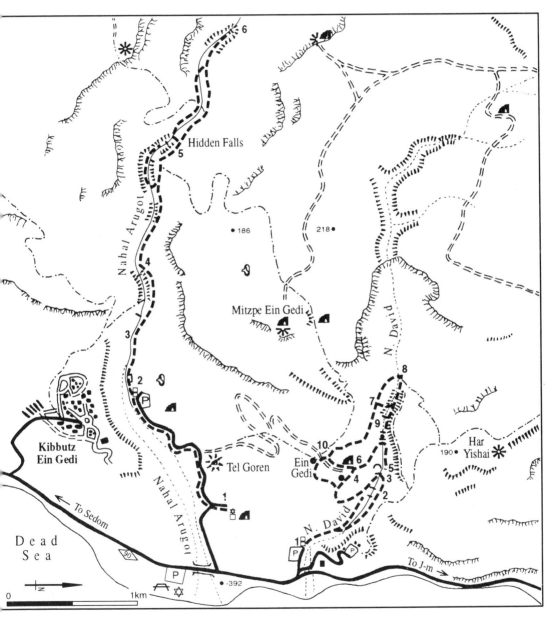

Hike 33, Nahal David and Ein Gedi, and Hike 34, Nahal Arugot

stream level, note a small new wall of rocks parallel to the stream. The wall protects a water pipe.

One hundred and fifty meters ahead, reach a small waterfall and pool, at the end of a tiny gorge. The spot is also adorned by two showers that fall from the pipeline above (4). After enjoying a refreshing shower, continue up the waterfall. If you have difficulty, climb up from the shower to the trail, which is 10 m. above the stream on the right (north), where a droopy-leafed moringa tree stands by a few reeds. Return to Nahal Arugot above the waterfall. Here you can see how some of the waters are channeled into the pipe. The waters are used by Kibbutz Ein Gedi.

Three hundred meters beyond the showers, the banks narrow and the trail reaches the gorge that ends at Hidden Falls (5). Before entering the gorge, note for later use the trail that ascends to the right, marked by a mosaic arrow. Head to Hidden Falls, 15 m. high and decorated by maidenhair ferns, the popular highlight of Nahal Arugot.

After thoroughly resting, retrace your steps to the gorge mouth and go left up the northern bank on the trail seen previously. At cliff-level you have two options:

Option 1: Return back to the starting point; continue up the trail for 50 m. and reach the red-marked trail (there is a sign). Go right and gradually descend parallel to Nahal Arugot back to the entrance (2).

Option 2: Continue on to the "Upper Pools"—a matter of half an hour (a bit more than a kilometer). Either follow the red-marked trail (50 m. above) to the left or head left off the trail where you are, and walk above the Hidden Falls gorge. At the top of Hidden Falls, enter the stream bed full of large boulders and wade upstream.

Three hundred meters from the gorge, the stream bed opens up. Opposite a wadi that enters from the right by acacia trees, there is a thick growth of tamarisk trees where the red trail ascends the towering cliffs. This ascent is Ma'ale Isi'im. Do not ascend, rather continue in the wet wadi.

After a few hundred meters, reach the canyon of the Upper Pools. Take it from the right. The canyon curves left and then right and dead-ends at a waterfall and pool (6).

This is the farthest point you will reach along Nahal Arugot. Beyond this canyon, Nahal Arugot is a running stream, emerging at Ein Arugot one kilometer west of the Upper Pools. This upper part of the oasis of Nahal Arugot is a closed nature reserve.

Returning to the starting point is very simple. From the Upper Pools, return the way you came until reaching a wadi coming from the north (now left) by a few acacias. Here, join the red trail on the left. The trail remains loyal to the northern bank all the way to the parking lot (2).

Before the descent to Hidden Falls, pass a couple of large green trees. On the slope to your left you should catch a glimpse of some hyraxes (rock-rabbits) doing their routine. Note the descent to Hidden Falls. From here, it is 2 km. to the entrance booth (2).

35

Ein Bokek

Three options

See map on page 279

Points of interest: *A lush desert oasis of a warm-water stream in a deep canyon teeming with wildlife. The route includes views of the Ein Bokek hotel complex, the Dead Sea and two Roman water systems.*

Length and nature of hike: 3 kilometers, loop trip or 2.5 kilometers, back-and-forth.

Hiking time: 1-3 hours.

Preferred season: All year.

Suitable for: All.

Maps: Judean Desert (south) hiking and touring map.

Special preparation: Swimsuit.

Starting & ending point: South of the bridge over Nahal Bokek on Road 90, behind the Ein Bokek Hotel. Here is an orange sign marking Ein Bokek and a black trail mark (1).

To reach starting point:

Arrival by private transportation: Park the vehicle on the western side of Road 90, by the sign in orange with a black trail mark, that reads in English, "Ein Bokek" (1). The sign is just south of where the road crosses Nahal Bokek, by kilometer post 212.

Arrival by public transportation: Take the Arad, Beersheba or Jerusalem bus to the Ein Bokek hotel complex. The closest bus stop is in front of the Ein Bokek Hotel. From here, find a way down to the dry wadi of Nahal Bokek, just north of the hotel (1). Follow Nahal Bokek beneath Road 90.

If the bus does not stop at the Ein Bokek Hotel, it is best to get off at the northern turnoff to the hotel complex and walk south for 400 m. along Road 90 to the starting point (1).

Geography

Ein Bokek is the only hike in this book in the southern Judean Desert.

The southern Judean Desert is more arid than the northern Judean Desert. The northern Judean Desert resides east of the Judean Hills that have a Mediterranean climate. The southern Judean Desert is east of the Northern Negev. One of the differences between the two sections can be seen following a rainy winter. While colorful flowers cover the slopes of the northern Desert, in the Ein Bokek area, only the wadi beds bloom. The slopes are sparsely dotted with annual growth.

The Fault Escarpments towering above the Dead Sea shore near Ein Bokek are 400 m. high, compared to 600 m. north of Ein Gedi.

The Nahal Bokek canyon is only 2 km. long. It begins at two dry falls of 100 m. and 60 m. Altogether, the nahal is 13 km. long, draining 21 sq. km.

Plants and animals

Common Acacia (*Acacia reddiana Savi*): This tree can be easily seen in the wadis that cross Road 90. Its Hebrew name is *shita selilanit*.

Shita is mentioned 24 times in the Bible, 19 as a tree and 5 times related to a site. "And Joshua the son of Nun sent two men secretly from Shittim as spies..." (Joshua 2:1). Although the Land of Israel has five acacia species, only the "common" one has construction-grade wood. The wood was used for the Tabernacle: "And you shall make upright frames for the tabernacle of acacia wood" (Exodus 26:15).

The tree grows to 8 m. The long, sharp white spines of the twigs are the stipules of the leaves. The minute flowers are borne on long stalks. The main flowering season is spring and the secondary is late summer. The fruits are twisted pods which accumulate beneath the tree and are consumed by various animals (not edible for man). Gazelles in particular enjoy acacia leaves.

As the largest desert tree, the acacia needs large quantities of water. It usually grows along large wadis and provides important shade for humans and is a food source for animals.

Fan-tailed raven (*Corvus rhipidurus*): Resting at a view point you might notice fan-tailed ravens putting on a show.

Originating in Ethiopia, this bird lives in desert and semi-desert regions. In Israel, it is found along the Syrian-African Rift south of Jericho. Its population is concentrated in the southern Judean Desert between Ein Gedi and the Sedom. The bird is often seen drinking at oases or gathering round garbage dumps.

The raven's body length can surpass half a meter. Its bill is shorter than most species. The fan-tailed species is distinguished in flight. Its broad wings and short tail turn it into a real performer. It catches feathers and papers in the air. It even plays by dropping objects in flight and catching them in mid-air.

Like other birds of its kind, the fan-tailed raven is omnivorous, preferring insects, fruit, carrion and young birds.

Breeding takes place on steep remote cliffs. Nesting begins in March. Sometimes a few pairs nest as neighbors.

History

Ein Bokek was inhabited during two periods: Late Second Temple and the late Roman, until the Early Arab period.

The first settlement occured during or just before the reign of King Herod. The settlers constructed a large agricultural estate that covered the alluvial fan of Nahal Bokek, and took advantage of every drop of water of Bokek and No'it springs. The crops were similar to the ones grown at Ein Gedi: valuable perfumes, spices and possibly dates. Ein Bokek represented the frontier of the government in the Judean Hills due to its location as a vital oasis in the arid southern Judean Desert.

The spring stands by two travel routes: the western Dead Sea shore and the Edom Route (today Road 31), which crosses the southern basin of the Dead Sea and climbs (5 km. south of Nahal Bokek) towards Arad. During the first centuries of the era, the southern basin of the Dead Sea was dry and the Edom Route was well-travelled.

Ein Bokek gave its name to a fort, Metzad Bokek, erected during the late Roman period. Its strategic location overlooks both the agricultural installations and the travel route. The site was occupied until the Arab conquest; since then, the spring has been nothing more than a rest-stop for weary travellers.

From Metzad Bokek, Ma'ale Bokek climbs to the plateau above, where it passes a Roman-Byzantine fort, Metzad Hatrurim, and merges with the Edom Route southeast of Arad.

H.B. Tristram describes how the oasis looked in the 19th century:

> About one o'clock we reached the mouth of Wady Um Bagkhek and turned up it in search of water. We soon found a little trickling rill of sweet water, lost at intervals in the sand and reappearing as a moist ooze through the gravel. Following up the gorge, the horses had a copious drink, and we sat down to eat our bread and cheese... I climbed alone up the ravine, where I found the stream expanded as the gorge deepened and contracted, till I reached a deep clear pool under a little cascade, where the sun never penetrates, and having laid down my clothes on a soft cushion of maiden-hair fern, enjoyed a delicious bath.

> The contrast of these lovely glens, few and far between in the rugged wilderness, is very enchanting, and one might have expected an exuberance of animal life collected in such a spot: but beyond the trace of ibex, gazelle, and porcupine, I saw no sign of living things. Plants, indeed, there were in rich profusion-tall canes, acacias, oleanders, ferns and willows... There are traces of an old road up the glen, which appears to have led down from the wilderness; and at the mouth, but quite in the open space in front, and doubtless connected with the road, are the ruins, very perfect, of a square fortress, with corner bastions... It had no other name...than Kulat Um Bagkhek.

In the early 1970s, Ein Bokek Hotel was established on the southern bank of Nahal Bokek. The hotel drew its water from Ein Bokek. Two more hotels were soon built nearby and a third one 3 km. to the south, requiring additional sources of water. In the 1980s the area went through intense development that continues today.

Site description

Ein Bokek: The spring emerges 1,300 m. up the canyon, 290 m. below sea level. Its discharge is 20-40 cubits per hour. Its salinity is 1,680 mg. per liter. Its waters create a 1-1.5 kilometer long stream.

Ein No'it: Also called the Roman spring due to its proximity to Metzad Bokek. Its chemical composition (2,000 mg. chlorine per liter, 6,850 mg. total dissolvents per liter) are believed to be curative. Discharge is 4-8 cubits per hour. The water is 39° Centigrade. It emerges 100 m. above today's Dead Sea level.

Remnants of a water system can be identified from the spring downslope. The system was built during Herodian times and renovated with the construction of Metzad Bokek. The waters were transferred downhill via a channel. The channel runs down the slope, in an east-southeast direction.

Where the slope becomes more gradual, north of Metzad Bokek, there are remains of a water tower which controlled water distribution to the agricultural lots. From the tower downhill, no remnants have been found. However, up by the sources there are the remnants of a 3.6-square-meter structure which resembles a Hellenistic altar, but was probably a bath house, typical of Roman culture.

Metzad Bokek: The fort dates to the late Roman and Byzantine period.

Upon entering, note the staircase on the left leading to the roof or second floor. It seems that the fort is composed of rooms in the inner court and external rooms built along the walls. Note the masonry of the four entrances by the four corners of the main structure. By the northeastern external room you can see remains of wood by the entrance. The wood was used as a roof. Signs of fire are evident at ground level in the room.

The inhabitants drew their water from two pools built on the southern bank of Nahal Bokek (near the trailhead). In the northwestern wall of the fort is an opening where water from jars was spilled into the fort for immediate use.

The Antiquities Authority plans to renovate the Metzad Bokek complex.

To begin hike:

Descend on the dirt road and note the remnants of two water-collection pools on your left. They provided the fort with drinking water and issued water to the farming sections where the hotels stand today. The pools were fed from an aqueduct that began at the opening of the canyon. Nearby, its remnants line the bottom of the southern cliff. Continue along the southern bank. This dry part of Nahal Bokek is adorned by a few tamarisk trees.

Two hundred meters from Road 90, the wadi sharply changes its west-east direction to a south-north one. Along this part you have two options, for the next 250 m.:

Option 1: Follow the dirt road that crosses the wadi and continues south along the western bank. Along the cliff, note remnants of the aqueduct that led water to the two pools.

<u>Option 2</u>: Follow the marked trail in the wadi bed. It will take a couple of extra minutes but sometimes this part of the wadi is already trickling with water.

Before choosing, look up at the cave on the northern side of the wadi's sharp curve. The cave is formed at the contact of a layer of hard sedimentary rock on top of a layer of soft shales. The easily-erodible shales have rolled down the slope, creating the cave. Note how the layer of rock of the cave dips steeply to the east. Above the dipping layer, is a thick layer of gravel which does not present a sharp tilt like the strata below it.

The northward direction of this part of Nahal Bokek can be explained as being "caught" by a north-south fault. (The fault is one of the many faults of the Syrian-African Rift). The tilted strata overlying the cave is most likely rock dragged down by the block that was lowered by the fault. After the faulting occurred, during the Lisan (Lashon) Lake stage of the Dead Sea, debris from the scarps and wadis was deposited, becoming the thick layer of gravel. This is the Lisan Formation (Marl). Outcrops of this formation can be seen stuck onto the canyon's walls, such as above the dirt road.

Where the dirt road reconnects to the stream bed, the lush part of the route begins. A trickle of water appears and saltbush and reeds adorn the sides. Enter the canyon via the wet wadi. The canyon was hit by a severe flash flood in 1993, uprooting most of the water foliage. Ascend cement steps (once a dam) that cross the wadi. The dam was created to collect water before piping it to Ein Bokek Hotel. In a similar way, a bit more downstream, 2,000 years ago, water was dammed and directed to the aqueduct. Here, the marked trail ascends to the left and soon descends back to the stream. Continue in the stream bed until reaching the waterfall (2).

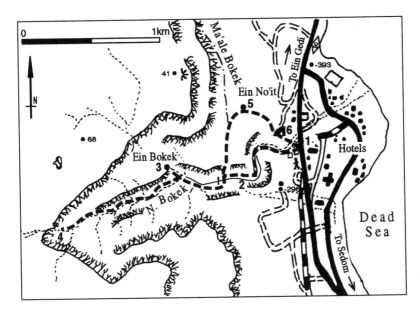

Hike 35,
Ein Bokek

From the waterfall, the loop route heads along the black trail that ascends the northern bank of Nahal Bokek (for an easy way out, of course, it is possible to retrace your steps back to the starting point (1)).

Ein Bokek emerges 350 m. upstream (3). Nahal Bokek's dry waterfall is 1 km. west of Ein Bokek (4). To head to these sites, follow the trail that ascends just left of the waterfall. The trail runs along the lower part of the canyon's southern slope and hits the wadi beneath the greenery of Ein Bokek (3). Ascend amid the reeds growing upon travertine, to the captured source of the spring. The pipes release a small amount of water in order to keep the green waterscape alive. Note the warmth of the water. To reach the bottom of the dry waterfall, head up the dry wadi from the spring (by the railing) for 1 km. and then return back to the spring going the same way.

From the spring return back to the waterfall (2).

From the waterfall ascend the northern bank along the black trail. The old trail heads to the right around a protruding rock. The newer trail is blocked by flattened reeds from the 1993 flood. After the rock, the trail ascends a rocky slope running above a fault line, hidden by debris.

Further up, the trail follows a shallow gully. Looking up, note a small cliff close to the ridge crest. The gully dissects the cliff. Looking south, note how the cliff on the southern bank is cracked by a fault. This is evidence that the gully runs along the continuation of the fault. This trail running up the gully, is a good example of how a human route follows the geology of the terrain. It takes advantage of the fault to ascend the slope easily, without needing to get blocked at a cliff. In late winter, small, round, yellow flowers dot the slope. These are called *Aaronsohnia faktorovskyi* after two Zionist botanists from the first half of the 20th century.

At the top of the ridge, enjoy a view of the hotel complex, perpetually under development. To the south, you can see the northern tip of the Sedom Mountains ending by the large Zohar alluvial plain.

The black trail passes a flat arena and heads north along the slope. One hundred and fifty meters from the flat area, a red trail descends to the right. Take it down to Ein No'it, which once emerged by the clump of greenery (5).

From Ein No'it, the red trail descends to the right of the spring and reaches an ancient agricultural terrace supported by a rock wall (by the lone acacia tree). Continue down to Metzad Bokek (6). Explore!

From the ruin it is easy to return to the starting point (1). Pink dock (sorrel) bloom along the trail in the spring and late winter. The leaves are edible and have a tangy taste.

Negev

Geography

The Negev is shaped like an isosceles triangle with its base to the north, running from a point near Gaza on the Mediterranean coast to the southwestern shore of the Dead Sea. From these two points the sides of the triangle run some 200 km. south to the apex, the city of Eilat, at the northern end of the Gulf of Akaba. The vast triangle measures about 12,500 km., roughly 60% of the State of Israel.

Its western boundaries coincide approximately with the Sinai Desert. The border is a political one with Egypt—it is indistinguishable on the ground. However, sharp agronomic differences between the two countries in the north have made the border quite apparent from the air—the Israeli side is covered with shrubs, while on the Egyptian side, uncontrolled Bedouin flocks have devastated the vegetative cover inhancing desertification. From the ground, the Negev's only sharp-boundary is the eastern one: the multiple-fault-lined Arava valley (part of the great Syrian-African Rift) which separates the Negev from the highlands of Edom. Toward the northwest, the Negev blends gradually into the Coastal Plain. Toward the north it merges into the Judean Foothills and Hills and further east into the Judean Desert without any clear line of demarcation.

Geographers divide the Negev into four main regions: Northern Negev, Central Negev, Arava and Southern Negev. The Eilat Mountains at the southern tip of the Negev are sometimes defined as a fifth region.

Northern Negev, whose center is the city of Beersheba, drains into both the Mediterranean Sea and the Dead Sea.

Central Negev, with the ruins of the ancient town of Avdat roughly at its center, is composed of basins of a number of large wadis, a majority of them draining into the Arava.

The Arava is a long, narrow strip extending from the town of Eilat in the south to the Dead Sea Valley in the north.

Southern Negev extends from the Eilat Mountains to the Paran fault line (by Nahal Paran). The fault is 50 km. south of Makhtesh Ramon and crosses the Negev in an east-west direction.

The jagged and dark-colored appearance of the Eilat Mountains easily displays its unique geology: Precambrian igneous and metamorphic rocks. They form the northeast extension of the high mountains of southeastern Sinai.

The hikes in this book take place in Northern and Central Negev. Northern Negev has two subregions: the coastal strip and the northwestern plains and foothills. The coastal strip is where the Negev borders on the Mediterranean to the south of Gaza. It consists of recent mobile and semi-mobile sand dunes, sand fields and material that has been deposited by floods in the wadis that flow into the Mediterranean Sea. These alluvial deposits form brown arid soils that are fertile when irrigated. The topography is relatively flat.

The northwestern plains and foothills contain the ruins of the ancient towns of Shivta, Nitzana, Rehovot and Halutza. It is an area of rolling plains some 30-60 km. wide, separated by hills and ridges between 200 to 450 m. above sea level. The lithology is mainly Eocenian chalk with thin layers of dark chert. The soil, mainly fine-grained loamy silt, sometimes reaches a depth of several meters. The soil particles originate from the sky: silt-size particles, known as loess, are transported to the Northern Negev by the wind, mainly from the Sinai. After the loess lands, winter rains transform it from dust into dirt. The subregion also contains two complexes of desert sand: sand fields and sand dunes which are not geographically connected to the coastal dunes.

Central Negev has three subregions: the northwestern hills, the anticline ridges and the lower sedimentary Negev. Although most of the region drains into the Dead Sea, the northwestern hills have a Mediterranean drainage system. These mountainous hills are out of Eocenian limestone and chalk. They average 600-900 m. above sea level. The anticline ridges are composed of a series of parallel anticlines and valleys (synclines) running in a southwest-northeast direction. These anticlines form ridges with gentle northwest facing slopes and steep southeast facing slopes. They are 500-1,000 m. high. Lithologically, the ridges consist of Upper Cretaceous hard sedimentary rock. White Senonian chalk and dark chert are exposed on the ridge sides.A unique and spectacular feature among three anticline ridges are pseudo-craters (erosional cirques) called makhteshim. Each makhtesh has eroded hundreds of meters into a different anticline, creating a deep semi-oval valley surrounded by cliffs and drained by only one wadi. Each of the three are named after the anticline in which it is located. Small (Hatzera) Makhtesh is an oval 4 by 6 km., while Makhtesh Ramon is 40 km. long and about 10 km. wide.

Har Ramon, overlooking western Makhtesh Ramon, at 1,035 m. is the highest spot in the whole Negev. About half of the subregion contains the same soils as the northwestern plains of the northern Negev. The other half is made up of rock outcrops, hammadas and shallow desert soils, as well as gravelly slopes and coarse desert alluvium.

The lower sedimentary Negev is found south of Makhtesh Ramon. The rocks are a mosaic of Eocenian and Mesozoic limestone, chalk, soft shales and chert beds. The bleak landscape is of vast plains covered by barren plains, whose regularity is broken by plateaus, mesas and buttes. Elevations range from 300 m. in the south to 900 m. in the northwest. This arid land has never sustained human settlement. There are no hikes in this book in this subregion due to the lack of waterscapes.

Climate

The Negev is located along the fringe of the Old World desert belt. Northwestern Negev is a transition region as the summers are warmer and the winters cooler than in the Mediterranean zone. Average annual rainfall is 200-350 mm. The climate south of Makhtesh Ramon clearly belongs to the Old World desert belt, which extends from the Sahara to the desert of Sind in India. Annual rainfall in this part of the Negev ranges between 0-150 mm. with an annual average not exceeding 70 mm.

The Central Negev highlands (north and west of Makhtesh Ramon) is a temperate desert, with cool winters and warm summers. Total yearly evaporation is much lower than in hot deserts. The mean temperatures for December through March are below 15° C. The mean minimum temperatures reach freezing point with snowfall occurring sometimes. The climate of Mitzpe Ramon resembles that of Jerusalem: its mean temperature is 17° C, from an August high of 24° C to a January low of 8° C. Average rainfall is 100 mm. Heavy dew is common in this region, especially in the fall. The annual amount measured at Avdat is 37 mm.

Vegetation

Desert plants are continuously exposed to harsh conditions and must consequently adapt morphologically, physiologically and behaviorally. Foremost, they must adapt to the scarcity of water. In the desert there are usually short periods and specific locations of abundant water. Most desert plants adapt themselves to the short durations of these periods and to the special habitats where runoff collects. Since rainfall greatly varies, plants must be able to survive several consecutive drought years. High soil salinity and high temperatures make adaptation to water stress even more difficult.

The prevention and protection methods of desert plants include:

1) Habitat: limited to areas that will receive more water and release the water at a slower rate than the average. Most species are found in wadi beds or growing from cracks of rock that collect runoff in amounts that sometimes equal Mediterranean conditions (over 500 mm.).

2) Evenly spaced dispersion of plants on open slopes. Density corresponds to physical conditions and species characteristics.

3) A summer dormant stage with summer leaves, no leaves or even branchless modes. Summer leaves are much smaller than winter ones. This adaptation radically reduces transpiration. Plants will also adapt their growth to the amount of available water. Thus, some desert dwarf shrubs can be 200 years old while achieving less than 75 cm. in height.

4) Anatomical adaptation includes a lower and upper epidermis along the external part of the leaf which protects against water loss. Holes in the epidermis, called stomata, are formed between special guard cells which control their opening and closing. Opening is necessary for intake of carbon dioxide, but the cost is loss of

water to the atmosphere. Consequently, the stomata in some plants are located only in the shaded underside of the leaf. The stomata open only in the early morning and late afternoon. Desert plants have fewer stomata than their non-desert counterparts.

Roots may probe deep to underground water or spread over a wide area (such as along a wadi).

Desert plants are usually small.

5) Plant germination requires a certain threshold of moisture. It will not occur in the summer even if there is an unexpected rainstorm, since the following days will consequently dehydrate the fragile sprout. Germination tends to occur after at least two seasonal rainfalls, which does not happen every year.

Since germination occurs only during specific years, populations of mature bushes include specific age groups only. Thus, these groups will be identified by their uniformity in size. Also, they will represent years that had at least two major rainstorms.

There are two types of seeds among bi-seasonal annuals. One type germinates immediately if the requirements are met, while the other unit becomes germinable later but for a longer period of time.

6) High levels of soil salinity. Due to the high level of evaporation and shallow penetration depth of rainfall, salt accumulates near the soil's surface, causing osmotic problems for the plants. Usually, desert plants solve the problem with thick succulent leaves, laden with water which neutralizes osmotic pressure.

Most vegetation of the Negev belongs to three of Israel's four phytogeographic zones. Over 1,200 species have been identified. These are divided into ten districts. Each hike in this book is in a different district.

In the northwestern plains and foothills, agriculture long ago destroyed the natural vegetation cover. In uncultivated fields the main components are the desert henbane and the yellow yarrow, whose pungent smell lingers when severely trampled. In the aeolian (wind blown) and stream-driven loess regions, the jointed saltwood dominates, accompanied mostly by the feather grass. The feathery grass awns when moved by the wind are like white waves moving over the ground.

On the hammada-like slopes and the shallow rocky soils of the anticline ridges, two dwarf shrubs predominate: the well-known bean caper and the gray sagebrush. Other common plants are the sunrose, Sinai bluegrass, sedge and three dwarf shrubs.

The depressions and gravelly wadis north and a bit south of Makhtesh Ramon harbor the Atlantic terebinth. After rainy winters, colorful flowers cover the wadi beds and bloom on the slopes. The multi-colored tulip, the Juno iris, and the blue flowered ixiolirion are common geophytes which bloom in spring around Makhtesh Ramon. The white Damascus crocus blooms in the fall at elevations over 800 m., while the delicate pink autumn crocus appears all over the Central Negev highlands.

The vegetation of hammadas is very poor. In hammadas, soil and consequently plants are found only in interstices between the stones. The dominant plant is the leafless anabasis which is sometimes mistaken for the bean caper.

Wildlife

Israel's geographic location, at the conjunction of three vast zoogeographic units, is the key to understanding the Negev's abundant animal life and the great variety of adaptive patterns to desert conditions. The Negev's variegated topographic relief, past climatic changes and the numerous varieties of rock formations create an abundance of biotopes, thus the wealth in animal species.

While the Negev is easily defined into phytogeographic zones, the zoological geography is more difficult to determine. The only outstanding demarcation of animal distribution runs near the northern edge of Makhtesh Ramon, continuing northward to the Hatzera Anticline. This 'Ramon Line' is the southern border for animals that have a Mediterranean distribution pattern. This line is mainly a function of Israel's climatic gradient (it gets hotter in the south and east of the national watershed). Interestingly, this line is the biblical southern border of the Israelite tribes, most likely due to these climatic reasons. The climate south of the Ramon Line is not suitable for profitable domestic animal cultivation.

Water is the most essential ingredient of animal life. Between sixty and seventy percent of the body mass of animals is water. The major problem of animals living in deserts is the maintenance of so great a water reservoir in the dry and hot desert atmosphere. Warm-blooded creatures need to keep a stable temperature. Sharply fluctuating temperatures increase the problem of survival. Furthermore, the low productivity of the desert requires increased activity to provide oneself with sufficient food, which makes the water problem and heat burden more acute. Small animals have a more difficult time as their high surface-mass ratio causes overheating.

Animals cope with the desert climate by many adaptations:

1) Mammals: Domestic mammals usually have large drinking and water storage capacities. The most notable is the camel, which can withstand desert heat for a number of days. Gazelles, in comparison, receive all of their liquids from eating plants, yet they will never overlook water.

Rodents never reach water sources and they lack evaporative cooling systems. Life in cool, moist subterranean shelters help rodents regulate body heat without losing water.

Carnivores receive sufficient amounts of liquids from their prey. Footprints of carnivorous animals found near water sources may mean that the animal followed its prey to these places rather than searching for water to drink.

A majority of desert mammals are nocturnal and release dry dung that conserves body water.

2) Birds: Birds are active in the day. In the heat of the summer they restrict activity to early morning and early evening. Flight makes their survival in the desert relatively easy. It eases their access to water sources and cool shelters. Flying high above the earth's surface distances them from mid-day heat. The rising hot desert air makes gliding and soaring an easy task for birds of prey searching for lunch. Feathers, like sheep wool, protect against heat. Solid uric acid waste also helps conserve water. Carnivorous birds that prey on arthropods, snails or vertebrates ingest great amounts of water in their food, but seed-eaters need to drink water.

3) Reptiles: Subterranean shelters help reptiles escape unfavorable conditions. They are cold-blooded. Once in shelter their temperature drops, metabolism slows and energy consumption falls. The main adaptation of reptiles is not physical but behavioral: each creature selects the season and the time of day in which to be active. Adaptations include raising legs to distance the body from the hot soil and panting and flattering of the upper part of the throat, which leads to evaporative cooling. Most desert reptiles are carnivorous and their food contains large amounts of water. Vegetarian lizards mainly eat succulent plants. As with other animals, urine is a semi-solid mass of uric acid.

4) Arthropods (insects, spiders and crabs): Being small, arthropods are more susceptible to overheating than are large vertebrates, but they can also tolerate greater water loss (up to 90% of their body water). Their size eases their search for cool, shady spots. Their small water needs can be supplied from dew. Spiders can even absorb water from the atmosphere. Daily active insects have a wax layer impervious to water vapor.

Snails are very common in the desert (and are an important food source for small mammals). Shells help them overcome water loss. Theoretically, a snail can tolerate 500 summer days of water loss.

Even though most desert animals roam at night, there are reasons that you may see them during the day. What to look for:

Animal	Notable characteristics and/or locaton
common agama	NW of Ramon Line; sunbathes on large rocks
sinaitic agama	SE of Ramon Line; sunbathes on large rocks
small desert lizard	seen on rocky slopes
fringe-toed lizard	darts from bush to bush in wadi beds
venomous snakes	most common is the Burton's carpet viper
pygmy gecko	smallest reptile (2-3 cm); under rocks by day
vegetarian dabb lizard	monstrous (60 cm); lives in deep borrow holes in southern Negev and Arava
gazelle	found on desert plains
Nubian ibex (mountain goat)	prefers cliffs
hare	look for them darting from a wadi
rodents	prolific; often seen during daytime
fat jird	common in Makhtesh Ramon vicinity
gerbil	common
golden spiny mouse	feeds on snails; heaps of crushed snail shells marks den
hyena, fox, wildcat }	all common at night;

lynx, leopard, jackal }	leopards are rare and have not attacked man in Israel
wolf, wild dog }	packs of wolves tend to disturb hikers' food (only!) at night

Birds are often the most common wildlife seen during the day. The Negev attracts raptors more than any other place in Israel. Species of particular interest in the Negev include houbara bustard, cream-colored courser, pin-tailed and black-bellied sandgrouse, hoopoe and Temminck's horned larks, spectacled warbler, mourning wheatear and desert wheatear.

black raven	widespread and shows no fear of humans
sandgrouse }	can often be seen flying to a source of
trumpeter bullfinch }	water to quench their thirst
black scoty falcon	nests during summer along the Tzinim Cliffs
kestrel (the common falcon in Hebrew)	winters throughout Israel
Golden eagles	have made a comeback in the Negev as throughout the country.

Human Involvement

Today the Negev is recognized as a desert, but there is evidence that its climate was not always as arid as it is today. A previously more hospitable climate may help account for the abundant historical and archaeological evidence of human involvement in the area. Current research is addressing the link between prosperous past cultures and the prevailing climate. Correlation between the two can help explain the question of socialized human adaptability to the Negev.

The overall dry desert climate has helped preserve material evidence of the past. Thousands of flint artifacts scattered widely over the area give primary evidence of prehistoric habitation. The raw material for these flints (chert) derives from concretions or strata in limestone or chalk layers throughout the Negev. The hard flint tools, when undisturbed, remain remarkably intact over thousands of years.

According to this evidence, man has inhabited the Negev since Paleolithic times. During the latest stone age (the Neolithic) the Negev was relatively well-populated. Men of the Paleolithic and Mesolithic were roving hunters and their artifacts are found mainly upon topographic highs. Neolithic sites lie in wadis and on loess plains, suitable for agriculture. Thus the Neoliths may have introduced desert agriculture to the Negev and may have been the first non-nomadic intrusion into the Negev desert.

During the Chalcolithic and Early Bronze period only the Northern Negev was populated. A common Middle Bronze remnant is a large stone mound called tumuli found upon hill-tops or ridges, especially between Makhtesh Ramon and Yeroham. The mysterious tumuli seem to have been burial sites. From the same time period, archaeologists have found some agricultural and village relics. Some researchers see the Middle Bronze period as one of dense inhabitance of the Negev. This culture was destroyed at the end of the 19th century B.C.E. leaving the Negev void of settlement.

Only 900 years later did human life return to the desert.

During the interim, the Children of Israel crossed the Central Negev. They came from Kadesh Barnea which is today under Egyptian control, not far from the Israel-Egypt border. They then followed the northern brink of Makhtesh Ramon to Nahal Tzin and then crossed the Arava. Interestingly, this route roughly coincides with the southern border of the lands given to the tribes of Israel: "Then your south quarter shall be from the wilderness of Tzin ... from the south to the Ascent of Akrabim and pass on to Tzin and the going forth thereof shall be from the south to Kadesh Barnea ..." (Numbers 34:3-4). Ma'ale Akrabim is in the Hatzera Anti-cline.

In biblical times only the area north of this border was known as the Negev. The name in ancient Hebrew meant "south" and may derive from the root *ngv* which means "dry."

With the expansion of the Israelite Kingdom in the 10th century, soldiers and peasants occupied the Negev. The works of King Uzziah are mentioned in Chronicles II 26:10: "Also he built towers in the desert and dug many water cisterns." Open water cisterns, along with house remnants and potsherds, remain from this period. Most of these are found just north of Makhtesh Ramon such as the Lotz Cisterns. The desert's features, such as the flash flood, were known in biblical times, according to Psalms 126:4: "Turn again our captivity, O Lord, as the streams in the Negev." The Israelite settlement weakened with the decline of the central government and disappeared after the Babylonian invasion in the 6th century B.C.E. Only during the reign of the Hasmonean King Alexander Jannaeus (103-76 B.C.E.) was the Negev, including the towns of Halutza and Avdat, briefly occupied by Judeans.

The Negev's most flourishing period began at the end of the 3rd century with the Nabatean-Roman-Byzantine era which lasted 800-900 years. The Nabateans most likely originated in southern Arabia. We first read of them as a successful opponent of General Antigonus Monophthalmus, one of Alexander's generals. The two battles in 312 B.C.E. are documented by 1st-century Greek historian Diodorus Siculus, who describes the Nabateans as commercial nomads. Using camels, they transferred precious perfumes, spices and silks from Gerrha on the Persian Gulf to Gaza, via their capital Petra, and Avdat. The merchandise originated in India, China and Arabia. Hundreds of surviving Nabatean graffiti mark their routes which were first described by a 1st century Greek geographer named Strabo. To protect their monopoly of this trade route, the Nabateans built urban centers at strategic positions. Five Nabatean towns stood in the Negev: Avdat, Shivta, Halutza, Kurnub (Mamshit) and Nitzana. With the rise of the Romans and a new Roman trade route, the Nabateans were weakened but remained in the Negev. They gradually transformed themselves from traders to farmers. The Romans guarded the Negev as a frontier province and sent army legions to maintain control, sometimes unsuccessfully.

During Byzantine times the Negev fell under the jurisdiction of the Eastern Byzantine Empire. Commercial enterprises were revived. Eilat became a port town, the hub of two caravan routes through the Negev. The desert was also a military buffer against the numerous groups of desert nomads. The constant threat of attack compelled residents of desert towns to engage in military service and civilian life (farming, commerce, religion) at the same time. Consequently, the Byzantine period left two imprints on the Negev: numerous churches and many kilometers of terrace walls.

Between 637-641 the Negev fell to the Moslems. Lack of a supportive central government slowly brought the inhabitants to abandon their homes. Some researchers see the flourishing Byzantine Negev as a result of a wetter climate at the time, and the fall of the settlement as a result of aridization. However, the prevalent opinion is that the Moslems had no interest in maintaining the desert economy. It therefore fell into Bedouin hands for the next 1,300 years.

The unindustrious Bedouin nomads only brought desertification. They used Byzantine constructions, but never maintained them. Three fierce tribes ruled Central Negev and their hostility kept the territory clear of visitors for hundreds of years. Not much is known regarding the sequence of events between the Bedouins. The dominant and most ancient tribe was the Azazme'. The Azazme' was pushed out of the Northern Negev by the Tarabin and Tiaha tribes in the 16th century. History may be re-written as recent archaeological surveys have found many small-scale Moslem remnants throughout the whole Negev.

In the middle of the 19th century the Turks began to achieve some order in the Negev and European explorers began to visit the region and document their finds. In 1906, the Rafiah-Taba line was measured in accordance with an agreement between Britain and Turkey. With the British conquest of Palestine in 1917, a number of changes took place. Some police stations were established, water facilities were improved for Bedouin use, and land ownership registration and scientific research began. Jews, though, were forbidden to enter the region. In search for resources during WWII, the British developed the first roads in the Negev.

Zionist settlement reached the Negev when Kibbutz Revivim was established in 1943. In 1949 I.D.F. units crossed Makhtesh Ramon for the first time and, upon reaching Eilat, annexed the Negev to the State of Israel. The new state worked in three directions regarding the Negev: creating a road infrastructure, locating and exploiting natural resources, and developing settlements. For resources, Makhtesh Ramon looked promising but did not deliver. Today, the Makhteshim support tiny plants for locally-quarried raw materials, such as quartz and clay. Otherwise, the only prosperous resource found is phosphate rock in the synclines of the northeastern Negev where the Tzin and Oron mines operate today.

In 1952 Kibbutz Sdeh Boker was founded, then the southern-most kibbutz in the world. In 1953 Prime Minister David Ben Gurion retired to this kibbutz, calling for mass development of the Negev (which has yet to happen). Ben Gurion and his wife Paula are buried by Sdeh Boker College overlooking Nahal Tzin.

In 1956 the Beersheba-Eilat Road 40 via Mitzpe Ramon was completed. Previously, the only route to Eilat was along the treacherous Ma'ale Akrabim via Hatzeva in the Arava. The new road opened Israel to the Negev and to the towns of Eilat and Mitzpe Ramon. Fifteen years later, the new Arava road to Eilat made Mitzpe Ramon one of the most distant and backward development towns in Israel.

With the signing of the Israel-Egypt peace treaty in 1979, which forced Israel to evacuate the Sinai, the Negev returned to Israel's focus of attention. The I.D.F. had to locate its strategic and routine infrastructure in the region. The Negev became one big firing zone, except for designated locations for Bedouin settlement (in Northern Negev) and nature reserves (such as the southern Eilat Mountains, Makhtesh Ramon and Tzinim Cliffs). Today, internal tourism is developing in the Negev, increasing the average Israeli's awareness of this area.

Water

The availability of water is the key to survival in a desert. Three principle factors determine the water requirements of man in the desert: air temperature, body characteristics and activity. Only the latter is controllable. Of all mammals, man is one of the least adequate for desert life. The human body constantly perspires in order to maintain a very specific temperature, making man highly dependant on reliable water sources.

There are two main sources of water: underground water and surface water. The origin of underground water in the desert is one of the leading puzzles for desert geographers. Underground water has two possible sources, local and distant.

Local underground water can originate from slope runoff or from flood water seeping through gravel wadi beds during and immediately after floods. Due to the steepness and lithology of the slopes, runoff water moves too fast in order to sink in. Thus underground water certainly sinks in through the wadi bed gravel. The wadi bed gravel also hosts underground streams of water that seep downstream for different spans of time following a flash flood. But it also seems unlikely for this water to seep into deep underground reservoirs through many layers of rock, some of which are impermeable. Therefore, the main Negev springs are most likely not fed from local sources.

Shallow underground reservoirs known in Arabic as *thamila*, meaning a place where water remains, are found by digging in the shallow wadi bed gravel, especially at the bottom of falls or in water hollows. A *thamila* can produce 0.25-0.5 cubic meters of water per day. Some *thamila* are made into shallow wells dug into the wadi bed. It seems that these types of wells, usually not surpassing ten meters in depth, were the wells dug and used by the nomadic patriarchs.

Deep wells are also found in the Negev, some reaching tens of meters in depth and some being over 2,000 years old. These wells penetrate strata until reaching an aquifer. Today, water which originates locally is drilled in the Negev, mainly along the Syrian-African Rift.

Underground water of distant origins may come from as far as Central Africa, by very slowly percolating its way northward through Nubian Sandstone deposited in the Early Cretaceous. This African water is a few thousand years old. There is also a theory that this Nubian Sandstone aquifer is fossilized water. This means that the water is not from Africa. The explanation is that thousands of years ago the aquifer was filled and that today it is not being replenished.

The springs of Nahal Besor are the only reliable water source in the northwestern Negev. Springs that feed perennial stream flow are mainly found in the Central

Negev, usually flowing upon Eocenian strata. A number of small springs can be found in a number of canyons throughout the rest of the Negev seeping off Cretaceous rock. Even more meager springs that are unreliable sources of surface water emege along the Arava.

Throughout history, humans have developed ever more sophisticated ways to capture surface water, from primitive natural rock holes to open cisterns toroofed cisterns excavated in rock and dams. Shaded cisterns can endure the entire hot summer.

The simplest waterholes offer the desert's most spectacular stagnant water-scapes. They form at impermeable lows such as at the bottom of falls and along narrow canyons. These unreliable waterholes or hollows serve travelers, settlers, herders, and wildlife, as mentioned in Jeremiah 14:3: "They come to the waterholes and find no water."

Open cisterns were first dug in the Negev during the reign of the Israelite Kingdom. A large number of them have been found north of Makhtesh Ramon dug into impermeable Turonian marl and lined with uncut stones. The cisterns were most likely covered with logs or mats. They were fed from directed runoff. Some of these cisterns have been restored. One of them is just north of Haruhot Junction, east of Road 40.

Roofed cisterns, requiring strong metal tools, date to the Nabateans. Three types are found: hillside, public town and private town. Hillside cisterns (*ma'agora* in Hebrew, *harabeh* in Arabic) were usually built along a wadi bed but were occa-sionally hill slope fed. Public town cisterns were fed by street flow and catchments, while smaller private domestic cisterns were fed by roof water. Nabatean cisterns were carved into chalk and the cistern's roof was usually a natural layer of hard limestone. Large cisterns required pillars for roof support and mortar to seal the cracks.

Life in a desert like the Negev includes the problem of unpredictable flash floods. High-intensity rainfall in small areas is most common during the fall and spring. One wadi may have a flash flood while its adjacent tributary stays dry. Low-intensity rainfall covering large areas takes place between mid-December and March. If this type of rainfall endures long enough, a relatively continuous stream flow can develop.

In the northwestern Negev there are dams that block some of the large wadis, where collected flash flood water is returned for storage via drill holes or seepage to underground aquifers. Northwestern Negev receives water from the northern area of Israel via the National Water Carrier while Southern Negev utilizes piped water and water from the Nubian Sandstone aquifer.

Hiking in the Negev

Only in the Negev can a hiker find a real wilderness, distant from modern civilization. But even here, space is very limited and every kilometer is defined. Most of the Negev is used by the military. The government has protected some unique landscapes as nature reserves, while others await consideration. There are also firing zones *inside* nature reserves. Thus many hiking routes are limited to days when the I.D.F. is not practicing, such as the Sabbath and Independence Day. Some firing zones are open to the public during holidays; *some* are inactive on Fridays. Information regarding firing zones can be obtained at S.P.N.I. offices.

The hikes in this book are *not* in firing zones, although occasional military activity may be seen. Please keep a distance.

Beersheba, capital of the Negev, is at its northern tip and is an hour and a half drive from Jerusalem and Tel Aviv. Mitzpe Ramon is one hour from Beersheba. Yeroham is half an hour from Beersheba. Three roads run north-south through the desert, bringing every spot in the Negev within a two-day hike. East-west roads cross only in the North. Public transportation is centralized from the Beersheba central bus station.

Safety precautions are especially vital for desert rambles. Even on water hikes it is important to supply yourself with water. In the summer, water consumption for a hiker is a liter per hour while in the winter 4-5 liters will do for a day. Since sunny days are prevalent throughout the year, please remember sunguard lotion and a hat. In the nature reserves, hiking is limited to trails only. For organized groups, outdoor camping is permitted at locations specified by the N.R.A. Animals may visit overnight campers in search for food (wolves enjoy meat so try to keep it in the car overnight).

Important Phone Numbers

S.P.N.I. Field Study Centers and Information: (area code 07)

Beersheba F.S.C.: 238527; fax: 237019
Sdeh Boker F.S.C.: 565016, 565828; fax : 565721
Har Hanegev F.S.C. (by Mitzpe Ramon): 588615/6; fax: 588385
Hatzeva F.S.C.: 581576, 581546; fax: 581558
N.R.A. Visitors Center, Mitzpe Ramon: 88620, 88691
Information Booths:
Shoket Junction, Bet Kama Junction, Beersheba central bus station
Northern Negev Tourism: 295546

Safety Assistance

I.D.F.:
Arava (Ein Yahav): 07-581450
Southern Command (in Beersheba): 07-902283, 07-902977

Police: 100
Beersheba: 07-462744
Mitzpe Ramon: 07-588444
Yeroham: 07-580144
Dimona: 07-559444/5

Ambulance:101
Beersheba: 07-279691
Mitzpe Ramon: 07-588333
Yeroham: 07-580133
Dimona: 07-559111

Sites worth Visiting

The Negev, forming 60% of the State of Israel, has many interesting sites. It is beyond the reach of this book to supply this long list. Information booths usually have a detailed brochure regarding the Negev.

Overnight Options

Indoors

S.P.N.I. Field Study Centers (see above).
Israel Youth Hostels: Mitzpe Ramon, Beersheba.
Ramon Inn, Mitzpe Ramon.
Sdeh Boker Guest House, at Kibbutz Sdeh Boker.
Orhan, hostel and guest house, Kibbutz Mash'abei Sadeh.

Outdoors

Haroeh campground, east of Road 40 opposite the entrance to Ben Gurion's home at Kibbutz Sdeh Boker. Offers shade, picnic tables and water.

J.N.F. Forest by the northern entrance to Mitzpe Ramon. Picnic tables and water.

Yeroham Reservoir Picnic Site, by western entrance to Yeroham (see Hike 37).

Be'erot campsite in Makhtesh Ramon. Five kilometers east of Road 40. Wind shelter, huts, bathrooms, water. Fee. Tel.: 07-588868, 07-586188.

Borot Lotz (Lotz Cisterns) campsite. Wind shelter, water, bathrooms.

Gas Stations

In all the cities and towns. Gilat Junction. Ramat Hovav, Mash'abei Sadeh Junction, Mitzpe Rimon and Avdat on Road 40.

36

Nahal Besor

See map on
page 301

Points of interest: *A large wadi bed cut through badlands holding pools of water and thick vegetation; a couple of ancient tels offering encompassing views of the western Negev. Nahal Besor runs by Eshkol National Park where there are lawns, recreation facilities and a landscaped spring.*

Length of hike: 8 kilometers, loop trip, 6 kilometers back-and-forth.

Hiking time: 4-6 hours.

Preferred season: Winter and spring.

Suitable for: All.

Maps: Gaza Region topographical map (1:50,000) or Negev Coastal Plain (Western Negev) hiking and touring map.

Special preparation: Upper parts of Nahal Besor drain in-dustrial zones and their toxic wastes. Swimming in the pools of Nahal Besor is not recommended. The region is heavily populated with snakes (not necessarily poisonous) so wear high shoes.

Starting & ending point: Eshkol National Park (a fee may be required) at the parking lot beneath Tel Shalala.

To reach starting point:

Arrival by private transportation: The entrance to Eshkol National Park (1) is off Road 241 between Ma'on Junction and Urim Junction. Turn south onto the paved entrance road. The road is lined with grey-leaved saltbush. Pass by the entrance booth. At the road split, take the right option. Pass the swimming pool (the largest one in Israel) parking lot on the left (olive trees on the right) and at a T-junction take a right. Pass a turnoff to the left to Ein Besor and 100 m. further north reach a shaded parking lot (2). Park the vehicle.

Arrival by public transportation: From the Beersheba central bus station take the bus that reaches the northwestern Negev settlements. Check that the bus line stops at the Eshkol National Park. Descend by the park entrance (1), and follow as described above in 'Arrival by private transportation.'

Geography

The expansive flat terrain of the region is out of loess. These loess plains thinly cover layers of different rocks that inform us of the events that shaped this dynamic region. Nahal Besor cuts through the loess and incises itself into the rock layers beneath. The revealed strata reveals four main geological stages which have shaped the Besor Region:

1) Formation: Eighty million years ago the Beersheba Valley was first formed. The valley drained large wadi beds from where Jordan stands today, into the Mediterranean Sea. Rocks originating east of the Syrian-African Rift are found in deposits of the ancient Nahal Besor.

2) Canyon: Millions of years later, the sea level dropped and a deep, wide canyon was cut in the Nahal Besor area. By sixteen million years ago, seawater engulfed the canyon depositing marine sediments. With the opening of the Syrian-African Rift, ancient Nahal Besor was severely shortened.

3) Deposition: Five million years ago the Mediterranean Sea dried up and conglomerate was deposited in Nahal Besor. Three million years ago the sea invaded again. Evidence of this period are beach rock, kurkar and conglomerates exposed beneath the carpet of loess and sand that cover the northwestern Negev.

During the last thousands of years, nature has deposited sand and loess. Israeli researchers claim that during the last 27,000 years, 0.5 m. of loess has been deposited, originating from Northern Sinai. The loess layer reaches 30 m. in depth at some places. Along Nahal Besor, about 8-10 m. of loess has been deposited, possibly by the stream. Since the loess is impermeable, rainwater runoff runs upon it and, when dropping to a low place such as Nahal Besor, creates a dissected topography of badlands.

The kurkar ridge cut by Nahal Besor along this hike is far from today's seashore. The deep invasion of the Mediterranean Sea took place between Ice Ages. Today kurkar is exposed in ridges ranging from 30-100 m. in height (there are three lining the Coastal Plain). Sometimes the ridges do not stand out since the low points have been filled in by different materials. Such is the case in Nahal Besor. The ridge has eroded partially and sand and loess have filled the depressions.

4) Erosion: A new Nahal Besor cuts into the kurkar ridge between Tel Sharuhen and Ein Besor. In other places, Nahal Besor cuts through other ancient deposits. Where it deepens to a pebble stratum of the ancient stream bed, water emerges, forming the springs of Nahal Besor.

The section of Nahal Besor that runs south of the Eshkol National Park is a nature reserve.

Plants and animals

Along the narrow nature reserve of Nahal Besor lie three vegetational habitats; the flat fields (plateau), the stream bed and the badlands between the two. Each hold different types of vegetation.

The stream bed is not too variated. It yields reeds that are either dislocated or flattened during flash floods. Perennial water sources support cattails. Animal husbandry and agriculture have decimated the natural plateau vegetation. Lone acacia, tamarisk and eucalyptus trees create important shade sites.

Along the badlands and slopes of Nahal Besor there is a variety of plants depending on the face of the slope and the soil and rock type. Sunny slopes have desert vegetation while more shady areas sustain Mediterranean and Irano-

Turanian plants such as the thorny burnet, usually found at the base of slopes where moisture is highest.

Crane (*Grus grus*): The impressive size and sharp contrast of these white birds against the bleak desert scenery make cranes a noticeable roadside sight. Migrating cranes pass through Israel in September en route south. Wintering cranes land between October and December. Spring migration begins in January. In March the population here heads north. They winter in the northwestern Negev, the Coastal Plains, the Jezre'el Valley and around Lake Kinneret and the Hula.

Cranes reach a height of 1.4 m. Wingspan reaches 2.4 m., making it one of Israel's largest birds. The long neck is the fowl's most noticeable feature. In flight the neck is stretched out straight. Its grey body has a white stripe going down the side of the neck that usually fades in winter. Their deep pitched call is loud and carries far, resembling hooting or trumpeting.

Wintering cranes have well-defined patterns of behavior. They roost for the night in large flocks, returning year after year to the same location. The site is chosen for gastronomic reasons. With sunrise the flock flies to the feeding site where it spends the day seeking food. In winter they are mainly vegetarian, forgetting their principles only for beetles. They eat vegetables and mushrooms. In spring a diet change takes place and they become omnivores attacking frogs, snakes, rodents and small birds like warblers. In order to get to water, cranes fly long distances.

The birds are cautious and are calm only when their field of vision is clear. Spotted eagles are enemies while many other raptors, such as kites and buzzards, are not.

The crane is known to put on dancing displays. The function is unclear. They are most frequent in spring. The display expresses excitement and involves various wing and body movement. The display of young energetic members includes leaps, bows, pirouettes and tossing of leaves and twigs.

Cranes are monogamous and territorial. Each pair guards its territory, usually a few square kilometers. Breeding does not take place in Israel, but usually north of the 49th parallel. One to three eggs are laid, incubated by both male and female for about 30 days. Aggressiveness naturally increases after the birth of the young.

History

Arabic names often resemble biblical ones. This has helped researchers identify many biblical sites. This is not the case regarding Nahal Besor, so its identification is problematic. Besor is mentioned in the Bible only once: "So David went, he and the six hundred men who were with him, and came to the brook Besor, where those who were left stayed behind" (I Samuel 30:9). The biblical Besor is not necessarily today's stream, but it most likely refers to one of the wadis in the area.

Being on the wide desert fringe of the Negev, Nahal Besor was a political border throughout history, either between the nomad-ruled desert and the cultivated land held by the dominant administration or between Egypt and the rulers of the land of Israel and Gaza.

Throughout pre-history human involvement in the region was sporadic. In the Old Stone Age man first penetrated the region during comfortable weather periods. Many hunting campsites from the Epi-Paleolith have been revealed. At the end of this period, the Harifian and Natufian Cultures began domestication. During the Neolithic period, constant dust storms kept people out of the region.

The Chalcolithic period brought to the area numbers of people yet to be equalled. The reason for the influx is unknown. The first settlements developed various functions, such as agriculture, art, commerce and copper work. Settlements centered around water sources and stream banks.

During the Early Bronze people neglected the area. Scarce remains teach of nomadic involvement only, yet three small villages (one of them by Ein Besor) give evidence of some settlement. The structures found reveal that there was no political tension in the region (no fortifications etc.). At the end of the Mid-Bronze, the area began to populate. Tel Sharuhen, as the most southern Egyptian post in Israel, was fortified. Only during the Late Bronze did the Besor Region fall under external administration. With time, the villages were fortified in an Egyptian fashion. At the end of the period as security conditions improved, small villages developed along the Besor banks. Nahal Besor was Egypt's northeastern border for 500 years.

During the beginning of the Israelite period, the Philistines had strong control, as mentioned in the book of Judges. Later in the period, the region was in constant conflict between the Philistines and the Israelites. Some researchers claim Nahal Besor to be the biblical Nahal Mitzra'im, though most think that Nahal Mitzra'im refers to Wadi El-Arish in Northern Sinai and a few even believe it is the Nile! Remnants of small-scale stream bank settlement from the 11th and 12th centuries are seen as an intrusion of the tribe of Simeon. Later in the 11th century, the region fell to the Philistines. During the time of King David, in the 10th century, the area was fortified by the tribe of Judah who later lost the region to invading Arab tribes. King Hezekiah dealt with these tribes during his fortification of the region, in preparation for the Assyrian invasion. The Assyrians invaded in the 7th century and held the region for a short time. The tribe of Judah filled the land that was soon neglected by the Assyrians. This also lasted for a short time as the area again became a main route for the Egyptians.

During the 6th-4th centuries B.C.E., the Persians controlled the whole Fertile Crescent. The Besor, being along the main route to Egypt, became a commercial center. The spice trade flourished until taken over by the Nabateans in the 4th century. Farms were also established in the region by Jews, Arabs and Edumites.

The Greeks invaded in the 4th century but did not change much. Hasmonean King John Hyrcanus in 125 B.C.E. widened the estate of Judah to the southern Besor Region in order to control the Nabatean spice route.

The Romans divided the Besor into two: its eastern section was annexed to Gaza while the more western area was administered from Maresha in the Judean Foothills. Herod marked his southern border along the Besor. Consistent with its policy elsewhere, the Roman government developed the area after the Great Revolt. Large barley and sheep farms were established. Here ran the *Limes*

Palestina, the border of Roman Palestine, holding a series of fortifications and roads. These government moves attracted people to the area, who continued to develop the region with sophisticated Roman technology for water collection.

Prosperity continued during the Byzantine period, although Christianity seeped in more slowly here than in the center of the country. Only one synagogue has been excavated in the region, in the ruins of Ma'on. The Byzantine government offered economic incentives to the region's Christian residents: exemption from taxes, allocation of churches in every settlement, economic assistance to converts and more. The first wells were dug, tens of meters deep, reaching the level of cobbles of the ancient Nahal Besor.

A Moslem-Byzantine battle took place in 634 along Nahal Besor. The villagers fled. The remaining settlers held on for 2-3 generations. At the end of the 7th century, the region was deserted and Bedouins invaded. The Crusaders kept the region clear as a buffer zone between themselves and the Egyptians. In the 13th century, the Mamelukes opened the Besor to Bedouins who spread throughout the area. The Bedouins grew primitive watermelons and barley. The barley, known as 'barley of the land of Gerar,' was exported to Europe and was well received by the brewing industry.

Following the opening of the Suez Canal in 1869, the Turkish Army established itself along the Besor and encouraged Bedouins to settle by erecting structures and cleaning out wells and water cisterns. The improved security situation was another incentive which brought on both Bedouin settlement and landholding by Gazan peasants.

The British did not involve themselves in internal Bedouin feuds. Nor did they assist Bedouin settlement, outside of drought relief. During WWII, Bedouins assisted (for pay) the British in logistics. The close interaction brought British support of settlement and modernized agriculture.

Three pre-independence Jewish settlements were established in the Besor Region: Gevulot (1943), Urim (1946) and Nirim (1946). These early Jewish settlements lived hand-in-hand with the neighboring Arabs, both Bedouins and peasants. The settlers purchased water from Arab-owned wells. After the U.N. partition gave the northwestern Negev to Israel, Egyptian influence provoked local Arab attacks upon Jewish settlements. In 1948, upon Egyptian invasion, some of the Arab villagers left toward Gaza in order to clear the way for the invading forces. Others were evacuated by the I.D.F. The Egyptian Army did not achieve long-term success in the region and the northwestern Negev Arabs remained in Egyptian-controlled Gaza.

Site description

Nahal Besor: This part of the stream is called in Arabic Wadi Shalala, meaning puddles. The stream is the largest in western Israel, draining 3,400 sq. km. The stream bed drains the national watershed from the southern Judean (Hebron) Hills in the north to Sdeh Boker in the south. The section of the described hike is fed by two main tributaries: Nahal Besor from Sdeh Boker and Nahal Beersheba running by the city. Nahal Revivim from the Yeroham area (Hike 37) is also a tributary. Further downstream, the biblical Nahal Gerar flows into Nahal Besor.

Magnitudal flash floods (usually 4-5 per year) tear down Nahal Besor. The floods, carrying millions of cubits of water, last from a few hours to a few days. The strong power of the water, at 3-7 kmph. has quickly ruined many storage attempts throughout the centuries.

Eshkol National Park: Covering over 3,000 dunams, the Eshkol National Park was founded by Kibbutz Urim in 1967. The kibbutz gave pasture lands for the project, which continues to develop. Hundreds of palms, olives, tipuana trees, California peppers and salt adaptable plants such as acacias were planted, along with vast lawns—all irrigated by the waters of Ein Besor. Today the park is a popular recreation area.

Tel Shalala: During the 6th century, the Shalala Church stood atop a loess hill. The worshippers drank water from the nearby cistern. The church boasted a decorative mosaic floor similar to one found at the Ma'on Synagogue 9 km. to the west, dating back to the same period. The church seems not to be connected to a specific village, but was a regional place of prayer; then, like today, Ein Besor was a common gathering place on special occasions. The spring and church were a rest stop on an ancient road running east-west to the north of the hill and in use today as Road 241.

The Pools of Ein Besor

The hilltop was a Turkish military post during WWI. During battle against an Australian-New Zealander unit (A.N.Z.A.C.), a shell hit the site and exposed part of the mosaic. The A.N.Z.A.C. chaplain, an amateur archaeologist, excavated the floor and eventually transferred it to Canberra, Australia for a war memorial. The excavation exposed the hill to intense erosion and today's hilltop is smaller in space than 100 years ago. The vegetation recently planted on the slopes should stabilize the degradation process. The cistern, renovated in 1970, is sometimes used as a water reservoir for the park.

Ein Besor Springs: These layer springs are the largest in the northwestern Negev, making it an important site. The springs produce 60 cubits per hour of water at 20°C and 1,296 mg. chlorine per liter year round. Swimming is prohibited by the Ministry of Health.

The site was used throughout nearly all of history, according to pottery fragments and a number of nearby archaeological sites. In 634, for example, a battle took place nearby between Byzantine forces and Moslems. During WWI, the springs offered water for British military encampments on their way to capture Gaza.

Tel Sharuhen: The hilltop was inhabited during Canaanite and Roman times and is identified with Sherikhan of the tribe of Simeon (Joshua 19:6). Fourteen layers of settlement have been uncovered. The settlement was 70 dunams large. The tel offers one of the best vistas of the region. At its base, by Nahal Besor, are remnants of a Roman retaining wall built of large blocks to combat erosion.

Be'er Sharuhen: Known in Arabic as *Bir e-Shalala* after the stream's name. The well is hidden amidst the dense reed thickets but the lofty palm trees mark the the site. Since the whole stream bed is moist, it is interesting how the banks do not carry palms. The palms of the well are most likely the result of date pits from the lunch of a Bedouin who came to water his flock.

Beside the well are remnants of a simple structure, possibly a guard house and remains of a British-era pumping piece. A large Paleolithic site was revealed in the badlands nearby, where pre-historic hunters left flint tools and bones.

To begin hike:

From the parking lot (2) head up to Tel Shalala rising to the east. The artificial mound has two access routes. From the tel, look toward the south, where the described route takes place. Note Tel Sharuhen (5), the green wadi bed of Nahal Besor, the flat fields and the badlands between the fields and the stream.

Return to the parking lot and take a left on the gravel road. Take the first right and reach Ein Besor.

Head left along the pond and take a right on the gravel road that leads south, parallel to Nahal Besor. You should be above and east of Nahal Besor.

The loop trip begins where a dirt road descends to the wadi bed. It is possible to go in either direction. The described text first runs along Nahal Besor to Tel Sharuhen and then leads you back via the edge of the badlands east and above the wadi. Thus, those who wish to hike back-and-forth can follow the description to Tel Sharuhen (5) and then retrace their steps. Returning via the eastern bank is longer since it involves looping around many ravines.

Take a right and descend to the wide wadi. This part of Nahal Besor has large puddles. Due to the easy accessibility, the water is visited by a variety of fowl and also shepherds with their flocks. Note the rounded cobbles, evidence of many kilometers of travel. Cross over to the western bank and go left. For the first 250 m., walk parallel to the 'Besor Way,' a gravel road that runs along the western bank of Nahal Besor. The 'Besor Way' veers west by what's left of the ramp of the British-built Rafiah-Beersheba Railway (3). Note the bridge's foundations in the stream bed.

Continue south along the wadi, here closed in with vegetation, mainly reeds. Four hundred meters south of the ramp, reach a mini-canyon. Here the stream cuts into

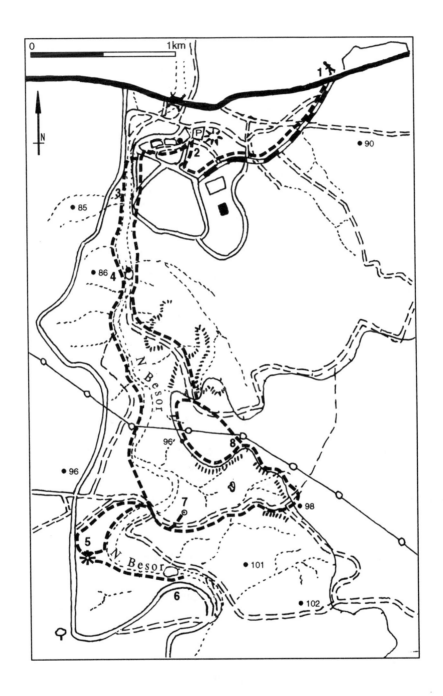

Hike 36, Nahal Besor

hard kurkar and a spring emerges somewhere in the thickets. Hard rock is exposed along the trail (there is a green sign), which was once a quarry. Here a trail drops to a beautiful large pool (4).

Continue south. At a narrow point between a steep slope and the stream bed many small yellow-flowering bushes called rest harrow grow.

As the trail curves left and where it veers right, note flash flood debris flattened on the tamarisk branches. This assortment of organic material indicates the level of flash flood waters. One hundred meters further, a dirt road crosses Nahal Besor. Go right on the sandy road ascending to the plateau. Take a left and ascend Tel Sharuhen (5). On the way up, note the dry moat to your right.

From the tel, face downstream and look for a large pool, the Besor Water-Hollow (6). A clear trail runs from your present spot to the site atop a badland ridge. The most convenient way back to Tel Sharuhen is the same trail.

Descend from Tel Sharuhen toward the northwest to Nahal Besor via the black-marked trail. The descent is stepped. Along the gully on the left you can observe a classic example of slope difference; the southern slope, facing the north, is covered with wildflowers in springtime while the northern slope which is more exposed to sunlight is nearly barren.

Along the bottom, note the cross-bedding of the layers in a small kurkar sandstone cliff on your left. Upon rejoining the dirt road, go right and wade across Nahal Besor. After 100 m. a green sign directs you toward Be'er Sharuhen (7), to the left among palm trees. Head there.

The trail returns you to the dirt road. From here either return the way you came or begin the return route for the loop trip.

Ascend to the left, between the badlands to the surrounding plateau. The closest settlement is Kibbutz Urim, 4 km. to the northeast. Atop the flat plateau, go left and head along the serrated edge of the badlands. An unmarked wide trail runs along this line between the badlands and the fields to the east. The trail offers nice views of the region and of the badlands that in the spring burst with wildflowers. Here, cranes pass the time during the spring and fall. The white posts mark the border of the nature reserve.

After about 800 m. reach an intersection (8). Two choices are present:

(A) To the left, the trail runs along the badland edge past a small clump of large, leafless tamarisk trees, the only shady spot in the area.

(B) Heading straight (northwest) on the trail past the high power wires traverses a 'peninsula' of flat field into the badlands and saves 0.5 km. of steps.

The two options merge by a post where you continue north on another 'peninsula' of badlands. The wide trail then descends a bit onto a watershed of two lengthy ravines, ascends to a small butte and descends straight to Nahal Besor by the large pool (4) hidden by thickets. Follow the dirt road along the eastern bank into Eshkol Park to Ein Besor and on to the starting point.

Yeroham Reservoir

*See map on
page 307*

Points of interest: *An artificial desert lake nestled between an evergreen forest with picnic facilities and a steeply sloping ridge. The scenic ridge carpeted with wildflowers in the spring offers interesting geology topped with ancient relics. In the fall, the bloom of the rare yolk-colored sternbergia crocus colors one of the nearby steep wadis.*

Length of hike: 5 kilometers, and an additional 4 easy kilometers for hikers arriving by public transportation, loop trip.

Hiking time: 3-5 hours.

Preferred season: October-May.

Suitable for: All.

Maps: Northern Negev (west) hiking and touring map.

Special preparation: Fishing pole.

Starting & ending point: Entrance road to Yeroham Reservoir.

To reach starting point:

Arrival by private transportation: Drive to the Yeroham Junction. Head south for 400 m. on Road 204. Opposite the western entrance of Yeroham, turn on to a blue-marked paved road (1), that leads to Yeroham Reservoir (there is an orange sign marking Metzad Yeroham). The road heads through eucalyptus trees and then forks. Take the right (paved) option, cross a gully and head between a pine forest and a slope. The road becomes a dirt one as it passes between the slope and tamarisk trees lining the lake's shore. Two kilometers from Road 204, the road ends by a dam (2) where the hike begins. Here stand a mysterious structure and on the right a dark outcrop of chert belonging to the Mishash Formation.

Arrival by public transportation: Take the direct bus from Beersheba to Yeroham. Get off by the western entrance road of the town. Opposite the turnoff is a blue-marked paved road leading to the Yeroham Reservoir (1). Follow it as mentioned in 'Arrival by private transportation.'

303

Geography

Nahal Revivim is one of the largest wadis in the northern Negev. It begins in the Yeroham area and drains into Nahal Besor 20 km. southwest of Beersheba. Intense flash floods surge along the stream every year.

Beyond the reservoir dam, Nahal Revivim begins to cut deep into the anticline of the Yeroham Ridge. Wadis do not often cut through anticlines. This phenomenon is found also in Nahal Yorke'am by Makhtesh Hatira and in Upper Nahal Besor. Usually, a wadi runs around an anticline ridge rather than through it.

Thousands of years ago, the stream of Nahal Revivim flowed unobstructed into the sea, for the Yeroham Ridge had yet attained an impressive height. As the anticline gradually rose, the stream maintained its course by cutting at a successive rate into the rising strata. The initial cut is narrow, which made it easy to construct a dam at that spot.

Plants and animals

Sternbergia clusiana:: Israel's most outstanding crocus. In Israel it is found at a number of specific sites. In the Negev a few clusters stand sharply out in the brown landscape, mainly on northern slopes. In Mediterranean regions, the bright aromatic flower also stands out among the fall thorns. In both places it is a pilgrimage site for flower lovers.

Having a Mediterranean and Irano-Turanian origin, the desert existence of the flower suggests that it is a remnant of a more humid climate. The surviving species found shelter in limestone cracks that receive runoff off large rock surfaces. Thus, the water the plant receives is similar to the amount it would get in a more humid Mediterranean climate.

The blooming season lasts from late October to December. The flower reaches 10 cm. in length, and blooms for up to 10 days. During this period, the flowers color changes from a greenish-yellow to a bright yellow. During its first days, the flower closes at night.

The fruit develops underground. It emerges only at the end of the winter and opens in spring. The black seeds contain a body of fat that attracts ants, which, collecting the seeds, help disperse the plant. The *sternbergia* also has vegetative reproduction: the bulb divides at a certain stage. This method explains why the flowers are found in clusters, each plant's flower a genetic twin of its neighbors.

History

Since Yeroham Ridge holds no perennial sources of water and is not along an ancient international trade route or boundary, human settlement developed here only during certain periods. Even today, Yeroham is known to be the most desolate town in Israel (even though it is only a 25-minute drive from Beersheba). The numerous military firing zones in the region hint that the land suits no better use.

Very few prehistoric settlements have been found in the region, since in those days the Negev was mainly inhabited by roaming hunters seeking game. They did most of the hunting near perennial water sources like those along the Tzinim Cliffs (see Hikes 38 and 39).

The Early and Mid-Bronze periods are the only periods that have left numerous remains along the Yeroham Ridge. During the Mid-Bronze, it was the core of Negev settlement, the focal point for semi-nomadic hunters. Three types of societies have been discovered: towns, settlements of 20-30 dwellings and many small sites of only a few buildings and enclosures.

In later periods the region was between the two main Negev thoroughfares: the Avdat-Gaza Road and the Petra-Mamshit-Beersheba Road. The course of today's

Yeroham Reservoir adorned by tamarisks

(Sdeh Boker-Yeroham) Road 204 that runs along the comfortable terrain of a synclinal valley was used to connect Mamshit with Avdat. Metzad Yeroham prospered in those days beginning as a stop along the way.

Site description

Yeroham Reservoir: Constructed in 1953-54. In 1954, it held a million cubits of water. The water was intended to irrigate the fields of Kibbutz Mash'abei Sadeh, 12 km. to the west. Since 1954, large amounts of sediments have accumulated in the reservoir, decreasing its capacity. The sewage of Yeroham also flows into the reservoir. Today the lake is used for recreation and carp fishing. During flash floods in plentiful years the overflowing dam is a magnificent sight.

Har Ruhama Site: This village is one of six central ones found in the Negev from the Mid-Bronze I. Only here, though, do the remnants show two building stages:

The first stage is homes, consisting of rooms and yards in a square or rectangular shape. Some were part of the village wall. Round post pieces were found, which most likely supported a roof of branches or leathers (that were not found). The round holes in the bedrock were used for home utilities such as grinding. Two small idols of a horned animal were found along with pottery. These finds hint that the inhabitants were involved in grazing. The settlement was abandoned for an unknown reason—no evidence of destruction, war or fire were found.

The later settlement was smaller, as the eastern portions were turned into a pen and used for tumuli construction (though not for burial purposes). Round structures were built on the ruins of their predecessors. At the top of the site in the west is a rock face with small holes—possibly an altar. The exciting find from this settlement was 18 copper bars, 15-20 cm. long. The copper source is unknown. The bars are exhibited at the Israel Museum in Jerusalem.

The village's regular water source was most likely Be'er Yeroham, located by Yeroham Junction.

Tumuli-Hill: Tumuli are usually believed to be burial mounds. They have a distinct construction pattern: an external circle of large stones encloses an internal burial box of large stones. A filling of gravel separates the two parts. Tumuli sometimes are bi-level: the lower floor of natural rock holds pottery and the second floor carries the body, covered with stone slabs. Pottery artifacts have been dated to the Early Bronze and Mid-Bronze I. Bone remnants have also been found inside, although most have been found empty. Tumuli Hill is the edge of a huge burial ground (150 mounds) continuing to the southwest upon the ridges.

Metzad Yeroham: Though known as a *metzad*, a fort, it is actually 100 dunams of ruins. Opposed to widespread Bronze period settlement on the nearby Yeroham Ridge, Metzad Yeroham developed during the Roman-Byzantine period. The site was possibly a caravan stop between Avdat and Mamshit, turning into a village in the 5th-6th centuries. The village was in two sections, dissected by Nahal Shu'alim. Archaeological surveys came up with interesting finds such as Nabatean pottery, whole lamps, cooking and perfume vessels, jewelry and a Greek ostracone. A dinar coin from 187/188 C.E. was found. Recently, the site underwent excavations.

To begin hike:

Follow the blue-marked trail beneath the dam, across Nahal Revivim and ascend the right (northern) side of the ridge. Along the ridge's lower sections in February through April bloom tulips, yellow and purple sun-roses, and many other flowers. Where a ridge merges from the left, enjoy a colossal view of Nahal Revivim cutting through Yeroham Ridge. Note the changes in plant density along the wadi's slopes. This is due to large quantities of water running down the tilted cliffs accumulating at its merge with the slope.

In the same direction, right across the way, notice the hill topped by soft limestone of the Shivta Formation. The formation is easily identified in the desert due to the non-uniform appearance of erosion holes and niches. Geologists refer to it as 'porridge.'

After hiking 700 m. and ascending 100 m., reach ruins (3) known as Har Ruhama Site, that cover the crest of the east-facing ridge.

From the ruins you can see your next stop, Tumuli-Hill (4), the next rise along the ridge. Head due south along the ridge crest for 350 m., past the topographic saddle to Tumuli-Hill (4).

The blue trail runs to the right of the hill-top, and continues 2 km. into an active firing zone, to one of the highest points of the Yeroham Ridge. From this spectacular viewpoint the blue trail descends to Nahal Revivim. Tumuli-Hill is the outer edge of the firing zone; thus, only on Friday afternoons, Saturdays and holidays is it safe to lengthen the described route.

From Tumuli-Hill, the described hike does not follow a clear trail.

The next site (5) is the hill-top upon the ridge that runs down to the reservoir, parallel to the last ridge. A platform stands here, encompassed by a wall. The site was most likely a pagan altar. The site also offers a grand view of the reservoir, the town of Yeroham and Hatira Ridge behind it. It is 400 m. to the platform and only an option, for the hike continues south of Tumuli-Hill. The ridge-route to the

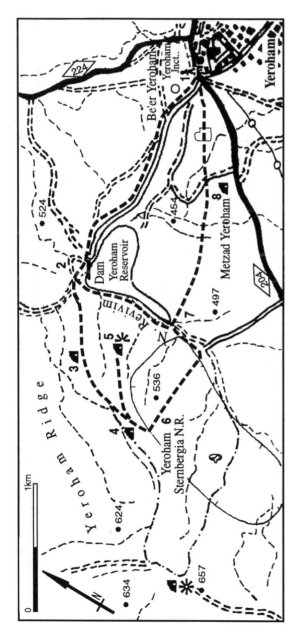

Hike 37, Yeroham Reservoir

platform is the quickest way to go and it offers more (unimpressive) ruins. From the platform head back to Tumuli-Hill (4).

From Tumuli-Hill head south for 250 m. along the ridge crest, to a semi-circular slope to the east (left) which becomes a small wadi. In the winter, this is a blooming site for the asphodel that displays light pink flowers atop tall stalks. Descend along the steep slopes that merge into a gully. Where two gullies meet, the incline levels out and thick bushy vegetation covers the wadi (6). Note the intense lichen covering the rocks of the north-faced slopes, which harbor vegetation different than the arid south-faced slopes.

Continue down the wadi that boasts the *sternbergia* in fall and many other Mediterranean plants, such as the round thorny burnet bush, sage and asphodel. Note the strong dips in the strata that the wadi dissects. One of the rock layers is hard and the wadi runs past it as a mini-canyon holding two waterholes that fill after floods. A cave appears where the wadi cuts into the Shivta Formation, up and to the left. Here is a large concentration of *sternbergias*.

A hundred meters downstream the brown limestone landscape that has been the prevailing stratum beneath your feet, begins to change. Distinct dark chert layers of the Mishash Formation create short cliffs. Between the cliffs and the wadi is a slope that is quite different than the rest of the slopes. It is uniform and is covered with vegetation. The prevailing plant is the mallow. Its small round fruit is edible and in rough times have sustained populations, such as the Jews of Jerusalem who were under siege in 1948. The slope is of soft Senonian chalk—the Menuha Formation. Jerusalem's Mount Scopus is out of the same white rock. By the wadi is a rest stop for camels marked by dung and saltbushes. The soft chalk is a comfortable bedding compared with the nearby rough limestone and dolomite.

Go left upon reaching Nahal Revivim. The trail runs along the western bank of the wadi. After 100 m., a small tributary runs into Nahal Revivim from the east (7). In winter and spring the reservoir's waters reach this point. From here, the route is different for those who have private transportation and those who do not.

Free-walkers should ascend the tributary (no defined trail), following the left (northern) option to the top of the low ridge. Descend the northeastern slope and head freely around the southern side of the reservoir. The landscape is disturbed at this part. To the south of the pine forest stands Metzad Yeroham and its adjoining remnants. Continue through the pine forest back to the western entrance of Yeroham (1).

Returning to the vehicle is quite simple. Follow the lakes banks back to the dam (2) where you began to hike. Along the way note the white outcrops, creating a cliff across Nahal Revivim. This is Eocenian chalk that was deposited in a sea that engulfed the region after the Yeroham Ridge was created. The Eoceninan sea was not deep here and only filled the low spots — the synclines, between the ridges.

Here, Nahal Revivim finds a soft spot, cutting between the chalk and the flanks of the ridge.

38 Ein Avdat Canyon

*See map on
page 316*

Points of Interest: *A scenic route to an oasis deep in a canyon including waterfalls, thriving wildlife and vegetation.*

Length of hike: Option 1: Back-and-forth walk, 3 kilometers.

Option 2: 5 kilometers, loop trip. *Recently, the park has been limited to one-way uphill hiking for an experimental period of time. For up-to-date details contact 07-550954.*

Hiking time: 3-4 hours.

Preferred season: All year.

Suitable for: All. There is a steep descent and ascent along the way.

Maps: Northern Negev (west) hiking and touring map.

Special preparation: Swimsuit. Entrance fee.

Starting & ending point: For the loop trip, you can begin at either of the two entrances to the Ein Avdat National Park. The one-way version begins at the upper entrance and finishes at the Sdeh Boker College.

To reach starting point:

Arrival by private transportation: Turn off (Beersheba-Mitzpe Ramon) Road 40 between kilometer post 123-124 to the Ein Avdat National Park. The turnoff onto a gravel road is marked by a sign. Follow the gravel road for 1 km. to the parking lot.

Arrival by public transportation: Take the Beersheba-Mitzpe Ramon bus. Get off and follow as mentioned above in 'Arrival by private transportation.'

Geography

Ein Avdat Canyon, holding the springs of Ein Avdat and Ein Ma'arif, is part of Nahal Tzin. Nahal Tzin, 120 km. long, is the largest wadi that begins in the Negev, draining altogether some 1,550 sq. km. The wadi bed of Nahal Tzin suddenly becomes active amidst and following torrential rainfall and drains into (what used to be) the southern end of the Dead Sea. Due to its size, sometimes only part of the wadi is active.

Nahal Tzin begins along the northwestern rim of Makhtesh Ramon, 20 km. south of Avdat. There and along its upper western tributaries, it originates along the national watershed and heads north. The Ein Avdat Canyon section cuts into the northern edge of the Avdat Plateau. The canyon marks an abrupt change in Nahal Tzin's route. Below the canyon the wadi breaks east beneath the hanging Tzinim Cliffs. Among these cliffs many spectacular canyons, rich in water sources, drop into Nahal Tzin. The Tzinim Cliffs are a nature reserve.

Two sharp changes in Nahal Tzin take place by the Ein Avdat Canyon:

1) Nahal Tzin suddenly drops 150 m. in a series of waterfalls, creating an impressive canyon. The sharp drop helps Nahal Tzin meet the elevation (400 m. below sea level) of the Syrian-African Rift where it merges into the southern tip of the Dead Sea.

2) Nahal Tzin changes its direction from north to east. At one time it merged into Nahal Besor (see Hike 36). The theory of this abrupt change in the stream course is based on finds of stream pebbles upon the slopes and ridges of Nahal Tzin by the Ein Avdat Canyon and also north and above of todays wadi bed, by Sdeh Boker. In some places the pebbles were cemented together, forming conglomerate. Prehistoric artifacts were found among the pebbles of Sdeh Boker, helping to date the change in direction of Nahal Tzin to a few hundred thousand years ago.

Ein Avdat Canyon cuts into Eocenian sedimentary rocks: hard chalk, limestone which has thin layers of imbedded chert, and grey layers of bituminous rock, rich in organic remains.

The springs in the canyon emerge on layers of tilted marl which lay beneath the chalk and limestone. The source of the water still baffles geologists. The region is arid, and during rainfall the runoff does not infiltrate, but drains away along the wadis. The current theory is that the springs come from flash flood water that has seeped down through the stream bed gravel (and the strata further down).

Plants and animals

Euphrates poplar (*Populus euphratica*): Common to stream and spring banks that have a high salt content, this tree appears along with the date palm at many desert oases. The tree's sweet scent is a good sign of a nearby source of water.

In the Bible the poplar is mentioned a number of times (in the English translation it is called a willow). The Talmud discusses the poplar's role on *Sukkot*, the festival of the Feast of Tabernacles. The tree's Arabic name is *hawr* meaning white. In Hebrew it is called *tzaftzefa*.

The Euphrates poplar has two kinds of leaves. Younger shoots and branches bear oblong leaves, similar to those of the willow. Older shoots have oval or rhombic leaves.

Some say that the presence of the Euphrates poplar at Ein Avdat and also at Ein Zik and Ein Shaviv are a relic, representing a previous wetter climate. When botanists studied the poplars at Ein Avdat, they found a difference between the trees growing along the stream and the trees growing on the slope. The main water source for the slope-growing trees is the rain, not the stream. Consequently, the stream-growing trees grow more rapidly and their water-leading vessels are more porous. The two groups also have different leaf shedding seasons.

Mourning wheatear (*Oenanthe lugens*): The most common wheatear in the rocky deserts of Israel. Nearly every desert hike passes by this beautiful bird perched on a boulder, its sharp black and white colors standing out in the brown landscape. The songbird is Saharo-Arabian.

It is about 15 cm. long. The forehead, crown, breast and belly are white. The wings, cheek and throat are black. A pale patch appears in the center of the wing during flight.

The female builds a nest in a rock crevice, under a boulder or in a hole in the ground, usually on a slope but sometimes in cracks of walls in ruins. She lays 4-5 eggs between February and April. The young hatch after 14 days and 14 days later they are able to fly, though their parents continue to feed them for another 35 days.

Other common birds here are the raven, especially the brown-necked raven which soars through the desert skies for many hours of the day.

The sand partridge is much more difficult to find, for its brown hues blend in with the hues of the color of the desert landscape.

History

The Ein Avdat surroundings have been visited and inhabited by different people for thousands of years. It seems that the region was penetrated by man in a sporadic pattern. Though during historical periods the motivation for immigration into the Negev may have been political, in prehistoric times it was most likely determined by the prevailing climate. Throughout the Avdat Plateau and Sdeh Tzin by Sdeh Boker, numerous prehistoric flint artifacts have been found. By Rosh Ein Mor, thousands of Musterian flint tools in a 0.5 m. layer were found. The tools belonged to the *Homo Erectus* man. The amount of artifacts suggests either a large population or mobile groups who returned to specific sites.

By the head of Ma'ale Divshon is a large concentration of flint tool remnants and samples of man-made knives and other hand held stones. The tools date to the Paleolithic and Mesolithic periods (60,000-10,000 years ago).

Between Ein Avdat and Ein Mor, on a small hill in the canyon, there are remains of a small settlement consisting of several round structures from the Mid-Bronze I (2200-2000 B.C.E.).

The next phase of building did not appear until a thousand years later, during the Israelite period. We find remnants of their forts and smallscale farms. By Ein Avdat there have not been any finds from this time.

During the Hellinistic period, Avdat became a station along the Nabatean spice route. Other regions in the Negev were not inhabited and there was no agriculture at the time. Between 37 B.C.E. and 70 C.E., the Nabatean Empire peaked as the forts of the spice route became thriving cities with many public buildings along with farming in the outskirts. Avdat was destroyed by Arab tribes who invaded the Negev between 50-70 C.E. Tribal insignias can still be seen in the rock engravings around the city.

The Byzantine period developed Avdat into a Christian city and a large church was built. The Ein Avdat Canyon was inhabited by monks. After the Moslem conquest in 636 the region slowly fell into shambles. The Ein Avdat Canyon since then has been neglected by man, used only for refreshment purposes.

With the establishment of Kibbutz Sdeh Boker and the road to Eilat in the 1950s, the Ein Avdat Canyon became easily accessible. The trail going through it was constructed in 1956. Recently, it was turned into a national park; the access roads were paved justifying an entrance fee. The trail going through the canyon is part of the Israel National Trail.

Site description

Ein Mor: This spring is neither easily distinguishable nor greatly distinguished. It amounts to nothing more than the trickle behind the parking lot. Mor is the Hebracization of the Arabic *mora,* meaning bitter, similar to the Hebrew *mar. Mor,* in Hebrew, is an aromatic spice plant—what a difference! At one time the canyon was known as the Mor Canyon; Ein Avdat Canyon is a new name.

The spring emerges at the contact between the Takiya marl and the Mor chalk above it. Because there are also impermeable layers further up the geological sequence (at the Mor-Avdat Formation contact), most of the spring's waters emerge there and only leftover water seeps down to the Ein Mor level. Tamarisks and bullrushes are the main plants that adorn the spring's surroundings.

Ein Avdat: This spring is the highlight of the hike. It emerges at the base of the waterfall. By the waterfall there is an accumulation of brownish travertine rock upon which the maidenhair fern grow. The water of the spring is a bit salty (1,600 mg. chlorine per liter) as the plants surrounding the pool are hydrohalophytes (saline water loving). The pool is 8 m. deep, fine for a refreshing swim, but please watch your step as the rock surfaces around the edge are slippery with algae! The water is very cold so if your body temperature is hot, it is best to enter the pool slowly in order to prevent body shock!

Hermits Caves: Dug into hard, white, chalky limestone 60 m. above the stream bed and 40 m. below the plateau. Find them on the western cliff, north of the ascending trail.

Ein Avdat

It seems that the main use of these hermitages was in the 6th century by monks from Avdat. Archaeologists have investigated four caves. In the caves are various sculpted shapes, carved for various reasons: closets, shelves, bars for hanging clothes, benches, stairs, water systems and more. In the second cave to the north a Greek inscription was found. It is a prayer to St. Theodoros, whose name adorns a monastery found in Avdat. The inscription was written by someone named Zachary, a common name at that time. A tomb bearing the name of Zachary was found at the Theodoros Monastery in Avdat.

Rosh Mor Site: The site contains thousands of flint artifacts of the Musterian Culture. The site is located at the top of the northwestern cliff of the Ein Avdat Canyon right above Ein Avdat.

It seems that members of the Musterian Culture (80,000-90,000 years ago), occasionally occupied this site. A few ostrich egg shells and onager bones help describe the fauna of the epoch. The abundance of flint in the outcrops nearby were utilized by the Musterians for many types of tools such as arrows, sheaths, points, etc. This archaeological site assists physical geographers in understanding the development of the Ein Avdat Canyon. The remoteness of the site, along the cliff, hints that in those days there was possibly no cliff, rather a shallow stream bed like the one present today along Nahal Tzin, 1 km. upstream. This theory would date the canyon as no more than 80,000 years old!

Rosh Tzin: The point marked by some piles of rocks is 537 m. above sea level. It is possible that, during different periods, a lookout or message station was posted here, for it overlooks vast parts of the Tzin Valley and a number of the anticline ridges of the northern Negev. In early morning and late afternoon the hues of the landscape make the view from Rosh Tzin spectacular.

To begin hike:

Follow the trail from the parking lot across the tributary of the canyon. Note the layer of flint exposed by the trail along the bank of the wadi. At the trail split, follow the arrow to the right, to the observation patio. Continue 50 m. along the cliff but not too close until reaching the top of the dry waterfall (5). Sixty meters beneath you emerges Ein Ma'arif, the initial source of the Ein Avdat Canyon.

From here you have two choices:

1) Back-and-forth: Follow the description of Hike 39, 'Avdat, Ein Avdat Canyon and Nahal Akev' all the way down the canyon to the lower entrance by Ein Mor. Anywhere along the way you can head back the way you came. If you are lucky, you can hitch a ride on a bus that dropped off hikers at the bottom and is driving to the upper entrance to pick them up. Heading back follow the hiking description of this hike, toward the end of the text.

2) Loop trip: Return to the trail split but do not follow the arrow to the descending trail, rather head up to the square Nabatean building on the slope. The building was two stories; note the staircase along one of the walls. The building guarded

the trail down to the canyon and commanded the nearby farming plots during Roman-Byzantine times. From the building you can see the city of Avdat, atop a hill, 3.5 km. to the south.

The next two kilometers run along the edge of the canyon cliff. There is no trail but the going is not rough at all. Proceed parallel to the edge of the cliff (careful!), enjoying spectacular views of the canyon. The plain is dotted with squills that bloom here in early fall. Along the whole route you have a good chance to meet ibex.

Two hundred and fifty meters from the Nabatean guardhouse, the canyon turns to the right (northeast) and there is a short descent. Note the flint fragments scattered on the ground.

At certain parts of the walk beside the cliff, you can notice round cobbles covering the ground. This is scientific evidence that, in earlier times, Nahal Tzin's level was where you are standing now, over 100 m. above the present day level! A hundred meters beyond the short descent, still by the cliff, there is a pile of earth and a wide shallow hole by it. This is known as the Rosh Mor Site (6).

Continuing by the cliff side, cross a wide wadi that is terraced upstream. The ruin on the wadi's southern bank was most likely the farmhouse or storage building.

A half-kilometer along the cliff, reach a descent to another tributary of the canyon. Head left and reach a dirt road. Take a right on the dirt road which runs on the northern side of the ridge, giving vistas of Nahal Havarim, and in the distance, the valley of upper Nahal Besor. The road ends by the pointed edge of the plateau, between Nahal Havarim and Nahal Tzin. This unique site is known as Rosh Tzin (7).

The descent from Rosh Tzin is on a clear unmarked trail. It runs along the sharp ridge descending northeast from Rosh Tzin. The route is also the divide between Nahal Havarim and Nahal Tzin. In other words, the trail can't be missed. Take it and watch your step! At first the path is steep as it heads down the hard rock, which is the strata composing the canyon walls. Further down, the descent reaches the soft greenish-grey shales and clays of the Ghareb-Takiya Formations. The protruding white rock that the trail passes is a layer of chalk signifying the upper part of the Takiya Formation. These two formations are one of the few recognizable geological layers found all the way from Eilat to the Galilee. The soft, unstable rock hosts the old city of Safed. In 1837 an earthquake shook the city and all of the structures built on the Ghareb-Takiya were ruined. These formations are exposed very clearly here and have allowed much research about ancient stream levels of Nahal Tzin, runoff and vegetation. Note the amount of plants growing on the green-grey hills around you, the badlands of Israel. It is fun to roll and climb in the soft shales.

Continue along the backbone of the ridge until a clear trail crosses your path at a topographic saddle in the shales. Take a right onto this trail which comes from Nahal Havarim, a popular hike. The trail first runs along the base of the cliff and then crosses Nahal Tzin, reaching the paved access road (6) to the lower entrance of the Ein Avdat National Park. Enter the park and look for Ein Mor, emerging on your right in the stream bed of Nahal Tzin by two tall Euphrates poplar trees. The tiny spring is an ideal rest stop.

From Ein Mor head into the narrowing canyon. Here the canyon is wide, since the flowing waters, millennia ago, carved away the soft shale of the Ghareb-Takiya Formations which underlies the harder chalk and limestone of the cliff walls.

Look for a lone Atlantic terebinth tree on your left at the bottom of the slope. This tree sheds its leaves in winter and buds in spring. This particular tree is estimated to be 350 years old.

After the terebinth tree the stream bed begins to carry water as you near the two pools of Ein Avdat. Reaching Ein Avdat remember that the 8 m. deep pool holds cold water which can cause body shock for those who immediately jump in! The spring here yields different amounts of water depending on the season.

Backstep 100 m. from the pool and head up stairs carved into the cliff. These stairs, first sculpted by Israeli teenagers in 1956, have been improved by the National Parks Authority.

Cross and recross the stream and reach the grove of beautiful Euphrates poplars. Very experienced hikers can ascend to the upper pools and source pool of Ein Ma'arif at the bottom of the dry waterfall (5). This is one of the most 'out of the world' landscapes in the Negev, accessible via slippery rock stairs. A carved rock water channel is evidence of human activity here. It is possible that the area of the poplar grove was once a vegetable garden cultivated by the monks who lived in the nearby caves. The water was channeled from the elevated pools of Ein Ma'arif to agricultural sections where poplar trees stand today.

From the poplar grove head up the clear trail. This modernized trail is along the route of an ancient one. Along the trail, before the ladders and stairs, an improved trail leads to the right along the base of a cliff. Take it for 125 m. to reach a two room man-made hermit cave. This cave is one of the caves that were inhabited by monks during Byzantine times. It is decorated by a cross, incised above a niche that was cut open as a window.

Return to the main trail and ascend to the brim of the canyon back to the starting point.

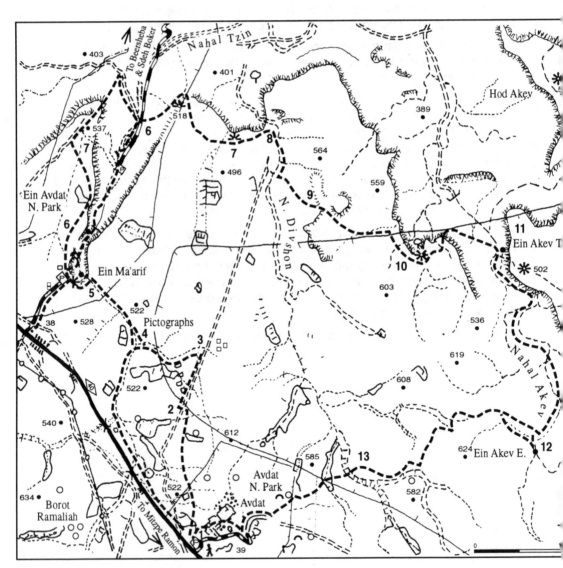

Hike 38, Ein Avdat Canyon and Hike 39, Avdat, Ein Avdat Canyon and Nahal Akev

39

Avdat, Ein Avdat Canyon and Nahal Akev

*See map on
page 316*

Points of interest: *A hike through a desert plateau between canyons, springs and streams, with spectacular views, ancient agriculture and rich wildlife.*

Length of hike: Option 1: 20 kilometers, loop trip. Option 2: 17 kilometers, one-way (more suitable for hikers arriving by public transportation). *Recently, the park has been limited to one-way uphill hiking for an experimental period of time. For up-to-date details contact 07-550954.*

Hiking time: 8-10 hours.

Preferred season: October to May.

Suitable for: Experienced hikers.

Maps: Northern Negev (west) hiking and touring map.

Special preparation: Swimsuit. Entrance fee.

Starting & ending point: The parking lot by the entrance to the Avdat National Park. For the one-way route, the starting point is at the turnoff to the upper entrance of the Ein Avdat National Park. At both places there are bathroom and drinking water facilities. Official visiting hours are 8:00-16:00.

To reach starting point:

Arrival by private transportation (one-way option): The Avdat National Park is located near kilometer post 120 on (Beersheba-Mitzpe Ramon) Road 40. Park beside the gas station (1).

Arrival by public transportation: Take the Beersheba-Mitzpe Ramon bus to Avdat National Park. Descend and head to the gas station (1).

The one-way hike begins at the turn-off from Road 40 to the Ein Avdat National Park (3 km. north of the Avdat National Park). Get off here and follow the road for 1 km., and pass the entrance booth. Reach the Ein Avdat Canyon and take a right along the rim to the dry waterfall (5). From here follow the hike description.

Geography

See Hike 38, 'Ein Avdat Canyon.'

Plants and animals

Leafless Tamarisk (*Tamarix aphylla*): One of the first plants mentioned in the Bible, the leafless tamarisk grows in the open in the loess soils of the Northern Negev. The trees are usually planted by Bedouins for their shade and soft branches, eaten by sheep. "Abraham planted a tamarisk tree in Beersheba, and called there on the name of the Lord, the everlasting God" (Genesis 21:33).

Classical Hebrew calls the tamarisk *eshel* (*atl* or *ethl* in Arabic). In post-biblical literature, eshel became a generic term for trees. Botanists assume that tamarisks developed in the vast salt plains of Central Asia during the Pliocene. The tamarisk has the most species of any tree genus in Israel—13 species. Israel has two predominant types, the leafless tamarisk and the Nile tamarisk (*Tamarisk nilotica*). The more common Nile tamarisk is a bush-like tree that grows in marshes, on sand and in nearly every deep wadi of the desert where high underground water is present.

The leafless tamarisk is a richly branched evergreen tree up to 10 m. high and up to 1 m. in diameter, with an oval crown. Its green or green-greyish twigs are leafless, but their green joints function as photosynthesizing and transpiratory organs. The small, spiked white flowers bloom in autumn. After pollination by insects such as Myriad flies and small bees (and also by wind), they quickly produce capsule-like fruits, which are full of minute seeds and topped with a tuft of hairs. The leafless tamarisk is common in the Beersheba region.

The tamarisk is known to be one of the plants best adapted to salinity. Being a tree of hot deserts, it excretes a salty solution through special glands in its leaves. As the moisture evaporates, crystals of concentrated salt accumulate on the leaves and eventually drop to the ground. This salt creates a saline micro-environment surrounding the tree, inhibiting plant growth. Accordingly, tamarisks are surrounded by a sterile zone, devoid of any seedlings or plants. They have root systems running both laterally and vertically in order to maximize moisture absorption. The strong roots also stabilize the tree during powerful flash flood events.

In the early 19th century, Europeans introduced tamarisks to the deserts of southwestern North America. It was planted as a shade tree. The tree quickly invaded both wild and human habitats and became a pest as it replaced poplars and willows. There, the tree is known as the salt cedar. The famous Israeli botanist, Michael Zohary, notes an interesting fact: In the Bible, the cedar of Lebanon is mentioned more often than the native tamarisk. He explains that the name 'cedar' was also applied to the tamarisk, especially in connection with the cleansing of lepers and their houses (Leviticus 14:4).

Long-legged buzzard (*Buteo rufinus*): The long-legged buzzard is one of the most common breeding raptors in all of Israel. The bird has been spotted many times in the Ein Akev vicinity. It was decimated by the pesticide poisoning of the early 1950's but has since recovered.

A predator of average size, it resembles an eagle, being heavy-set with broad wings and a short neck. While standing it is distinguished by the long, unfeathered legs. The most common color of the bird is rusty brown, with a cream-colored head. The long-legged buzzard also comes in a darker, chocolate-like color. In flight the raptor displays white patches in the center of the wings that are tilted upwards when gliding.

It has a southern Palaearctic range and most of its populations do not migrate. Its preferred habitat ranges from mountainous landscapes with sparse vegetation to steppe environments. It spends most of its time perched on vantage points but often glides in search of prey. Most individuals have a varied diet: small mammals, various reptiles, songbirds, insects and locusts.

Long-legged buzzards live in pairs, each in a territory of 6-8 sq. km. Courtship begins in February: the pair perform display flights and emit sharp and short mewing sounds. The twig nest is 80 cm. in diameter and usually on a cliff. Two to four eggs are laid in March, incubation is 28 days and by June the young begin to fly.

History

See Hike 38 , 'Ein Avdat Canyon.'

Site description

Nahal Akev: Nahal Akev is a large wadi beginning at the northern edge of Makhtesh Ramon, 800 m. above sea level. It twists and turns for 20 km. through the Avdat Plateau and collects many tributaries before draining into Nahal Tzin at 300 m. above sea level. The lower course of the wadi is cut deep into Eocenian strata and two springs emerge in the stream bed; Ein Akev Elyon and Ein Akev Tahton.

Ein Akev Tahton: This is one of a series of stratum springs which gush along the Tzinim Cliffs. This spring, like the others, appears in the Eocenian limestone and chalk which constitute the Avdat Plateau. Among the horizontal layers of chalk and limestone are strata of marl which is impervious to water. When water percolates through the cracked limestone or chalk it collects over the marl layers and flows along the tilt of the rock layer, here being toward the north. The canyons of the Tzinim Cliffs expose these rock layers and thus the water flows out.

Ein Akev Tahton flows from beneath a layer of conglomerate which protrudes at the top of the narrow canyon walls. The waterfall is covered by a thick layer of travertine which is coated with green moss and maidenhair ferns. Other common water-loving vegetation add to the oasis atmosphere of Ein Akev Tahton.

The spring's pool is 7 m. deep and is home for a rich variety of animal life. Green toads, leeches, water bugs and backswimmers. Hornets and dragonflies hover noisily over the water.

The pool is also a meeting place for fowl and mammals. Five pairs of charcoal-colored sooty falcons have been spotted by the spring. The falcons arrive in late summer for breeding and with their fledglings fly to East Africa at the end of autumn.

Avdat: This magnificent ancient city cannot be accurately described in the layout of the present book. The city stands upon a flat hilltop 619 m. above sea level in the northern section of the Avdat Plateau.

The Nabateans founded the town. They entered the Negev in the 7th century B.C.E, apparently from Saudi Arabia (like many invading Bedouin tribes). They were traders, first with bitumen from the Dead Sea and later with spices and perfumes that originated in the Far East. Their trade route, coming from their capital Petra, crossed the Negev via Avdat.

Fourth century B.C.E pottery shards are the most ancient artifacts found at Avdat. Then the site was a small Nabatean campsite. While conquering Gaza in 100 B.C.E , Hasmonean King Alexander Jannaeus destroyed the city of Avdat. Soon afterwards, King Avdat II renewed settlement in Avdat, and the city flourished. A new temple was constructed. New invaders, this time Arab tribes, destroyed the city again between 50 and 70 C.E. In the mid-80s, Rabal II renewed settlement in Avdat most likely along the western slope of the hill (a farm was established nearby). After Rabal's death in 106, Rome annexed the Nabatean kingdom and the city continued to develop. In the 3rd century a new temple was built and a new community was created on the southern side of the acropolis. The new community expanded to the eastern side of the city also.

In the 4th century, the city became Christian: the temple became a church with an adjacent immersion cell. In the next hundred years a new church and monastery were constructed. The expansion of the town created a housing crisis, and burial caves were turned into homes, pens and wine presses. At this time agricultural sections were established along the ridge of Avdat and in the nearby valleys. The town's glory faded after the Moslem conquest in 636.

To begin hike:

There are two options for the first two kilometers of the hike. The shorter and easier option (#1) runs along the main road for a kilometer. The more peaceful option (#2) runs parallel to the main road but 500-1000 m. east of it. The two routes meet at the boulders with the rock drawings (4).

Option 1: begin to walk by the main road on a dirt road that begins by the gas station (1). After 200 m. there is a sign marking a trailhead with the I.N.T. mark. Follow the marked trail for 1 km. along the main road until reaching Nahal Tzin. The trail crosses the shallow bed of Nahal Tzin and continues atop its western bank between two rows of stones. After 300 m. two wadis merge into Nahal Tzin (across the way) with an interval of 150 m. Between these two small wadis, Nahal Tzin drops a small fall and begins to create a canyon atmosphere. One hundred meters north of the merge of the northern wadi of the two, at the top of the eastern cliff, (across the way) lie a few dark boulders. Cross the wadi and climb up to the boulders (4) to see their rock drawings. These insignias may have been done by the Arab tribes who invaded Avdat between the years 50 and 70 C.E.

Option 2: from the gas station (1) head 100 m. north to a building, a Byzantine bathhouse. From here follow the dirt road to the north through terraced silty fields covered with desert hammada bushes. Along the way on the right there are a couple piles of shards and marble fragments from the public buildings of Avdat. What the remnants are doing here is unclear. They may have been dumped here during the digs.

The dirt road narrows to a trail as it goes over a crumbling rock fence. Follow the trail over the saddle to the right of the small hill, 548 m. above sea level. The trail continues north through rocky fields covered with bean caper bushes, soon passing a small wadi draining west into Nahal Tzin. Looking west you see the flat tops of Har Arkov. The openings in the

Ein Akev

white chalk at its base are active water cisterns, fed from flash floods in Nahal Tzin.

Three hundred meters later the trail passes another wadi, ascends a low ridge and drops to a terraced wadi (2). Today Bedouins grow wheat here. Take a left down the wadi and soon a dirt road crosses it. Take a right onto the dirt road and follow it up to a plain where Bedouins sometimes reside. Follow the dirt road which curves to the right around the encampment. One kilometer from the terraced wadi, a dirt road merges from the right and the road you are on curves left to the north. Here a white wadi cuts 1.5 m. into the plain (3). Go left into the wadi and follow it to the west and then for 400 m. to the northwest, where it merges with the impressive Nahal Tzin.

Head north 100 m. atop the eastern cliff of Nahal Tzin to a pile of dark-colored boulders, adorned with rock drawings (pictographs) (4). From the rock drawings head freely along Nahal Tzin 0.5 km. to the dry waterfall (5).

Forty meters below in the dark pool emerges Ein Ma'arif. Here begins the Ein Avdat Canyon. Follow the cliff to the left, cross a spur and soon reach the observation patio overlooking the spectacular canyon.

If you want to walk above the canyon, follow Hike 38, 'Ein Avdat Canyon.' Just beyond, before the Nabatean guardhouse, is the trail which you take down to the bottom. Half-way down at the end of the section with the ladders, where the sheer canyon wall turns into a steep slope, a trail leads to the left along the cliff base for 125 m. and reaches a two-room cell once inhabited by monks of Avdat (see Hike 38). Return to the main trail and descend to the grove of Euphrates poplar trees. There is an opinion that this grove is a relic, indicating that the Negev was damper in the historical past. Among the trees grow bushes of the meaty-leaved golden samphire.

On hot days it is worthwhile for very experienced hikers to climb up the slippery wet waterfalls to the pool of Ein Ma'arif. This is possibly the most exquisite place in the Negev. If you are not in such an adventurous mood the best you can do is to take a right to the edge of the grove and peek into the dark canyon of Ein Ma'arif.

From the bottom of the ascent follow the trail to the left, cross and recross the stream reaching the top of the Ein Avdat waterfall. The trail from here is hewed into the rock at the base of the cliff on your left. It descends beneath a tamarisk tree to the end of the long pool.

From Ein Avdat head down the stream which gradually runs dry. An Atlantic terebinth tree stands to your right. Continue down the wadi to Ein Mor. Beside the spring grow a few poplars. Notice that nearby tree branches hold debris left by high flash flood water. To the right (southwest) of the spring is the park entrance and parking lot where there are facilities. Head there and continue down the paved road along Nahal Tzin. Ahead of you atop the ridge is the Sdeh Boker College with David and Paula Ben Gurion's grave on the cliff's edge.

Five hundred meters from the parking lot, a trail merges into the road from the left and soon on your right there is a signpost with a green mark, indicating Ma'ale Divshon (6). Go right and ascend the cliffs (125 m. high) on the moderate, ancient trail to the Avdat Plateau. At the top, enjoy the view of Nahal Tzin, Nahal Havarim (in the west) and the Sdeh Boker College across the way. Here you might spot an Egyptian vulture soaring above the valley.

The trail circles a wadi and then crosses a flat ridge covered by flint fragments. These are remnants and samples of man-made knives and other stone tools, made by the people of the Paleolithic and Mesolithic periods. A half-kilometer on the plain brings you to a wadi right before it drops in a spectacular fall (7) to Nahal Divshon. In the shade of this fall grows a large Atlantic terebinth tree.

Continue 500 m. east along the cliff, leaving the marked trail to where Nahal Divshon drops in a 60 m. fall (8) similar to the previous one. Along the way, note the rounded rocks, evidence that during earlier times the wadi ran a different course than today. These two falls are known as horse-shoe falls as the wadi is shallow preceding the fall and the resulting canyon has an elliptic horse-shoe shape.

Head up the shallow wadi of Nahal Divshon for 500 m. where the green-marked trail crosses the wadi. Take a left onto the green trail which ascends a small tributary of Nahal Divshon. The tributary, holding terraces, used by Bedouins for wheat, curves south and widens. The trail runs aside the terraces to the end of the wadi at the watershed of Nahal Divshon and Nahal Akev (9). Follow the trail into a valley along the main wadi. After 1 km. the trail leaves the wadi and veers to the right. Beyond this spot to the left, the wadi curves north, cuts into the rock, creates a small canyon and then falls 100 m. to a wide valley where it merges with Nahal Akev. The canyon offers a shady rest stop.

The trail follows the cliff to the right to the next fall 250 m. from the first one. Beneath this fall are a few palm trees that live off high underground water (10).

After crossing the wadi the trail passes interesting rock formations on the right; this small cliff is out of chalk and limestone. The chalk has eroded more than the limestone, which protrudes out.

The trail heads over a small ridge where there is a nice view of the protruding cone-shaped hill of Hod Akev. Descend on the trail to the top of a wide gorge. Ein Akev Tahton emerges at its head. Fifty meters west of the gorge head, descend a blue-marked trail to the green oasis of Ein Akev Tahton (11).

Leave the small canyon to the top of the waterfall via the same path you descended.

Head upstream for 3 km. Along the way, follow the hard-to-find black trail mark. The trail cuts the curves of the stream bed. Nahal Akev becomes a dry wadi, but not for long as Ein Akev Elyon feeds a one kilometer long stream of water accompanied by lush vegetation of bullrush, reeds and tamarisk trees. Ein Akev Elyon (12) emerges by a small 1.5 m. fall and usually creates a pool suitable for a dip. Here the stream bed curves left and 200 m. beyond the pool, the water vegetation ceases to grow.

Take the blue trail, which heads up the western bank of Nahal Akev along and above a small canyon that merges into Nahal Akev by the spring. It is also possible for climbers to ascend through the narrow walls of the canyon and to connect to the marked trail to the right, where the canyon ends. The blue trail heads northwest along the wadi of the canyon and reaches its watershed. Here again are remnants of ancient stream-rounded cobbles.

The trail continues westward climbing another ridge. From this ridge the trail descends to the left of a terraced wadi and drops into Upper Nahal Divshon. Note how wild vegetation grows only by the crumbled walls that cross the wadi. This is due to the larger quantities of water the earth absorbs from the rock runoff and the shade the rocks give. Also, this part of the field is not touched by humans. In the summer, yellow flowering stalks of the mullein bloom in the wadi.

Follow the blue trail along the eastern side of Nahal Divshon for 1 km. Cross Nahal Divshon (13) and 150 m. further, cross a wide tributary. Here you head up the blue trail which runs to the left of a protruding hill. As you are now nearing Avdat, remnants of civilization become more apparent in the landscape: terraces along the slope (not only in the wadis), walls and a wider trail.

Eight hundred meters from Nahal Divshon the blue trail reaches the plateau where Avdat stands. The plateau is dissected by many walls, most likely of ancient farming sections, and it may be hard to follow the trail mark. Avdat is 500 m. ahead to the west, by the silhouette of the Nabatean camel convoy on the ridge. From the upper parking lot enter the city of Avdat and follow the arrows through the impressive structures. The marked trail will eventually take you down the hill to the National Park entrance by the starting point (1).

Lotz Cisterns

See map on
page 327

Points of interest: *A Negev highland kilometer-high atmosphere with ancient agriculture relics, open water cisterns
brimming with water, colorful flowers and unique vegetation.*

Length of hike: 3-4 kilometers depending on route, loop trip.

Hiking time: 1-3 hours.

Preferred season: All year except in mid-day summer.

Suitable for: All.

Maps: Negev Mountains (west) hiking and touring map.

Special preparation: None. Swimming is not allowed in the
cisterns.

Starting & ending point: Borot Lotz Campsite.

To reach starting point:

Arrival by private transportation: On (Mitzpe Ramon-Beersheba) Road 40, 5
km. north of Mitzpe Ramon is Haruhot Junction. Turn west (it is the only paved
option) and follow Road 171 for 27.5 km. until a gravel road marked by an orange
sign pointing to the 'Lotz Wells' begins on your right. Take this blue-marked road
for a bit more than a kilometer until reaching the Borot Lotz Campsite (1) where
there are palm-covered stone huts and bathrooms.

Arrival by public transportation: Currently there is no bus route on the road
leading to the Lotz Cisterns.

Geography

Nearly all of the Lotz Cisterns (Borot Lotz) are carved into marl of the Ora Shales
Formation from the Turonian epoch. The soft marl of the Ora Shales is easy to
dig and is impermeable to water. Lying upon the marl is a layer of hard limestone.

The founders of the Lotz Cisterns knew their geology. They kept the limestone
layer in place as a roof for the cisterns that they carved into the marl below. This
type of closed cistern is known as *ma'agora* in Hebrew. The open cisterns are cut
into the marl and lined with limestone rocks in order to maintain stability.

The landscape of the area is profoundly flat with semi-deep wadis cutting into the
general plain. To the southeast you can see the ridge of Makhtesh Ramon which
is a bit higher than the Lotz Cisterns area. Eighty million years ago the Makhtesh
Ramon area rose to an elevation of 2,000 m. (only later was the Makhtesh
formed), standing high above the nearby Lotz Cisterns area. During the Eocene
epoch the area now known as Israel was engulfed by sea and the Ramon Ridge
stood out as an island. The Lotz Cisterns area was covered by a shallow sea.

Sediments of the sea created sedimentary rock which composes the Avdat Plateau of today. The Eocenian rock becomes thicker as the distance north from Ramon Ridge increases, since there the sea was deeper. For example, by the Ein Avdat Canyon, the depth of the Eocenian rock reaches hundreds of meters, whereas at Rosh Elot the Eocenian cliffs are only a few meters thick.

Around the Borot Lotz Campsite, 2 km. south of Rosh Elot, there are no remnants of Eocenian rock. Thus, the Lotz Cisterns area was for millions of years a seashore or shallow sea. Through the passing eons, the sediments deposited by the shallow sea were washed away, exposing the hard parts of the Turonian rock beneath. Beneath a hard layer of the Turonian rock is the Ora Shales Formation in which we find the Lotz Cisterns.

The receding Eocenian sea 40 million years ago that eventually turned into the Mediterranean Sea of today has dictated the direction of today's streams. The wadis drain north off of Ramon Ridge and generally head in a northerly-northwest-erly direction to the Mediterranean. The long distance has kept the slopes of the streams fairly gradual, creating few canyons along the stream courses.

Plants and animals

Atlantic Terebinth (*Pistacia atlantica*): Israel's largest tree. Also known as the Atlantic pistachio. Like the oak (*alon*), the terebinth's Hebrew name, *elah*, stems form the Hebrew *el*, meaning god. The tree is associated with might and sturdi-ness. Like the oak, the terebinth was revered by the ancient Hebrews and other peoples. They used terebinth sites for worship and incense burning, and as burial places: "And took away the body of Saul and the bodies of his sons and brought them to Jabesh, and buried their bones under the terebinth in Jabesh ..." (I Chronicles 10:12). Many biblical stories are connected with the terebinth.

These trees are among the most aged and widespread species from Dan all the way to the Central Negev! In Arabic the tree is known as *butem*. Many sites in Israel bear the Hebrew or Arabic name for terebinth, such as Nahal Elot — *Wadi Butema*.

Four species of *Pistacia* are Israeli natives but only two, the Atlantic terebinth and the Palestinian terebinth are biblical. The leaves of both species are composed of two or more pairs of leaflets and are shed in winter. The green flowers are minute and clustered. The fruits are small fragrant drupes. The two species differ in structure, leaves and distribution. The Palestinian terebinth is typically Mediter-ranean, often found in the company of the common oak.

The Atlantic terebinth is a dryland tree with modest needs. It is usually found on the border between the evergreen Mediterranean woodland and the dwarf-shrub steppes. It is found in the Negev, mainly between Makhtesh Ramon and Nahal Tzin, growing along wadis. A couple of specimens grow in the Judean Desert. In the Lotz Cisterns vicinity there are 20-30 per sq. km., the highest concentration in the south. Some specimens are over 1,000 years old. Some researchers see its presence in the Negev as a relic of past, moist climatic conditions.

History

The Lotz Cisterns are a series of 17 water cisterns concentrated in 4 sq. km. Fifteen of the cisterns still fill with water nearly every year, even though they are probably 3,000 years old. Borot Lotz is a Hebracized name of the Arabic *lotzan* which refers to the Lotz Mountains 8 km. south of the cisterns. The cistern's Arabic name is *Hirbet um Varitma*.

Ten thousand years ago, people settled at Har Harif, 5 km. west of Lotz Cisterns. They were hunter-gatherers using flint tools. Many sites have been found in the vicinity. Archaeologists use the term "Harifian Culture" to describe the special characteristics of these people.

During the Mid-Bronze I, shepherds lived in the area. At central campsites, they constructed round dwellings on rock foundations. Their grave sites were also round—large round rock piles known as tumuli. Tumuli are found atop many ridges in the Central Negev.

During the 10th century B.C.E., King Solomon brought men into the wilderness to create a barrier between the desert nomads and the settled land. The frontier passed along the northern fringe of Makhtesh Ramon to Kadesh Barnea in the west. Cisterns were dug for drinking water for man and for flocks of friendly nomads. This lasted until the destruction of the First Temple in 586 B.C.E.

Five hundred years later, Nabateans travelled through the Negev and, after a few hundred years, settled the region. At Lotz Cisterns, they most likely found infrastructure for farm settlements. Their descendants prospered in the 5th-7th centuries.

After the Moslem conquest there was no organized settlement in the area and Bedouins used the cisterns. The agricultural terraces were neglected.

The British, during their brief control of the area, began to train Bedouins in farming. Kadesh Barnea had an experimental farm.

Site description

Rosh Elot: Also known as the 'Small Masada.' The 980 m. peak has a limited view. Here the uniformity of the landscape can easily be seen. Five kilometers to the southeast you can see Israel's highest mountain south of the Galilee, Har Ramon (1035 m.). Looking 6 km. southwest you can see the antennae of Har Harif (1012 m.) along the Israel-Egypt border.

The upper part of Rosh Elot is Eocenian hard limestone of the Nitzana Formation. Looking north you can see the Eocenian cliffs of Nahal Elot. Two kilometers to the north, the Eocenian strata gradually takes over, covering the whole landscape.

The large amount of chert strewn beneath the cliffs of Rosh Elot represent the edge of the sedimentary deposition of the Senonian sea. The chert belongs to the famous Mishash Formation and appears here as a thin layer. This layer at Rosh Elot sits between the Turonian marl and limestone below and the Eocenian limestone above. The Mishash Formation is prevalent throughout the Judean Desert and Negev, where its dark color, thickness and strong durability make a distinct impression on the landscape. Rosh Elot, being close to the seashore at the time of chert deposition accumulated no more than a few centimeters of chert.

Looking across the way, note how the bushes grow more densely at the bottom of the cliff. The reason is a better water economy. Rainfall hits the cliff at an angle due to strong winds. The water slowly drips down to the base of the cliff and soaks in. The cliff shades its base more than open areas and less water is evaporated, creating an ideal home for plants.

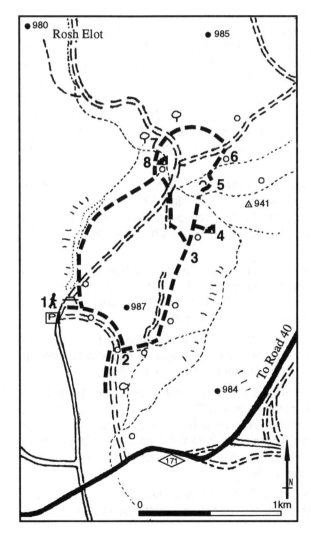

Hike 40, Lotz Cisterns

To begin hike:

From the faucets at the Borot Lotz Campsite (1) take a right up the wide red-marked dirt road and after 100 m. reach the 'Small Cistern' with a tamarisk growing from it. The crescent-shaped channel leading to the cistern is 350 m. long.

Following the dirt road, cross a topographic saddle and drop to 'Lotz Cistern,' the largest in the area (2). Its depth is 4 m. and it is fed by four channels. In 1980 the cistern overflowed and the whole depression turned into a lake. The adjacent hill to the cistern is composed of sediment that accumulated in the cistern and was evacuated every few years. This type of bare white hill is an easy sign in the desert of a well or water cistern.

There are remnants of many buildings in the proximity of this large cistern. A hundred meters southwest of the cistern is a house from the Israelite period that was most likely a single-family farm. Some researchers see this site as the core or the Israelite settlement in the area.

It is possible to continue on the dirt road for 200 m. to the next wadi to see the Fig Fruit Garden and Fig Cistern a bit upstream. In 1980 the terraces were renovated and figs, pomegranates and olives were planted in memory of Yossi Yaffe by youth. Return back to Lotz Cistern (2).

The red-marked trail, lined by rows of stones, descends from Lotz Cistern into a small wadi and after 200 m. reaches a pair of cisterns. Do not let small children run ahead! One of the cisterns is covered with cement with two small openings camouflaged by vegetation and gravel! Falling through one of these openings can be treacherous!

Two cisterns are fed from separate wadis that merge here. These cisterns are of the type known as *ma'agora* (see Geography, this hike). The Nabateans usually built *ma'agora* cisterns, so it is possible that the *ma'agorot* were built or renovated by the Nabatean settlement here. The roof of the cisterns here has been modestly renovated by Bedouins.

Follow the trail along the slope to 'Saltbush Cistern,' named for the saltbush plants growing beside it. The roof is most likely a Bedouin addition from this century. Continuing along the trail you reach the 'Open Cistern' and soon afterwards 'Ma'agora Cistern,' also known as 'Mushroom Cistern.'

By the next cistern a dirt road veering to the left (3) gently ascends the ridge. The dirt road reconnects to the loop red-marked trail, so if you want to shorten the trip take the dirt road to 'Clogged Cistern' (8) by the Nabatean House.

Continue on the red-marked trail. Note a small trail leading right after 75 m. Here is a round threshing floor on the small ridge (4). Continue down the red trail and pass another threshing floor on the left. When reaching a triple wadi junction, look 100 m. across the way to the wadi coming in from the east. Note a green bush on a short cliff and a small pile of earth beneath it (5). Head there. The red trail heads up the opposite side of this wadi.

This triple junction of wadis was most likely a farm section. Note the walls and terraces in the wadis and on the slope between them. By the bush there are two ruins. Beside them is the pile of earth and a lot of greenery. Most likely at one time the opening beneath the cliff was deeper and was a *ma'agora* cistern. Along the slope today there are no remnants of a water channel.

Head up the wadi for 50 m. from the two ruins. Go left onto the red trail which crosses the ridge and drops down to the parallel wadi to the north. Here is a section, known as the 'Tamarisk Fruit Garden' that was renovated a few years ago, but has not been maintained (6). Above the farmed section is a large cistern marked by a tall tamarisk. Head there. The cistern is a semi-*ma'agora* that was dug beneath a layer of hard rock.

Keep with the marked trail over two small ridges and into a wadi by a terebinth. Descend the wadi to the west. Along the way step over a few rock outcrops that hold dark snail shaped fossils called *Nerinea cretacea*. The site is marked by a sign. From here the trail leads to another Atlantic terebinth by a wadi junction (7). From this area is a nice view of Rosh Elot, the protruding hill standing out 1 km. to the northwest. Take a left up the wide trail to the Nabatean house (8).

Beneath the Nabatean house, in a gully, lies 'Clogged Cistern.' The cistern is simply clogged by debris and only the upper row of bricks is exposed. The house was built during the 1st or 2nd century. The builders most likely chose the spot based on the adjacent cistern. Here, the dirt road from the 'Mushroom Cistern' joins the red trail.

The clear red trail encompasses the ridge, beginning along the water channel of 'Clogged Cistern.' The slope is evenly covered with many wormwood plants. Right before finishing back at the Borot Lotz Campsite (1), you reach 'Goodwater Cistern' named by travelers who quenched their thirst here in the pre-campsite days.

Mud cracks at the bottom of a dry cistern

Map Legend

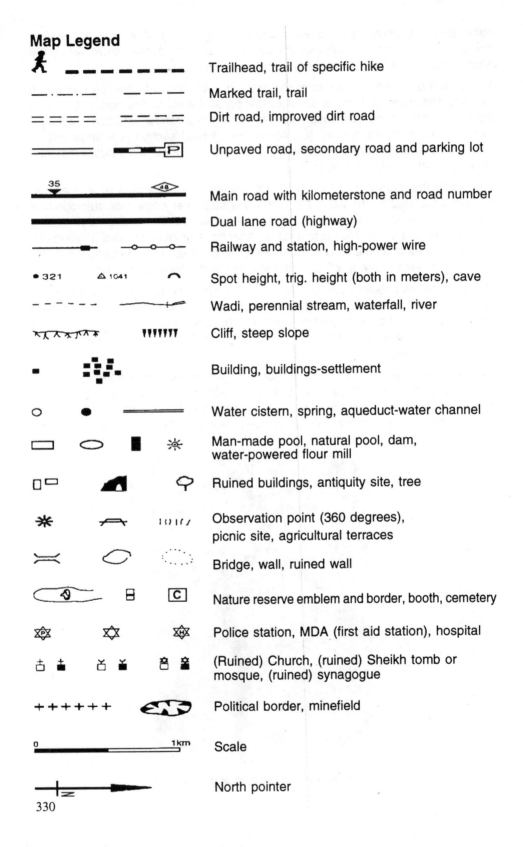

	Trailhead, trail of specific hike
	Marked trail, trail
	Dirt road, improved dirt road
	Unpaved road, secondary road and parking lot
35 48	Main road with kilometerstone and road number
	Dual lane road (highway)
	Railway and station, high-power wire
● 321 △ 1041	Spot height, trig. height (both in meters), cave
	Wadi, perennial stream, waterfall, river
	Cliff, steep slope
	Building, buildings-settlement
	Water cistern, spring, aqueduct-water channel
	Man-made pool, natural pool, dam, water-powered flour mill
	Ruined buildings, antiquity site, tree
	Observation point (360 degrees), picnic site, agricultural terraces
	Bridge, wall, ruined wall
C	Nature reserve emblem and border, booth, cemetery
	Police station, MDA (first aid station), hospital
	(Ruined) Church, (ruined) Sheikh tomb or mosque, (ruined) synagogue
+ + + + + +	Political border, minefield
0 1km	Scale
N	North pointer

Hebrew-English Glossary

Some of the following words and terms appear frequently throughout this book. Many are part of the Hebrew name of a geographical site.

Be'er	Well
Berekhah, Berekhat	Pool, pool of
Bayit, Bet	House, house of
Bik'ah, Bik'at	Valley, valley of
Ein (Ma'ayan), Einot	Spring, springs
Emek	Valley
Eshed	Cascade
Gesher	Bridge
Giv'ah, Giv'at, Giv'ot	Hill, hill of, hills
Har	Mountain, Mt.
Hirbet	Ruin (Arabic)
Hurbat	Ruin
Kefar	Village
Khan	Caravansary, roadside hotel (Arabic)
Kibbutz	Communal settlement. Less than 3% of Israel's population dwells in kibbutzim.
Ma'ale	Ascent (trail)
Makhtesh	See explanation in the Scientific Glossary
Mapal	Waterfall
Metzad	Fort
Moshav	Agricultural settlement
Nahal	Perennial or ephemeral stream
Nahar	River
Rosh	Head or top
Sadeh, Sdeh	Field, field of
Sharav	Barometric high bringing hot temperatures
Tel	Artificial mound created by human settlement containing accumulated debris.
Tzuk, Tzukei, Metzokai	Cliff, cliffs of
Tzomet	Junction
Wadi	Dry stream bed (Arabic and Hebrew)

Scientific Glossary

Alluvium: Stream-laid sediment deposit found in stream channels and in low parts of stream valleys subject to flooding.

Alluvial Fan: A fan-shaped deposit of coarse alluvium, the apex pointing upstream, laid down by a stream where it issues from a constricted coarse, e.g. from a canyon, on to a more open valley or plain.

Anticline: An arched-shaped upfold of rock layers, caused by compression of the earth's crust, the layers dipping down and away from the central line (axis). An anticline has the oldest rocks along its axis in the center.

Aquiclude: A porous rock which, although usually permeable, becomes impermeable because of the saturation of its pores by water.

Aquifer: A water-bearing rock layer, sufficiently porous to carry the water and sufficiently coarse to release it.

Basalt: Dark, volcanic rock. Occurs as lava flows, dikes, and cinder cones.

Batta: A Mediterranean plant formation of dwarf bushes and grasses.

Beachrock: Fragments of shells and sand, hardened by solutions. Its presence indicates that the site was once a beach.

Breccia: Volcanic rock consisting of broken fragments ejected from a volcano, cemented together with lava or volcanic ash.

Chalk: Variety of limestone that is soft, earthy and white, formed of hard parts of planktonic marine organisms (foraminifers, algae).

Chert (Flint): Variety of sedimentary rock, usually dark-colored, composed of chalcedony and various impurities in form of nodules and layers.

Cobbles: A naturally-rounded water-worn stone, larger than a pebble, 6-20 cm. in diameter.

Cross-bedding: Obliquely slanting beds between the main horizontal layers of sedimentary rock, usually sandstone. Formed by currents of wind or water in the direction which the bed slopes downward.

Cubit (meter): 1 meter in the third power (1,000 liters of water).

Dike: (geological) Thin layer of igneous rock, often nearly vertical or with a steep dip, occupying a widened fracture in the surrounding older rock and typically cutting across the older rock planes.

Discharge: The volume of water flowing through a cross section in a given unit of time. In this book it is usually described in cubic meters per second (cms). The Missouri River in Nebraska, USA has a discharge of 280-2,800 cms.

Divide (Watershed): A water parting, the elevated line of which may or may not be sharply defined, separating two contiguous drainage areas. From here, the head streams flow in different directions, into different drainage basins.

Doline: A karstic depression of different sizes caused by underground collapse of dissolute carbonate rock.

Dolomite (Dolostone): Carbonate mineral or sedimentary rock made of calcium magnesium carbonate.

Drainage Basin: The tract of land drained by a sole river system.

Dunam: 1,000 square meters (one tenth of a hectare).

Ephemeral: Lasting for a short time.

Escarpment: A continuous line of cliffs of gently inclining strata resulting from a fault or erosion.

Fault: Sharp break in rock with displacement (slippage) of the block on one side with respect to the adjacent block.

Garrigue: (French) Scrub vegetation, especially of stunted evergreen oak occuring in limestone in drier areas of Mediterranean climate. It is believed to result from human settlement, fire and the browsing of domestic and wild goats.

Geophyte: An earth-growing plant whose bulbs are buried.

Gorge: A rocky-walled, steep-sided, deep and narrow river valley.

Graben: Trench-like depression representing the surface of a fault block that has dropped between two normal faults.

Hammada: The rocky desert of flat areas stripped of sand and dust by wind, the surface smoothed by abrasion.

Hexagonal Column: There are a number of theories explaining their formation. A well-known theory explains that during the cooling and contraction process of lava into basalt, joints are formed due to tension since the outer sections cool more quickly. Scientists claim that the natural order of this type of jointing is in a hexagonal pattern. This occurs when lava movement is slow, upon a gently tilted field.

Horst: Fault block uplifted between two normal faults.

Hydrohalophyte: A plant associated with salinity and water.

Hydrophytic: A plant living in water or wet ground.

Incised Meander: A meander (loop-like bend of a sluggish stream) deeply sunk into the general level of the surrounding country. This may result when a mature river, with extensive meanders, changes its landscape by an uplift of the land and begins to incise its bed.

Irano-Turanian Zone: A phytogeographic zone of southeastern Europe, northern Iran and Iraq, stretching to Tibet. The climate is a cold and dry (max. 350 mm. annual precipitation) and the vegetation is bushes and grasses.

Joint: Internal bedrock fracture surfaces of hairline thickness along which no slippage has occured.

Karst: Landscape or case of topography dominated by surface features of limestone solution and underlain by limestone cavern systems.

Kurkar sandstone (Calciferous sandstone): A fossilized sand dune cemented by limestone solution. Usually the rock exhibits thin layers of wind-blown and hardened sand, sometimes crossing one another, known as cross-bedding. The dunes appeared beyond the seashore. The location of kurkar ridges represents ancient shorelines.

Layer (Strata) Springs: A spring emerging upon an impermeable underground rock layer (such as marl or clay) where the layer is exposed.

Lava: Magma that reaches the surface, or rock hardened by it.

Limestone: Non-clastic sedimentary rock in which calcium carbonate is the dominant mineral.

Loess: Silt-size airborne particles that have been deposited in the last thousands of years during rainfall. The source of the loess is dust from the deserts to the south and in Africa.

Magma: Molten rock in or from the earth's interior.

Makhtesh: An erosional cirque (steep-walled basin) hundreds of meters deep, formed in an anticline. It usually is drained by only one wadi system.

Maquis: Form of dense low scrub vegetation of evergreen shrubs and small trees found throughout the Mediterranean

Marl: A soft impermeable sedimentary rock composed of clay and calcium carbonate, usually deposited in lakes.

Mediterranean Zone (Climate): A phytogeographic zone characterized by a rainy winter (400-1200 mm.) with a meager amount of snow and a hot dry summer, such as in the hills around the Mediterranean Basin and in parts of California. The zone is rich in fauna and flora. Non-desert Israel enjoys this type of climate.

Outcrop: Surface exposure of bedrock.

Palaearctic: A zoographic term relating to the northern hemisphere of the Old World (without America).

Perennial: Applied to plants and streams that continue to grow or flow year to year without a stop.

Phytogeographic Zone: Classification of plants into zones based on their geographic distribution.

Raptor: A predatory bird.

Reg: Desert surface armored with a pebble layer, resulting from long-continued deflation.

Rendzina: A grey soil developing on chalk and marl in a Mediterranean climate.

Rift: Trench-like valley with steep parallel sides; essentially a graben between two normal faults; associated with crustal spreading.

Permeable: Capable of being wholly penetrated by fluid.

Plant Association: A group of plants of a certain composition that repeats itself in certain ecologic conditions. The association is named after the one or two most common plants.

Pothole: Also called a water hollow. A more or less circular hole in the bedrock of a wadi or stream created by the whirl of stones during swift flow.

Saharo-Arabian Zone: A phytogeographic zone that includes much of northern Africa and the southern Middle East of typical desert climate where annual rainfall does not exceed 200 mm.

Salinity: The amount of salts in the medium. In this book salinity is usually described in milligrams (mg.) per liter. Drinking water in Israel has about 200 mg. of salt per liter.

Sedimentary Rock A rock consisting of material derived from pre-existing rocks, or from organic debris or chemical precipitation, formed in layers.

Shard: A broken piece of a brittle substance, such as an earthen vessel; a potsherd.

Sill: A thin body of magmatic rock intruded between horizontal rock layers.

Sporangium A sack in which asexual pores are produced endogenously, as in certain algae and fungi.

Steppe: Plant association class in the form of grassland, consisting of short grasses distributed in clumps, and some shrubs; widespread in areas of semi-arid climate in continental interiors such as Eurasia and the Irano-Turanian zone.

Strata: Layers of sediment or sedimentary rock separated from one another by stratification (bedding) planes.

Sudanian Zone: The arid tropical phytogeographic zone between Western Africa and the Sahara and Arabian Deserts. The typical climate of this zone has a hot, rainy summer and a warm, dry winter. The typical vegetation that develops is a savannah—an open forest of multi-trunked trees such as acacias and tall shrubs, dominated by perennial grasses.

Syncline: A fold of rock layers that is concave upward, dipping inwards towards a central axis. A syncline has its youngest rocks along its axis.

Tectonic: Crustal processes of bending ("folding") and breaking ("faulting"), usually concentrated on or near active plate boundaries.

Terra Rossa: 'Red Earth.' A residual soil of chemically weathered dolomite and limestone, rich in clay and iron. It is the common soil of the non-desert hilly regions of Israel.

Travertine: Carbonate mineral matter, usually calcite, accumulating in limestone caverns and on hot spring and external surfaces where calcium carbonate saturated water is flowing or has flown.

Tuff: A rock composed of particles of volcanic ash.

Water Hollow: See "pothole."

Anthropological Glossary

Many of these names and terms appear in different hikes.

Bedouin: Nomadic Arabs originating from the Arabian Desert. Today many are more sedentary.

Cairn: A mound or heap of stones for a memorial or marker.

Dolmen: A megalithic sepulchral monument of several large, unhewn stones, that are set on one end and covered with a single huge stone, as to form a (burial) chamber.

Druze: Religious sect deriving from Islam, founded in the 10th century in Egypt. Today its members reside in Israel, Lebanon and Syria. Their religion is kept secret from all but a select few who learn at their religious college in Hatzbaya, Lebanon. In Israel they are concentrated in 18 villages: two in the Carmel, four in Northern Golan and the rest in the Galilee. Druze serve in the I.D.F.

Episcopacy: Government of a church by bishops.

F.S.C.: Field Study Center. An outdoor center belonging to the S.P.N.I., mainly composed of guides who lead trips in the adjacent region. Most centers offer overnight facilities at a low cost.

Hamula: Arabic word for a large family clan.

I.D.F.: Israel Defense Forces.

J.N.F.: Jewish National Fund. In Hebrew, Keren Kayemet le-Yisrael. Institution of the World Zionist Organization for the acquisition, development and aforrestation of the land of Israel. Founded in 1901.

Makhrab: Arabic word for a niche in the wall of mosques and *makams* establishing the direction toward Mecca.

Mishna: Jewish oral books of law edited and arranged in 190 C.E.

NAHAL: Hebrew acronym for "Fighting Pioneer Youth." A branch of the I.D.F., training combat soldiers for agricultural (and recently development town) settlement. Also means stream.

N.R.A.: Nature Reserves Authority. Israeli government agency in charge of nature protection throughout Israel.

N.W.C.: National Water Carrier. The plan was first developed in the 1930s as a project to exploit all the water sources of Israel. The main conduit was completed in the mid-1960s, one of Israel's marked technological achievements in the 1960s.

The main reservoir is Lake Kinneret. Water is pumped from its northwestern corner into pressure pipes that raise it 256 m. From this point the water runs for 16 km. in an open channel to the Tzalmon pumping station. En route, the water crosses Nahal Ammud and Nahal Tzalmon via a siphon. The waters eventually reach the northwestern Negev.

Palestine: A shortened version of Palestinian Syria, a name imposed by the Romans in order to minimize the Jewish association of the country. The Romans took the name from Philistine, the enemies of King David.

PALMACH: Hebrew acronym for "shock companies." The striking arm of the Haganah—Israel's underground defense force before 1948. It numbered only 6-11 companies during its existence from 1941-1948, but has had a strong impact on the I.D.F until today.

P.I.C.A.: Palestine Jewish Colonization Association, founded by I.C.A. after WWI to administer colonies in the Holy Land. The association was funded by Baron Edmond de Rothschild.

Saladin: Salah e-Din. A great Moslem sultan of Egypt and Syria who led the successful campaign against the Crusaders in the land of Israel.

Saracen: In ancient times, a nomadic Arab of the Syrian-Arabic desert. A Moslem enemy of the medieval and Byzantine Christians in the region.

S.P.N.I.: Society for the Protection of Nature in Israel. Israel's largest non-profit nature conservation group, with over 25 field study centers. Close to 10% of Israel's population participate in S.P.N.I. activities annually.

Talmud: Explanation of the Mishna as records of academic Jewish discussions.

Templars: A military order founded in 1119 for the defense of a Latin kingdom in Jerusalem, and for protection of pilgrims; a German Christian sect that settled in Jerusalem and the Haifa region in the late 19th century. During WWII, the British imprisoned and then expelled them.

Tigart Fort: A network of police stations planned by the Briton Charles Tigart during the Arab Revolt of 1936-1939. The forts have a distinguished, uniform appearance.

Tosefta: A supplement to the Mishna.

Tristram, Henry Baker: Father of the modern nature research in the Holy Land. Canon Tristram grew up and studied in England. Although his interests went beyond natural science, he emphasized biology. He conducted four research outings to the Holy Land and published his most extensive journey in 1863-1864. This diary has invaluable information on the land's flora and fauna.

Archaeological Periods of Israel

Period	Sub-period	Main Events
Stone Age 600,000-4,000 B.C.E.	Paleolith *Old Stone Age* 600,000-12,000	600,000-200,000: Old Auchelian culture: pre-cave culture, hand axes, hunters, fire known. 200,00-100,000: Upper Auchelian: first cave deposits.
	Mesolith 12,000-7,500	Natufian culture: gathering grain, hoes, picks, beginning of agriculture.
	Neolith *New Stone Age* 7,500-4,000	Jericho
Chalcolithic Age 4,000-3,200 B.C.E.	Copper Stone Age	Houses, towns, trade, geom. designs on pottery. Introduction of copper.
Canaanite (Bronze) 3,200-1,200 B.C.E.	Early Bronze 3,200-2,200	Fortified towns, temples.
	Middle Bronze 2,200-1,550	1,900-1,750 Age of the Patriarchs.
	Late Bronze 1,550-1,200	Egyptian domination 1,300-1,200: Exodus and conquest of Canaan by Israel
Israelite (Iron) Age 1,200-587 B.C.E.	Early Iron 1,200-1,020	Period of the Judges. Occupation of Canaan by Israel.
	Middle Iron 1,020-842	United Israel under Kings David and Solomon. Jerusalem capital of Israel. First Temple.
	Late Iron 842-587	722: Exile of the Ten Tribes. 587: Exile of Judah.
Persian Period 587-332 B.C.E.	Babylonian and Persian Periods	587-536: Babylon captivity. 536-322: Persian domination post-exile restoration, Second Temple, Ezra and Nehemiah.
Hellenistic Period 332-63 B.C.E.	332-141 Greek domination 141-37: Hasmonean Dynasty	332: Alexander the Great. 312-198: Rule of Ptolemies. 198-167: Rule of Seleucids. 167-141: Hasmonean War of Liberation.

Roman Period 63 B.C.E.-324 C.E.	37 B.C.E.-70 C.E.: Herodian Dynasty 70-324: Period of the Mishna and Talmud	37-4: Herod the Great. 66-70: Great Revolt. 70: Destruction of Temple. 73: Fall of Masada. 132-135: Bar Kokhva Revolt. 200: Yehuda Hanasee and Mishna completion.
Byzantine Period 324-640	379: Partition of the Roman Empire 614-628: Persian conquest	326: St. Helen builds Jerusalem. 352: Galilean Jewish Revolt. 425: End of Patriarchate and completion of Jerusalem Talmud.
Early Arab (Moslem) Period 640-1099	661-750: Omayyad Dynasty Abasside Dynasty	996-1100: El-Hakim be-Amer Allah, founder of the Druze sect.
Crusader Period 1099-1291	1187: Saladin reconquers Israel 1250: Rise of Mameluke Dynasty	1099-1187: Crusader Kings in Jerusalem. 1291: Fall of Acre.
Mameluke Pariod 1291-1516		Expansion of Jerusalem. 1492: Spanish Jews settle in Israel.
Ottoman Period 1517-1917	1831-1840: Egypt conquers Palestine	1538: Walls of Jerusalem. 19th century: Return to Zion, agricultural Jewish settlements.
British Mandate 1917-1948	1917: Balfour Declaration	1920: Arab rioting. 1929: Arab rioting, Hebron massacre. 1936-1939: Arab Revolt.
State of Israel	1948-1977: Labor Government 1977-1991: Likud Government	1947-1949: War of Independence. 1967: Six Day War. 1973: Yom Kippur War. 1979: Peace Treaty with Egypt. 1995: Murder of Prime Minister Yitzhak Rabin.

Geological Time Table

Period	Epoch	Millions of Years Before Today	World Events	Regional Events
Quaternary	Holocene		Modern man	Formation of present landscape.
		0.01		
	Pleistocene		Worldwide glaciations. Neanderthal Man	Lashon Lake in Syrian-African Rift. Slight uplift. More volcanism. Shaping of S.-A. Rift.
		1.6		
Tertiary Neogene	Pliocene			Basalt flows. Last great uplift forming today's prominent landscape features. Continuation of rifting.
		5.3		
Neogene	Miocene		Opening of Red Sea	Beginning of the Syrian-African Rift. Mountain building.
		24		
Tertiary Paleogene	Oligocene		Collission of India with Asia	Uplift and erosion.
		37		
Paleogene	Eocene		Early horses	Last Tethys Sea transgression.
		54		
Paleogene	Paleocene		Early primates Extinction of dinasaurs	
		66		
Upper Cretaceous	Senonian Turonian Cenomanian		Early flowering plants	Anticlinal ridges begin to appear in the Negev with phosphate rock deposited between them. Thick sediments. A fluvial regime deposits sandstone.
Lower Cretaceous				
		144		
Jurassic			Early birds and mammals	Tethys Sea transgression deposits sediments.

Period	Age (million years)	Life	Geological events (this region)
	208		
Triassic		Opening of Atlantic Ocean	Deposition of gypsum in marshes.
	245		
Permian			*The region is intermittently*
	286		
Carboniferous		Early reptiles	*covered by the Tethys*
	360		
Devonian		Early trees	*Sea and then exposed*
	408		
Silurian		Early land plants	*causing erosion.*
	438		
Ordovician		Early fishes	
	505		
Cambrian		Early shelled organisms	Erosion of the A-N. Massif creating sandstone.
	570		
Precambrian Time		Early multi-celled organisms. Formation of early supercontinent	Uplifting of the Arabian-Nubian Massif in southern Israel and Sinai.
	4,500	Formation of earth	

Plant and Animal Index

Plants

Animals

Selected Bibliography

English

Chronic H.: *Roadside Geology of Arizona*, Mountain Press, Missoula, 1991.

Clark A. N.: *Dictionary of Geography*, Penguin Books, London, 1990.

Dalley T., Brubacher G. and Rape D.: *The Scripture Garden*, Biblical Resources Study Center, Jerusalem, 1990.

Evenari M., Shanan L. and Tadmor N.: *The Negev, The Challenge of a Desert*, Harvard University Pres, Cambridge Mass., 1971.

International Association of Sedimentologists: *Sedimentology in Israel Guidebook*, part 1 & 2, Israel, 1978.

Mottana A., Crespi R. and Liborio G.: *Guide to Rocks and Minerals*, Simon & Shuster, Milan, 1978.

Orni E. and Efrat E.: *Geography of Israel*, Israel Universities Press, Jerusalem, 1976.

Parmelee A.: *All the Birds of the Bible*, Keats Pub. Inc., New Canaan Conn., 1959.

Paz U.: *The Birds of Israel*, Stephen Greene Press, Tel Aviv, 1987.

Press F. and Siever R.: *Earth*, W. H. Freeman and Company, New York, 1986.

Robinson E.: *Biblical Researches in Palestine* vol. 2, London, 1856.

Roskin J.: *A Guide to Hiking in Israel with 40 selected one day Hikes*, Jerusalem Post, Jerusalem, 1991.

Roskin J.: *Hikes in the Jerusalem Hills and the Judean Desert,* Efrat Ltd., Jerusalem, 1987.

Strahler A.H. and Strahler A. N.: *Modern Physical Geography*, John Wiley & Sons, New York, 1987.

The Holy Scriptures. A Jewish Bible According to the Masoretic Text, Hebrew and English, Sinai publishing, Tel Aviv, 1972.

Tristram H. B.: *The Land of Israel, A Journal of Travels in Palestine 1863-4*, London.

Wigoder G.: *The New Standard Jewish Encyclopedia*, Massada Press Co. Ltd., Jerusalem-Ramat Gan, 1977.

Zohary M.: *Plants of the Bible*, Cambridge University Press, Cambridge, 1982.

Journals

Archaeological News, all editions, Antiquities Authorities, Jerusalem.

Eretz, Eretz Ha-Tzvi Inc., Jerusalem, all editions, (1987-1994).

Israel Land and Nature, S.P.N.I., Jerusalem, all editions during 1979-1991.

Hebrew

Alon A. (chief editor): *Encyclopedia of the Plants and Animals of the Land of Israel*, all volumes, Ministry of Defense, 1990.

Alon A. and Bukhman Y. (editors): *Touring in the Lower Galilee*, S.P.N.I. and the Ministry of Defense, Israel, 1993.

Amirav M.: *Ein Kerem-A Journey to the Village of the Lord*, Ariel, Jerusalem.

Amit D., Hirschfeld Y. and Patrich J. (editors): *The Aqueducts of Ancient Palestine — Collected Essays*, Yad Yitzhak Ben-Zvi, Jerusalem, 1989.

Amitai P.: *Scorpions!*, Massada Ltd., Israel, 1980.

Ben-Dror M.: *To the Delightful Corners, A Guide to the Land of Water Rivulets*, Ariel, Jerusalem, 1993.

Braun D.: Geology of the Afikim Region, M.Sc. thesis, the Hebrew University of Jerusalem, Jerusalem, 1992.

Carta's Atlas, all volumes, Carta, Jerusalem, 1974-1991.

Dafni A.: *Edible Wild Flowers*, S.P.N.I., 1984.

Danin A. and Itzchaki A.: *A Wild Flowers Tour Guide in Israel*, Cana, Jerusalem, 1985.

Dvir O. (editor): *Hiking and Touring Maps*, all regions, S.P.N.I. and Israel Map Center, 1983-1991.

Flavius J.: *War of the Jews*, Massada, Giv'atayim, 1986.

Glickson: Geology of Upper Nahal Ammud, M.Sc. thesis, the Hebrew University of Jerusalem, Jerusalem, 1964.

Goren M.: *Freshwater Fishes of Israel Biology and Taxonomy*, Hakibbutz Hameuchad Publishing House Ltd., Tel-Aviv, 1983.

Hare'uveni, E.: *Go Walk in the Land, A Guide to Israel's Nature Reserves*, Ministry of Defense, Israel, no date.

Heinzel H., Fitter R. and Parslow J.: *The Birds of Britain and Europe*, Hakibbutz Hameuchad Publishing House Ltd., 1981.

Harel M.: *Nature and Man in the Bible*, Am Oved Publishers Ltd., Tel Aviv, 1984.

Heiman A.: Geology of Banias Plateau and Northern Hula Valley, M.Sc. thesis, the Hebrew University of Jerusalem, Jerusalem,1985.

Ilan T.: *The Land of Golan*, Am Oved, Tel Aviv, 1980.

Inbar M. and Schiller E. (editors): *The Golan Heights*, Ariel, Jerusalem, 1987.

In Continuous Flow (no authors), 12 Hiking Routes, S.P.N.I., no date.

Itzchaki A. (editor): *Israel Guide Encyclopedia*, all volumes, Keter Puublishing House, Jerusalem, 1978-1980.

Krispil N.: *Moshe Ben Maimon Medicinal Plants*, Efrat Ltd., Israel, 1989.

Livneh M. and Meltzer A.: *The Rock Hyrax*, Massada Press Co. Ltd., Israel, 1982.

Marcus M.: *The Northern Judean Desert*, Keter Publishing House Ltd., 1986.

Marcus M.: *The Bet-El Hills*, Keter Publishing House Ltd., 1991.

Marcus M.: *The Jerusalem Hills*, Keter Publishing House Ltd., 1993.

Marcus M.: *The Central Negev Highlands and Makhtesh Ramon*, Keter Publishing House Ltd., 1986.

Mazor E.: *Geology with an Israeli Hammer*, Everymans University, Tel-Aviv, 1980.

Mazor E., Shefrn N. (editors): *Courses in the Geology of Israel*, Everymans University, Tel Aviv, 1987.

Meshel Z. (editor): *The Negev Highland — Landscape and Journeys*, Ministry of Defense, Israel, 1991.

Mor D.: Volcanics of the Central Golan, M.Sc. thesis, the Hebrew University of Jerusalem, Jerusalem, 1971.

Mor D.: Volcanics of Golan, Phd. thesis, the Hebrew University of Jerusalem, Jerusalem, 1985.

Mor U.: Geology of the Mitzpe Shalem area, M.Sc. thesis, the Hebrew University of Jerusalem, Jerusalem, 1974.

Nir D.: *Geomorphology of Israel*, Akademon, the Hebrew University of Jerusalem, Jerusalem, 1970.

Paz U., Eshbol Y.: *Photographic Guide to the Birds of Israel*, Keter Publishing House Ltd., 1990.

Raz E.: *The Dead Sea Book*, Keter Ltd., 1993.

Shalmon B. (editor): *The Gazelles in Israel*, S.P.N.I., 1987.

Shalmon B.: *A Field Guide to the Land Mammals of Israel, Their Tracks and Signs*, Keter Publishing House Ltd., Jerusalem, 1993.

Saltzman U.: The Geology of the Tabgha Hukok Majdal Region, M.Sc. thesis, the Hebrew University of Jerusalem, Jerusalem, 1961.

Scenes and Sites, Ministry of Defense, Israel, 1979.

Schlein: The Geology of the Alma Region, M.Sc. thesis, the Hebrew University of Jerusalem, Jerusalem, 1961.

Shavit Y. (chief editor): *The History of Eretz Israel*, all volumes, Keter Publishing House Ltd., Israel, 1990.

Shimron A.E., S. Peltz: *Early Cretacaous Pyroclastic Volcanism on the Hermon Range*, G.S.I. Bull. 84, Jerusalem, 1993.

Shmida A. et. al.: *Pictorial Flora of Israel*, Massada, Israel, 1983.

Shmida A., Darom D.: *Handbook of Wildflowers of Israel, Mediterranean Flora*, Keter Publishing House Ltd., 1990.

Shmida A., Darom D.: *Handbook of Wildflowers of Israel, Desert Flora*, Keter Publishing House Ltd., 1989.

Shorer Y.: *Israel Field Trips—The North*, Keter Publishing House, Jerusalem, 1990.

Shpanier Y. (editor): *Judean Hills—An Assortment of Routes*, S.P.N.I., Har Gilo.

Yehuda Hanassi (editor): *Six Tractates of the Mishna*, Lower Galilee, ‎90.

Ziv Y.: *Travellers Trails in Nature Reserves*, Ministry of Defense, Israel, 1982.

Ziv Y.: *Back Pack*, Maxwell-Macmillan-Keter Publishing Ltd., Jerusalem, 1991.

Joel Roskin, born in 1966 in Fort Worth Texas, began hiking in the Pacific Northwest of the United States. In 1979 he moved to Israel with his family from Chicago, Illinois. Following a course of study at Yeshivat Ma'alot Ya'akov in the Upper Galilean town of Ma'alot, he served as a combat officer in the I.D.F.

Joel has led a navigation and hiking youth club of the Society for the Protection of Nature in Israel for five years. Today he is working on a M.Sc. in physical geography and geology at the Ben Gurion University of the Negev in Beersheba, where he resides with his wife and daughter.

His first publication, *Hikes in the Jerusalem Hills and Judean Desert*, was published in 1987, successfully followed by *A Guide to Hiking in Israel* (1991). He is currently working on *Hikes in Southern Israel* and *Hikes in Judea*.